MW00489396

Certificate of Membership

This Certifies

That **Rogers B. Toy**

is a member of

The Old Guard

of the

GATE CITY GUARD

Atlanta, Georgia

John L. Morison
Commander Old Guard Battalion

C. P. Crosby
Adjutant-General

Date **February 5, 1990**

CHRONICLES

OF

THE OLD GUARD

OF THE

GATE CITY GUARD

ATLANTA, GEORGIA

1858-1915

BY

HENRY CLAY FAIRMAN

ATLANTA, GA.
BYRD PRINTING COMPANY
1915

NEW MATERIAL Copyright ©1986
by The Old Guard of the Gate City Guard,
a Georgia Corporation, Atlanta, Georgia

All rights reserved. No part of this publication may be reproduced, stored in
a retrieval system or transmitted in any form or by any means without the prior
permission of the publisher.

SOUTHERN HISTORICAL PRESS, INC.
c/o The Rev. Silas Emmett Lucas, Jr.
P.O. Box 738
Easley, South Carolina 29641-0738

ISBN 0-89308- 594-4

PREFACE TO THE THIRD EDITION

The First Edition of these Chronicles of the Old Guard covered the period from the date the Gate City Guard was chartered, January 8, 1957, to August 1, 1915. The Old Guard was organized in 1893 as a separate organization from the Gate City Guard, by former members of it, and chartered May 27, 1910, with the name "Old Guard of the Gate City Guard."

The First Edition was supplemented in 1933 by the publication of a booklet entitled "A Brief Resumé of Worthy Achievements." In 1964 the Second Edition of the Chronicles was published which included the First Edition, of 1915, the 1933 "Resumé," an additional resumé of the years from 1933 to 1945 and Commandant's Reports for the years 1949 through 1963. Unfortunately, there are no records of activities during the years 1946-1948. No photographs were included in the Second Edition.

The Second Edition having been out of print for several years, the Command decided by unanimous vote on May 5, 1986, to authorize a reprint of the First Edition, complete with original photographs. At that time it was determined that it will be necessary to publish a second volume recording the history of the Old Guard from 1915 to the present.

It is interesting to note that at the time of publication of the First Edition in 1915 there were 116 active members of the Old Guard. The Resumé published in 1933 lists 101 active members. The Second Edition published in 1964 does not contain a roster of members at that time. Today we have 104 active members. Although few in number, the members of the Old Guard and the Gate City Guard have carried on through more than 129 years of civic and patriotic activities.

With pride in our illustrious history, we look to the future with confidence.

A.M.W., Jr.

Atlanta, Georgia
May 31, 1986

List of Illustrations

Foreword

T HESE "Chronicles" emanate from the desire of many members of the Guard to have a permanent and detailed record of its achievements and the spirit that inspired them. This record is of particular interest to the members, their families and friends; for them it is printed, and not for readers in general.

The narrative, to the year 1897, was written by the late Henry Clay Fairman, and from that date to the end by Prof. Joseph T. Derry, who served in the same regiment with the Gate City Guard in the sixties.

These gifted writers tell the story which will not only entertain, but will aid in perpetuating the ideals expressed in events both great and small.

ARCHIBALD H. DAVIS, Chairman,
BEN LEE CREW,
JOHN W. MURRELL,
FRANK M. BERRY,
                    Committee on Chronicles.

Introductory

IN compiling these chronicles, I have relied almost entirely on extracts from the Georgia press and from the press of the country generally, therefore, I am rather the editor than the author, there being but little original matter in the book; the personal sentiments and opinions which I have written are the result of conversations with our citizens and friends of the Gate City Guard, and from editorial and local matter in newspapers from different parts of the Union. I found it often very difficult to obtain accounts of events connected with the Company, but as a full history would require more than one volume, I have confined myself more to that part of it which relates to the higher and patriotic work of the corps, rather than to details of competitive contests and social events, which are features common to nearly all military organizations. I do not claim any literary merit for the work, my object being to preserve for the members and their relatives and friends, a condensed history of the unselfish efforts of the Gate City Guard to create and maintain a fraternal and patriotic sentiment among the people of all the States for the preservation of our common country.

H. C. FAIRMAN.

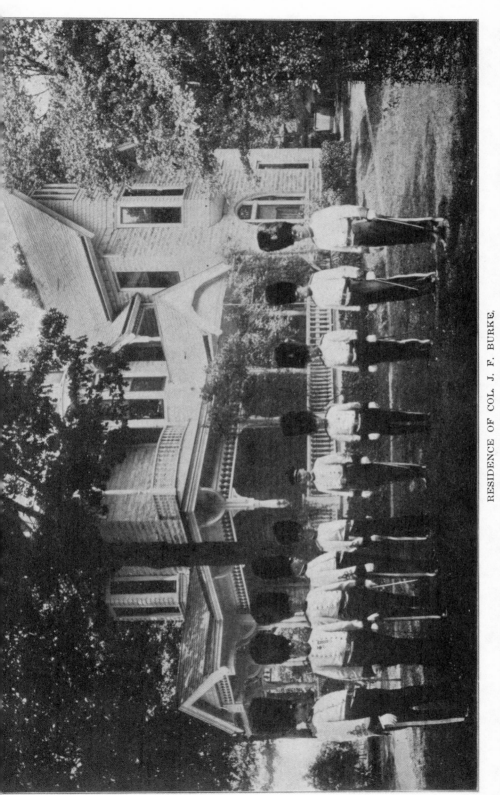

RESIDENCE OF COL. J. F. BURKE,

Where the erection of the Old Guard (G. C. G.) Monument in Piedmont Park, Atlanta, Georgia, was conceived and carried to completion. Reading from left to right: Col. Edward Wight, Gen. A. J. West, Maj. A. H. Davis, Col. George M. Napier, Maj. B. B. Crew, Col. J. F. Burke, Capt. W. M. Crumley, Maj. Chas. P. Byrd, Capt. Jno. J. Woodside, Lieut. Geo. R. Donovan.

CHAPTER I

Organization of the Gate City Guard—Roll of Members—Uniforms—John Cobb Executed—In Camp—Stars and Stripes Presented—Beginning of the War between the States—New Officers—War Sermon—Presentation of Another Flag—A Gold Watch to Miss Hanleiter—Ladies Present War Flag—Little Miss Avary's Speech—Off for Pensacola, Macon and Virginia—Fight of Carricks Ford and Cheat Mountain—Flag Lost in a Ravine—First Loss by Death.

THE ORIGINAL ORGANIZATION

THE GATE CITY GUARD was first organized on the 8th of January, 1857, at Atlanta, Georgia, and was named after the City of Atlanta, which bore the cognomen—"Gate City."

The first place of meeting was in a room over a bank building, located on the corner of what is now Wall and Peachtree Streets, then belonging to the Georgia Railroad and Banking Company. The election of officers resulted as follows:

THE ORGANIZERS.

Geo. Harvey Thompson	Captain
Wm. L. Ezzard	1st Lieutenant
S. W. Jones	Sr. 2nd Lieutenant
Jno. H. Lovejoy	Jr. 2nd Lieutenant
John T. Lewis	Ord. Sergeant
Wilson J. Ballard	2nd Sergeant
Willis P. Chisolm	3rd Sergeant
J. H. Purtell	4th Sergeant
Thos. M. Clark	1st Corporal
Jas. E. Butler	2nd Corporal
Ed. Holland	3rd Corporal
Jos. Thompson, Jr.	4th Corporal

Dr. Jas. F. Alexander.................Surgeon
Daniel Pitman............Secretary and Treasurer
M. O. Markham   ⎫
                       ⎬ ....Markers
J. Edgar Thompson   ⎭

PRIVATES

Marginius A. Bell, David W. Brown, J. M. Blackwell, A. J. Buchanan, G. W. Burr, M. N. Bartlett, Thos. M. Beaumont, E. A. Center, Nath. Center, A. G. Chisolm, J. L. Crenshaw, R. W. Craven, W. B. Cox, J. L. Cutting, P. N. Calhoun, D. H. Connally, Phillip Dodd, Vines Fish, F. S. Fitch, R. A. Fife, T. P. Fleming, F. W. Farrar, Jno. Ficken, H. H. Glenn, Henry Gullatt, Zach Gatewood, Elias Holcombe, C. R. Hanleiter, W. G. Herndon, Albert Howell, F. E. Henson, Jno. Haslett, C. A. Harralson, W. H. Hulsey, R. O. Haynes, L. L. Jones, Warren Jourdan, T. C. Jackson, Marion Jackson, Jas. F. Jackson, Jas. H. Johnson, Peter F. Jones, Harry Krouse, O. G. Kile, J. J. King, Austin Leyden, Jas. W. Loyd, Jas. M. Love, Wm. Mims, R. F. Maddox, H. A. Mitchell, N. A. McLendon, Jno. McLendon, Jas. H. Neal, A. J. Orme, David Prince, C. A. Stone, P. M. Sitton, W. J. Tanner, Joe B. Tanner, Robert Winship, George Winship, Frank Watkins, David Young, W. F. Peck.

The membership was representative of the best element of Atlanta's citizenship. The uniform of the company was a remarkably brilliant one, being dark blue, with dark epaulettes and trimmings, edged with gold. The hat was a black French shako, with drooping white plume. The service uniform was gray. The company, even in those ante-bellum times, were well drilled, and noted for their proficiency in the manual of arms and company movements, and were the favorite corps of gala festivities.

On all occasions when necessary, the company was called on by the authorities. When Jno. Cobb was hung during July, 1859, and it was rumored that his friends would make an attempt to rescue him from the sheriff, the company was called on to act as a guard to the sheriff; and again in November, of the same year, when ten or twelve stores on Whitehall and Alabama Streets were destroyed by fire, Capt. Thompson called out the company to assist the city authorities in preserving order and guarding the property of the merchants saved from their burning stores.

CHARTER OF THE GATE CITY GUARD

An Act to Incorporate the Gate City Guard, of Atlanta, and to Grant Certain Immunities and Privileges to the Members of the Same.

SECTION 1. Be it enacted, &c., that from and after the passage of this Act, George Harvey Thompson, Captain; W. S. Ezzard, First Lieutenant; S. W. Jones, Second Lieutenant; John H. Lovejoy, Third Lieutenant, and others, the officers and members of the Gate City Guard, a volunteer infantry corps of the City of Atlanta, and in the County of Fulton, and State of Georgia, and their successors, the officers and members which hereafter become members of said corps, be, and the same hereby declared to be, a body politic and corporate under the name and style above expressed; and in their corporate capacity shall have power to sue and be sued, plead and be impleaded, in all and singular the courts of law and equity in this State; to have a common seal, and to hold such property, real and personal, whether obtained by gift or purchase, as may be deemed necessary or convenient for the purposes of said corps, and to make all by-laws, rules and regulations for their own government that they may deem necessary, and which are not contrary or repugnant to the Constitution and laws of this State, and to the laws of the United States; and by their commanding officers to constitute and hold courts of inquiry, to enforce said by-laws and regulations, and to punish delinquents; *provided*, always, that said courts of inquiry shall be governed and controlled by the rules and regulations of other courts of inquiry of this State.

SEC. 2. And be it further enacted, That the number of men composing said corps shall never exceed the number of eighty privates, exclusive of the commissioned and non-commissioned officers.

SEC. 3. And be it further enacted, That all persons who are now enrolled, or who may hereafter enroll themselves, as members of aforesaid corps, *provided*, always, that the number does not exceed the number recited in the second section of this Act, shall be, and they are hereby declared to be, exempt from all duty, patrol duty and militia duty, further than such as may be required of them as members of such corps, and such drills and inspections as may be ordered by the Commander-in-Chief; *provided*, always, that the said corps shall, at no time, drill and parade a less number of times yearly than is now required by the militia laws of this State.

SEC. 4. And be it further enacted, That the officers of said corporation shall be a President and Secretary; that the commanding officer of said corps shall be, by virtue of his office, the President of the said corporation, and that all acts performed by him, in behalf of said corps, and which he may lawfully perform as President of said corporation, shall be held good and valid in any court of law and equity in this State; *provided*, that all contracts in writing shall, in addition to the signature of the President, be countersigned by the Secretary of said corporation.

SEC. 5. Be it further enacted, That the immunities and privileges aforesaid shall continue no longer than during the membership of said corps, and that the certificate of the commanding officer of said corps shall be sufficient evidence of such membership to entitle said member to all the immunities and privileges as aforesaid.

SEC. 6. Be it further enacted, That the members of said corps, after seven years' service as such, be, and they are hereby declared to be, exempt from all militia duty forever, except in cases of insurrection, invasion, rebellion or war.

SEC. 7. Repeals conflicting laws.

Approved December 14, 1859.

On the 10th of July, 1860, the company went into camp at White Sulphur Springs, Meriwether County, and remained ten days, during which time they were under strict military discipline. They afterwards went to La-Grange and camped for two days, and were highly entertained by the La-Grange Light Guards, and the citizens generally, everyone doing all that could be done to make it pleasant for them. From LaGrange they marched to the Springs, a distance of sixteen miles, a disagreeable march in the hot mid-summer sun.

During November, 1860, a convention of the military companies of the State was called to meet at Milledgeville, to devise means to perfect the military system of the State. The delegates from the Gate City Guard were Capt. Thompson, Lieut. Lovejoy, E. Holland, Harry Krouse and Lieut. Ezzard.

NATIONAL FLAG PRESENTATION

Without woman, the society she affords, the smiles she bestows, and the thousand and one innocent, yet refining and elevating pleasures she invents to

THOS. M. CLARKE.
Oldest Member of the Corps, and One of the
Organizers in 1858.

JOSEPH THOMPSON.
One of the Organizers in 1858.

GEORGE WINSHIP.
One of the Organizers in 1858.

HARRY KROUSE,
One of the Organizers in 1858.

beguile the hours and "drive dull care away", this world would be, indeed, a desolate waste.   But for them to love and to fight for, to make home dear and endearing to us, chivalry would be known only in name, and patriotism expire.   These little reflections have been suggested by a charming little episode which occurred yesterday afternoon.

The ladies of Atlanta, having resolved to present the Gate City Guard with a flag, procured one, and April 16, 1860, was appointed for the presentation.   About four o'clock, the gallant corps took the line of march for the residence of William Barnes, Esq., where it had been determined the presentation should take place.   On reaching the house, the Guard formed in line in front, when they were greeted by a numerous company of invited guests, and of the ladies of Atlanta.   The eyes of this gallant corps will not quail quicker, nor their cheeks blanch more, before an enemy in battle-array, than they did when the glances from that formidable array of bright eyes flashed upon them.   Everything being in readiness, Miss Josephine E. Hanleiter, the chosen representative of the ladies, and the brave and amiable daughter of the soldierly Lieutenant of the Guard, C. R. Hanleiter, approached, and with womanly tremulousness, presented the flag, delivering the following neat and patriotic address:

Miss Jos. E. Hanleiter's Address

Gentlemen: In the name of the ladies of Atlanta—your wives, sisters and daughters—I have the honor to present to the Gate City Guard, this flag—the ever-glorious "Star-Spangled Banner."

It is not to be regarded as the reward of heroic actions, performed on the battle-field, where men seek

> "The bubble reputation,
> Even at the cannon's mouth,"

but rather as a mark of respect for you—a portion of our citizen soldiery— whom we feel confident will be found ever true to the motto of your corps, "Always Ready," should occasion arise, to quell the riotous disturbers of our domestic tranquillity, suppress servile insurrection, or crush the daring usurper of our rights.   Unlike other nations, ours keeps no large standing army; but, relying upon you, and such as you—its citizen soldiery—as a bulwark in time of war, it bids a proud defiance to the combined armies of the world.

Beautiful in conception, and still more beautiful and exalted in the sentiment it embodies, is our National Flag. May the day never, never arrive when either of the stripes, representing the glorious "Old Thirteen," shall be sundered from their blood-cemented companionship, or one of the stars, forming that resplendent constellation, be blotted out and lost to its sisters; but may others be added, until the light of their combined rays penetrate all parts of the earth, diffusing the light of rational freedom to all nations.

Memories of which we, as a nation, may be proud, cluster around this flag. It has only been unfurled in the defense of Right; it has never floated over the field of dishonor; it has never been disgraced by inglorious retreat. It is now respected by every nation, and floats most gloriously on every sea, the emblem of Justice and Honor. Under it the last man of you may die, but from it he cannot desert. In peace it will remind you of the esteem of the donors; when the war cry summons to the battle, let it inspire each of you to deeds of daring.

Assured, officers and members of the Gate City Guard, that it is about to be confided to those who will gallantly maintain, with their lives if need be, the high renown it has won, I now commit it to your custody, and bid you

"Unfurl the glorious banner,
    Let it sway upon the breeze,
The emblem of our Country's pride,
    On land and on the seas.
The emblem of our liberty,
    Borne proudly in the wars,
The Hope of every Freeman,
    The gleaming Stripes and Stars."

SERGEANT STONE'S REPLY

On receiving the flag, Sergeant C. A. Stone said:

Miss Hanleiter: In behalf of the Gate City Guard, I return you our most sincere and grateful thanks for this magnificent and appropriate gift, so gracefully presented to us, through you, by the ladies of Atlanta, and rest assured that as long as life shall last, these colors shall never trail in the dust.

Nothing cheers the soldier's heart as the approving smiles of lovely woman; and for this cause, as much as any other, is attributed the reputation of

American soldiery in matchless courage.   Here, as you have aptly observed, we have no standing army, but we have a citizen soldiery, taken from the bosom of our people, not by force, but by their own free choice, who in the "piping times of peace" attend to those sacred duties of the civilian—build up the industry, the commerce and prosperity of their own beloved country; but when the battle alarm sounds are ready to flock to their country's standard to protect their hearthstones, their wives, their sisters, their mothers, and last but not least, their sweethearts, too.   But the soldier's pride is in action, not words.

We thank you, kind ladies, for this beautiful gift—still more for the delicate manner in which you have presented it.   May the earth on which we tread sink beneath us if we ever suffer one stain of dishonor to blacken the graceful folds of our National Banner.

On the conclusion of Sergeant Stone's response, Capt. Geo. Harvey Thompson, the gallant commander of the Guard, seizing the staff, gave expression to the patriotic emotions, which well nigh overpowered him, in a few brief, but appropriate remarks.

As Sergeant Stone faced about, the company was commanded to "present arms," when the usual salute was given; after which the flag was escorted to its position in ranks.   As soon as this was done, upon the signal being given, the band marched along the line and saluted by playing most spiritedly, the "Star-Spangled Banner."

The arms being stacked, at the word of command, the company broke ranks preparatory to a destructive assault upon the various bountifully supplied delicacies, which had been provided and temptingly arranged by the whole-souled wife of the large-hearted host.   For an hour or more time passed pleasantly in giving toasts and receiving responses, when the Guard and the guests retired, leaving the field in the undisputed possession of the ladies present.

The Guard then paraded through our principal streets to display their flag, going through with promptness and precision many military evolutions. They then marched to a position in front of their armory, where they were dismissed.   The occasion throughout was made one of exceeding pleasantness by all who participated in any manner in it, and fully evinced the cordial good-will which pervades our community.

The flag is made of rich rep silk, and is six feet long by four feet six inches wide.   On the obverse, surrounded by the stars in the blue ground, are the words, "Gate City Guard, from the Ladies of Atlanta, 1860." On the reverse, surrounded in the same manner by the stars, is the motto, "*In hoc signo vinces.*" ("In this sign thou shall conquer.")

The flag is handsomely fringed, and the staff is surmounted by a Liberty Cap, with gold cord and tassels depending.

The occasion was enlivened, and the interest much increased, by the excellent music of the brass band.*

OUR FIRST LOSS BY DEATH

ARMORY HALL, GATE CITY GUARDS,
Atlanta, July 16, 1860

"Oh what a shadow o'er the heart is flung,
When peals the requiem of the loved and young."

For the first time since the organization of the Gate City Guards, we are called upon to mourn the loss of a comrade. A name has been stricken from our roll by the hand of Death. Mankind's great enemy has invaded our corps and borne from its ranks one who lately moved among us in all the buoyant pride and exultant hope of young and joyous manhood.

Private David Y. Tomlinson is no more. He died of consumption on the 11th inst., at the residence of Mr. J. J. Thrasher, in this city. The many virtues of our deceased comrade had endeared him to our hearts. He was warm in his attachments, generous in his impulses, noble in his nature, and now that he is gone these qualifications will

"Keep his memory green in our souls."

We know that it becomes us to bow in humble resignation to the will of the Almighty, but when one so young, with such bright prospects for a long, useful and happy life is cut down, 'tis hard, hard, indeed, to recognize God's hand and repress the murmuring sigh.

The deceased was one prompt and punctual in the discharge of his duties as a member of the company. We all remember how much interest he took in our recent encampment, and how zealously he attempted to participate actively in its exercise, despite his fearful cough and wasted form; but alas, Death's cold hand was even then clutching at his heart, and he was forced to yield. As we

---

* The presentation of this flag indicates that in Atlanta there was but little thought of the war storm that soon followed.

have seen the bloom of youth passing from his brow and the flush of health fading from his cheek, we have feared this result, but our regret is no less poignant, the sorrow which it brings is no less bitter.

We have paid our departed comrade the last mournful tribute of respect and bade him at his grave, a soldier adieu. It only remains now for us to give some expression to the feelings of our hearts.

Therefore, Resolved 1st.—That we have heard with much sorrow of the melancholy demise of our fellow member, David Y. Tomlinson.

Resolved 2nd.—That we tender to his family and especially to his sisters (to whom in their orphanage he has proven a parent), our heart-felt condolence, that we mingle our tears with them in this their great bereavement.

Resolved 3rd.—That this preamble and resolutions be entered upon our minutes, and a copy be furnished the family of the deceased.

Resolved 4th.—That our banners be draped in mourning for 30 days and that we wear the usual badge thereof for the same length of time.

NEAL,

HOLCOMBE,

G. WINSHIP,

Committee.

True extract from the minutes of the Gate City Guards.

DANIEL PITTMAN,

Sec. *pro tem.*

The above resolutions are furnished by Mr. Walter E. Hancock, nephew of the deceased, who is a member of the Old Guard. His brother, Mr. W. L. Hancock, is also a member.

It seems that the company, in those times, had at least two competitive trials of marksmanship. At the first, the prize was won by Thos. M. Clarke, who still resides in Atlanta, a retired merchant, and a member of the Old Guard. On the 8th of January, 1860, there was another contest, and the prize, a gold medal, was awarded to Private T. C. Jackson. This interesting memento is now in the possession of Mr. Jackson's widow, who resides in Atlanta. On one side of the medal, the Georgia Coat-of-Arms is inscribed. On the other the following:

"Presented to Private T. C. Jackson, best shot, by the Gate City Guard, Jany. 8, 1860."

In the War between the States

All was harmony until the close of 1860-61. There was a marked division among the people of Georgia on the question of secession from the Federal Union. Some of the State's most illustrious men firmly opposed it up to and during the sittings of the Milledgeville Convention, which adopted the fateful ordinance of withdrawal from the Union. It was but natural that there should be some discussion in the Gate City Guard upon the momentous issue. (A test of the question arose among them out of the proposition to hoist the United States flag over the armory. There was a warm, if not angry discussion of the question, and the decision was averse to the banner of the Union. The State flag was unfurled.) It being thought probable about this time, that Governor Joseph E. Brown would accept troops for active service, a vote was proposed to be taken as to whether the Guard would volunteer. Preceding the ballot the flag issue was again raised, and was bitterly debated. Some members refused to remain longer in the company if the Stars and Stripes were not used. A temporary adjournment was resorted to in hopes of uniting all the members, but no agreement could be reached, and nearly one-half of the members resigned, including one or two commissioned officers. At the next meeting the resignations were accepted, and it was determined to offer the services of the company to the Executive, and place it on a war footing by electing officers to fill vacancies resulting from the resignations. A paper was passed among the company for the signatures of those who were willing to volunteer for active service, and forty-six members signed it at once. The remainder declined. The forty-six who signed decided to invite volunteers to join them, and in a few days the forty-six had grown to be about eighty. Then the company met and elected the following officers:

G. H. Thompson, Captain (afterward Major of 1st Regt.), W. L. Ezzard, 1st Lieutenant, H. M. Wylie, 2d Lieutenant, C. A. Stone, 3d Lieutenant, A. Leyden, Ensign, T. C. Jackson, Orderly Sergeant, Peter F. Jones, 2d Sergeant, A. G. Chisolm, 3d Sergeant, Wm. Mims, 4th Sergeant, P. M. Sitton, 5th Sergeant, A. J. Orme, 1st Corporal, Albert Howell, 2d Corporal, Joseph Thompson, Jr., 3d Corporal, Harry Krouse, 4th Corporal, Dr. W. F. Westmoreland, Surgeon.

The Privates seem to have been the following: Alton Angier, Ed. Atkinson, Jas. Barnes, William Barnes, Dave Brown, M. D. Bass, A. E. Brooks, Charles Barrett, James Crockett, J. L. Crenshaw, Warren Jourdan, Wm. W.

Johnson, James Loyd, James Love, W. M. Leatherwood, Charles Lattimer, Jep. N. Langston, Joe Montgomery, H. A. Mitchell, Robt. J. Mitchell, Wm. L. Corley, Dave Connally, Tom R. Clingham, Ed. A. Center, Nath. Center, Richard Craven, Phillip Dodd, Thos. M. Darnell, Albert Dudley, Joe Eddleman, Vines Fish, Robt. Farris, M. Friedenthall, Frank Farrar, J. H. Furcrum, Robt. Fife, Henry Gullatt, Dave S. Guard, Adolphus Gant, Zack Gatewood, Jno. A. Hill, F. Henson, R. O. Haynes, G. A. Loftin (now a noted Baptist minister), Joe Harrison, Richard Hammond, Nat. M. Mangum, Thomas Moon, Seab Ozburn, W. F. Peck, W. H. Ozburn, John Pilsbury, M. Rote, J. L. Rodgers, Zack Smith, Alf Suttle, G. A. Strick, James Stokes, John Sanders, Jesse Thornton, W. J. Tanner, Gus. Tomlinson, James Turner, Stephen Turner, Hiram Wing, Marcus V. Wood, M. Witgenstein, Charles Wallace, David Young, Mike White, John Warwick, J. J. King, W. R. Key, David Prince, F. S. Fitch, Robt. Farris, J. Furguson, C. A. Haralson, Marshall Hibler, Ed. Hill, C. Harwell, Wm. H. Joiner, L. L. Jones, Marion Jackson, Jas. H. Johnston, J. M. Blackwell, Robt. Badger, John Bankston, J. C. Barrett, Wm. Connally, J. C. Connally.

The Governor accepted the offer of the company's services, and ordered them to hold themselves in readiness for active duty. The company now had 104 men, and daily and nightly drills were had to prepare the new members for efficient service. They had secured one hundred Springfield rifled muskets, then the best arms in use, and on March 18, 1861, orders came to rendezvous at Macon, on April 1, 1861, for regimental organization. Before leaving Atlanta, many marks of kindness were shown them. Among these patriotic courtesies was the presentation to them of a Confederate flag by the ladies.

A Sermon to the Gate City Guard

Yesterday morning, March 31st, 1861, at ten o'clock, the spacious room in the City Hall was crowded to its utmost capacity to hear a sermon from the Rev. J. S. Wilson—well known and universally beloved throughout this community—before the Gate City Guard, previous to their departure for Pensacola, which took place today at half past two o'clock. It was a bright and glorious spring morning, and the glorious orb of day seemed prodigal of his cheering light, as if in mockery of the sadness within many hearts at the parting with those who were near to them, and whose patriotism called to the point of their country's danger. At half past ten, the Guard, with solemn tread, entered the room, under command of Capt. Ezzard, and quietly took the front seats which had been reserved for them. After some excellent vocal music, the venerable minister arose and with evident emotion read the morning lesson, which consisted of the 1st, 46th and 99th Psalms. He then offered to the Throne of Grace, a fervent, heart-moving prayer for the safety and protection of our gallant soldiers, the salvation of all hearers, and the peace, prosperity and glory of our beloved land.

He selected his text from the 13th verse, 6th Chapter of Paul's Epistle to the Ephesians: "Wherefore take unto you the whole armor of God, that ye may be able to withstand the evil day, and having done all, to stand."

The first portion of his sermon was addressed to the congregation at large, urging the necessity of a Christian's wearing the armor of Godliness, with which to successfully fight the great battles of life and win the never-fading crowns of glory, which were reserved for the faithful to the end. The learned divine then took up the causes which have, for forty years, been agitating the public mind and exciting apprehensions for our safety on the part of the people of the South, and which have brought about our present difficulties. With a master hand he portrayed those causes, pointed out their remedies, and established the justice of our cause. He implored the blessings of Heaven on our threatened country, and her gallant defenders. His features glowed with earnestness and his eloquence and power as a pulpit orator are peculiarly his own.

All who were present listened spell-bound to his burning words, and were deeply impressed. Many mothers, wives and sisters of those who would soon leave for the war earnestly lifted up their hearts in silent prayer for their safety. May their Christian spirits, like guardian angels, hover over and protect our gallant soldiers from every temptation and evil, and from all harm.

ANOTHER COMPANY FLAG PRESENTED TO THE GATE CITY GUARD, APRIL 1, 1861.

(Taken from the "*Southern Confederacy*")

Within a few days past, it became known to a few that Miss Josephine E. Hanleiter had prepared a most elegant flag of the Confederate States, to be presented to the Gate City Guard, and that the presentation ceremonies would take place this morning, which it did, in front of the large buildings of the Franklin Printing Company. The sky was overcast with dense clouds at early dawn, which continued to grow more threatening, 'til it terminated in a rain about 9 o'clock. Notwithstanding this unfavorable aspect of the weather, early signs of preparation for the approaching ceremonies were observable in the rapid passing to and fro of men wearing military dress, and the gathering of a large multitude of people on the platform and under the eaves of the Macon & Western Depot. The windows of all the surrounding buildings were filled with ladies. The long veranda in front of the Franklin Building was crowded with ladies and misses, who stood there with umbrellas to protect them from the falling rain. Every window of the large building, and, indeed, almost every room in it, was crowded with human beings, all eager to get a sight of the interesting proceedings. There was also a large number of people on the house-tops, despite the falling rain—so anxious were the people to see all that transpired.

At a quarter past ten o'clock the heavy roll of the drum and shrill notes of the fife gave notice of the approach of the military. The procession was headed by the Fulton Dragoons, commanded by Capt. W. T. Wilson; next came the Georgia Volunteers, under command of Lieut. Johnson; next the Fulton Blues, Capt. J. H. Purtell; next the Atlanta Cadets, Capt. Willis Chisolm; and the Gate City Guard brought up the rear. It was a splendid and imposing military array, every way worthy of our city and the military spirit of the people.

The Dragoons took their position in the rear, fronting the Franklin Printing House—the Georgia Volunteers on the right flank, with the Blues and Cadets on the left. Into this hollow square, just in front of the Dragoons, the Guard were marched in fine style. The rain and the travel over the street had made any amount of mud and slush, but the soldiers heeded it not.

When all were arranged, Miss Hanleiter, accompanied by Miss Emeline Shaw and Miss Mary Parr, emerged from Col. Hanleiter's residence and took their position on the front of the pavement. Miss Hanleiter bore in one hand the beautiful flag which she had prepared, and in the other an elegant bouquet of spring flowers. She rested the flag-staff upon the pavement, while Gen. Z. A. Rice, on the part of the ladies made the presentation speech, as follows:

"Captain Ezzard and Soldiers of the Gate City Guard:

"Why this assemblage here? Why peals forth the note of martial music? Why this paraphernalia of war which I see before me now? But a few short months ago, the citizens, of what was then the United States of America, were living in peace and harmony with each other. But in the course of events, a fanatical party usurped the reins of government, foisting themselves into power by the assertion of a principle that was destructive to our very existence, to-wit: The infamous dogma of an equality of the white and black races. While I, for the sake of not being contentious, would admit that, in many respects this doctrine would apply to many of the people of the Abolition States of the North, yet we of the South rightfully insist that the black race are, and should be, our servants, and we their masters; and such relative status was given by the decrees of God; and which law of our society was recognized by the Constitution of the United States, and which they were bound by such solemn compact to observe. Regardless of this compact, led on by their lust of power, and guided by their fanaticism, and relying upon our submissiveness, in consequence of our known veneration for the Union of our fathers, there was no indignity that was not heaped upon us, and finally the last feather was laid upon the camel's back. The Union was dissevered by them. They forced us to resume our State sovereignty. We have done so and declared ourselves a free and independent State; have entered into a new alliance, and now when we have a right to suppose that we should be permitted to depart in peace—as the consciences of the Abolitionists would be relieved of the sin of slavery—they refuse to allow us to depart, for fear their pockets will be depleted also.

"For asserting our independence, the superiority of our race, and the contracting of a new alliance, the old and decrepit government of the North is threatening us with war and subjugation.

"I am proud to know, in defense of this principle and this action—in defense of our own honor, and the honor of our own native South, that we now see you clad in the habiliments of war—ready in a few hours to take up your line of march for what may soon be a field of gory strife. To preserve unsullied and untarnished one's own honor, and the honor of his country, is the highest, the noblest ambition of the patriot-soldier.

'For gold the merchant plows the main,
　　The farmer plows the manor;
　　But *glory* is the soldier's prize:
　　The soldier's wealth is *honor*.'

"Captain Ezzard: As the humble representative of a lady donor, I have the honor of presenting to your noble company, this flag—the flag of the Confederate States of America—in whose service you have enlisted. Under the guidance of those *seven stars*—the emblem of Eternal Truth—you will march; and under its bright folds, upon the field of battle, you will rally to meet enemies of your country. In conclusion, I will only say that the fair daughters of Atlanta are proud of the Gate City Guard—we are all proud of you—proud of such noble defenders. They already feel confident that, upon the field of battle, this flag will wave as long as one of the Guard survives; and I doubt not that the remembrance of the fair donor will nerve the arm of each one of your noble patriot band to deeds of daring that the future historian will inscribe in letters of light upon the historic page.

"And now, in behalf of the fair donor, and for myself, I bid you farewell. Put your trust in God, in Truth and in Right. May His blessings attend you; His kind providence protect you, and vouchsafe to you a safe return to your homes, your kindred and your friends."

At the conclusion of his address, he took the flag from the hands of Miss Hanleiter and gave it to Private C. A. Harralson, who received it on the part of the company in an appropriate address, of which the following is the substance:

"General Rice and Ladies: It is a well-spring of pleasure to me that I am called upon to receive, at your hands, this beautiful and well thought of present. The ladies of the South have ever been heroic and true to their country, and thoughtful to provide for those who go forth in its defense. Their encouragement and cheering smiles have ever beamed on patriotic hearts; and it is peculiarly gratifying to us to receive from your hands this token of regard for us, and for the cause in which we are engaged.

"Ladies: The signs of the times indicate that we, perhaps, are not called upon to do duty as mere peace soldiers, but that with strong arms and stout hearts we may have to meet our country's foes before our service shall end. The boast has been made that our homes and firesides should be invaded, our country despoiled, and our manhood humbled in the dust. It is the duty of our young men to come forward, strike for the protection of our country—our honor—our wives, sisters and mothers; and if necessary, die in their defense. We accept the issue, and with gratitude we accept this beautiful flag, which your fair hands have wrought. Our motto shall be that which was given by the Spartan mother to her son when he was departing to fight in defense of his country: 'Return with this, or upon it.' Again, ladies, accept our heart-felt thanks."

He then turned and gave the flag to Color Sergeant Peter F. Jones, the standard bearer of the company, and addressed him as follows:

"Sergeant Jones, as color bearer of our company, I give into your hands for safe-keeping this token of love and esteem from the ladies of this city; and I enjoin you to cherish and protect it, as you would a prized gift from a mother; do not hesitate to shed your blood in defense of the honor of this flag.

"And now (addressing his company), brother soldiers of the Gate City Guard, behold your flag. I know you will never see it dishonored. Brothers: This is a gift from 'God's best gift to man.' If nothing else inspire you to heroic deeds, the fact that this beautiful flag has been wrought by the fair hands and given us through the kind heart of a woman should. I know you will never suffer its folds to be sullied, or see it trail in the dust, while an arm remains with which to raise it, or a hand to strike. Cherish, then, our banner, and should it be our duty to meet our foes in deadly conflict, let us show by our valor that we are worthy of the confidence which the ladies have placed in us, and the flag with which they have honored us." Mr. Harralson's remarks were received with applause by the vast audience, and when he appealed to his gallant co-patriots not to suffer the honor of the flag to be sullied, a universal shout was the response of the whole company.

When he had concluded, Sergeant A. G. Chisolm advanced, and on the part of the company, presented to Miss Hanleiter, to whom the credit of getting it up, making and presenting this flag is principally due, a lady's beautiful gold watch, accompanied by an elegant and appropriate speech, which was handsomely replied to by General Rice, on the part of Miss Hanleiter. The watch has the following inscription:

"Gate City Guard to Miss J. E. Hanleiter, April 1st, 1861."

Three cheers were then given with a will by the vast throng for the ladies, and three more for the Guard, after which the company marched to their armory, escorted by the Dragoons, Blues, Volunteers and Cadets, and the crowd dispersed.

Watch Presentation

The crowded state of our columns yesterday, prevented us from inserting the speech of Sergeant A. G. Chisolm, of the Gate City Guard, on presenting a lady's beautiful gold watch to Miss Josephine E. Hanleiter, which we now annex:

"Miss Hanleiter: It becomes my pleasing duty, in the name of the Gate City Guard, to present you with this watch, as a small token of their good will. Your repeated acts of kindness toward us render this present but the more appropriate. Whether we are called upon to struggle amid the fearful scenes of the bloody battle-field, or are permitted to walk quietly 'in paths of pleasure and paths of peace,' be assured that the Gate City Guard will long remember your encouraging smiles and valuable advice. Let the beauty of this watch as you bear it to learn the hour as it passes ever remind you that it cannot be more faithful in telling you the time of the day, than we will be in procuring, with our lives if necessary, your best interests, as the chief earthly good will of all true Southern women. We are now, in many particulars, in the midst of the greatest revolution the world has ever known. So far as we are concerned, we are *unalterably determined* that this revolution shall be a success. We have placed our hands to the plow, and rather than look back, in this glorious delivery from Northern tyranny and insult, we confidently believe that the fair women of the Sunny South will cheerfully join us, if need be, in giving up their heart's blood to secure to our posterity the priceless blessings of Constitutional liberty. But we shall not fail. Armed with Justice— and hence doubly armed—supported in our movements by the voice of Heaven—beckoned onward by the fair hands of our own fair country—women— in the name of Justice—of Woman—and of God, we have determined to

'Strike till our last armed foe expires,
Strike for our altars and our fires,
Strike for the green graves of our sires,
God, and our native land.'

"On one side of this watch, you will find thirteen jewels; these will remind you of the thirteen original States so famous in history for their deeds of heroism and noble achievements. These States were at first controlled by honest men, disposed to do each other justice. But times have changed. The thirteen grew to thirty-three, and a dominant and unconscientious majority, acting under the false philosophy of the 'higher law,' and the senseless statesmanship of the 'Irrepressible-Conflict-Rail-Splitter,' thinking that the spirit of '76 had fled from the dwellers in the 'Southern land,' foolishly prepared to place upon our necks social and political inferiority, regardless of written compacts and fraternal ties. On the other side you will find seven jewels; these will remind you that the North sadly mistook the people of our States, taking our forbearance in times past for cowardice, and that the spirit of '76 still lives among us, and that the 'Confederate States of America' have been compelled to inaugurate a new government—we believe a better one than the old. Your smiles and your countenance, and the smiles and countenance of such as you, will inspire us to stand by the immortal 'Seven.' The memories of the 'Thirteen' will turn your mind to the patriot women of the Revolution which delivered us from the tyranny of the British Lion. The memories of the 'Seven' will point you (God bless them) to many a living woman who will live in history, gloriously connected with a revolution which has freed us from a bondage worse than England placed upon our fathers.

"Having written your name among the patriot women of '61, you have proved yourself to the world to be a worthy descendant of the women of '76. Again, I say, accept this watch, as but a humble testimonial of the kind regards of the Gate City Guard."

General Rice then replied as follows:

"Sergeant Chisolm: In the name of Miss Hanleiter, the recipient of this valuable present—so unexpectedly presented—permit me to assure you she accepts, with inexpressible pleasure, and that it will be worn with a grateful remembrance of your noble company, who are about to take the line of march to the tented field, and if need be, to fight the battles of our country. And also, to thank you for the kind terms in which you have tendered the valuable gift. Rest assured that you, and the noble company you represent, will be presented to the Throne of God daily, that His providence may watch over and protect you. And again in her behalf, and for myself, I express our devout prayer that God will preserve you, whether in camp or battle, and again return each one of you to your homes and your friends."

Miss Avary's Speech

Enthusiasm on the departure of the gallant Gate City Guard pervaded the schools of Atlanta, especially the Atlanta Female Institute. Over two hundred of these young girls in procession, led by the President and teachers and each girl bearing a little flag, marched to the depot, and formed in line fronting the company. Then just before the moment when the Guard were to take the train, Dr. A. G. Thomas, Professor of Belle Lettres, presented a little girl, Miss Sallie Avary,* who delivered with grace and enthusiasm the following little speech:

"Soldiers, your country has called for your services, and with a promptness never excelled by Greek nor Roman you grasped your swords, buckled on your armor, and now wait but the neighing of the iron horse to bear you on with thunder tread to the scene of action, and it may be to the field of bloody glory. In you we present to the sacred cause of patriotism the jewels of Georgia.

"To each of you we give, as a token of admiration, a tiny flag, inscribed on one side, 'From the young ladies of the Atlanta Female Institute,' and on the other the true legend 'None but the brave deserve the fair.' "

Miss Kane, on the part of the ladies, made a few appropriate remarks, when all the young ladies in a body stepped forward and presented to each member of the Guard one of the very beautiful miniature flags which they held in their hands. Three cheers for the ladies of the Female Institute were given with a hearty good will by all who were present, and then three more were given by the crowd for the Guard.

At this point there was a call for the Hon. T. R. R. Cobb, who was present, and he, in response, came forward and made a most felicitous speech. We are sorry to be unable to lay before our readers a copy of this most excellent speech. After he had concluded, a large number of the relatives, acquaintances and friends of the Guard bade them an affectionate farewell. This was, indeed, an affecting scene.

At two o'clock all the soldiers had taken their seats in the cars, and the train of the Macon & Western Road moved off with thirteen passenger cars attached, amidst the booming of cannon and the cheering and shouting of the unnumbered throng, and the waving of handkerchiefs of the ladies from the windows and balconies contiguous.

The greatest gathering that was ever witnessed in this city took place to witness their departure. The Trout House, Atlanta Hotel, Concert Hall, depots, carsheds, tops of cars—and, indeed, every available space—was crammed with living masses of men, women and children, all eager to see and to cheer the departing soldiers.

---

* Miss Sallie Avary, named above, afterwards became the wife of Gen. Clement A. Evans, of the Confederate Army.

Many were the prayers that followed them to their destination. Many were the tears that were shed at parting with them, and many anxious hearts will sigh for their return, with peace and plenty smiling over our happy land.

The editor has given the foregoing speeches in full to show the prevailing sentiment at the outbreak of the war, that the reader may contrast that exciting period with the sentiment expressed by the Gate City Guard and the people of Georgia in 1879, in which they manfully accepted the result of the war without surrender of former convictions, and labored for a restored Union and the destruction of sectionalism.

On arriving at Macon, the company was ordered to camp in the Fair grounds below the city. All the companies having arrived, the First Regiment of Georgia Volunteers was organized on the 16th of the month.

J. N. Ramsey was elected Colonel; J. O. Clark, Lieutenant Colonel; Capt. G. H. Thompson, of the Gate City Guard, was elected Major. First Lieut. Ezzard succeeded to the captaincy of the company. Hugh M. Wylie now became First Lieutenant, Chester A. Stone, Second Lieutenant, and A. Leyden, Third Lieutenant.

"While in camp at Macon, Governor Brown ordered that we should give up to the State our fine Springfield rifled muskets, and take the old smooth-bore muskets. This created much indignation and the fine guns were shipped secretly to Atlanta and concealed. The company accepted the old muskets, and kept them until their return to Atlanta from Pensacola. On starting to Virginia, the Guard were put in possession of their favorite weapons again.

"On arriving at Pensacola, the company was placed under the strictest military discipline by General Bragg, and required to build batteries for heavy guns, do heavy picket duty along the bay, and about the Perdido swamps. During our service there General Bragg determined to make a night assault on Fort Pickens, located on Santa Rosa Island, and held by the Federal troops. He ordered 1,200 select men to be taken from the army stationed there. Twenty-five of the Gate City Guard, with Capt. Ezzard and Lieut. Leyden, were taken as part of this body. They were marched to the Navy Yard after night, where boats were ready to convey them across the bay to the island. Then they were furnished with scaling ladders to cross the ditch around the fort and to climb the walls. They had forty rounds of ammunition to the man, and were at the boats ready to push out into the bay, when the Federals began to throw up rockets. General Bragg, supposing that our purpose was discovered, postponed the assault, and marched us back to await a more favorable opportunity, which did not come until after the regiment went to Virginia."

"The First Regiment was ordered to leave Florida and proceed to Virginia about the 1st of June, 1861. Passing through Atlanta they gathered some recruits, and exchanged their old muskets for their fine Springfields, as already mentioned. 'Probably, if we had been more experienced soldiers,' says the historian in the 'Cartridge Box,' 'we would not have been so anxious to take the long-range rifles when the rest of the regiment had short-range guns; for when there was any skirmishing or sharp-shooting to be done, the Gate City Guard rifles were ordered to do it, as they were more on an equality with the Federals, who were well armed.'

"On arriving at Richmond, we were ordered to Northwest Virginia, where our troops had just met a slight reverse at Philippi. We went by rail to Staunton, and from there marched over the mountains for a long distance to Laurel Hill, on the western slope of the Allegheny Mountains. Here we were placed under the command of General Garnett, an excellent officer and strict disciplinarian. We were hurriedly put to active duty picketing and preparing our position for an expected attack, which was not long in coming. Our company had suffered, like all new troops, from the different camp diseases and the great change of climate from Florida to the mountains of Virginia. We had almost constant rains, keeping the men wet for weeks at a time, and the Gate City Guard could only turn out about sixty men for daily duty. As picketing was very heavy, it required all the company to go out at once. And it so happened that the night before the Federals attacked us, the Gate City Guard were sent out as the outside pickets next to the enemy (except cavalry scouts). Lieutenants Wylie and Stone were the commissioned officers with the company during the night. Capt. Ezzard and Lieut. Leyden were to command during the day, but Capt. Ezzard, being indisposed, could not go out, and Lieut. Leyden relieved the two night Lieutenants at daylight. A little before sunrise, our cavalry videttes were driven in very rapidly, and in a few minutes the Federals were upon us; Lieut. Leyden posted the Gate City Guard on each side of the Parkersburg Turnpike, in the edge of the wood, and as soon as the enemy came within range we opened on them, and sent word back for reinforcements. The advance of the Federals was checked, as they found that they had other than cavalry to deal with. They immediately formed lines of battle, but before they could advance, the whole of the First Georgia

Regiment had come to the assistance of the pickets who were in line to receive them. Sharp-shooting was kept up until about ten o'clock, when the enemy made a bold rush across the open space between the lines, and penetrated the woods in which the First Georgia was in line of battle, getting within range for smooth guns before they were opened on by the whole line. In a very short time they were running back faster than they had come up. After this there were no charges made, but a constant skirmishing was kept up until our little army was flanked by the capture of Rich Mountain in our rear, and compelled to commence a disastrous retreat. For three days and nights the fighting continued. On the fourth night about twenty of the Gate City Guard were on picket duty next to the enemy, under Lieut. Leyden. It was raining, and very dark; about twelve o'clock pickets were withdrawn from the front. In doing so, the officer in charge had to pass along the lines and touch each man giving him orders in a whisper to follow, keeping the touch to prevent being lost in the dark woods. When the Gate City Guard pickets arrived at camp about two o'clock in the morning, they found our army all gone. It had left as soon as it was dark. They were then ordered to form the rear guard, and follow over the mountain through rain, mud and darkness, worn out and hungry as we were. After marching all night, and until ten o'clock next day, they came up with the army and resumed their places with their regiment. The enemy had possession of the road in front. Our Generals then ordered us to file off into a mountain road leading to Carrick's Ford, on Cheat River. The First Georgia Regiment was made the rear guard for the whole of Garnett's army, allowing all the troops, trains, etc., to get a mile ahead of them. The regiment marched all that day and into the night, having nothing to eat. At last they lay down where they were, famished and without fire, and in a pelting rain, until just before daylight, when they were aroused to continue the march. By this time numbers of the soldiers had given out, and were so broken down that they were allowed to go with the baggage train, and in that way escaped the suffering and dangers of those who kept up for duty. On this day, the First Regiment was still kept as rear guard; and about eight o'clock in the morning, just as they were filing into the Cheat River, the Federals came in sight and commenced firing on us while we were in the water, making it rather lively for us. It being a wet, foggy morning, the Federals got very close to us before we could see them. We had depended on cavalry videttes who unaccountably disappeared. We lost no time in getting on the opposite bank of the river, where

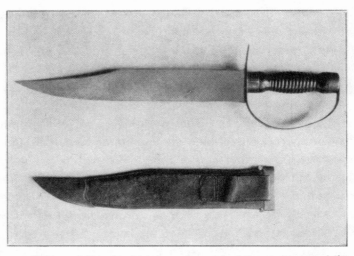

Knife and Sheath which formed a part of the equipment of the Gate City Guard when they left Atlanta for the seat of war. The length of the knife was 16 inches and the width of the blade about 2½ inches.

we formed a line of battle, hoping the Federals would come to the river, where we had been; but the stratagem failed. After waiting for them some hours, we continued our march, while they resorted to skirmishing. At the next crossing of the Cheat River, our regiment was formed in line of battle, with the right resting on the river, and extending at right angles from it into the woods. Immediately the enemy commenced cannonading our lines, and using their long-range rifles on us. Here occurred an unaccountable blunder of our field officers, which was of a very serious nature. While under fire, the officers allege they ordered the regiment to move by the right flank into and across the river, and they may have done so, as the four companies of the right did file into the river and cross; but the six companies on the left did not hear such an order, and maintained their position. The Colonel and Lieutenant-Colonel went with the four companies. This blunder cost our company many lives. The Federals, supposing that all the Confederates had crossed, pressed forward to the river and beyond it at once, thus cutting the First Georgia Regiment in two, and leaving a part of that regiment—the six companies mentioned —in their rear. The Gate City Guard was one of the companies so cut off, and as they lay concealed in the woods, the enemy, unconscious of their proximity, marched their entire force past them, and crossed the Cheat River in pursuit of Garnett's army. Some of the officers and men were anxious to make an attack, which would have been a surprise, but the commander, Maj. Thompson, forbade the movement, and commanded silence.

"When about two brigades of the enemy had filed past us, not knowing that we were within twenty-five yards of them, and all chance of our joining our army was gone, we held a consultation of the commissioned officers of the six companies thus cut off, as to whether we should go out and surrender, or try to pass through the succession of unknown mountains to the Valley of Virginia. By a unanimous vote it was determined to take to the mountains.

"We immediately began the terrible task by moving up the mountain in single file, having no path to guide us through the unbroken wilderness, and no one with us who had ever been in that country before. Many of us had nothing to eat for forty-eight hours but a few crackers before the start (the writer—Major Leyden being one of them). We marched all day, and when night came, laid down, with no fire nor food, and wet to the skin. At daylight we started again in single file, passing over a succession of mountains all day long. On the second night, we lay as in the first, wet, cold, starving and lost. The third day was as the first two, except that the forest became denser with spruce and laurel undergrowth—so thick, indeed, that we had to cut our way with knives and swords. Numbers of the men broke down and declared they could go no further. Some became delirious, and had to be watched. Our condition on the fourth morning was extremely wretched. Many of the men could not move, and there was no prospect of escape for those remaining on their feet. During our wanderings we had met no human being except our comrades, not a bird nor beast, nor habitation of man; no path nor signs of settlement—nothing but a dark, trackless wilderness. Those who were able were sent to the front with knives to continue to cut the way. As soon as one would give out another would take his place, and then we continued to work until about ten o'clock in the day, when word was passed from man to man along the line that a hunter had come up to the rear of the column, and proposed to lead us out. It proved to be a Mr. Parsons, who knew the mountains. He stated that he had heard that troops had passed into the mountains, and knowing that they must perish if not succored at once, had resolved to follow and rescue us. After consultation with the officers, who rather suspected him of being a spy of the enemy, we agreed to accept his guidance with the condition that two riflemen, Phil Dodd and Harry Krouse, were to be near him, and would shoot him if he proved treacherous. As soon as we came to this agreement, those that were able started on the trail of the hunter, leaving their disabled companions lying along the path where they gave out, and others to take care of them until relief could be sent back. By the fourth night the head of the column had arrived at a hunter's hut in the mountains. Parsons, with three assistants, went farther on, and by one o'clock in the night he brought two sacks of meal, some corn bread, salt and four small beeves along the path to the hut. Two of them were shot at once, and the soldiers rushed at them, and scarcely waiting for a pretence of cooking, devoured their flesh. Many of the men were so far gone that they could not be gotten up to take their meat, but had to be served by stronger companions. When daylight came relief was dispatched back along the path to those who had been unable to travel, and by the next night, all had arrived at the hut. There we remained another day, then we moved by short marches out to the settlement, and arrived at Montercy, Virginia.

"A great many of those who had suffered so much died of fevers and other ailments in a few months. Most of those who had become crazy, recovered for a time, but either died soon afterward or became permanently deranged.

"The remnant of the Gate City Guard was now ordered to McDowell to recruit and refit for a month or two, when they were again marched up to Cheat Mountain, for the purpose of driving away the Federals entrenched there. During the retreat from Laurel Hill, our General, Garnett, had been killed while trying to organize another rear guard after the First Georgia was cut off.

"The Gate City Guard had the misfortune to lose its flag on this disastrous retreat. It had been used as the regimental flag, being the finest in the regiment, and was at the colonel's headquarters. On the night of the retreat it was raining hard and the flag was placed in a baggage wagon for transportation. When wagons could not be passed over the bad roads, they were tumbled down the mountains. The wagon containing the flag met this fate, and so fell into the enemy's hands. The Gate City Guard, being part of the rear guard, did not know of the loss until too late to retrieve it.

"After the death of General Garnett, General R. E. Lee was appointed his successor. He soon reorganized the army, and ordered us up to Cheat Mountain, where for three days we lay before the enemy's work, ready to assault them as soon as other portions of the army got into position; but the combination failed, and we were ordered to Green-Brier River, where we were almost daily and nightly in contact with the Federal troops.   Night skirmishing was very frequent in those dark mountain gorges, where we could only detect the presence of the enemy by hearing him.   Finally, the Federal General, Rosecrans, determined to attack us.   Accordingly he advanced, driving in our pickets about daylight.   As usual, a detachment of the Gate City Guard formed part of the pickets, and their reserves made a stubborn resistance, holding the enemy back until the army could get into position to receive the attack.   The battle was fought in the valley of the Green-Brier River, and resulted in the defeat and retreat of the Federals.   General Harry R. Jackson, of Georgia, commanded the Confederate forces immediately in the field, with General Ed Johnston as second in command.

"A private, David W. Brown, of the Gate City Guard, who was one of the pickets killed in this action, was found after the battle on his knees leaning against a sapling, with his empty rifle held firmly as if taking aim.   He was shot through the heart.

"The regiment remained on the Green-Brier River until the last of November, when it was ordered to join Stonewall Jackson in the lower valley for his winter march on Hancock and Romney.   It went through that severe winter march with credit, and after returning, was ordered to Lynchburg to be disbanded, its term of service (one year) having expired.   When mustered out, the Gate City Guard's organization was temporarily suspended, and the remaining members joined different organizations of the Confederate Army, as the ranks of the company were too decimated to reorganize, and they fought to the close of the war.

"In October, 1861, Lieut. Leyden was promoted to Major of Light Artillery, and ordered to Georgia to enlist a battalion of artillery.   He succeeded in mustering five companies, with many of the Gate City Guard, in all about nine hundred men, and remained in active service until the surrender at Appomattox."

In December, 1861, Capt. Ezzard resigned, and on December 18, 1861, Lieut. C. A. Stone was elected Captain of the Gate City Guard.   T. C. Jackson was elected Second Lieutenant, and Sergeant Wm. Mims Third Lieutenant, at the same time.   For the foregoing outline of the company's war service, the compiler is indebted chiefly to the brief history printed in the Gate City

Guard's paper, called the "Cartridge Box," issued during their fair in 1880; also to Mr. J. S. Peterson.

During the visit of the Gate City Guard to Philadelphia, in 1879, an interesting article was printed in one of the newspapers there with reference to the retreat from Laurel Hill, and the Carrick's Ford affair. From it we take the following extracts:

"The visit of the Gate City Guard to Philadelphia recalls to our recollection, the scenes of the battle of Carrick's Ford, in which they were conspicuously engaged; the battle was fought on the soil of Virginia, July 13, 1861. An account of the engagement was written shortly afterwards by Lieut. Thos. M. Ward, of Company H, 14th Ohio Regiment."

"The force of the Gate City Guard," says Lieut. Ward, "numbered about seventy-five muskets, being between the minimum and the maximum of a full company. The rascals fought well—*I was there!*

"They belonged to the First Georgia Regiment, * * * and formed part of the brigade under the command of General Garnett, who fought the Union troops at 'Carrick's Ford.' In July, 1861, the Confederate troops under the General, were strongly fortified on the heights of Laurel Hill. A few miles in their rear, Confederate Col. Pegram was entrenched in the Modern Gibraltar of America, known as Rich Mountain. Pegram had 1,760 men. On the 11th of the month he was attacked by General Rosecrans, and driven from his position.

"At twelve o'clock, the same night, intelligence reached General Garnett of the defeat of Pegram, whereupon he immediately destroyed his works and fell back to a more tenable position on Cheat River, near Carrick's Ford.

"The Union forces were in front of the Confederates at Laurel Hill, and were not aware of the retreat of the enemy until fifteen hours after his flight. As soon as it was known in the Union camp, the troops were put in motion, and with Steedman's Regiment, the 14th Ohio Regiment, at the head of the column, followed by Col. Milroy's Ninth Indiana Regiment, commenced the pursuit. Early in the forenoon of the next day (13th) the enemy's rear guard was overtaken. The Gate City Guard was part of it. They immediately drew up on the left bank of Cheat River, and fired upon us while we were fording the stream, which at that place is very wide, and has a swift current. As my position, Company H, was in close proximity to these men, I hailed them: 'What company is that?' An officer answered: 'The Gate City Guard

—you damned abolition devils!' At this juncture we received additional re-inforcements, and the Georgians retreated. They were finally cut off in their attempt to retreat, by Capt. Dodd's Waterville Company, 14th Ohio Regiment, who succeeded in capturing about twenty prisoners, including two officers, Lieut. W. B. Turner, of the Southern Guard of Columbus, Ga., being one of them, and who proved to be the officer with whom I had had the parley. The maneuver of the rear guard, we afterward learned, was only a feint, in order to afford Garnett time to array his men in line of battle. * * * *

"Whitelaw Reid, of the New York *Tribune*, may be said to have received his christening at Carrick's Ford, for he was under fire there, acting as war reporter for the Cincinnatti *Gazette*. The road over which the enemy made their retreat was strewn with playing cards, which gave origin to the remark of the witty reporter of the *Gazette*, that 'the game was up; the trumps being against the enemy, they had thrown down their hands in disgust.' "

NAMES OF THE PARTICIPANTS IN THE RETREAT FROM CARRICK'S FORD

Effort has been made to obtain and record the names of the members of the Gate City Guard who were cut off at Carrick's Ford, and participated in the terrible retreat across the Virginia Mountains. According to the recollection of Maj. A. Leyden, one of the most noted survivors, they are about as follows. The Major, in supplying these names has not relied exclusively upon memory, but has been aided by referring to a printed list of the company's rank and file that entered the service under General Garnett, at Laurel Hill:

Maj. G. H. Thompson, Capt. W. L. Ezzard, First Lieut. H. M. Wylie, Second Lieutenant C. A. Stone, Third Lieutenant A. Leyden, T. C. Jackson, Peter Jones, A. G. Chisolm, William Mims, P. M. Sitton, A. J. Orme, Albert Howell, Harry Krouse, Alton Angier, E. A. Atkinson, Robert Badger, W. D. Bass, John Bankston, William L. Corley, R. T. Clingham, M. C. Casey, R. W. Craven, J. C. Connally, Albert Dudley, Phil Dodd, Joe Eddleman, Vines Fish, Robert Farris, Frank Farrar, F. S. Fitch, D. S. Guard, W. H. Joiner, James H. Johnston, J. W. Langston, J. J. King, William R. Key, Joe Montgomery, R. J. Mitchell, N. M. Mangum, Seab Ozburn, L. H. Smith, John Sanders, W. J. Tanner, J. B. Tanner, A. Tomlinson, James Turner, Stephen Turner, Jesse Thornton, John Wylie, M. V. Wood, Charles Wallace, M. Wigenstein, John Warrick, Mike White and David Young.

Of this list, the following never recovered from the effects of exposure and starvation, and died in consequence:

E. A. Atkinson, Robt. Badger, Albert Dudley, Joe Eddleman and Joe Farris, died in the Valley of Virginia.

Frank Farris, died at McDowell, Va.

L. Gatewood, died at Staunton, Va.

M. Rote, died near Culpepper, Va.

Jesse Thornton, became deranged on the retreat, and died at home.

John Wylie, died of exposure.

M. Wigenstein, died at Staunton, Va.

H. L. King, became deranged in the mountains.

Killed in the Confederate Service

From the same authority is obtained the following list of members of the Guard killed during the war:

First Lieutenant W. H. Wylie, at Franklin, Tenn.

David W. Brown, at Green-Brier, Va., October 3, 1861.

John Bankston, on Battle Hill, near Atlanta.

R. T. Clingham, near Richmond, Va., while serving as courier for J. E. B. Stewart, who lost his life in the same fight.

J. H. Furcrum, at same place, same fight, and in the same capacity.

R. W. Craven, by being blown up in the explosion of Grant's mine under the Confederate lines at Petersburg, Va. This was the celebrated "Crater."

Jas. H. Johnston, in a cavalry skirmish on the Rappahannock, in Virginia.

J. J. King, at the battle of Lynchburg, Va.

CHAPTER II

REORGANIZATION OF THE GUARD

THE Gate City Guard was reorganized in 1870 by many of the old members, and with younger men made a full company. Major Austin Leyden, of the old company, was elected Captain—W. H. Wooten, First Lieutenant; W. W. Austell, Drill Sergeant. After organizing, it was found that under the Federal statutes, no State military organizations were allowed or recognized. The company continued to exist in this condition until July, 1876, when it was reorganized permanently, with the following officers:

Austin Leyden, Captain.
T. J. Dabney, First Lieutenant.
W. R. Biggers, Second Lieutenant.
John W. Butler, Junior Second Lieutenant.

At this new beginning there were only about thirty men, but it grew apace by accessions.

Maj. Leyden, who was a lieutenant in the war company, resigned, and J. F. Burke became Captain by unanimous vote (March 21, 1878).

The old company had had its days of tragedy and heroism. The new organization, under the active and liberal leadership of their new captain, entered upon a career of civic and military usefulness and honors which have made its name celebrated. The first of these was the friendly invasion of South Carolina by the Gate City Guard in May, 1878.

COL. JOSEPH FRANCIS BURKE.

Capt. Joseph F. Burke is a South Carolinian, and a Charlestonian. It was a happy conjunction of circumstances that brought him the leadership of the Gate City Guard about the same time that his native State had been redeemed from the misrule of negroes and Northern camp followers.

The illustrious Wade Hampton, whose soldierly qualities and deeds had glorified the old commonwealth during the bloody war between the States, was now become her civil ruler. His name was upon every Southern tongue. For many years after the war South Carolina had been subjected to the hated rule of alien adventurers and the hordes of black followers. Foremost she stood at the beginning of the great civil conflict, and deepest in the slough of disaster and humiliation she sank at its close. Only Mississippi, Louisiana, and Arkansas could bear comparison with her in respect of the low state of her fortunes. Those devoted States, after a long experience of those black depths of despair that breed political earthquakes, had suddenly shaken off their oppressors, and all eyes had been turned to the old Palmetto State to witness the upheaval that seemed imminent. For it was generally felt in the South that the people who had lowered the national flag in 1861 would not fail, when driven to the last extremity, to send or drive away their tormentors. And when this faith, founded upon observation of centuries of the great deeds of a heroic race, was verified; when South Carolina was redeemed, and stood in line with her sister States in the Union, greeted with tumultuous cheers and congratulations from the entire South, there was no more exultant heart than that which beat in the bosom of the new commander of the Gate City Guard.

Capt. Burke was a thorough believer in the theory that the South was justified in the act of secession as the best mode of maintaining the principle of local self-government; at the outbreak of the Civil War, he belonged to a corps of cadets in the First Regiment of Rifles, and took part in the firing of the "Star of the West," January 9, 1861, and he was a participant in the bombardment of Fort Sumter and other battles. Though not more than a boy at that time, he rejoiced in that assertion of the Southern manhood and State rights; he had mourned for his native State in the hours of her defeat and humiliation, and his heart was thrilled with unspeakable delight at the announcement of her disenthrallment. What could be more natural than that under these affecting circumstances he should dream of returning to the house of his fathers, and testifying by grasp of hand, and flash of eye, and music of eloquent words, his joy at the glorious change that had come in the fortune of his mother State? He determined to visit Charleston and look again into the beaming faces of her people. Not only that, but he would take the Gate City Guard with him, and spend a week in military encampment at the historic city—not with any design or expectation of reaping honor to himself or his splendid company, but simply to gratify his own desire to visit his native State at such a propitious moment, to give his men another taste of camp life and military discipline, and afford them an opportunity of visiting a locality so celebrated for its civic and warlike reminiscences.

The project was warmly received by the members of the Gate City Guard, and by the public of Atlanta generally.

Governor A. H. Colquitt was 'invited by Capt. Burke to go with the company as its guest, and consented to do so.

Schoolboys have sometimes made a little fire in the dry leaves of the forest for a bit of private amusement, and been horrified a few hours later to find the whole neighborhood at war with conflagration.

Capt. Burke's modest request for leave to visit Charleston and rejoice with the Carolinians for their disenthrallment, and camp for a few days by the shore of the Atlantic for recreation and instruction of his men, produced effects as surprising, though not at all tragic, in consequence.

The South Carolinians are a combustible people. When they are mad or glad it is their habit to swell to the point of bursting. If anger happens to be the nature of their ailment, they, like glass, should be "handled with care." In dealing with them the world has learned to look carefully before taking hold to see which side should be kept up.

In 1860-61, for example, shocks of every character were studiously avoided. One dared not tread heavily on the Charleston pavements. Even lovers were observed to avoid smacks. Kisses were of a soft and sibilant character—but probably none the less refreshing for that reason.

But to return: Capt. Burke's request for permission to march on Carolina soil was answered by Governor Hampton in a most cordial acquiescence, and an invitation to visit Columbia, also.

Soon after this correspondence with Governor Hampton, the military authorities of his State began to take steps preparatory to the reception of the Guard upon its arrival, and the affair assumed a magnitude not dreamed of at the beginning. The newspapers took the subject up, and it continued to furnish abundant material for news and comment until the Guard had effected the visit and returned to Atlanta.

The Charleston press devoted columns to the topic. The following is quoted from the *News & Courier* of May 24, 1878.

Gate City Guard—Grand Preparations for Their Reception and Entertainment.

The visit of the Gate City Guard to this city promises to call forth a much larger and grander military display than was at first anticipated, and the festivities attending their arrival and during their stay will be of an exceedingly interesting character. * * * * A meeting of the Committee of Arrangements and the commanding officers of the several military companies was held at Military Hall last evening, and the following programme was agreed upon:

Each of the city companies is ordered to detail a squad of twelve men, two non-commissioned officers, with a lieutenant commanding, and to report at the Military Hall at half past five o'clock on Saturday morning, to act as escort to the Gate City Guard from the depot on their arrival at 6:30 A. M., to the Charleston Hotel, where they will breakfast. This escort parade will be under the command of Major G. Lamb Buist, with Lieut. J. S. Baynard, of the Lafayette Artillery, as Adjutant.

The Committee of Arrangements, together with Major Sale, who has been invited, will meet the visitors at Sineath's Station, and will leave South Carolina Railroad Depot at 5 A. M. in a special train.

After forming into line at the Military Hall, the escort will march to the South Carolina Railroad Depot, and upon the arrival of the train will then escort the Gate City Guard down to the Military Hall headed by a band of music. Upon the arrival of the column at the Military Hall, the parade will be dismissed, and arms will be stacked and left under a guard of six men. The visitors will then be turned over to the committee who will escort them to the Charleston Hotel to breakfast, and after which will assign them to the spot selected for their camp-ground.

It is ordered that the Gate City Guard will have a special place assigned in the column of parade of the Fourth Brigade in the afternoon, which will pass in review of Governors Colquitt and Hampton on the Battery.

On Sunday, the Guard will attend early service at St. Mary's Chapel, and have been invited to attend morning service at the Wentworth Street

Lutheran Church, where the annual sermon before the Charleston Riflemen will be delivered by Rev. W. S. Bowman, the Chaplain of the company.

It is also understood that on Monday and Tuesday the Regatta Association will tender the visitors an excursion around the harbor, after which they will go into camp on Sullivan's Island for a few days. * * * *

LETTER FROM CAPTAIN BURKE

The following letter from Capt. J. F. Burke, of the Gate City Guard, in response to a letter from Capt. G. Follin, the Chairman of the Committee of Arrangements, details the object of the visit of that command to this city, and their proposed programme during their stay:

ATLANTA, GA., MAY 20, 1878.

Capt. G. Follin, Commanding Lafayette Artillery, Charleston, S. C., Chairman Committee, &c.

MY DEAR CAPTAIN: Your valued favor of the 19th, informing me of the action of the commissioned officers of the Fourth Brigade, before me.

It is not necessary for me to attempt an expression of gratitude for the flattering courtesy which they so generously proffer to me and my command.

The extent and display of the reception you have arranged for us is far beyond anything I had anticipated, and I feel that I have already incurred obligations of courtesy which I shall never be able to cancel.

The object of our visit is to give the younger members of my command a taste of camp life, combined with recreation; consequently, only the younger members of the company will be permitted to wear uniform; the older ones have seen camp life in all its dread reality during the late unfortunate war. Our further object is to rejoice with you on your disenthrallment from negro rule.

Camp discipline will be rigidly enforced, and under no circumstances will any one of the men be permitted to live at the hotels. This *regime* is in conformity with my published orders, issued at request of the men, as they are desirous of a radical change from home-living, table-fare and other domestic comforts; consequently, they will draw the usual quantity of "commissary stores." So you see it is our purpose to have a complete change of living for the week that we shall remain in camp.

Our "band" is composed of two drummers and a bugler, and our daily routine will be bugle reveille at sun-rise, breakfast-call, guard-mounting, fatigue duty, morning drill, after which the men will be "off" until adjutant's call for dress parade, bugle tattoo 10 P. M., and "taps" at 10:20. *These rules will be varied whenever occasion requires.*

There are a few of my men who have never seen the ocean. This may appear remarkable to you who have lived for years on its border; but there are some persons in the mountainous regions of Georgia who have yet to see a railroad.

I wish to give the command an opportunity to sail around the harbor, and visit the forts, and if they desire it, bathe in the surf, if I have to muffle my drums, drape our colors, reverse our arms, and return with three or four of them drowned.

In regard to our camp, I have issued the same orders to the commissioned officers, and though my family will be at the Charleston Hotel with other ladies from this city, I shall remain in camp with the company.

I have received an invitation to attend with my company, military services at St. Mary's Church, Hasel Street, on next Sunday morning, and I have accepted. I am informed that another invitation is about to be sent to me to attend service at St. Michaels (Episcopal) Church, of Revolutionary fame, on Sunday afternoon, which we shall be pleased to do.

It will be impossible to send our quartermaster-sergeant down before we go; he is very busy, and if you will do me the favor to wire me the location you may select for our encampment, we shall go there on our arrival in your city.

Our camp will be pitched in ten minutes—all the tents go up together by command; there will be no noise or confusion. The good people of Charleston will hardly know we are there until they see our row of tents at daybreak.

I wrote to Mr. S. Elliot Welsh, formerly of Paul, Welsh and Brandes, about having a large wagon to meet us at the depot to take our baggage. If you would confer with him, he would tell you what he has done in the matter. I would suggest that you have the reception parade on the day following our arrival (Saturday) and we shall be more than pleased to conform to anything that you may command.

Please offer, for myself, and those of my command, our warmest appreciation for the very great courtesies which you and your committee have so generously extended to us, and believe me,

Very truly yours,

J. F. BURKE,

Capt. Commanding Gate City Guard.

P. S.—We cannot reach Charleston before 12 or 1 o'clock on Friday night.

Adieu.

A MONSTER DEMONSTRATION AHEAD—DEPARTURE OF THE GATE CITY GUARD FOR CHARLESTON

The military demonstration that will be made on the occasion of the visit of the Gate City Guard to Charleston, will be one of the grandest ever seen in the South.

The Fourth Brigade, and all other commands in Charleston—artillery and cavalry—to the number of seven thousand men, will be drawn up in line on the arrival of the Guard in that city.

Gov. Colquitt will be escorted to the depot here by the Gate City Guard, who will be his body guard until the arrival in Charleston, when the Washington Light Infantry, of that city, will act as special escort, as they have invited him and the Gate City Guard to be their guests during their sojourn. Governor Colquitt accepted the invitation, and will be accompanied by his aides-de-camp. They will meet Governor Hampton and his staff at Columbia, South Carolina, whence all will proceed to Charleston under escort of the Gate City Guard, of Atlanta.

When Capt. J. F. Burke first thought of taking his company to Charleston, it was his intention to go there quietly, pitch his camp, and remain one week to give his company a taste of camp life, combined with recreation; and with this view he wrote to a few friends in Charleston signifying his purpose, but his intention became known to other friends, and the result will be one of the grandest military pageants ever held in the Southern country.

The military companies of Greenville, S. C., at which point the excursionists will make their first stop, have been ordered out to meet the Guard and their guest, and all along the route in South Carolina the local organizations will be drawn up at each stopping place to extend them military courtesies. On their arrival at Columbia they will be met by the combined military companies of that city, headed by Governor Hampton and staff, and it is significantly rumored that orders have been privately issued to uncouple the car containing the Gate City Guard and their guest; which doubtless means that Governor Hampton intends to exercise his executive authority over the invaders by placing a military guard over them, whilst the good people of that patriotic city overwhelm them with hospitable courtesies.

Capt. Burke has positively declined to accept the invitations of numerous friends in Charleston to take his command to the hotels, as that would defeat one of the principal objects of his visit to Charleston. He has, however, accepted invitations to several banquets to be given in honor of the Gate City Guard, and also to visit the various points of historic interest around the harbor and the neighborhood of the city. A very cordial invitation has been extended to the Guard to attend military service at St. Mary's Church on Sunday, which invitation has been accepted. They have also accepted invitations to attend services at the Episcopal Church during Saturday and Sunday afternoons.

The Gate City Guard has been ordered to meet at their armory at two o'clock, today, with their knapsacks packed, and will escort the Governor to the depot at half past four.

It will look like old war times to see the Guards marching with knapsacks and camp equipage, and thousands of our citizens will line the streets to cheer them farewell and a safe return.

Departure for Charleston

Pursuant to orders the Guard assembled at their armory at two o'clock P. M., on Thursday, May 23d, preparatory to departure, and at half past four escorted the Governor in his carriage to the railroad depot. Their appearance was truly magnificent as they went through the streets in their beautiful uniforms, and glittering arms and accoutrements. Stepping in perfect unison with the strains of martial music, and responding like pieces of perfectly adjusted machinery to the commands of the officers, they reminded the admiring spectators of a perfectly drilled and long-trained company of German or Russian soldiery.

The uniform was blue, trimmed with canary color, and a white drooping plume, and the materials were of the finest quality. Each man wore a knap-sack with blanket rolled upon it, and about his waist his cartridge box. In brief, they appeared as if going away to actual war.

Great crowds of people assembled on the streets to witness the display that preceded the leave-taking, and unbounded good feeling and enthusiasm prevailed.

At half past five the train pulled out of the station, and the Guard was off for the Palmetto State amidst rousing cheers, smiling female faces, and waving handkerchiefs.

The following is a list of the officers and men who participated in this memorable campaign into South Carolina:

THE COMMISSIONED OFFICERS

Captain J. F. Burke, First Lieutenant J. G. Scrutchin, Second Lieutenant W. R. Biggers, Jr., Third Lieutenant J. W. Butler.

NON-COMMISSIONED OFFICERS AND PRIVATES

M. B. Spencer, E. W. Reinhart, Thomas Flemming, Edward White, C. E. Sciple, A. C. Snead, J. Hollingsworth, E. H. Snead, P. N. Hewin, G. A. Dunn, W. H. Evans, F. Fenn, J. H. Lumpkin, Will M. Camp, W. B. Cummings, W. R. Boring, E. W. Hewitt, A. B. Andrews, J. L. Jackson, J. B. Joiner, B. R. Allen, Peter F. Clarke, J. H. McGhee, H. O. Buice, J. E. Mann, Jos. A. Gatins, O. D. Burnette, T. R. Malone, Joseph Gatins, H. A. Daniels, R. Braselton, R. Bird, O. Bohnefield, H. T. Craft, C. W. Connally, R. J. Gilbert, E. S. Hart, J. H. Martin, Robt. H. McCrystal, John Mahoney, Charles Mullins, W. B. O. Quinn, C. E. Pyron, W. J. Pelot, C. R. Simonton, S. A. Swearinger, Paul Tuggle, J. S. Wallace, H. Witcher, W. B. Winburn, Edw. Young, W. A. Martin.

ATTACHES

Drummer, John Wesser; Bugler, John Buchler; Cook, George Holmes (colored); Baker, Albert Hill (colored).

Governor A. H. Colquitt was the invited guest of the Guard during the journey, and became the guest of the Washington Light Infantry of Charleston, commanded by Capt. Wm. A. Courtnay. Upon arrival in that city the Governor was accompanied by Col. I. W. Avery, his private secretary, and about twenty prominent ladies and gentlemen of Atlanta.

THE GREENVILLE SURPRISE PARTY

According to the planning of the expedition, no stop was to be made until the arrival at Charleston. But the usually wide awake Capt. Burke was overreached and entrapped by lurking, though not blood-thirsty foes, at Greenville, in the Palmetto State, which place was reached at midnight, and the train was stopped. There being no appointment the captain inquired into the cause of the delay, and found the Greenville Light Guard and the Butler Guard waiting to receive the party with military honors. They declared that the jolly Georgians should not pass without paying the tribute of a handshake, and measuring glasses with the descendants of the nullifiers. The Gate City Guard capitulated, the terms being that they were to be allowed to retain their side-arms as a means of defense at Charleston against the assaults of Wade Hampton's Legions. This point was readily conceded by the Greenvillians, and the whole party, with Governor Colquitt in the post of honor, were escorted to the Mansion House amidst throngs of cheering citizens through the brilliantly illuminated streets. A banquet had been prepared at the hotel, and Governor Colquitt, Col. Avery, J. H. Lumpkin, and others entertained their hospitable hosts with appropriate speeches and toast responses.

Gen. Garlington made a great hit by announcing that the Mayor of Greenville sent greeting to the Gate City Guard, and declared that he had discharged all of his civil officers for the time being, and that the city was surrendered to the Georgia Company. A messenger inquired for Governor Colquitt and was told that he was in the banquet hall and completely intoxicated. "What," said the messenger, "Governor Colquitt intoxicated!" "Yes, sir," was the response, "thoroughly intoxicated with gratitude for this generous reception."

As for Capt. Burke, he slipped away to seek repose by way of bracing himself against the wear and tear of the morrow's campaign.

About daybreak Capt. Burke was awakened by voices in front of the hotel, and as he rubbed his eyes and sought to locate himself he distinguished these words: "Attention, Battalion!"

Wondering what this warlike sound could mean at such an untimely hour, he ran to the window and looked out, as the stentorian voice continued, "Right dress!"

An inextricable mixture of Greenville Guards, and Butler Guards, and Gate City Guards were making a whimsical pretence of forming lines under orders of some self-appointed leader who was finishing the night of hilarity with a ludicrous practical joke. The boys were humoring the jest, by improvising all manner of absurd contrasts. Long men sought short mates and blue uniforms consorted with any color except their own. The unexpected was true to its ancient record on this ridiculous occasion. When the drill officer said "Order arms!" each soldier promptly ordered something else as far reversed as possible from the maneuvre he was commanded to perform. It was immensely funny, and no one laughed more heartily at it than the captain, who, unknown to the jolly performers, stood *en dishabille* at the hotel window and looked down upon them. The boys had been up all night, but with no trace of dissipation, not withstanding the farce they were enacting by the faint light of dawn. The motley assembly was commanded by Private Joseph Henry Lumpkin, of the Gate City Guard, now associate Justice of the Supreme Court of Georgia.

And when a few hours later the Guard was ordered into ranks by the bugle call, they were as erect and bright as if they had just been awakened from eight hours of undisturbed repose.

Capt. Burke and the Guard were the recipients of a profusion of bouquets from the hands of Greenville ladies, and fair fingers failed not to send flowers for the button-hole of each member of the Guard.

Atlanta's crack company began to realize after leaving Greenville that their visit to South Carolina was regarded by the Carolinians as no everyday event. The remainder of the trip was one continuous ovation, schools, seminaries, military companies all along the route assembled to see the Guard pass. The bugler of the Guard awakened the echoes of the Carolina Hills with the reveille and other warlike notes, and veterans of the war roused from their cottage and fields by the old familiar sounds, came forth to welcome the Georgians with the old Rebel yell, and the village and country maidens waved their 'kerchiefs, floral wreaths and palm branches and smiled, and spread their choicest nosegays beneath the wheels of the puffing iron horse, until Columbia was reached.

The Guard at Columbia

The train arrived at Columbia about half past five, P. M. Here Governor Hampton met the Guard, and their guest, Governor Colquitt. Forgetting that martial law was out of fashion, and yielding for the moment to the dictatorial instinct which often takes cat-naps, but never sinks into complete unconsciousness in the bosoms of warlike natures, Hampton commanded the train to halt, detached the locomotive, and captured the whole tea-party for the delectation of his capital.   Seldom has the chief executive of a great State displayed greater weakness than did Governor Colquitt upon this occasion.   He not only yielded to Hampton's demands, but he yielded meekly—even smilingly.   Indeed, he stood not upon the order of his yielding, but yielded at once.

And as for Capt. Burke and his stalwart Guard, they offered no resistance whatever.   No blow was struck, no sword drawn, no bayonet fixed, in defense of Georgia, and Georgia's chief executive.   With great alacrity Capt. Burke commanded his men to stack arms.   So great is the power of champagne guns, and salad of the devoted chicken, and so potent the tie that binds together the sisterhood of American States.

The Columbia papers, under great display headlines, contained full accounts of the Gate City Guard's stop and short sojourn in the capital.

"Our citizens," said one of these journals, "were on the *qui vive* yesterday, in anticipation of the brief visit of Georgia's distinguished Governor, and the crack company of Atlanta, the Gate City Guard.   By four o'clock the streets leading to the Greenville and Columbia Railroad Depot were thronged with people, and shortly after, our military companies, with the Silver Cornet Band, marched to the depot.   As soon as the train hove in sight, about half past five o'clock (P. M.), the Columbia Artillery fired a salute of nine guns, and thousands of spectators cheered loud and long.   Governor Hampton and the State officers were present. * * * *

The Gate City Guard have with them fifty-five men with two drummers, a trumpeter and a fifer.

An extensive collation was ready for the Georgians, and short speeches of welcome, earnest and eloquent, were made, and fervent responses were loudly applauded.   It was clear that the Carolinians were themselves again, reflecting the spirit of their revolutionary forefathers, and having buried the relics of an ignorant supremacy, and redeemed their State from the shackles that camp followers, through an untutored race had placed upon her, were glad to welcome the Georgians and tell them the interesting story of their fight for liberty.

Thoughtful ladies furnished the boys with tasteful button-hole bouquets. The balconies and windows along the line of march were filled with ladies. About half past seven the line was reformed and marched to the South Carolina Depot, and amidst the earnest and hearty cheering of all parties, the train moved off, having captured Governor Hampton; they now had two Governors in charge to Charleston.

THE GUARD IN CHARLESTON

Governor Hampton with his staff and several of his associate State officers were now become members of the party, and the trip was made to Charleston without any interrupting event. In that city the climax of welcome and hospitality was experienced and heartily enjoyed by the visiting Georgians.

The people of the place, and the organized military, under the inspiring example of Governor Hampton and his associates, entered with all their hearts into the business of entertaining the visitors. Their stay at Charleston was characterized by cannon salutes, magnificent military pageants, martial music, receptions, banquets, speeches, steamship excursions, and other entertainments too numerous to be enumerated. The papers of the city joined in heartily with the movement to show honor to the Georgia soldiers. The columns of matter written about the Guard during their stay in the historic city of Fort Sumter would, in themselves, make a small volume. We must content ourselves with a few extracts from the great number of good things printed on that occasion by the press of Charleston.

The *News & Courier*, of May 23, 1878, spoke as follows:

OUR GUESTS FROM GEORGIA—HOW CHARLESTON WILL HONOR THE GATE CITY GUARD

Charleston will welcome to-day Governor Colquitt, of Georgia, and the Gate City Guard, of Atlanta, and as the representatives of a sister State, endeared to us by many holy ties, the hearts of our people will go out to them as the heart of one man. Side by side, with naught between them but the yellow ribbon called the Savannah River, Georgia and Carolina have stood through more than a century and in two bloody revolutions. It is hard to say whether in peace or in war the States have been dearest to each other. To Georgia's soldiers, and Georgia's Governor, Charleston bids a whole-souled welcome.

The Committee of Arrangements and Mayor Sale will meet the Gate City Guard and Georgia visitors at Sineath's Station and Capt. Follin and Mayor Sale will welcome the visitors on behalf of the military and of the city, respectively. On reaching the depot, Capt. Follin will introduce the visitors to Major Buist, who, as commander of the escort, will welcome them in appropriate terms.

THE REVIEW AND INSPECTION

Of the Fourth Brigade will take place at six o'clock this afternoon. The Brigade will form in front of Charleston Hotel, and when the line is formed will be turned over to General Seigling, who will command the parade.

Capt. Wm. Aiken Kelly will act as Adjutant. After being reviewed by their excellencies, Governors Colquitt and Hampton, the line will move off down Meeting Street to South Battery, around South Battery to East Battery, where the parade will pass in review of the Governors, and will then be turned over to the several regimental commanders.

The line will be formed in the following order:

Gate City Guard, Capt. J. F. Burke, commanding. Carolina Rifle Battalion, Col. C. I. Walker, commanding. Seventeenth Regiment, Maj. W. J. Gayer, commanding. First Regiment of Rifles, Col. W. L. Trenholm, commanding. First Regiment of Artillery, Maj. A. T. Smyth, commanding. German Hussars, Capt. Gerhard Reike, commanding. Charleston Light Dragoons, Capt. Jervey, commanding. The Gate City Guard will be assigned the post of honor on the right of the line. The company will be attached for the parade to the Carolina Rifle Battalion, which will be stationed on the right of the brigade.

A GRAND EXCURSION

(Charleston *News & Courier*)

The many entertainments given in honor of our Georgia visitors, culminated yesterday afternoon in a grand excursion around the harbor, which afforded a rare fund of pleasure not only to the Georgians, but also to the many other guests present.

Through the courtesy of Messrs. James, Adger & Co., the fine Steamship Charleston was placed at the disposal of the Committee of Arrangements, and the start was arranged for four o'clock. Long before that hour scores of ladies and gentlemen could be seen wending their way towards Adger's Wharf, where the steamship was moored, handsomely decked out in bunting. A few moments before four o'clock the Gate City Guard, under command of Capt. J. F. Burke, and headed by the drum corps, marched down to the wharf and boarded the vessel, where they were welcomed by Capt. G. Follin, the chairman of the committee. A few minutes later the steamship glided out into the bay with her decks thronged with gay excursionists. * * * *

After steaming down the harbor past Fort Sumter and Sullivan's Island, the steamship turned just before reaching the bar, and headed for the city again. The handsome and abundant preparation provided by the committee for their guests was then made apparent, and ices, cakes, fruits and etc., were handed around by waiters. After the ladies had been provided for, the gentlemen were invited down stairs, and were equally well taken care of

A Surprise

The committee had provided for their guests, the Gate City Guard, a pleasant surprise in the shape of the presentation of a large 24 x 12 inch photograph of Governor Hampton, taken by Barnard, and handsomely framed in wood and gold. The pleasant task of making the presentation, of course, fell to the lot of Capt. Follin, the chairman of the committee, and the place selected for the ceremony was on the after deck. The company was drawn up in line on either side, while every available inch of space elsewhere was occupied by the ladies and their gay escorts. Capt. Follin, with the souvenir in his hand, mounted a chair, and turning to Capt. Burke, said:

Captain Follin's Remarks

"Captain Burke, and gentlemen of the Gate City Guard, the pleasant duty devolves upon me, as chairman of the Committee of Arrangements, to present to you, on behalf of that committee, a picture of our honored Chief Magistrate, Wade Hampton. I feel, sir, that it would be superfluous for me to make any extended remarks. I feel, sir, a perfect assurance that the feeling which exists between Georgians and Carolinians makes this little souvenir acceptable to you and your command, and that you will cherish and prize it.

"Ladies and gentlemen, I have the honor of introducing to you, Capt. Burke, of the Gate City Guard."

CAPTAIN BURKE'S SPEECH

"Capt. Follin, Ladies and Gentlemen: I receive your gift with feelings of regret; I am sorry that you have so suddenly called upon me, not only to pay tribute to another evidence of your overwhelming generosity, but to offer tribute to one of the grandest characters that nature ever molded into form of man. I regret that I had not time to prepare a fitting response for the occasion; for I accept this picture of your noble Governor as an offering which unites the friendship and political fortunes of two great and prosperous States.

"In the terrific struggle that during four years deluged our country in misfortune, the sons of Georgia were found side by side with the bravest of those of Carolina's Commonwealth. The same spirit moved them both, the same principles inspired them both, the same cause united them both, and they went forth hand in hand, prompted by that spirit, to maintain those principles, and uphold that cause, the memories of which will live forever, from generation to generation, in every household where the vacant chair speaks silently, but eloquently, the terrible sacrifices that were demanded to maintain the sacred honor of our beloved South. We do not come to your city to find evidences of that unfortunate conflict, for we have but too many of them in our own. We come from a city that sent encouragement to you in the darkest hours of misfortune, and now we bring from that city a hearty greeting to you in your bright hours of prosperity.

"Welcome from a city whose location but a few years ago was marked by ruined homes, blackened walls and spectre chimneys, that stood like grim sentinels over the spirit of departed happiness, but by our progress we have shown to the world that the Southern people, despite the ravages of fire and sword, shorn of wealth and engulfed in penury and universal ruin, they still live, they still have energy, they still have enterprise, they still have persistence, they still have the power of recuperation, and the secret of success.

"We come among you to bear witness to your generosity, to praise your hospitality, to acknowledge your patriotism, to clasp the warm hand of friendship in peace and prosperity as we clasped it when Georgia's devoted children stood shoulder to shoulder with Carolina's bravest sons, at a time when faith, and principle and truth and hope and liberty's cause all struggled and went down together.

"In these piping times of peace we can exchange courtesies without getting a furlough or a surgeon's certificate, and if we are hereafter to be received with the same attention and liberality that has marked our reception by your hospitable citizens, I hope that the peaceful times may continue to pipe, at least until the generation shall have passed into Paradise, and not have to explain their bank accounts at the gates.   In these times Georgia sends greeting to Carolina.   Atlanta extends her hands to Charleston, and Charleston, with unprecedented magnanimity, surrounded by the grandeur of her own ruins, offers a fraternal welcome to Massachusetts.   The trappings of war are hung up as souvenirs; and the past is buried in the caverns of human reflection.   White winged peace has visited us, and a brilliant future is in store for us.   Georgia is proud of her sister State.   She encouraged her in her struggle for supremacy when she was battling against hired emissaries, camp followers and political vultures, that sapped her very heart's blood after having mounted into power on the shoulders of an ignorant and deluded race.   And now she congratulates the people of South Carolina in their deliverance from the shackles of political thralldom, and unites her paeans of joy with yours, freighting the gentle zephyrs that steal a passing kiss from the bright flowers of our own sunny land, and waft onward and onward to startle the solitude of a boundless eternity with the gladsome dactyls of peace, prosperity, and the glorious future that is heralded in the magic name of Hampton."

This pleasant little episode in the excursion was followed by a handsome champagne collation in the cabin.   The steamship by this time had headed up Cooper River, and after running in this direction for about a mile, the course was again changed, and the steamer ran down toward Sullivan's Island.   After giving the excursionists an opportunity of observing all points of interest in the harbor, the genial and popular Capt. Lockwood, who was in command, turned his vessel towards the city, and arrived at the dock a few minutes after seven o'clock.   The Gate City Guard, upon reaching the wharf, were formed into line, and marched up to their encampment with the Helicon Band at their head.

The *News & Courier* goes on to tell about how the old Irish Volunteers of Charleston took possession of Capt. Burke and his company for the remainder of the evening and entertained them at their armory in capital style.   Speeches were made by Capt. W. L. Trenholm and Capt. McCabe, of Charleston, and Lieut. Scrutchin and J. H. Lumpkin, of the Gate City Guard.

The company enjoyed special entertainments also at the hands of the Washington Light Infantry.   Capt. Courtenay spoke on behalf of his company (The Light Infantry) and was responded to appropriately by Col. Avery, of Atlanta. Maj. A. T. Smythe also spoke. Afterward the Lafayette Artillery captured the Guard and conducted them to their armory and set them down to a feast. A speech of welcome was made by Capt. Follin, responded to by Capt. Burke. He was a little fatigued, but did not fail to sustain his reputation as an extemporaneous orator.

THE EXHIBITION DRILL

The Charleston *Journal of Commerce* had this paragraph: "The exhibition drill of the Gate City Guard attracted several thousand persons to the Citadel Green at six o'clock yesterday afternoon. The company were out in full uniform under the command of Lieut. Scrutchin, who put them through the manual, and then through the entire school of the company, including some of the most intricate maneuvres of Upton's tactics. The wheeling company front was pronounced to be as admirably done as any set of men could do it. The company next wheeled in double time, with the same precision. Then they marched, and wheeled backward, at which the spectators opened their eyes with astonishment; and when the serried ranks marched backwards and wheeled backwards in double time, still keeping the alignment unbroken, it was more than the average Charlestonian could stand. Some of the crack militiamen of Charleston were simply amazed, so thunderstruck that they forgot to join in the hearty applause that greeted the maneuvre. After drilling about an hour the company was drawn up for dress parade under command of Capt. Burke. The orders of the day were published and the company marched back to their camp."

THE MILITARY MASS

Among the most striking incidents that attended the sojourn of the Guard in Charleston, was the military service at St. Mary's Church under the conduct of the pastor, Rev. Harry Northrop. Though a common enough spectacle in France and other Catholic countries, this stately service was a novelty in Charleston, and hence the announcement that it was to take place brought a vast assembly of people to the sacred edifice.

Under military regulations, the soldiery, while in the church, is under command of a subordinate officer. If it is a company, the first sergeant is in charge. As the building is entered, the commissioned officers bring up the rear, and the soldiers are seated uncovered in the neighborhood of the altar. At St. Mary's the acting first sergeant brought the Guard in and seated them, and all went well until at the solemn moment when the bell began to toll and the muffled drums rolled, Sergeant Reinhardt called out, "Attention, Company!" "Present Arms!"

Instantly, and with one lamentable exception, in perfect union of movement, the Guard formed in two lines on each side cf the center aisle, with covered heads and at the command, present arms, when Private James F. O'Neil had the sad distinction of supplying the exception. In the act of placing his white plumed shako upon his head, he dropped it, and was placed in a dilemma. Under military rules he could not present arms with uncovered head, nor could he break ranks to recover his lost head-piece. So he stood in his place, the blushing observed of many smiling observers until a friendly spectator passed him his cap. His firm adherence to military etiquette recalls a singular experience of one of the French kings. The monarch's chair was before a very hot fire. Decorum forbade that he should shift his position without assistance. The only servitor who was authorized to move the chair was temporarily absent. And although the royal sufferer was in vigorous health, and was surrounded by courtiers, yet he was compelled to blister and perspire until the proper officer could be summoned to attend him. Private O'Neil is now a prominent member of the Atlanta bar, and represents Fulton County in the Legislature. In the afternoon the Guard attended service in the historic St. Michaels Episcopal Church, the Rev. Dr. Frapier officiating. The church was crowded to its utmost capacity.

Among other things published by the Charleston press during the visit of the Guard, was the following in relation to the reception in that city:

Capt. Burke responded to the warm welcome by Major Sale, alluding in commendatory terms to Carolina and Carolinians, and referred to the historic record of the State and her chivalrous people, and said the proverbial hospitality of the South Carolinians was the best assurance to him that their stay would be an enjoyable one. He then called on Private Lumpkin to respond for the company. Mr. Lumpkin spoke as follows:

SPEECH OF PRIVATE J. H. LUMPKIN

"Your Honor and Fellow-Citizens of South Carolina: I am aware that it is considered a requisite of every good soldier to be ever on his guard and never be taken by surprise; yet when you employ such kindly weapons as you have today, and call upon me to respond without a second's warning, I confess that you have introduced a Trojan horse into my citadel, and have so completely taken me unawares, that as a military man, I consider my best course to surrender at discretion before your generous attack. On behalf of the company whom I represent, allow me to return our heart-felt thanks for the welcome you have bestowed upon us. We are not surprised at it. Your city, as well as your State, is famed alike for its bravery in war and generosity in peace. Throughout the American continent, from the bleak hills of Maine to the prairies of Texas, from the ocean that roars to the ocean that sleeps, wherever the name of South Carolina is mentioned, it is understood to be the synonym of courage, chivalry and generosity.

"Sir, like Anthony of old, I am no orator, but only a 'plain, blunt man, that knows his friends'; but permit me to say, both for myself and those whom I represent, that when we come to reckon our friends, whenever or wherever it may be, we shall never forget the gallant South Carolinians."

The Guard left Charleston for home early in the morning of May 31, 1878, amidst the cheers of the compatriots who had so generously entertained them, and arrived back in Atlanta on the following day. The *Constitution* alluded to the event of their arrival in the following words:

Welcome Home—Return of the Gate City Guard from Charleston

Yesterday morning before the hour of the arrival of the Air Line train, a very large crowd had assembled at the depot to welcome Capt. J. F. Burke and his gallant command, the Gate City Guard.

The Governor's Guards, under command of Capt. Milledge, were in line to tender an escort to their comrades-in-arms. This mark of esteem from one of our volunteer companies to another was very appropriate, and typical of that true spirit of soldierly generosity which we hope to see abound among our companies. Capt. Milledge and his men presented a very fine appearance.

As the train slowly rolled into the huge depot, the voices of the Gate City Guard could be heard in mellow harmony, singing "Home Again," which was suddenly interrupted by prolonged and enthusiastic cheers from the immense crowd which filled the depot. As soon as the train stopped, hundreds pressed forward to shake hands with the "boys" and inquire how they were received in South Carolina. The men were dressed in fatigue coats, and each wore on his left breast a badge of one or other of the Charleston companies. Attached to each belt was a fan sent to the company by Messrs. McLoy and Rice, of Charleston, and every man wore a straw hat with an immense brim. Soon the command was heard to "fall in," and the men began to file out of the car, the first man carrying the picture of "brave Hampton" that was presented to the company by the officers of the Fourth Brigade, South Carolina Volunteer Troops, Charleston. As soon as the crowd caught sight of the picture, the thunder of voices that greeted it was deafening. The men marched off at the "right shoulder, arms!" Capt. Burke, without halting his company, commanded: "A rocket for the Governor's Guards." Instantly, every throat in the Gate City Guard yelled: "One, two, three, siz-z-z-z, boom-ba-a-a-a-h!" The effect was electrical, and every word was sounded together. This was the cheer they learned in Charleston, and they will continue to use it in memory of their Charleston friends.

The procession marched to the armory of the Gate City Guard, headed by Bentley's excellent band. After the usual salutations between the Governor's Guard and the Gate City's, and their officers, the escort marched to their armory. Capt. Burke then addressed his men as follows:

"Comrades: Our return to our own house closes one of the grandest ovations that was ever given to a military organization. From the time we left the city, to the hour of our return, we have been the recipients of uninterrupted generosity. Were the whole State of Georgia to unite in one grand jubilee of welcome to our friends of South Carolina, we could not cancel the obligations we owe to them for their reception and entertainment of us as Georgians. If our friends of South Carolina will give us an opportunity, we will show them what we can do. We can entertain their Governor in return for their royal reception of our own. We will endeavor to 'punch' them on the ragged borders of strict military discipline and pay the bill with alacrity; but a Carolinian thinks he is not treating his guest with becoming courtesy unless he pays his bar bill twice. If they will come to us, they will find our latch strings ever on the outside, and we will put an additional piece to it, that the smallest of them may reach it. Now for a parting cheer for our friends of South Carolina."

Capt. Burke then enumerated with wonderful accuracy, all those who were prominent in their courtesies to the company, beginning at Greenville, and ending at Charleston, both ladies and gentlemen, and more than fifty voices responded to the call, Governors Colquitt and Hampton receiving their share. The company then "broke ranks," cheering their captain lustily. Thus ended one of the most enthusiastic and grandest receptions ever extended to a military organization in this country.

SERGT. W. M. STEPHENSON.

HENRY H. HIRSCH.

J. CHARLES GAVAN.

FRANK M. AKERS.

CHAPTER III

DRILL AT MACON, GEORGIA

IN October, 1878, Captain J. F. Burke accepted the invitation of the mayor and citizens of Macon, and took the Guard to that city, and engaged in the inter-state competitive drill, where they won the first prize. Col. Wm. M. Wadley, President of the Georgia Central Railroad, generously offered his private car to Capt. Burke to take the company to Macon and return.

THE OVATION TO MRS. KNOWLES

In the early part of the year 1879, the Mendelssohn Quintette Club, of Boston, Mass., a celebrated musical organization, on its tour through the South, visited Atlanta, and one of its most charming and popular members was Mrs. Etta F. Knowles, the noted vocalist of Boston. Aside from her personal claims to consideration, she could not fail of courteous attention in Atlanta military circles, because of the fact that she was the wife of Captain H. F. Knowles, of the Boston Light Infantry. In accordance, therefore, with the fitness of things, the Gate City Guard complimented her in a most pleasant and gallant manner. The newspapers of the country contained many references of the incident, and room is made for one or two of them:

(From the Augusta, Ga., *Evening News*)

Atlanta always likes to be ahead in everything, and she often succeeds in her ambitious purposes. It is well known to our readers that the military of Charleston and Augusta paid their respects to Mrs. H. F. Knowles, the charming vocalist with the Boston Quintette Club, as her gallant husband commands the Boston Light Infantry, one of the companies composing the Centennial Legion in 1876.

Capt. J. F. Burke, commander of the Gate City Guard of Atlanta, the prize drill company of the last State Fair, seeing what Charleston and Augusta had done in honor of a brother officer's estimable lady, resolved to do even better, so far as a military display was concerned.

On Tuesday night after Mrs. Knowles had returned to her hotel from the concert in Atlanta, the Gate City Guard appeared in the rotunda, in full uniform, and with full ranks announced their desire to meet her in the ladies' parlor, which request was promptly granted, and after stacking arms "the boys" marched up to the parlor.

Before the formal ceremony took place, however, His Honor Mayor W. L. Calhoun; Senator E. P. Howell, of the *Constitution;* Alderman B. B. Crew; Maj. Sidney Herbert, of the Savannah *Morning News;* Maj. John A. Fitten, of the Atlanta Battalion; Capt. Philip Ellis, of the 13th United States Infantry; Lieut. Eugene Bruckner, of the Governor's Guards, and other gentlemen, were presented to Mrs. Knowles, who received them with her usual grace, dignity and cordiality, and a brief time was passed in pleasant conversation.

After this came the formal presentation of the company by Capt. Burke in a speech of rare beauty and appropriateness, in which he referred to pleasant remembrances on the part of Boston's hearty greeting to the Georgia troops in the Boston Centennial, at the Centennial, and announced that in honor of her visit to Atlanta, the Gate City Guard had, by unanimous vote, elected her an honorary member of their organization.

Mrs. Knowles was deeply moved by this marked tribute of respect, and in a feeling manner thanked Capt. Burke and his comrades for the high honor done her by their visit, which, as a soldier's wife, she knew how to fully appreciate. In other cities she had been most kindly greeted by Southern soldiers, but nowhere with such a grand and cordial welcome as in the "Gate City." Her praise of the Company was unstinted and deserved, for "the boys" looked their best.

Returning to the rotunda, Capt. Burke reformed his company, and put them through the manual of arms, Mrs. Knowles and a large number of ladies looking down upon the exhibition from the ladies' rotunda, while a large crowd of gentlemen filled the spacious area below. The Guard never appeared to better advantage, and their movements were like clock work, winning the most lavish praise from all classes of spectators.

After three cheers and a "sky rocket" for Capt. H. F. Knowles of the Boston Light Infantry, "the boys" marched out of the hotel with a step as proud and as steady as that of a conquering legion returning home from victorious fields.

It was generally remarked, during the visit, that such courtesies as these serve to unite more closely in the fellowship of good feeling the people of the North and South.

Captain Knowles Gets the News

There is nothing perhaps that stirs the heart of a husband more profoundly than courtesies extended to his wife when she is far from home, and among strangers. The ovation extended by the Guard to Mrs. Knowles, "got very close" to Capt. Knowles—as appears from the following, which was clipped from the *Constitution* of March 1, 1879:

The grand ovation paid to Mrs. Knowles, of the Boston Quintette Club troupe, during her recent visit to Atlanta, by Capt. J. F. Burke, of the Gate City Guard, seems to have had a most happy effect upon the Boston people. In a letter to Maj. Sidney Herbert, in referring to the subject, Capt. Knowles says: "I hardly know how to express myself in regard to the high compliment paid the Boston Light Infantry, which I have the honor to command, by the military of your good city. I assure you that my company fully appreciate it, and when the report of the affair was read from the Boston *Journal*, at parade last night, the members could not restrain themselves from bursting forth into rapturous applause, and cheer after cheer went up for you and the noble Gate City Guard, and by acclamation, they were placed side by side with our brothers in Charleston and Augusta."

This reference is to the Charleston, S. C., Washington Light Infantry, and the Clinch Rifles, of Augusta, who were with the Boston Light Infantry in the Centennial Legion, at Philadelphia, and whose officers also extended military courtesies to Mrs. Knowles while in Charleston and Augusta, in compliment to her gallant husband.

Capt. Knowles further says: "Such acts as these do more to unite the two sections in the bonds of good fellowship than congressmen can do, and what we need is more of such interchanges of courtesies. I trust, however, that it may be our turn next to pay honor to some representative of the military of your section. But this ovation has touched me very deeply for, although given as a compliment to the Boston Light Infantry, it was paid to my beloved wife, and I feel that simple words can not express the depth of my gratitude. I hope I shall soon have an opportunity to repay, in part, at least, this debt of gratitude."

After the parade alluded to, the Boston Light Infantry adopted a series of resolutions complimentary to the Gate City Guard of Atlanta, which were neatly engrossed and forwarded to the Guard, at Atlanta, Ga.

THE GUARD AT ROME

In 1879, the Gate City Guard made two visits to Rome, Ga., at the earnest request of the citizens of that city. The first was on the occasion of the annual Southern custom of decorating the graves of Confederate soldiers, and the other an encampment and competitive drill for a State prize—a large silk United States flag. The first occurred in May, and the latter in July.

The May meeting was for the double purposes of honoring the dead heroes with flowers, and also laying the cornerstone of a monument to their memory. Governor Colquitt was the guest of the company on this occasion.

As usual, the movements of the Guard were watched with interest by the press of the country.

THE CHARLESTON NEWS & COURIER SAID

This crack Georgia Corps (Gate City Guard) and their prince of good, Captain Joseph F. Burke, who are so pleasantly remembered in Charleston, participated in Memorial Day at Rome, Ga., on the 9th inst. The corps acted as escort to Governor Colquitt, who went to Rome to lay the cornerstone of the Confederate monument and deliver the address. The trip was greatly enjoyed, and is regarded as another event in the history of this truly representative and splendidly drilled organization.

THE ROME DAILY BULLETIN STATED:

That the city was crowded with visitors upon the occasion. There was an excursion on the Coosa River, and a "Hop" in honor of the Guard. The ladies favored the Guard with boutonieres and bouquets, and this won a permanent place in the recollections of "the boys."

The programme of the morning consisted of a drill of the Gate City Guard. This announcement began to draw the crowds early to the platform of Berry's warehouse, and when the company filed on the parade ground they were greeted by a large and appreciative audience. They are emphatically perfect in tactics. The ladies showed their appreciation of the performance by numerous bouquets showered on the company.

At the July encampment, at Rome (1879) the anticipated interesting event was the competitive drill. The prize to be won was a very fine silk United States flag, and the Gate City Guard enjoyed the glory of bringing the great banner home with them in triumph.

The Atlanta *Daily Post*, of July 9, 1879, said:

THE GATE CITY GUARD—THEY BRING THE BEAUTIFUL BANNER HOME

The encampment at Rome is virtually at an end, and all the visiting companies, except the Griffin Light Guards, have returned to their homes. The Gate City Guard arrived yesterday at 12 M., bringing with them the silk prize banner, won at the competitive drill. This company, soon after its arrival in Rome, won the respect and confidence of all. It soon became an acknowledged fact that Atlanta would be the home of the banner, and that the Gate City Guard would be the custodian.

So well did the company maintain their reputation, that when the day for the drill arrived, only one of the military organizations in the encampment was willing to compete with them. This, the Griffin Light Guards, gave the first exhibition drill and were loudly applauded by the Gate City Guard; their drill was admirable, and was followed by the Gate City Guard.

So thorough and perfect were their maneuvers that the other companies declined to attempt to procure the prize. Their score, as announced by the military judges,* lacking but one-tenth of one point from being complete.

After the banner had been awarded to the Guard it was presented by Corporal J. R. Saussy, of the Chatham Artillery, in a handsome speech. The banner was received by Capt. Burke, of the Gate City Guard, who expressed

---

*Brig.-Gen. William M. Marshall, then a captain in the U. S. Army, was chairman of the board of judges of the drill.

the appreciation of his company for the uniform kindness shown them during their sojourn in Rome.

The prize is, indeed, a handsome one, and well worth the efforts that have been put forth to procure it.

An Amusing Incident

There occurred during the visit to Rome an incident which strongly illustrates the respect for discipline which characterized the Gate City Guard. On Saturday night quite a number of the members of the company stayed late in town visiting the young ladies, and attending receptions by the good people of the city, and on their return succeeded in evading the pickets, and instead of seeking their beds and quieting down to their repose as good soldiers ought to do, they amused themselves awhile by making cat-calls and other hideous sounds, greatly to the discomfort of those who were disposed to sleep.

Capt. Burke sought vainly to locate the individual law-breakers, but he "had it in" for them as the next morning's events proved to their satisfaction, if not their comfort.

A great many of "the boys" had made appointments to go to church at 11 A. M. with young lady friends and by 10 o'clock they were ready, in their elegant uniforms and spotless linen and white gloves and shining buttons, to keep their appointments. But just as they were proudly putting the finishing touches to their faultless toilets, the drummer began to sound the "assembly," and the sergeant to call out "Fall in!" To say the men were astonished is but feebly to express their state of mind. But they were soldiers first, and inquirers afterward. It was "theirs not to reason why."

So with their usual alacrity they seized their rifles and fell into line; Capt. Burke at once began to drill them. Hither and thither he marched, and counter-marched, and wheeled them, with face as solemn as that of an undertaker, until finally he called halt as they stood facing a road and on its very edge. On the bed of this road there was dust of a remarkably "fine" quality, and three or four inches deep.

The Captain now put the company through a variety of those evolutions which belonged to loading and firing in upright posture, and followed it up suddenly by the command to "fire lying down!" In an instant the discomfited men were stretched on their faces in the dust, and loaded and fired, by command, with machine-like regularity, as if they were on a grassy lawn. A rumor has been handed down through the intervening years to the effect that a wave of quasi profanity passed down the line. This report is not well authenticated, but it is thought to be quite probable, considering the provocation, that some homely cuss words were done in a whisper.

Readers can imagine better than words can describe the appearance of the company when they arose from the ground, and how incapable they had become of keeping engagements with the lovely Roman belles. But that afternoon they obtained leaves of absence, and it is to be hoped succeeded in making satisfactory explanations. It was a lesson in "tactics" never to be forgotten. A lesson of punishment, but nevertheless, a lesson of discipline.

THE NORTHERN TOUR—PATRIOTIC MISSION OF THE GATE CITY GUARD

When Capt. Burke, in March, 1878, accepted the command of the Gate City Guard, he was moved by a high and serious purpose. The opportunities to be afforded for display on holiday occasions, if they entered his thought at all, played but an insignificant part in the considerations which induced him to assume the responsibilities of a trust so tedious and burdensome. A student of history, a thoughtful observer of public affairs, and a lover of his country he was quick to perceive that representative military organization belonging to one of the extreme Southern States—composed of men, and the kindest of men, who had faithfully defended the Confederacy, and bearing at their head the flag of our united country—might, even in times of peace, be so used as to do valuable service in the cause of our great Union, whose sovereignty that banner represented. He was among the first of Southern men to turn his thoughts to the great subject of national pacification. Only very short-sighted or very selfish men on either side lent themselves to the policy of continuing the strife after the armed conflict had ceased. Those of broader minds and nobler views soon grasped the truth that a Union pinned together by bayonets would be worse than no Union at all. The theories of Calhoun and Webster, after many years of unsatisfying parliamentary combat, had at length met on the battle-field where the sword had arbitrarily decided that the federation of American States was to be "inseparable now, and forever." Further armed opposition being out of the question, why not make the partnership as designed by its founders, a union of hearts, as well as of hands? Patriotic and thoughtful Southern men were wont to say in those melancholy days, "We have vindicated our courage and devotion to principles." The world acknowledges this.

What have we lost? Our honor, the most precious of our possessions, is still our own. Defeat no more robs of that than violence, a noble woman of her virtue. What then have we lost? Only slavery, and the asserted right to withdraw from the Union. But the most priceless of our constitutional jewels remains unimpaired—the right of *local self-government*. And this our victorious Northern brethren will help to maintain. For they can not fail to perceive that any movement of government which imperils a Southern State in this particular, becomes a deadly precedent for their own enslavement. Therefore all the States, without regard to section, do now, and shall forever occupy common ground.

Moved by such sentiment, Capt. Burke conceived and planned in 1879, the "Northern Tour" which became so celebrated, and which forms an event of no small importance in the history of the reconstruction period of our country.

At that time the appeal to sectional prejudice formed largely the stock in trade of many Northern men whose trade was politics. In the political parlance of the time it was called "waving the bloody shirt."

As illustrative of this style of party tactics, we cite the advice given by one of the Northern speakers to an audience composed largely of Northern veterans. "Boys, vote as you shot—Southwards!"

Capt. Burke was one of those Southerners who believed that such methods were not approved by the thinking people of the North, whether civilians or soldiers, and he proposed to his company that they should visit the Northern cities, dressed in their blue uniforms and bearing the United States flag, and test the temper of the Northern people and testify that the Georgians, at least, were reconstructed, were willing to let by-gones be by-gones, and bury the "bloody shirt" with all its bitter memories.

This expedition of the Gate City Guard is especially notable as being a pioneer among those unification movements which became afterward so fashionable. The patriotic spirit which moved the commander of the Gate City Guard is abundantly shown in the many speeches that he made during the sojourn in the North. Like many gifted extemporaneous speakers, he rarely prepared and furnished his speeches to the press. This will be lamented by readers of this compilation, as the newspaper reports of his Northern addresses are crude and imperfect.

The many friends of the Guard were divided as to the opportuneness of their visit to the Northern and Eastern States. It was argued that the time was not ripe for such an undertaking, that sectional feeling was yet deeply rooted, and the Guard might find themselves received with chilling courtesy. On the other hand, friends of the company advised the fraternal mission to proceed, among whom was Governor A. H. Colquitt, who visited the armory when the company was ready to march to the train. The Governor's address was deeply impressive. He pictured the historic importance of the undertaking, calling to mind that no such extensive movement with the same unselfish and patriotic purpose had been undertaken by the military since the close of the Civil War. It is true that companies of State militia had exchanged short visits, North and South, but it was for the Guard, at their own expense, to undertake a protracted mission of fraternity and peace under one national flag.

The press of the country editorially approved the project of the Guard, and in flattering terms promised a most hearty welcome for the Atlantans.

On to the North—The Grand Northern Tour of the Gate City Guard

A *Constitution* reporter called on Capt. J. F. Burke, of the Gate City Guard yesterday, determined to ascertain as far as possible, all the details of the tour for which the company is preparing.

"When will the Gate City Guard leave for the Northern cities?" asked the reporter.

Capt. Burke replied, "On Monday, October 6th, at 3:30 P. M., we will go by the Piedmont Air Line Railroad and reach Washington the next night. We will remain in Washington on Wednesday; spend Thursday in Baltimore; Friday, and part of Saturday, in Philadelphia; Saturday afternoon and three additional days in New York; thence to New Haven, Hartford and Boston, Lawrence and other places, spending one day in each city."

"What is the programme in each city on your arrival?"

"At Washington we will be the guests of the Washington Light Infantry. President Hayes, if he should be in Washington, will also give us a reception. In my conversation with him a few weeks ago, he spoke very kindly of the Atlanta people, of their hospitality, thrift and enterprise, and dwelt at some length on the good effect our visit to the North would have in promoting harmony and fraternal feeling between the extreme sections of the country, and expressed much pleasure at the prospect of meeting the military and civil representatives of Atlanta in Washington."

"Who will receive you in Baltimore?"

"We will be the guests of the Fifth Maryland Regiment. Here is an official dispatch from their headquarters just received, asking the exact time we will reach Baltimore, and how long we will remain. Here is another from the battalion of State Fencibles, at Philadelphia, asking for the same information."

"Who will receive you at New York?"

"We will be received by the Seventh Regiment. Here is an official letter from Col. Emmons Clark, tendering us an escort on arrival and departure, and some other flattering courtesies not necessary to mention here."

Among the early invitations received by the Guard, was the following:

HEADQUARTERS 7TH REGIMENT, N. G. S. N. Y.

NEW YORK, August 30, 1879.

Captain: Having been informed that you intend to visit New York with your command, the Gate City Guard, during the month of October, I desire to tender you a military escort upon your arrival and departure, and to extend to you such other military courtesies as may be acceptable and agreeable to you and your command. Commending warmly the patriotic purpose of your visit.

Hoping for a favorable reply, I am with respect,

Yours truly,

EMMONS CLARK,
Colonel Com'dg 7th Regiment.

To CAPT. J. F. BURKE,
Com'dg Gate City Guard, Atlanta, Ga.

"At Hartford, we will be the guests of Putnam Phalanx. About the same programme will be carried out at Boston, as I learn from a letter just received from there.   In addition to the military receptions, I learn there will also be receptions by the civil authorities in every city visited."

"Twelve hundred miles is a long journey.   Will all the members of your command accompany you?"

"Not in uniform.   Only one single rank company will go in full uniform, not exceeding fifty in all.   The whole party, including ladies, and other guests, will probably not exceed one hundred persons.   Mayor Calhoun will be among the guests, Governor Simpson, of South Carolina, and Senator Vance, of North Carolina, are also invited.   The object of the trip is to observe the militia systems of Northern States and at the same time, to promote, as far as possible, harmony and good feeling between the people of both sections of our country."

"The Gate City Guard have an extensive reputation for proficiency in drill, will they give an exhibition during their absence?"

"Probably not.   We have many requests to do so, but the disposition of the men is adverse to that kind of notoriety.   Besides, we confine ourselves strictly to the tactics, and ignore what are called 'fancy movements.' "

After thanking Capt. Burke for his information, this reporter took his departure.   He had not proceeded far when he met Lieut. J. H. Lumpkin, of the Guard, on his way to the Supreme Court, laden with law books and ominous looking papers.

"Mr. Lumpkin, is the Gate City Guard nearly ready for its Northern trip?"

"Yes, sir, they will leave positively on the 6th.   And I am glad to see so many flattering notices of our visit in the papers throughout the North. It is an extensive undertaking and will be productive of much good."

The reporter next called on Mr. W. J. Houston, General Passenger Agent of the Piedmont Air Line Railroad, and opened on him as follows:

"Mr. Houston, is there likely to be any delay about the Gate City Guard leaving on October 6th, for their Northern tour?"

"None whatever.   Their private car is being refurnished and carpeted. It will go through with the company to New York, and wait there for their return.   Everything is arranged along the line for this tour, and the most extensive receptions await the company in all the cities at which they will stop."

Mr. Houston, at this time, sent the following to the Gate City Guard:

ATLANTA & CHARLOTTE AIR LINE RAILWAY,
PASSENGER DEPARTMENT,
ATLANTA, GA., Oct. 6, 1879.

Capt. Burke, and Members of the Gate City Guard:

MY FRIENDS AND FELLOW-CITIZENS: Many years ago, on this very spot, I witnessed the departure of the old Gate City Guard under very different circumstances than the present. It was my desire then to go with the company, but circumstances rendered it necessary for my stay at home, and duty made it my province then, as now, to prepare the articles of transportation that carried your predecessors hence in the same direction you are now going, but by another route. The great Piedmont Air Line was not then under consideration, but it was proposed by our citizens to unite the sections now traversed by it with a plank road. Wisdom exhibited the folly of this, and capital and necessity compelled the building of the great line tracing the foot of the Blue Ridge on the east side to Virginia through the land of the sky.

This beautiful car, ordered for your special accommodation by a public-spirited manager, Maj. G. J. Foreacre, designed and executed by a skilled master of the mechanic arts, painted and decorated by an Atlanta boy, owned by those you are going to visit, I start you onward with the best wishes of the president, manager and employees of the Atlanta & Charlotte Air Line Railway.* You carry with you our God speed. May the Great Architect of the universe protect each and every one of you, and after you have received the hearty and hospitable welcomes awaiting you throughout the East, may you return to your homes, convinced of the importance of forever cherishing that brotherly love that should unite American citizens and soldiers wherever found, in one common cause, regardless of sections and political creeds.

W. J. HOUSTON.

At the appointed time for departure on the historic tour, Governor Colquitt visited the company at their armory, and made one of the happiest speeches, showing the good results that would reward the members. Then, with martial music, gazed at by applauding crowds of enthusiastic Atlantans, the

---

* Now a part of the Southern Railroad.

Guard marched down to the splendid special car which had been an object of admiration for days preceding, and moved on to Washington, and many "God speeds" and benedictions from loved ones followed the departing train.

To detail the incidents of this expedition would be to write a large volume. A large book could be made of extracts from Northern and Southern press in relation to the tour. In the main, the newspapers will be allowed to tell the interesting story—the editor only regretting that he has space for so small a part of the writing that was printed on the subject.

Following is a list of the officers and privates who boarded the car in uniform:

Capt. J. H. Burke, Lieut. W. C. Sparks, Lieut. H. W. Johnstone, (Lieut. J. H. Lumpkin was unable to make the tour), E. W. Reinhardt, Chas. E. Sciple, W. P. Horton, C. W. Connally, J. H. Hollingsworth, W. M. Camp, H. A. Daniels, J. S. Wallace, W. B. O. Quinn, W. H. Hart, Chas. P. Byrd, W. T. Kuhns, P. F. Clark, W. B. Buchanan, E. H. Sneed, J. H. McGehee, C. Howard Harris, J. P. Culberson, A. L. Sneed, E. W. Hewitt, T. Flemming, W. R. Boring, Edward White, Jr., R. J. Gilbert, E. S. Hart, W. B. Cummings, T. J. Cooper, S. A. Swerenger, J. L. Jackson, G. W. Sciple, Jr., E. S. Strobhar, S. Marion, Henry L. Collier, F. Hart, M. Bently, drummer.

In addition to the members in uniform, there were others detailed to attend to the guests, about forty ladies and gentlemen, honorary members and friends of the company accompanied them.

GEORGIA MILITARY—GRAND NORTHERN TOUR OF THE GATE CITY GUARD

(Special to the Louisville *Courier-Journal*)

New York, September 7th. The Seventh Regiment is making extensive preparations to receive the Gate City Guard, of Atlanta, Ga., the leading military organization of the State, which is expected soon. The Georgia company is to visit Washington, Baltimore, Philadelphia and other cities, being received in Baltimore by the famous Fifth Maryland Regiment. Here they will be the guests of New York's favorite regiment, and the city authorities will accord them a reception. Thence they go on to Boston, to become guests of the Boston Light Infantry and Veteran Corps of that place.

Patriotic Letter

(From the Hartford *Globe*)

A telegraphic dispatch was recently received and published in the *Globe* announcing a contemplated tour to the Northern States of the Gate City Guard, of Atlanta, Georgia.

ARMORY, GATE CITY GUARD,
ATLANTA, GA., September 1, 1879.

MAJ. F. M. BROWN, Commanding Putnam Phalanx, Hartford, Conn.

MY DEAR SIR: Your esteemed favor of the 28th inst. was received this day. Permit me to reciprocate the friendly sentiments expressed therein, and to join with you in the love and fraternity that should unite the people of all sections of our common country. The object of our visit is to engender and foster a proper appreciation and unity between the people of the North and the South. A great part of our misfortunes may be traced to a want of intimate intercourse between the people of this great nation, and no element is more peculiarly fitted for a reunion of all sections of our country than that element on which we depend for protection and preservation.

Thanking you, again, my dear Major, for your very flattering invitation, I remain,

Truly yours,
J. F. BURKE,
Capt. Commanding Gate City Guard.

(Charleston, S. C., *News & Courier*)

The Gate City Guard, one of Georgia's most active and efficient companies of citizen soldiery, will leave Atlanta on the 6th of October, next, for Washington and other cities, on a national mission of patriotic fraternity. They will be hospitably entertained by the military of that city. The purpose of the tour is to promote a friendly feeling with our Northern friends. They will go on a pilgrimage to Mount Vernon, the hallowed tomb of the immortal Washington. * * * *

It will be remembered that the Gate City Guard honored Charleston with a visit in the summer of 1878, on which interesting occasion they were escorted by the entire militia of the city. * * * * Capt. Burke, the worthy commander of the company (a native of Charleston), is an accomplished orator as well as a brave soldier. The kindest wishes of their Charleston friends will accompany them throughout the journey.

ON TO THE NORTH—GRAND TOUR OF THE GATE CITY GUARD
(Rome *Tribune* of Sept. 30, 1879)

This admirable organization is making preparation for their visit to Washington, Baltimore, Philadelphia, New York, New Haven, Hartford, Boston and Lawrence, Mass., and other cities, and will leave Atlanta October 6th. The undertaking has assumed a national character, and the grandest receptions await them in all these cities on their route, beginning at Washington by President Hayes. Their private car is being refurnished and will go with them to Boston and return. A large number of ladies and gentlemen of distinction will accompany the organization. The Guard will number about fifty men (the other members cannot leave business to go), and they will take with them the handsome Stars and Stripes presented to them by the people of Rome last July. We recommend them to our Northern friends. They visited our city, by invitation, on two occasions, accompanied by Governor Colquitt, and won the esteem of our citizens by their gentlemanly deportment, and captivated us by their superb drill. An army officer pronounced their drilling to be far superior to any military organization in America.

As to their commander, Capt. J. F. Burke, he is too well and favorably known in Georgia to need introduction. A graceful speaker and cultivated gentleman, he will make friends of all who may meet him.

Like all military organizations in the South, the Gate City Guard is composed of young men (the old war members being unable to make the tour), and they will appreciate and fully enjoy the hospitalities our Northern friends are preparing for them. The visit is calculated to have excellent effect in promoting a feeling of fraternity between the sections of our country, which is the prime object of the tour. We learn that some of our ladies intend sending beautiful floral wreaths to decorate the private car of the Guard on the eve of their departure.

The company proceeded on its way without exciting incident until its arrival at Belle Isle, Virginia. Here they were met by a delegation from Richmond Light Infantry Blues, headed by Hon. John S. Wise, and a large number of officers, which detained them for an hour and entertained them

CAPT. G. A. FALLIN,
Comd. Lafayette Artillery, Charleston,
S. C., May, 1878.

COL. WM. G. MOORE,
Comd. Washington Light Infantry Battalion,
Washington, D. C., Oct., 1879.

MAJ. F. M. BROWN,
Comd. Putnam Phalanx, Hartford, Conn.,
October, 1879.

MAJ. J. W. RYAN,
Comd. Battalion State Fencibles of Philadelphia, Pa., October, 1879.

with a luncheon, speeches, etc. It was an especially pleasant episode because it was a surprise.

AT WASHINGTON

Of the arrival at the Federal Capital, the Washington *Daily Critic* said:

A ROYAL RECEPTION

The Gate City Guard, of Atlanta, Ga., arrived here last night, and were received by Company A, Washington Light Infantry Corps, and several thousand citizens. The vicinity of the Baltimore and Potomac Depot, on Sixth Street, was illuminated by a calcium light, as was also Pennsylvania Ave. Sky-rockets, colored lights, and Roman candles were freely used. The company, after marching down Pennsylvania Ave., escorted by Company A, Washington Light Infantry, were quartered at the Metropolitan Hotel, their arms having been stacked in the armory of Company A. Upon the return of the visiting soldiers to the armory, and after stacking arms, Capt. Moore advanced, and made a brief speech of welcome. Capt. Burke responded saying he did not anticipate such a hearty reception as his company had received. He said that in order to dissipate the impression that some people in the North had that the Southern companies never carried a United States flag, his company brought the Stars and Stripes with them to show that they were fully reconstructed. This statement was received with tremendous applause. (Capt. Burke's very appropriate speech was not taken down at the time, and can not be inserted here.) The visitors were then invited to luncheon, which had been prepared for them. * * * *

This morning the Georgians visited Mount Vernon, and this afternoon they will have a dress parade with the Washington Light Infantry Corps, Col. W. C. Moore commanding.

OUR GEORGIA GUESTS—AN ENTHUSIASTIC RECEPTION ACCORDED THE GATE CITY GUARD

(From the Washington *Post*)

It is doubtful if any visiting company of military ever met with the reception that was accorded the Gate City Guard, of Atlanta, Ga., by the Washington Light Infantry and citizens on their arrival last night, en route for the North. Unusual activity was noticed during the evening at the armory, on

the Avenue above Sixth Street, which assumed a tangible form after ten
o'clock, when Company A, mustering sixty members in fatigue uniform, and
commanded by Capt. W. G. Moore, and Lieuts. Dalton & Ross, filed out
of the building, and headed by Douch's band, marched to the Baltimore &
Potomac Depot. Here they took up a position at the lower end of the platform, and awaited the arrival of the Southern train, which came in about
10:30 P. M. The visiting military alighted, accompanied by a party of thirty
or forty friends, including many ladies, and were received by Capt. Moore's
company. The Gate City Guard numbered forty men, nearly all of whom
were young and of splendid appearance, wearing a blue uniform with canary
color trimmings, white cross-belts, blue dress-coats and stiff hats with drooping
plumes. They were commanded by Capt. J. F. Burke, with Lieut. W. C.
Sparks and Lieut. Johnstone, and, as they appeared on the depot platform,
were greeted with loud cheers by a large mass of citizens in attendance. The
local organization escorted their guests to Sixth Street, and took a line of
march along the Avenue to Ninth Street, to F Street, to Seventh Street,
thence to the armory. From the depot all along the route, the greatest enthusiasm prevailed. When the two companies entered Sixth Street, they
were surrounded by a concourse numbering several thousand persons, who
participated in the street demonstration, affording the Southerners a mam-
moth escort. In addition to the generous excitement there was a fine display
of pyrotechnics. The scene on the line of march was exceedingly brilliant;
various colored lights, Roman candles, crackers, bombs and other fire-works
being discharged at every point. At the armory, the rooms of the Columbia
Club, and many private residences along the route, the display was taken up,
adding to the otherwise brilliant effect. During the march the visiting troops
performed a number of military maneuvers with a precision that won round
after round of cheers. At the armory other evolutions were gone through,
after which Col. Moore, in a neat little speech, welcomed the Southern troops,
to which Capt. Burke responded, stating the purpose of the Guards' visit, and
making an appropriate allusion to the beautiful United States flag which
they brought with them.

Company A then gave their peculiar cheer, after which the visitors were
served with a handsome collation. The Georgia troops and their friends have
been quartered at the Metropolitan Hotel.

The reception and arrangements were conducted by a committee of Company A, Col. Webster, Col. B. L. Blackford and Maj. Vandenburg, of the District Military Staff, also assisted in entertaining the visitors. This morning the strangers will visit Mount Vernon. On their return they will be met by the Light Infantry and escorted to the front of the Arlington, where a dress parade and drill will take place, to be succeeded by an inspection and review on F Street, between Seventeenth and Eighteenth Streets. This programme observed, both organizations will be entertained by Col. Webster at his residence. Tonight, at 10:15, the Southerners continue their journey to the North, stopping at Baltimore over Thursday, as the guests of the Fifth Regiment, M. N. G., two of the members of which (Capt. Charles H. Reeves, of Company G, and W. Bolton Fitzgerald, Commissary Sergeant) were present at the Washington reception last night.

(From the Washington *Post*)

The programme for the entertainment of the Gate City Guard, of Atlanta, Ga., yesterday as indicated in the *Post*, was faithfully observed, and the visiting military were afforded another round of enjoyment succeeding their enthusiastic reception Tuesday night. At 10 o'clock in the morning, clothed in fatigue uniforms, the strangers were attended to Mount Vernon by a committee of the Light Infantry, consisting of Messrs. George Evans, J. C. Entwistle, John G. Cowle, and George Van Sackel, accompanied by Maj. Vendenburg and Capt. Rodier, who catered in every way to the amusement of the guests. Having thoroughly canvassed the historical attractions at the tomb of the immortal Washington, the troops returned to the city, and repaired to the armory of the local military. At 4 o'clock, P. M., escorted by two companies of the Washington Light Infantry, one in full dress, and the other in fatigue uniform, and commanded by Col. Moore and Lieuts. Dalton and Ross, the line of march was taken up the Avenue to Seventeenth St., to F St., where the Gate City Guard gave an exhibition in military evolutions, which for proficiency and precision, is seldom equaled. Subsequently, they became the guests of Col. Amos Webster, and were entertained at his residence, near at hand, after which the column returned to the armory. Here a collation was served, and donning their fatigue uniforms again, the Atlanta command were escorted to the Opera House, and witnessed the production of the "Strategists." After the performance they were in turn escorted to the Baltimore and Potomac Depot, and left for Baltimore to become the guests of the Fifth Regiment, Maryland National Guards. On the march from the Cpera House to the depot, the Avenue was again brilliantly illuminated with a continued shower of pyrotechnics, and the Atlanta military left the National Capital as they were welcomed, in a brilliant and enthusiastic ovation, in which the citizens vied with the military to make it a success. During the afternoon Lieut. Bloomer, Surgeon of the State Fencibles of Philadelphia, arrived in Washington and arranged with Capt. Burke for the reception of his command in the Centennial City.

Gen. W. T. Sherman was to have met the Guard at Washington, but telegraphed his regrets at not being able to do so, and the reception at the White House was prevented by the absence of the Chief Executive from the Capital. The President was with General Sherman in the West.

The following dispatch was sent by the General to Captain Burke, when the Guard arrived in Washington:

"To Capt. J. F. Burke: Will not reach Washington until after you have passed through there. Hope to see you when you return.

W. T. SHERMAN."

RECEPTION AT BALTIMORE

THE GATE CITY GUARD—BALTIMORE'S WELCOME TO ATLANTA'S CITIZEN SOLDIERS

(From the Baltimore Sun of Oct. 10, 1879)

Never before, perhaps, in the history of Baltimore, was a more cordial and general welcome extended by its citizens to a visiting military organization than that which received the Gate City Guard, of Atlanta, Ga., yesterday. As already stated in the Sun, the Guard, under command of Capt. J. F. Burke, arrived at Calvert Station over the Baltimore and Potomac Railroad at 11:55 P. M., on Wednesday, and remained there in their special car all night. Yesterday morning, at 8:20 o'clock, they repaired to the Carrollton Hotel where breakfast was served, after which they returned to Calvert Station. A crowd had already begun to gather there, and by half past 9 o'clock, the throng filled the station and the neighboring streets, all eager to get a glimpse of the gallant Georgians. * * * *

At 9 A. M. Company B, of the Fifth Maryland Regiment, with 75 men in line, under command of Capt. Lipscomb, assembled at the armory on Howard Street, in full regimentals, preceded by the band and drum corps, marched to Calvert Station. Here Capt. Burke, of the Guard, was introduced by Lieut. H. E. Mann, of the Fifth. The Guard marched out of the depot, and on Centre Street, between North and Calvert, were received with a marching salute. The Georgians marched with the precision of veterans, and their well-executed maneuvers on the way elicited warm applause from the dense throng of spectators. Regular line of march was then taken, police sergeant and police officers leading to clear the way, and the Fifth taking the right of the line. The route was out Calvert Street to Madison Street, to Eutaw, to Wilson, to Madison Avenue, to Eutaw again, to Baltimore, to Gay, to Fayette, and to Holliday, front of the City Hall. When passing through Eutaw Place, the Georgians were greeted with warm applause by the ladies, who thronged the windows to witness the march, and they were frequently cheered on their way by the crowds along the streets for their admirable military bearing. Before the City Hall the manner in which they changed front and stacked arms was also warmly applauded. After stacking arms, the Guard, escorted by Capt. Lipscomb, of the Fifth, marched in column of twos into the City Hall, and were received in the Mayor's reception room by Mayor Latrobe, Gen. John S. Berry, Gen. Herbert, Maj. P. P. Dandridge, Capt. G. W. Wood, Dr. W. R. McKnew, Capt. J. Mason Jamison, Maj. Harry Gilmor, Adjt.-Gen. Bond, Capt. Anderson, Capt. Herbert, and Lieut. E. C. Johnson, of the Fifth. Gen. W. E. Ross, Col. Harrison Adreon, Comptroller Vansant, Register Rob, and other city officials.

Accompanying the Guard were Messrs. F. Ballon, J. C. Johnson, George Hunt, and Geo. Clegg, of Columbus, Ga., honorary members, T. K. Smith and J. H. Cole, of Atlanta, and a number of ladies. Capt. Lipscomb presented Capt. Burke and Mayor Calhoun, of Atlanta, to Mayor Latrobe, who said:

"I take great pleasure in welcoming you to Baltimore. You come from a section of our country with which the people of this city claim most close and friendly relation. The State you represent is known to us as one of the most prosperous of what are called the Southern States. Your people are gallant, active and energetic, and after the close of the war your State soon resumed her position as one of the great States of the Union. For if New York is called the Empire State of the North, Georgia is certainly entitled to the name of the Empire State of the South. You will find the people of Maryland prepared to extend you a cordial reception wherever you may go within her borders on your patriotic mission. I regret that your stay in Baltimore is so limited. I hope, however, that you may enjoy yourselves while in our city, and as its chief executive officer, I will be most happy to extend to you any facilities in my power to make your time here pass agreeably."

Mayor Calhoun, of Atlanta, responded, thanking the mayor for the kind and complimentary remarks which he had been pleased to utter, and for the warm and hospitable welcome with which the Guard had been received in Baltimore. He appreciated it highly because it came from the representative of a great city, and more highly still because it was given with the warmth of a true Southern heart. He was glad that Baltimore was so prosperous, and prayed that peace might ever dwell within her borders—nay, not only within her borders, but throughout the entire country.

The formal reception concluded, the visitors were shown through the City Hall, and at 1:30 P. M., the roll-call was beat to assemble again on the street. From here the line of march was resumed around the City Hall, via Lexington Street, to North, to Fayette, to Calvert, to Baltimore, to Charles, to Monument, to Park, to Madison, to Howard, and along Howard to the armory. The armory was decorated with flags and festoons, and in the centre of the drilling hall was a stand of tropical plants, among which the colors of the Fifth stood in pleasing contrast to the dark luxurious foliage of the plants. At 2:30 P. M., a banquet was served to the visiting military. There were present all the officers of the Fifth, in full regimentals, Mayor Latrobe, Mayor Calhoun, of Atlanta, Col. Geo. R. Gaither, Col. H. D. Loney, Rev. Jos. Reynolds, Chaplain of the Fifth, Hon. Charles G. Kerr and Gen. Herbert and staff. Capt. Zollinger presided, with Mayor Calhoun at his left and Capt. Burke at his right. A table laden with all the delicacies of the season and thorough good feeling among all present conduced to render the occasion one to be remembered with pleasure by all participants. Capt. Burke, in response to calls from the company, made an excellent speech, in which he said it was pleasing to him to respond to such evidences of hospitality as had met the Guard upon their arrival in Baltimore. There are no people in Georgia who can more fully appreciate the bountiful gifts of the culinary philosopher than those of Atlanta. They were proverbial for extending hospitality to the stranger, and he would be unjust to them if he should not say they were equally proverbial for knowing how to accept it when cordially bestowed. They rally around the alimentary condiments without flinching.

Touching upon politics, Capt. Burke said the Georgians are fully reconstructed, they believe the war is over. The Guard comes to the North that they may meet their fellow-citizens there and seal the bonds of friendship more strongly still. And continuing in a humorous vein he said the Georgians have just as much as they can do to feed the colored people and keep them out of office. It was contrary, he knew, to military usage for a company to carry a flag, but he had suggested that the Guard should carry the Stars and Stripes, which they had won at Rome, Ga., last July, if for nothing else than at least to show it to the people of the North and re-introduce them to the flag of their forefathers.

Unfortunately, Capt. Burke's eloquent speech was not taken down in shorthand.

Speeches were also made by Gen. Herbert, Adj.-Gen. Bond, Dr. A. P. Bloomer, of the State Fencibles of Pennsylvania, who assured the Guard of a hearty welcome in the City of Brotherly Love, Hon. Chas. G. Kerr, Capt. Burgwynn, of the Fifth, and Lieut. Sparks, of the Guard.

In the evening the visitors were taken up to the Academy of Music as the guests of the Fifth Regiment to witness the military drama of "Ours," with Lester Wallack, Maurice Barrymore, Chas. Collins, Miss Rosa Rand, Miss Kate Bartlett and M'me Ponisi in the principal roles. The house was crowded with beauty and fashion, several parties of ladies and gentlemen having also come in from the surrounding country.

The Guard occupied the stalls on the left, and were warmly applauded by the audience upon their entrance. They wore fatigue dress. The officers of the Fifth sat in the stalls to the right. The play was admirably set upon the stage—a noteworthy feature of the performance being the appearance of the full band and about 100 members of the regiment in marching order at the close of the second act, as British soldiers en route to the Crimea. Both Mr. Wallack and Mr. Barrymore, a companion of the unfortunate Porter, who was wounded in Texas last Spring, were warmly applauded upon their first appearance since the unfortunate affair with an outlaw in Texas, and the members of the Gate City Guard were warm in their welcome of them.

CHAPTER IV

The "Peace Mission" Continued—The Guard Arrives at Philadelphia—The State Fencibles in Waiting—The March
through the City—An Ovation—Bountiful Luncheon at
Fairmount Park—Banquet at the "Union League Club"
—On to New York—Received by the Seventh Regiment—
The March up Broadway a Continual Ovation—Review of
the Second Division of the National Guard—A Magnificent Pageant—Arrival at Hartford—Booming of Cannon
—Received by the Putnam Phalanx—Parade and Beautiful Ball—Banquet—Leaving Hartford with Regret

ALL the Baltimore papers contained elaborate accounts of the Guard's
visit. The *Daily News* remarked as follows:

UNIFORM OF THE VISITORS

The uniform is of dark blue cloth, the coats being trimmed with light
buff cloth, and ornamented with three rows of Georgia State buttons. The
epaulettes are of silver and blue fringe. The pants are of the same colored
cloth as the coats, with a buff stripe running down the side of the leg. The
caps are of the same style as those of the Fifth, surmounted with white drooping plumes. The men also wear the regulation white cross belts, which set
off their uniform to great advantage. A special feature of the Guard is the
gentlemanly and orderly conduct of the members; their polished manners
evidenced that they were gentlemen of culture.

A handsome silk United States flag, borne by a color sergeant, attracted general attention; upon inquiring, the reporter was informed that the
company won it at a competitive drill at Rome, Ga., on July 7, 1879.

The honor of carrying the National colors through the North with the
Guard belongs to Sergeant E. W. Hewitt.

IN THE CITY OF WILLIAM PENN

The Georgia soldiers arrived at Philadelphia at 8:45 on the morning
of October 10th. Of the event the Philadelphia *Press* spoke thus:

SOUTHERN SOLDIERS—ARRIVAL OF THE GATE CITY GUARD
OF ATLANTA, GEORGIA

Georgia's crack military organization, the Gate City Guard, arrived from the Monumental City at 8:45 yesterday morning, on their mission of patriotic fraternity, and were received at the Baltimore Depot by the Infantry Battalion State Fencibles, under the efficient command of Maj. John W. Ryan. The visitors arrived in a special car furnished by the Atlanta and Charlotte Air Line Railroad, and which will be used during the Northern tour of the soldiers.

In anticipation of the arrival of the Guard, many private residences, business establishments, and the various government, State and municipal, buildings were profusely decorated with flags and bunting.

At the point of arrival the scene was, indeed, an animated and interesting one. Long before the time announced for the arrival of the soldiers, people began to assemble around the neighborhood of Broad Street and Washington Avenue, and when the train containing the visitors rolled into the depot, the thoroughfare in front of that structure was almost impassible. As the Guard, under the escort of a committee of the State Fencibles, came on the scene, cheer after cheer went up from the crowd. The battalion of Fencibles were drawn up in line on Broad Street, and they saluted the visitors with military courtesy, after which both organizations were drawn up in line. First came McClurg's Cornet Band, next a fife and drum corps, and then the Fencibles, followed by the Gate City Guard.

As the men stood in the line they presented a fine appearance, and were frequently applauded by the assembled crowd. Everything being ready, the word to start was given, and the procession moved slowly up Broad Street to Chestnut, turning down the latter thoroughfare. The marching of the visitors was perfection itself, while the maneuvers were admitted by those versed in military matters to be really astonishing. Both organizations were heartily applauded all along the route. Arriving at the State House, the Fencibles took up a position on the pavement to left, while the Gate City Guard were commanded to "stack arms!" This movement was executed so quickly and so faultlessly that an instantaneous cheer went up from the immense crowd of spectators, and the air was made black with the shakos of the Fencibles, who waved them aloft.

The Guard was drawn up in line at the eastern end of the room. Mayor Calhoun, of Atlanta, Georgia, was then introduced to His Honor Mayor Stokley, and both took up a position alongside the old table on which the Declaration of Independence was signed.

Mayor Stokley was then introduced to Capt. Burke. After shaking the latter warmly by the hand, he addressed the visitors as follows:

"Captain and Gentlemen: It affords me a great deal of pleasure to meet you here in Independence Hall; here, where a little more than a century ago, the Declaration of Independence was signed, and here where we resolved to be a free and independent government. We should stand shoulder to shoulder to make this a government which will be respected throughout the length and breadth of the world. That respect we have thus far commanded, and can command throughout all time, provided the North and South stand shoulder to shoulder.

"I think it is only fitting that here we should renew our pledge where the Declaration was signed, and in the very presence of the signers, and before the table upon which the grand document was signed.

"If we but will it, we can command the respect of the world, and we owe it to ourselves, our families and our posterity to do it.

"I hope that your stay among us may be pleasant, and when you return to your homes in the South your recollection of Philadelphia and its people may aid to unite the ties of friendship and brotherly love which should exist between the North and South."

Mayor Calhoun made a brief response, and Capt. Burke spoke in substance as follows:

"I do not propose to inflict upon you, Mr. Mayor and gentlemen, a lengthy speech. I would simply refer to the fact that when you spoke of the table upon which was signed the Declaration of Independence, I thought of the Stars and Stripes, which we have brought with us to testify that it is our wish to cement together the lately divided sections of our country. That flag was presented to us by the citizens of a State which took an active part in the late unfortunate struggle—sometimes called the rebellion, but call it what you may those people accept the settlement reached in consequence of it in perfect and abiding good faith. Looking at that table, and thinking of its associations, we feel that we are all rebels and the sons of rebels. Nevertheless, we have brought the 'Stars and Stripes' with us, for we could not resist the temptation of introducing you to the flag of your forefathers (great laughter) ; that glorious banner that is destined to float forever over the greatest government the world ever saw. It will never be trailed in the dust, for if we of the South were unable to pull it down, nobody else can (great applause). I accept your invitation to renew our political vows over the table of the Declaration of Independence, and we pledge our fealty to the Constitution of our fathers."

These expressions were warmly applauded, and this concluded the reception in Independence Hall; and then the Guard, escorted by the Fencibles, proceeded to the Continental Hotel, the headquarters of the visitors during their stay in the city.

A Tour of Pleasure

At 2 o'clock "the Boys from Georgia," as guests of the Fencibles, took barouches at the hotel and were driven through Fairmount Park, stopping at Belmont Mansion, where a sumptuous dinner was served. The line of carriages extended for about half a mile. Returning by way of Girard Avenue Bridge, the party stopped at Girard College to witness a drill by the Girard College Cadets. A large number of spectators were present, including the State Fencibles, members of the Grand Army of the Republic, and others. The Cadets never appeared to better advantage.

A touching incident occurred during the parade, which testified to the fraternal feeling prevailing between the Gate City Guard and the Fencibles, and which is worthy of record. Sergeant Michael Brown, of the Fencibles, was an old prisoner of war, and during a seven-months' captivity had been guarded by one of the members of the Gate City Guard who was present yesterday. When asked by a companion to give the name, he replied, "No, not for $10,000," following up the emphatic remark by an equally emphatic embrace of a Southern brother. It was a grand sight—a scene never to be forgotten by those who witnessed it.

On leaving Girard College the visitors and their escort drove rapidly to the Continental, from whence, after partaking of tea, they proceeded to the Walnut Street theatre to witness the performance.

The Banquet

At the conclusion of the performance at the theatre, the Guard, escorted by the Fencibles' committee, proceeded to the Union League Club, on Broad

Street, and sat down to a great banquet. After the cloth had been removed, Judge Kelly, a member of Congress, was called to the chair, and made a few remarks appropriate to the occasion.

Of the banquet the Philadelphia *Times* remarked:

The most notable event of the visit of the Gate City Guard was the banquet given at the Union League Club House, beginning at half past 11 o'clock. Among those present, besides the Southern guests and their hosts, were Gen. Robert Patterson; Adj.-Gen. Latta; Brig.-Gen. Geo. R. Snowden and staff, in uniform; Brig.-Gen. Jas. A. Beaver, of Bellefonte; Lieut.-Cols. Geo. H. North and Silas Pettit, of Gen. Hartrauft's staff; Col. Theodore E. Weidersheim; Col. A. Loudon Snowden; Mayor Stokley; Hon. A. K. McClure; John Henry Puleston, member of the English Parliament, and Chief Commissioner Baldwin. Hon. Wm. D. Kelly welcomed the guests to the banquet on behalf of Maj. Ryan and the Fencibles in a speech in which he mentioned, incidentally, that he carried a musket as a member of the State Fencibles, forty-one years ago, before many members of the present company were born. After the banquet toasts were drunk, and speeches of mutual good will were made by Judge Kelly, Capt. Burke, Mayor Calhoun, Gen. Patterson, Major Ryan, Mr. McClure, and others. Capt. Burke's speech on this occasion was one of his best. His allusion to the late war, its sufferings and devastations, its heroism entwined with human sympathy, all pictured so pathetically that many a veteran felt the unbidden tear well up and course along his cheek as he applauded his approval of the patriotic sentiments. Capt. Burke was congratulated on all sides when he finished. Col. McClure, of the *Times*, made an excellent speech which was warmly received.

THE GUARD'S ARRIVAL IN NEW YORK

The New York papers, and also the press throughout the country, followed the patriotic mission of the Gate City Guard from place to place, from the time they left Atlanta, and their arrival in New York City was looked for with much interest by the military and citizens, particularly by the Southern residents in that city, and the streets in the vicinity of Courtland Street Ferry were thronged with people awaiting the arrival of the Guard. Col. Emmons Clark, commanding the Seventh Regiment of New York, had ordered a battalion of the regiment, under command of Capt. George P.

Barrett, acting Major, to meet and escort the Guard to their armory, and when the Guard arrived, they found the Seventh's escort, trim, soldierly and imposing, with full band and drum corps awaiting them. The little ceremonious episode that followed was indicative of the military knowledge and excellent training of the two bodies of soldiers—the "present arms" of the Seventh, in salute of the Southerners as they marched past them, executed with military precision, and a warm welcome to prompt it—and like a flash the return salute from the Guard, as with a snap, their rifles were brought to a "carry arms," with an easy grace of movement that awoke the immense crowd who saw this neat and well-executed exchange of courtesies and the welkin rang with an instantaneous outburst of applause for the soldiers. The New York *Herald* gives the story of the march to the armory.

THE GUARD IN NEW YORK CITY—RECEIVED WITH FULL MILITARY HONORS BY THE SEVENTH REGIMENT

(New York *Herald*, Oct. 12, 1879)

The Gate City Guard, of Atlanta, Ga., numbering forty men and commanded by Captain J. F. Burke, Lieutenants W. C. Sparks and J. W. Johnstone, arrived in the city from Philadelphia at two o'clock yesterday afternoon, and were warmly received and entertained by the Seventh Regiment. The Guard was accompanied by Mayor W. L. Calhoun, of Atlanta, and a number of ladies and gentlemen from that city.

The corps is considered the crack corps of the State of Georgia, and certainly sustained that reputation handsomely yesterday. Though commanded now by Capt. J. F. Burke, a veteran Confederate, most of the men are young soldiers, the descendants of Confederate veterans.

The Gate City Guard wore navy-blue uniforms with buff facings, similar to those in which the Gate City Guard of old were attired and mustered into the Confederate Army, and presented a very dashing military appearance when they landed in this city at Courtland Street Ferry. Shortly after two o'clock they were received by Companies I and E, of the Seventh, under Captains Barrett and Casey, the former commanding the battalion.

After the customary military etiquette the Seventh, headed by Grafulla's band, led the Georgians up Courtland Street to Broadway, amid the plaudits of the thousands who lined the sidewalks to view the pageant and welcome the Southerners. At the City Hall there was a great crowd of people awaiting their arrival, and the police had all they could do to keep the plaza clear when the drums and cornets in the distance told of the columns' approach. About a quarter to three the troops wheeled into Mail Street behind the Post Office, and at the same moment Mayor Cooper, accompanied by Col. Emmons Clark and Lieut.-Col. Fitzgerald, of the Seventh, descended the City Hall steps with Mayor Calhoun, of Atlanta, Ga., and took up his position in the old reviewing spot immediately in front. There was silence for a few minutes, during which Capt. Barrett visited the officials, and receiving instructions from his chief, hurried back to Mail Street. A second later the drums told that the column were again in motion, and soon after the imposing form of the drum-major of the Seventh was seen at the eastern entrance to the City Hall Park. Then the band struck up, and the Seventh wheeled into the "open" and marched past the reviewing station by columns of companies, followed by the visitors, whose well-dressed ranks and soldierly bearing elicited hearty cheers from the multitude of spectators. The thing was over in a few minutes, that is to say, as soon as the men reached Broadway, and all along the line were cheering multitudes for the visitors and their escort until they came to Eighth Street, where they turned to the eastward, and proceeded to the Seventh Regiment armory, opposite the Cooper Institute.

In the Seventh's Quarters

The Seventh drew up in line before the main entrance of their armory, on Sixth Street, and presented arms, when the Gate City Guard passed in column of fours with the short company step and entered the building. They ascended the stairs and were received in the great drill room by the "off" members of the Seventh, with cheers. The escort and band followed them quickly, and wheeled into line on the left of the Gate City Guard. Arms were stacked, and the men marched to the bountifully supplied refreshment tables opposite, and were left to themselves by the officers, who with Capt. Burke, Lieuts. Sparks and Johnstone, and Mayor Calhoun, proceeded to the room of the Board of Officers, where a magnificent repast awaited them. To receive the strangers there were present, besides the officers of the Seventh Regiment, Adj.-Gen. Woodward, Brig.-Gen. Varian and staff, the staff of Maj.-Gen. Shaler, who was unavoidably absent, Commissioner Thos. Brennan and many other civilians. An hour was spent in discussing the collation

THE GATE CITY GUARD AND SEVENTH REGIMENT OF NEW YORK, IN NEW YORK, OCTOBER, 1879.

Commissioned and Non-commissioned officers of the Gate City Guard in 1879. Reading from left to right: Sgt. E. W. Reinhardt, Lieut. Jos. Lumpkin, Sgt. E. W. Hewitt, Capt. S. A. Swearinger, Ajt. J. L. Jackson, Lieut. W. C. Sparks, Capt. J. F. Burke, Corpl. W. B. Cummings, Corpl. M. F. Amorous, Corpl. Gordon C. Neff, Sgt. Wm. M. Camp, Corpl. Chas. E. Sciple.

and friendly interchanges between the guests and their hosts, and then Col. Clark, in a few well-chosen words, on behalf of the Seventh Regiment, welcomed the Georgians to New York and the armory.

"I assure you, Capt. Burke," said he, "the kindly feelings evinced by your most praiseworthy visit are heartily reciprocated by us all."

BURYING THE PAST

Capt. Burke, who is a tall, soldierly-looking man, with iron-gray hair and brown moustache, arose and with much feeling spoke at length upon the past and the future of his State.

Following are extracts from Captain Burke's speech:

"It is with feelings of unalloyed gratification that I embrace the privilege so kindly accorded me to respond on behalf of myself and my command to the generous hospitality and noble sentiments of which we are the happy recipients. It is sincerely gratifying to find at this great distance from our homes, so many friendly hands to embrace us, so many words of kindness to greet us, so many noble sentiments to inspire us, and with all my heart I reciprocate them and assure you that they are indelibly photographed on its inmost recesses.

"It is a satisfaction to stand here in the garb of the commonwealth of Georgia, a proud and prosperous State, and be welcomed by the sons of a sister State with all the warmth of a soldier's magnanimity, and I can not but feel a pang of regret when I turn back a few pages of our country's history to the record of the unholy strife that deluged our people in direst misfortune, and reflect how speedily and peacefully our differences would have been adjusted had they been left to the citizen soldiers of our common country (applause)." * * * *

Capt. Burke continued in an interesting and reminiscent mood, describing the devastation that resulted from the Civil War and the return of the Confederate soldiers after heroic struggles on the battle-fields to ruined homes, blackened walls and a hopeless future for themselves and their families, which conditions were effectively and eloquently portrayed, and continuing, he said:

"But we have come among you not to recall sad memories nor to pass in panoramic tableaux the appalling portrayal of war's devastation, and if under the inspiration of the melancholy recollections these thoughts bubble to the surface and find expression in the impulse of the moment, charge them to the reminiscences which your unstinted kindness brings vividly to my mind, seducing from the deep recesses of memory the recollections of former years.

"We come among you divested of the pomp and circumstance of war. Our cartridge boxes are not lined with ammunition for our rifles, nor our 'haver-sacks' with 'hard-tack' for ourselves. The Southern flag under which my command assumed this character of equipment, has been furled, furled with all the aspirations and hopes that gave it to the Southern breeze and now entwined in the melancholy memories of the past—we are again in our fathers' house, and in the emblem that floats above, we recognize the Stars and Stripes of our forefathers, the colors of the Nation, the talismanic shield that will unite the growing States of this great country in one Union, inseparable forever hereafter (applause). * * * *

"Here on Northern soil the sons of those who were estranged in deadly conflict but a few years ago, meet and embrace in the bonds of fellowship—united once more under the same roof—breaking bread at the same table; it is a grand subject, this glorious re-union and the fraternal mingling of two great sections of our country, representing a brave and magnanimous people—and in evidence of our unity we have brought with us the Stars and Stripes of the Nation, that emblem of power and the canopy under which our progress and civilization will dazzle the nations of the future and imprint America's escutcheon on the eternal tablets of time."

Captain Burke's eloquent speech was punctuated throughout with loud applause.

The next feature in the reception was the drinking of the health of the mayor of Atlanta, and Col. Clark's statement of the regret of Mayor Cooper at his inability to attend. Mayor Calhoun, of Atlanta, responded. He was evidently overcome to some extent by his feelings, and in accents marked by emotion, told how difficult it was to express his appreciation of the high honor conferred on him.

"We feel," he stated, "that good may come of this visit to you. We know that the war and its evil consequences to us are things of the past and should be forgotten. The past is buried, we must look to the future."

He then told how much the people of Atlanta were indebted to the North, and New York itself for aid in the rebuilding of their homes and fortunes, and concluded with a genuine expression of his hope of a closer union between the Northern and Southern people.

MAJ. GEORGE BURGESS FISHER,
Comd. Governor's Foot Guard of Hartford,
Conn., 1879.

CAPT. GEORGE P. BARRETT,
Seventh Regiment, New York, 1879.

COL. EMMONS CLARK,
Comd. Seventh Regiment, New York, 1879.

CAPT. GEORGE B. RHOADS,
Seventh Regiment, New York, 1879.

Mayor Calhoun's speech was received with applause.

There were many other speakers introduced by Gen. Clark, but most of them contented themselves with very brief statements. For instance, Commissioner Brennan invited both commands to partake of the hospitalities of Blackwell's Island tomorrow. Col. Jusson, of Gen. Shaler's staff, asked Capt. Burke to take part in the first division parade on Wednesday, given in their honor, and Gen. Varian heartily welcomed the strangers, and Lieut.-Col. Fitzgerald of the Seventh, offered the hand of fellowship to them. In fact the reception was one of those genial affairs which soldiers alone can create when they have buried their differences and shaken hands as friends.

AN EXCELLENT DRILL

When the officers left the Board room they repaired to the drill room overhead, where Grafulla's band discoursed sweet music, and the North and South, in the persons of their citizen soldiers, forgot the past and fraternized once more. Then followed, at the request of the officers of the Seventh Regiment, the exhibition drill of the Gate City Guard, which astonished and delighted the members of the Seventh, who cheered the skillful execution of many evolutions to the echo. The precision and accuracy of the strangers was certainly marvelous, and were characterized by some of the veterans of the Seventh as unequaled by any visiting corps. Marching and counter-marching in line, column and platoons, firing front, right and left obliquely on the knee and lying down, were beautifully done, and the armory fairly rang with the plaudits of the Seventh.

At the conclusion of the drill the Seventh, leading the strangers, marched through Eighth Street to Broadway, up Broadway to Fourteenth Street, thence to Fifth Avenue, thence to Twenty-seventh Street, and up Twenty-seventh to the Coleman House, where the visitors are quartered. The Guard will attend the "Church of the Strangers" today, and will leave for Boston on the 15th of October.

All the great daily papers of the great American metropolis gave elaborate accounts of the movements of Atlanta's military representatives during their stay on the ancient Island of Manhattan. The New York *World* contained the following:

OUR SOUTHERN GUESTS—PARADING WITH NEW YORK'S MILITIA AND SUPPING WITH THE OLD GUARD

The entertainment of the Gate City Guard in this city ended Wednesday by the assignment to them of the place of honor at the review of the first division of the National Guard, and by a reception tendered them in the evening by the Old Guard at the armory of the latter on Union Square.

The Guard gathered at the Coleman House about 3 P. M., and marched out under arms and in full uniform, to join the Seventh Regiment at the corner of Fifth Avenue and Twenty-ninth Street. They were escorted by the Seventh Regiment down the line of the column of the first division, and back again to the place of honor at the extreme right. When the reviewing stand was reached they dropped out of column and took their places on the reviewing stand with Governor Robinson.

At 8 P. M., the Guard, dressed in fatigue uniform and accompanied by Col. Clark and many of the rank and file of the Seventh, entered the armory of the Old Guard. In the absence of Maj. George W. McLean, the commander of the Old Guard, the president of the Society, Mr. Alexander Henriques, welcomed the visitors. He said that these friendly meetings between the men of the North and South had the effect of strengthening the bonds of union between the two sections.

Capt. Burke, of the Gate City Guard, was absent, dining with Mayor Cooper, at the Union Club, and Lieut. Johnstone was called on in his place to respond for the visitors. He spoke of the cordiality of the reception they had met with and said:

"This trip has not been taken solely for a pleasure, but chiefly to bring the young men of the North and South together, to the end that by knowing each other they may join hands—not across any 'bloody chasm,' for we do not admit there is any such chasm—but in common interest and common friendship. And in conclusion, allow me to say, that if any enemy shall in future have the audacity to threaten the flag of our common country, we will come up from the South 200,000 strong to join you in maintaining its honor and dignity."

Lieut. Johnstone was loudly cheered. Major McLean, who had by this time arrived, made a short speech in which he said that the Mason and Dixon line, and every other line between the North and South has been obliterated by these pleasant reunions of the Northern and Southern soldiers. Speeches were also made by Col. Emmons Clark and others.

FRANK LESLIE'S ILLUSTRATES THE REVIEW

Not only did the great dailies assign special reporters to write up the honors shown the Gate City Guard while in New York, but the illustrated papers employed the pencils of their artists in the same direction. Frank Leslie's Weekly published an effective picture of the company as it passed in review before Governor Robinson, and remarked as follows on the subject:

"The Gate City Guard of Atlanta, Ga., occupied a position in advance of the division. In a column of fours, forty-five strong, they moved down the Avenue. To avoid the wagons, all of which at this time had not been removed from the west side of the Park, they moved to the right and left oblique, and changed from column of fours to double-file with such military precision as to call forth repeated bursts of applause from the thousands of spectators. Even the tall white plumes upon their caps seemed to sway from side to side in unison. They were given a position on the front row of the grand stand with Governor Robinson."

About 30,000 people were around the grand stand to see the Georgians. The whole first division, about nine regiments, infantry, cavalry and artillery, were in the parading column. It was a telling compliment to the Southerners. Their march down Fifth Avenue was a continual ovation by the populace.

The famous Seventh Regiment earned the lasting friendship of the Georgians by its many thoughtful courtesies, among which was their escort of the Gate City Guard to Blackwell's Island to partake of an elaborate banquet tendered them by the City of New York. And Mayor Edw. Cooper afterward invited their commander and Mayor Calhoun to dine with him and friends at the Union Club.

During the grand review in Madison Square, Ex-Governor R. B. Bullock, of Georgia, was on the reviewing platform with Governor Robinson, of New York. Among the ladies accompanying the two Governors were Mrs. Clark, wife of Col. Emmons Clark, of the Seventh Regiment of New York City, Mrs. J. F. Burke, Mrs. John A. Bowie and Miss Rosa Bowie, of Georgia, and many others.

On Thursday morning with the escort of the Seventh Regiment, under Major Kipp, the Gate City Guard marched from their hotel on Broadway to the Grand Union Depot, where they took possession of their car for Hartford, Connecticut, with many leave-takings and warm hand-shakes with the officers and members of the illustrious Seventh.

Speaking of the Guard's generous reception in the Metropolis of the Union, Lieut. Sparks, of the Guard, said of the march up Broadway:

"I was somewhat doubtful of our visit to Philadelphia, until after we arrived there, because the political feeling in that city had been strongly antagonistic to the South, but when I found that our mission of reconciliation was understood and so warmly appreciated, I felt that New York would understand the purpose of our visit at once, and when I heard the cheering crowds and saw the waving hats, and found myself stepping off to the inspiring music of the Seventh Regiment's magnificent band and drum corps, I just swelled up until I couldn't tell how many I was."

THE OVATION AT HARTFORD, CONN.

(From the Hartford *Times*)

Amid the cheers of a large crowd and a salute of thirteen guns, the Gate City Guard, of Atlanta, Ga., disembarked from the cars at the Union Depot, on Asylum Street, yesterday afternoon, and were escorted to Bushnell Park, where they were received by the historic Putnam Phalanx with military courtesies.

Very soon the line was formed and the two companies marched over the prescribed route, which embraced Ford, Trinity, Washington, Park, Main, High, Church, Trumbull, Pearl and State Streets, and Central and American Row. On all the streets there was a liberal display of the National colors arranged in the most tasteful manner. Prominent among the decorated buildings was that of the *Times*; in front of the office windows were two pedestals with an eagle at the foot of each. On these pedestals stood (nearly life-sized) figures of a sailor and a soldier, and between them a large shield with the word "WELCOME" on it. Above the shield rose a canopy of flags, surmounted by a large eagle. The windows above were draped with flags, and in the centre stood a large figure of the "Goddess of Liberty," her hand stretched forth toward the South, bearing a branch of palm. Above this, surrounded by flags and festoons of red, white and blue, was the inscription: "The Only Arms Today—Open Arms."

Conklin's Bazaar and Appo & Stevens, tailors, were almost concealed by the folds of bunting and flags with which the building was covered.

The "Home Circle" club rooms were beautifully decorated, the flags mingling with large palm trees and other plants and flowers. Other buildings were equally beautifully decorated, and the whole display was a really creditable one.

Along the route the visiting military were the recipients of hearty and frequent bursts of applause, and their marching showed them to be well-nigh perfect in drill. At the end of the march the Georgians were escorted to the United States Hotel, where they rested for a time preparatory to

THE BANQUET

This was given in the large hall of the Putnam Phalanx, which was tastefully decorated with streamers of red, white and blue. Over the stairway was a canopy of flags, so that the visitors to the rooms seemed as if coming from the open folds of a tent. Appropriate inscriptions of welcome appeared on all sides.

The feast was prepared by Messrs. Stickney and Fitzgerald, and was all that could be expected or desired. The tables were beautified by large bouquets of flowers, and vases full of brilliant colored grasses. The napkins were of paper, and each bore the coat of arms of Connecticut and Georgia, between which were clasped hands. On the bill-of-fare were all kinds of cold poultry, game and meats, salads, pastry, confectionery and fruits. The inner man's wants having been supplied, the speechmaking began.

MAJOR BROWN'S ADDRESS OF WELCOME

When the company had all taken their seats at the tables, Major Brown, the commander of the Phalanx, made the following address of welcome to the guests of the battalion:

"Capt. Burke, Officers, Members and Guests, of the Gate City Guard: It is my agreeable duty, in behalf of the Putnam Phalanx to extend to you a sincere and cordial welcome to these, their headquarters, and to such hospitalities as may have been provided for your comfort and pleasure during your visit to the Charter Oak City, and Capital of our beloved commonwealth. While coming here as strangers, we are not strangers to the high character which your organization maintains, and we welcome you in the spirit of unity and fraternity of a common brotherhood. We welcome you as coming from one of the old thirteen States, which stood steadfast and true to the cause of American independence 'in the days that tried men's souls.' We welcome you as citizens holding due allegiance, and entitled to all the rights and privileges, and willing to share the responsibilities pertaining to the government founded by the fathers of a grand republic, which challenges the admiration of the world. And we welcome you as the representative element from the Southern States, devoted to a nation's greatness and glory, and for the higher elevation and nobler purposes of a 'government of the people, for the people, by the people.' The object of your visit to the Northern States is of more than social importance, being, as I understand it, three-fold: pleasure, observation, and fraternity between the late divided sections of our country. It is significant, and of national interest. It says in no unmeaning words that you, of the South, with our people of the North, abide by the same laws, support the same constitution, revere the same old flag, and will maintain the same union indivisible and unimpaired for the inheritance of posterity. We trust as you shall meet with our people and observe their varied industries and institutions, you will find every pursuit so naturally interwoven with our national interests that you will be fully impressed with the idea that unity and a broad charity are alike demanded on all hands for their highest developments. That your coming among us and the acquaintances you shall make will tend to the desired result—pardon me for saying it—is manifested here today, and hence it is not to be questioned. May your journey culminate in naught but pleasure, profitable observation and fraternal good-will to the overflowing of your liveliest anticipations.

"Accept then, gentlemen, a hearty New England welcome, in the spirit that would bridge over the bloody chasm, and only treasure up the glories of the past as an inspiration to brighter glories in the future. And with amity of purpose let us sustain that which was planted for our inheritance, guided by the principles of justice, wisdom and moderation, to the fulfillment of the sublimest aspirations of the heroes of the revolution."

GEN. HAWLEY'S ADDRESS

As Gen. Joseph R. Hawley was obliged to leave the city on an early evening train, Maj. Brown called upon him to speak next, in order that he, might be able to fill his engagement. The General spoke briefly, saying:

"I was very willing and desirous to come here, being glad of the opportunity to tell you how glad we are to welcome you to this State, which for two hundred and forty years has governed itself. Connecticut has never failed to elect its own governor, and its people have always been obedient to its laws and prompt to any call of duty. I am exceedingly glad to welcome you, and am sorry that you must go away so soon, for we should like to show you something of the Nutmeg State, and some of our varied industries. We should be glad to show more of Hartford and welcome you to our thousands of hospitable homes where our people would be glad to see you. They are your homes; this is your and our land, and you have brought your delightful weather with you. We are sorry that you cannot stay longer."

Prayer was then offered by the Rev. John C. Kimball, the chaplain of the Putnam Phalanx. Col. Charles M. Joslyn was then announced as the toastmaster of the occasion. He said:

"Citizens of Georgia—Comrades-in-Arms: I can only repeat and emphasize the words of the commander, and welcome you, the sons of a sister State, to this city and State. Looking back to the past, and forward to the future, I doubt not that you will ever be found upholding the honor of our flag. The Putnams are a commemorative organization. Our mission is to honor patriotism whenever found, and strike hands with all whose watchword is 'God and our native land'. I give as the first sentiment, 'Our honored guests, the Gate City Guard.' "

Capt. Burke, the commander of the Guard, responded, saying it was with feelings of unalloyed gratification that he spoke for himself and comrades. He regarded it both a privilege and an honor to stand as he did, beneath the shield of the great commonwealth of Georgia, and be received and welcomed by a sister commonwealth with a soldier's magnanimity. He could not but be impressed with the fact that all the differences of our common country could have been settled had they been left to the soldiers of the two sections. Atlanta suffered from the ravages of war, but her people still have energy and enterprise, and the powers of recuperation and the elements of success. We have come here to clasp hands as did our fathers in the days of the revolution, when faith, truth, hope and liberty in a common cause, struggled and triumphed together. We come divested of the pomp and circumstance of war, bearing with us the Stars and Stripes.

The flag that is ours, the emblem of our power, destined to float over a great nation and a brave people(applause). We are here united as a common people and have broken bread together. It is a noble sight; we are here to grasp your hands in fraternal feeling (applause).

There is no record of Capt. Burke's eloquent speech on this occasion and the above are but a few of the sentiments expressed by him.

EX-GOVERNOR HUBBARD'S ADDRESS

"Georgia and Connecticut" was the next toast announced by Col. Joslyn. He said in looking around he saw a gentleman at one of the tables from whom, as his superior officer, he formerly took orders. He now would turn the tables, and order him to respond to the toast he had just given, and he introduced Ex-Governor R. D. Hubbard to the company.

Ex-Governor Hubbard said:

"I obey the orders of my subordinate with pleasure and alacrity, for I count it both a pleasure and honor to join with the Putnam Phalanx in welcoming you, gentlemen of the Gate City Guard, their comrades-in-arms. I say comrades-in-arms, and such they are in every word and deed; for the republic is and must ever be dependent upon the citizen soldiery of the States for defense against the enemies of her peace, and whilst you and they are defenders of your respective States against invasion, insurrection and domestic violence, you are also, and none the less, brethren in arms, in a common cause and duty, the common defense of a common flag and a common country, and so you are each and both knit together in one great and soldierly brotherhood for the defense of the whole republic and the entire sisterhood of States (applause).

"I have said the whole sisterhood of States, for whatever estrangements may have existed in the past, and however we may have followed for a time with differing faiths the fortunes of different flags, we are once more—thank God—a reunited sisterhood, with one flag, one country, and one destiny. And what we are today, that, by God's grace, we are resolved to remain, one and undivided under the constitution, not a score or more of severed or clashing nations bristling with standing armies and converted for self-defence into military barracks, but a constitutional unity—a nation (applause), or call it what we will, and wrangle about terms as we may, a federal government supreme for federal purposes, and capable of self-defense, not less against

CAPT. PETER F. CLARKE.

WALTER SCOTT COLEMAN.

DR. HENRY F. SCOTT.

FLOYD FENN.

enemies from within than enemies from without—every State abiding in the Union, not by leave and sufferance of any other, but of constitutional right, and remaining there, too, not of caprice, or grace, or favor, but by constitutional obligation, and every one moving in its own sphere of independent local self-government by its own law, as in the great gravitations of the heavens each star keeps harmony with the sun, but holds its own orbit, and refuses to be absorbed into the central mass (applause).

"And now, one word more; the contest to which I have already made allusion was one of the most unnatural of all unnatural wars known among men—a fratricidal war. Let us see to it as we value its cost in blood and treasure, and dread its possible recurrence, that the peace which it accomplished shall be the best and truest known amongst men, a fraternal peace; not a hollow truce, but a welcoming back to brotherly and lasting reconciliation of States that were dead and are alive again (applause), of brethren that were lost and are found (applause); for a Union, founded not on a common love of a common country, but on the brute force of swords and bayonets, is not the Union of our fathers, nor one which God will bless and men approve. It may exist; it can not last. A better peace than before was the purpose of the struggle. Anything less than this was subjugation in motive and will prove a miscarriage in the result. He, therefore, who, today, now that the sword has long been sheathed, seeks to stir up sectional disaffection—no matter from which side or to what party he belongs—he, who today, for personal ambitions, or party gain, seeks to uncover the embers of the war, and render its hatreds hereditary in the blood of unborn generations, is a traitor and fratricide in heart, and lacks nothing but courage and opportunity to become both the one and the other in fact (applause).

"Capt. Burke and gentlemen of the Gate City Guard, in this spirit you have accepted the decision of the Civil War, honestly and magnanimously, and you have left your distant homes to come here in a spirit of true patriotism and offer us the hand of national fellowship. We most cordially and sincerely accept the offer and with our hearts filled with gratitude we thank you for this visit (great applause)."

Following the ex-Governor there were speeches by Mayor Calhoun, of Atlanta, and Mayor Sumner, of Hartford, the same patriotic views being emphasized, and A. E. Burr spoke effectively to the toast "The Press." Letters and telegrams of regret were received from Hon. William W. Eaton,

Senator of the U. S. from Connecticut, and Governor Andrews. Dr. Paltier, the paymaster of the Phalanx, read the following letter from the celebrated author and humorist, Mark Twain:

ELMIRA, NEW YORK, Oct. 14, 1879.

P. D. PELTIER, ESQ.,

DEAR SIR: Please receive my best thanks for the invitation to meet the Atlanta soldiers, and the Putnams. I was on the point of starting when a committee requested me to remain here and introduce General Joseph R. Hawley to a political mass meeting. This was a great surprise to me, for I had supposed the man was comparatively well known. I shall remain, of course, and shall do what I can to blow the fog from around his fame. Meantime, will you kindly see that the portion of your banquet which I should be allowed to consume, if I were present, is equably distributed among the public charities of our several States and territories? I would not that any partiality be shown on account of political creed or geographical position, but would beg that all the crates be of the same heft.

I am glad to add my voice to yours in welcoming the Georgians to Hartford. Personal contact and communion of Northerners and Southerners over the friendly board will do more toward obliterating sectional lines, and restoring mutual respect and esteem than any other thing that can be devised. We can not meet as Northerners and Southerners, we grow in breadth and stature meantime, and part as *Americans*. There is not any name among the world's nationalities that can oversize that one.

Sincerely hoping that our guests will receive a welcome at our town's hands which will cause them to forget the length of their journey and make them willing to come again, I am truly yours,

S. L. CLEMENS.

ADDRESS OF JUDGE CALHOUN, OF HARTFORD

Judge David S. Calhoun, being called on for a speech, said he came under a safe conduct, and was assured that he should not be molested. If he spoke, it was because he was overawed by the military. He did not know why, he, as a representative of the law, should be called upon to speak, for it is a well-known maxim *"inter arma silent leges"*—in the midst of arms the laws are silent. For himself, however, he was pleased to express his personal respect and regard for the honored guests from the Gate City of Georgia, and assured them that he welcomed them to the Charter Oak City. Their State was the youngest of the old Thirteen, ours one of the oldest. He hoped we should be held together in an indissoluble union of fraternity and regard.

COL. L. A. BARBOUR

Col. Lucius A. Barbour, of the First Regiment, C. N. G., spoke to the toast of the National Guard.

A BOX OF WOODEN NUTMEGS

Ex-Comptroller C. C. Hubbard, of the Sunday *Globe*, presented Capt. Burke with a box containing six wooden nutmegs, carved from the wood of the historic Charter Oak of Hartford, in behalf of J. H. Most. The gift was accepted by the captain as a most interesting souvenir of the occasion.

Allyn Hall was made beautiful by red, white and blue festoons and flags, mingled with bouquets of grasses and flowers. The lights were reflected by numerous glass globes with gold fish swimming in the water, which were suspended around the hall, interspersed with gilded cages in which singing canaries were confined. On the stage was a coat of arms of Georgia and Connecticut, and on it the inscription:

"Welcome, Brethren of the Gate City Guard."

Early in the evening the crowd began to gather, and soon the galleries were filled with spectators. Colt's full band performed a selection of choice pieces, consisting of the overture and "Barber of Seville," selections from "Pinafore," "Resch's Waltz," etc., etc.

By the time the concert was finished the military guests had arrived, and very soon the band struck up the march "Welcome to the Gate City Guard" to the music of which the company opened the ball. Capt. Burke, of the visiting company, escorted Mrs. Maj. Brown, and was followed by his officers and the field staff of the Phalanx. Several hundred took part in this march, in which the elegant costumes of the ladies were shown to the best advantage. The variety of dress was infinite, and it would be impossible to describe the many rich and elegant costumes which were shown. A handsomer display of dress is rarely seen in one exhibition. Dancing began soon after ten o'clock, and there were twelve selections on the programme. Lieut. W. P. Chamberlin was the floor manager, and his assistants were Capt. C. H. Case, Ensign B. G. Baldwin, Ensign A. P. Moore, Corporal E. A. Parry, Corporal B. C. Porter, Drum-Major Theodore Colston, Quartermaster-Sergeant N. L. Harris, Secretary W. H. Barnard, Private Geo. H. Wooley, N. L. Hope, and Lieutenant B. Merriam. Adkins & Stevens Orchestra furnished the music and William Church acted as prompter. The members of the Phalanx were unflagging in their endeavors to provide for the wants of their guests, and everything was harmoniously managed.

The ball developed the fact that the members of the Gate City Guard were not only graceful dancers, but eclipsed many of our home folks.

The Departure of the Visitors

It was expected when arrangements were made for the reception of the Gate City Guard that they would remain in the city today. Arrangements for an exhibition drill, a visit to Colt's armory, an exhibition of the Gatling gun, an inspection of the Capitol, and visits to other places had been made; but during the evening telegrams from Boston were received, which made it imperative that the Georgians should leave on the midnight train. This move cut short the courtesies which the Governor's Foot Guard, the City Guard, Company K, the Hillyers and the Light Guard expected to show the visitors today. But large delegations of all these companies accompanied the visitors to the depot and bade them God-speed.

Short as the visit was, it was fraught with cordiality and good feeling. It showed the Southerners that the "Yankees" were ready with open arms to give them a hearty welcome, that all differences of the past were buried. It is greatly to be regretted that the company was compelled to go so soon, but the friendships formed last night will prove lasting ones.

One of the features of the decorations yesterday was in front of the Best Manufacturing Company's store, where there was a large drawing of a soldier in blue, and a soldier in gray, grasping each other by the hand. The artist cautiously made the Southerner the handsomer man of the two.

During the evening many of the visitors were taken to the City and Foot Guard armories, and to the Home Circle club rooms where they were hospitably entertained.

Mayor Sumner, by invitation, accompanied the Gate City Guard to Boston. It is not impossible that the Guard will return tomorrow night and spend Sunday in Hartford. One and all expressed themselves much gratified with their reception in Hartford. The men thought Hartford was more like their own city than any place they had visited.

Among the notable incidents of this Hartford visit was a banquet given by Marshall Jewell, ex-Postmaster-General, and ex-Minister to Russia, to the officers of the Guard, and Mayor Calhoun, in which some water from the Dead Sea was tasted only to prompt silent imprecations on its bitterness, which was more stringent than a green persimmon. It was a joke played by Mr. Jewell.

CHAPTER V

THE GUARD IN BOSTON

THE METROPOLIS OF MORAL IDEAS WELCOMES
THE GALLANT SOUTHERNERS

SOUTHERN soldiers in blue uniforms, and bearing the United States flag, received with plaudits, and martial music, and military salutes, in Boston! And all in less than twenty years after the most import-ant war in history! In 1859 New England and the South glaring at each other with fury in their aspects. In 1879 survivors of the Confederacy and their sons received with open arms in the old abolition city, and vowing mu-tual fealty to the restored Union with all the warmth and zeal that charac-terized the revered founders of the great structure! Verily, the mission of the Gate City Guard was patriotic in a very high sense.

Before the company had come to Boston, its progress through the coun-try had become widely known. Its pacificatory purpose was recognized, and approved by the better class of newspapers. New England had been reading the press reports and by the time the brilliant sojourns in Washington, Philadelphia, Baltimore, New York and Hartford were ended, she was preparing for her part in the grand reunion. Only a small proportion of the press comments in Massachusetts has been preserved, and of such material, space can be spared for only a small part.

THE GATE CITY GUARD—YESTERDAY'S COURTESIES TO THE SOUTHERN VISITORS

(From the Boston *Daily Advertiser*)

The Gate City Guard of Atlanta, Ga., one of the crack military organizations of the South, for whose advent here much had been arranged by the city government, military organizations and private citizens, arrived in this city yesterday at 6:15, from Hartford, Conn., via Boston & Albany Railroad. They were received at the station by Capt. Thomes and Lieut. Hobbs, of the Boston Light Infantry, and Capts. Shattuck and Hichborn, and Lieuts. Laughtons and Storer, of the Infantry Veterans Association. Capt. Burke and his company were informally welcomed by Capt. Thomes, after which special cars were taken to the Revere House, where the visitors are quartered during their stay in the city.

Mayor Calhoun, of Atlanta, and Mayor Sumner of Hartford came with the Guard as guests. The company is composed of veterans of the Civil War and young men, sons of Confederate veterans. Their uniforms consist of dark blue cut-away coats, dark blue pantaloons, trimmed with blue and buff, and a black shako hat with white drooping plumes.

THE RECEPTION CEREMONIES

The Boston Light Infantry and the Veterans Association assembled at their Armory in Boyleston Hall at 8 o'clock. The active company paraded in full uniform as a battalion of two companies, under Capt. Thomes and Lieuts. Lovett and Hobbs, the Veteran Association paraded in dark clothes, and wore red badges. The route was up Washington, School, Tremont, Court to Bowdoin Square, where the company drew up in line before the Revere House. At the Revere House the usual formalities of receiving the Gate City Guard were gone through, and then taking the visiting company under escort, line of march was taken through Court, Tremont and Bacon Streets to the State House.

Both companies marched into the rotunda. The commissioned officers then proceeded to the private room of Governor Talbot, where they were warmly welcomed by his Excellency. Mayors Calhoun and Sumner were of the party. Governor Talbot was accompanied by Cols. Kingsbury, Pulsifer, and Olin of his staff. After this reception the party descended to the rotunda, where Capt. Thomes introduced Capt. Burke and the Guard. In reply, Governor Talbot very feelingly expressed his pleasure and extended a genuine Boston welcome to the Georgians. His speech was most appropriate and enthusiastically received.

Capt. Burke responded eloquently, and was heartily applauded.

The line of march was again taken through Park, Tremont and School Streets to City Hall, where the companies were received by Mayor Prince and members of the city government. The battalion were marched in the City Hall grounds and were brought to parade rest. Capt. Thomes presented the visitors with the following remarks:

"Mr. Mayor, and Gentlemen of the City Government, as commander of the Boston Light Infantry, I have the honor of presenting to you, Capt. J. F. Burke, and the officers and men of the Gate City Guard, of Atlanta, Ga. The company under my command was not especially selected by the militia of Massachusetts to perform this most agreeable duty. It has fallen to us through our great good fortune. These gentlemen, citizen soldiers, have come from the most distant of the old original thirteen States. Their fathers fought the battles of the Revolution side by side with our fathers, and they helped to frame that good and glorious constitution under which we now live and prosper. They have come this great distance to breathe the bracing air of Faneuil Hall and Bunker Hill, to extend a friendly grasp of the hand to their brethren, the citizen soldiers of Massachusetts, and thereby help to keep alive those patriotic sentiments of Union and Liberty, one and inseparable, which now so happily fill the heart of every true lover of his country. I am most happy to add that Capt. Burke has with him, as a distinguished guest, His Honor Mayor Calhoun, of Atlanta.

Capt. Burke then said that as he had just finished the infliction of a speech at the Governor's office, he felt justified in entering a plea of oratorical bankruptcy, but he nevertheless in another short speech did honor to himself and the occasion.

Mayor Prince's welcome was as follows:

"Mr. Commanders and Mayors: It gives us great pleasure to see our military friends from Atlanta. As you have just told me, they have come from a long distance, and the City of Boston is honored by the visit. It bids you welcome. She offers to you her best hospitality, and all that I can say at this time is that your visit may be as pleasant to you as I am sure it will be to us."

The Mayor, members of the board of aldermen and the common council, heads of the departments, and invited guests then took their place in line, and the march was taken up through School, Washington, State Streets, and Merchants Row to Quincy Market, passing through the building down Commercial and Broad Streets to Row's Wharf, where the steamer Governor Andrew was taken for Deer Island.

At the front of Faneuil Hall Market, there were extensive and appropriate decorations consisting of large American flags and the State coat of arms of Massachusetts and Georgia. As the company entered Faneuil some ladies came forward and gave Capt. Burke a large bouquet of flowers.

All along the route the greatest interest was manifested in the company. The steamer made a quick run to the island, and landing at the wharf the visitors were welcomed by President Little of the Board of Directors for Public Institutions. The various buildings were then inspected, after which the company assembled in the Chapel, where they listened to a recitation and several musical selections by the boys and girls connected with the pauper and truant establishments. Chaplain Dadnum conducted the services and the guests heartily enjoyed the performance. Capt. Burke gave his bouquet of flowers to one of the poor children who sang "Little Butter-cup," which brought a suffusion of blushes to her cheeks. After the services, the visitors were photographed in a group, and then the steamer was again boarded.

A trip was made around the outer light, and from thence to Fort Warren, where the party landed and strolled about the grounds. In the absence of the commander, the mayor and several of the visitors were informally received by Lieut. Merrill. A bountiful collation was then served on the steamer, and the boat was headed for the city. On the trip up, "the boys" enjoyed themselves with a will. It is safe to say there was nothing slow about the return trip. The wharf was reached soon after three o'clock, and the company, disembarking, marched to Fort Hill Square, where an exhibition was given of the working of the Fire Department, under the supervision of the Fire Commissioner and Chief Engineer Green.

The line of march was then taken up through High, Sumner, Winter, Park and Beacon Streets, to the Common, where the Gate City Guard gave an exhibition drill at the request of the military and civil officers. A part of the Common was roped, and required a card of admission to get inside the line. In the drill many movements were executed, which received loud applause from the large crowd gathered on the Common. Although the grass was quite high, the marching movements and firing was remarkable in rythmic accuracy. At the conclusion of the drill, the line of march was taken up through Tremont and Court Street to the Revere House, where the procession was dismissed.

BANQUET AT THE REVERE HOUSE

The Guard enjoyed a splendid banquet at the Revere House as guests of the Boston Light Infantry, Capt. John K. Hall, Capt. Thomes and the Veterans.

The date was the eighty-first anniversary of the formation of the Boston company. Many distinguished persons were present, among them being Governor Talbot. There was excellent music, and abundance of toasting and responding. The first toast was that in honor of Georgia soldiers, and Capt. Burke, as usual, responded for them, in a speech of more than half an hour. Alternating from grave to gay, he held the closest attention of the assembly. His speech was most enthusiastically applauded throughout. He had no notes, and the speech can not be produced here.

Mayor Prince spoke to the toast "The City of Boston and its Memorable Motto, 'Not Under a Monarchy, Though Ruled by a Prince.'" Cheers greeted him as he arose.

"The City of Boston," he said, "bids you welcome. We are delighted to see you. You have come to us from a far-off city—far off because separating miles intervene between your city and ours—but only far off in this respect, for we are compatriots and fellow-countrymen, and therefore, near to each other, near in mutual interest, near in mutual regard, and near as members of the same political family. Georgia is dear to Massachusetts because of Revolutionary associations, because as was said to us today by Capt. Thomas, she is one of the original thirteen glorious colonies which stood united for the maintenance of their rights, because her soil is sacred by the blood of those heroic men who stood side by side with us in the great struggle.

We do not greet the Gate City Guard as citizens of Georgia, but as citizens of the United States—having the same government, recognizing the same flag, and sharing the same political destiny. We interpret this visit on the part of our guests as an assurance that all hideous recollections of the fraternal strife and discord which have so recently reddened and polluted their part of this great country are to be buried in perpetual oblivion, as an assurance of our reconciliation and amity never to be again disturbed (applause). It is sometimes unwise to look back. Sorrow and tribulation have been given to him who turns from the things before him to those behind. Let us not disturb the dead and buried past, let us look forward, let us anticipate. We are one people, all interested, share and share alike, in the common prosperity and glory (applause). Do not let the politicians and office-seekers make you believe that anything can come between the people of this great country, and prevent unity of heart, so essential to political unity (applause). Count him as the common enemy who would rekindle and keep alive the fires of sectional dissension and discord (applause). The newspapers tell us that your way to the North has been through miles of cordial welcome, and kindly greeting, that everywhere the people have been glad to see you. These demonstrations are sincere because they come from the people. What mischiefs could be averted if the people, and not the politicians could speak (applause)! If there was ever a time when we should stand united—if there was ever a time when the American people should stand shoulder to shoulder, forgetful of everything that caused our separation—that time is now. All the trans-Atlantic world bristles with arms. Six millions of soldiers are arrayed there to repress the emancipation of the spirit of liberty which is so gradually leavening the nations. Soon it will be fought out whether Europe is to be Cossack or Republican. Now our example will greatly aid to establish the result. If this experiment of popular government—of a government, as Mr. Lincoln said, 'of the people, by the people, for the people,' is to be finally dissolved, the advocates of liberty in the Old World, and in all nations, will be discouraged. Force and not right will prevail. But if our republican institutions shall stand the test that they are now being called upon to stand, there can be no doubt of the result.

"Let us then see to it that American citizens in every part of our broad domain, as well in the South as in the North, as well in the East as in the West, shall enjoy all the political rights and privileges, and the liberty of free speech and action, all the right to the sacred protection of which the constitution guarantees to the citizens of every section and of every race and color (applause). If this be assured our political house is founded upon a rock. Politicians may talk of a solid North and a solid South. A fig for such insinuations. I am here, a solid man for solid Americans (applause), for solid friends to each other, and solid enemies to all who divide us (applause), hence I most heartily endorse the fraternal purpose of our visitors from Georgia and I bid them God speed on their patriotic mission."

Then followed speeches by Col. Wilder of the "Ancient and Honorable Artillery," of Boston; Mayor Calhoun, of Atlanta, Ga., and Col. Merrill, Commander of the Loyal Legion of the United States. Col. Frank Boyd also spoke, and on his motion the Gate City Guard were unanimously voted to be honorary members of the Boston Light Infantry.

Capt. Burke wrote the following letter to Mr. John D. Hall, of Boston, to which the *Globe* referred editorially:

GATE CITY GUARD—CAPT. BURKE'S ACKNOWLEDGEMENT OF THE HOSPITALITIES OF BOSTON—A PATRIOTIC LETTER

Capt. Burke, of the Gate City Guard, Atlanta, Ga., whose recent visit to this city is fresh in mind, writes the following interesting letter to John K. Hall, Esq., President of the Boston Light Infantry Veteran Association, whose guests the Gate City Guard were in this city:

ATLANTA, GA., November 11, 1879

MY DEAR FRIEND HALL: I have but a moment to spare, and I desire to occupy it in a line to you. Owing to three weeks' absence, business has accumulated to such an extent that I have had time only to collect a scattered brain and apply it to hard labor. I can hardly express to you how gratified I am at the result of our tour. It was a tremendous undertaking. I had many misgivings. I did not know how we would be received. I did not know that the receptions that were offered us would not be so pregnant with chilling civility as to turn us back dispirited and hopeless. I did not know how many of those we met would

"Damn with faint praise, assent with civil leer;
And, without sneering, teach the rest to sneer."

There was no national occasion to take us from home; there was no celebration to invite us; but in the quiet meditation of evening hours I determined to test the real temper of our countrymen, to sound their patriotism and sacrifice their animosities on the altar of fraternal peace.

Good will in our hearts and our National emblem in our hands were all we had to offer, and we asked if you would accept them. You did not wait for us to knock at your gates; but, with open arms and fraternal welcomes, you met us beyond the walls. I feel that our peaceful mission has been successful, that the people of this country bear no ill-will toward each other by reason of State boundaries or a deplorable past, and that only the subtle schemes of designing men can keep the people of both sections from that unity and fraternization which we all so ardently desire. I believe our mission has been fruitful far beyond our most sanguine anticipations. Its memories are indelible and its associations indestructible.

Believe me sincerely yours,

J. F. BURKE.

(From the Boston Globe)

The letter of Capt. Burke of the Gate City Guard, to Mr. John K. Hall, of this city, ought to be a sufficient rebuke to the miserable agitators of sectional hatred here at the North. Capt. Burke confesses that when he set out on his tour he had misgivings as to the temper in which a Southern military organization would be received. Such a doubt could be possible only through the misrepresentations of the sectional press, which are, in fact, slanders on the whole people of the North; and these slanders which we here know to be only for political effect, have, as seen in this case, a wider influence for evil than their reckless authors imagine. But in the case of our Atlanta visitors this misapprehension of Northern sentiment has been dispelled. The words of Capt. Burke should be pondered by the organs of animosity in this section; that "the people of this country bear no ill-will toward each other by reason of State boundaries or a deplorable past, and only subtle schemes of designing men can keep the people of both sections from that union and fraternization which we all so ardently desire."

CAPT. THOMES AND THE GOLD MEDAL

The editor can not quit the Boston reception without special reference to Capt. W. A. Thomes' speech and presentation of a diamond medal to

Capt. J. F. Burke.   The Boston *Herald* contained the following acccount of the episode:

After spending an hour in discussing the excellent viands provided by mine host of the Revere, the company was called to order by the president. In calling to order, Mr. Hall briefly spoke of the pleasure it gave him to welcome the citizen soldiers of Georgia to the anniversary dinner of the Boston Light Infantry, and closed by introducing Capt. Thomes, who was received by three rousing cheers.   He responded as follows:

CAPT. THOMES' SPEECH

"Please pardon me if I, the youngest of the many official gentlemen, who are here present, find myself somewhat daunted; it is fearful enough to speak in behalf of a corps which has borne on its roster the names of Quincy, Winthrop and Adams, each distinguished for wonder powers of eloquence; but to address our honored guests, commanded as they are by a gentleman whom the public press of his own State has informed us is most gifted in speech in that land of fluent and fervid orators—all this is surely enough to cause a much bolder man than I am to tremble.   Pardon me, then, if I make no attempt at speech-making.   'Deeds, not words,' was the motto of our fathers at Bunker Hill, Saratoga and Yorktown.   'Deeds, not words,' have builded our railroads, spanned our continent and have stretched out magnetic wires, making Georgia and Massachusetts neighbors.   'Deeds, not words,' have expanded, filled our workshops and factories with wonderful machinery, transformed our western prairies into gardens and granaries for the world, and made our land the admiration of civilized humanity.

"Brethren from Georgia, again I bid you a hearty welcome.   If our tongues had been silent (and the cheers which greeted you today have shown that they are not) you would yet have known by the grasps of our hands, and the flash of our eyes where our hearts were and to whom we have given them. These hearts of ours, we assure you, are like a modern photographer's plate—capable of making permanent an instantaneous flash.   Such is your visit—a flash—but a bright and cheerful one, and the kind impression left is most vivid, and will be indelible.   Yes, friends from Georgia, your stay is altogether too brief; you give us no opportunity to extend to you those attentions, unceremonious and unofficial, that we would gladly show you.   If you have found the breezes of our beautiful bay too chilly—if you have looked upon our granite edifices as too solid and unimpressible, permit me to assure you that if you will prolong your visit, so that we may introduce you to our ladies, some of you might be induced to repeat your visit soon, and perhaps remain with us forever.

"Again assuring you that our hearts greet you, I give place to those who can better express New England's feelings on this occasion, and will offer as a toast, 'The chain of patriotic friendship; the only chain which the citizen-soldiery of the United States, throughout its entire length and breadth will ever willingly wear. May it be kept bright and untarnished 'til the mountains of our land shall crumble, and our rivers run dry.'"

Capt. Thomes, continuing, said:

"Capt. Burke, and Gentlemen of the Gate City Guard: A very pleasant duty has been assigned to me by my associates, in the performance of which, I must for a moment, interrupt the kindly intercourse of this occasion, only promising a word of explanation, which though not eloquent, will be at least with a willing heart.

"When in our revolutionary struggle, through the sagacity and skill of a Virginian (George Washington) the British were driven from this city—then the town of Boston—a congress of the State, in which Georgia was represented, presented him a gold medal commemorative of the event. That medal, after many vicissitudes, became the valuable and cherished property of this city. We regard and cherish it as a memorial of cherished interest. Believing that such memorials of interesting events are of great value in perpetuating recollections, both friendly and patriotic, hoping that we may cause you, after you have returned to your homes and your friends, to think of us and the few pleasant hours of social intercourse which we have enjoyed together—with this object in view, I am commissioned by the veterans of the Boston Light Infantry, and acting for the active company, to present you with this medal, as a slight token of friendship.

"Permit me to place it upon your breast. We trust that you will honor us by wearing it in all public parades and receptions of your command.

"The gold of which it is composed is typical of your own sterling qualities; the inscription will be a reminder of our friendship, and as the jewel which sparkles from its center is the most valued of jewels, so may this friendship be to you. And now brethren from Georgia, in the language of another, but a language that expresses our feelings, when your star of life shall set, may it

JAMES A. SHIELDS.

DR. HUGH M. LOKEY.

SERGT. HENRY C. BEERMAN.

LIEUT. FRANK T. RIDGE.

set as sets the morning star, which goeth not down behind the darkened West, but melts away into the brightness of eternal day."

THE MEDAL

is an elegant one of solid gold, and fine workmanship, and comprises a pin, bearing the words "Boston Light Infantry," with a tiger's head suspended beneath, and below that is a large Greek cross with a large diamond center, surrounded with the words "Gate City Guard, Atlanta, Ga."

As the medal was pinned to Capt. Burke's coat, a round of rousing cheers were given, joined in by both companies, and Capt. Burke, in the easy, felicitous style which is natural to him, accepted the gift amidst enthusiastic cheering.

Thus closed a forceful episode not without its effect in the reconstruction of the country. The late Henry W. Grady, of Atlanta, in following the same patriotic impulse, delivered in Boston his celebrated speech to the New England Society, about seven years after the visit of the Gate City Guard.

AT LAWRENCE, MASSACHUSETTS

As had been the case in other cities, the papers of Lawrence vied with each other in writing up the honors and attentions shown the Georgia Company. The Lawrence *Daily American* published the following:

The coming visit of the military company from the South will afford our people an opportunity to show that while victors in the late struggle, they have only the kindest feelings toward the section of country conquered by the national arms, and that the citizens of the North have only the most fraternal feelings toward those of the extreme section. As a representative military organization, and the first since the war visiting Lawrence, they merit a cordial and enthusiastic welcome, in which, we are sure all classes will join. Let us show our late opponents how magnanimous and friendly we can be in peace, and send them home with such memories as can not be effaced.

The *Daily Eagle* had the following report:

THE SOUTHERNERS—A BRILLIANT RECEPTION TENDERED THEM

The reception tendered the Gate City Guard, of Georgia, by the Sherman Cadets, their honorary members, the city government, and the patriotic citizens Saturday, was a grand affair, and a success in every particular. Capt.

L. N. Duchesney, Mayor Simpson, Congressman Russell, and Agent Fred E. Clarke left the city on the early Boston train, and shortly after ten o'clock met the Gate City Guard at the Boston and Maine Depot, in Boston.

They arrived in Lawrence at 11:30, where they were met by the committee having the reception in charge, and after an interchange of courtesies a line of procession was formed in the following order:

Drum-Major W. Binns; Lawrence Brass Band, 25 pieces; Maj. Geo. S. Merrill and staff, mounted; Sherman Cadets, Co. M, 8th Regiment, Capt. L. N. Duchesney; Gate City Guard, of Atlanta, Capt. J. F. Burke; Lawrence Light Infantry, Co. F, 9th Regiment, Capt. D. F. Dolan, and carriages containing guests of the Guard and members of the reception committee.

After the customary military salutes the line marched down Essex Street to Amesbury to the armory of the Sherman Cadets, where arms were stacked, and the companies were dismissed for half an hour to await the arrival of those of the Guard who had missed the 10:40 train. They arrived at one o'clock, and the line of procession was formed again, the military without arms marched to the City Hall, where the banquet was in waiting. About 250 plates were laid by the caterers. A handsomely printed menu in steel engraving and letter press represented a cut of a gate city, with a scene in the distance through the gate. Guards were on sentry duty outside, in the exact uniform of the Gate City Guard.

The menu comprised everything that the palate could desire, and was served in the most tasteful manner. The hall was very elaborately decorated by S. M. Patterson & Co., and with the presence of the ladies in the galleries and a host of pretty young ladies who waited on the Guard at the tables and the handsome uniforms of the military, the scene was one of unusual interest and splendor. Maj. Merrill, on behalf of the Sherman Cadets, who invited the Guard to Lawrence, welcomed the guests to the city. He expressed regret that their stay in Lawrence was to be so short, saying that the people of Lawrence would have been glad to show the representatives of the South the industries of the city, its marvellous growth, its complicated machinery, and as much as possible of its people. The welcome of the people of Lawrence is hearty. They gladly take the representatives from the South by the hand, and bid them welcome. We rejoice, he said, at every opportunity of cultivating the acquaintance of the people of the South, believing that it will prove of value in cementing the bonds of friendship. Had this been done earlier, years of bloodshed and sorrow might have been averted.

Capt. Burke made a happy and lengthy response, and Mayor Simpson was introduced as the chief magistrate of the city. He responded in a speech of hearty welcome, and was followed by Mayor Calhoun, of Atlanta, Ga., who, in conclusion, invited the people of Lawrence, particularly the ladies, to visit Atlanta. Capt. L. N. Duchesney said he had learned from Capt. Burke that they fought opposite each other at Charleston, and he was glad to meet so honorable a foe. The invitation to the Guard from the Sherman Cadets was made in good faith and the welcome was in earnest.

Col. Sherman was introduced as the patron of the Sherman Cadets, and who, for the honor of having them named for him, had promised to make all their speeches. He was glad to meet the men of the South. There would be no more trouble in that quarter. The people understood each other better than formerly, and if there comes any more trouble it will come from outside sources.

Maj. Merrill regretted the necessary absence of Congressman Russell, and called on ex-Congressman Tarbox. He said that when word came from the Southern men to the Boston patriots not to pay for an ounce of the d—d British tea (that is now sometimes called profane) spilt in Boston Harbor, that canonized the expression and made it fit for Christian lips. He was glad to know that the North had with them brave Southern men that fought manfully, and when defeated, manfully laid down their arms, and returned to the arts of peace. It is now a determination of the citizens both of the North and South that the old flag shall last with humanity and patriotism. If the politicians who brought sectional bitterness would only stop and ask the people to express their feelings, the country would have peace because they would see that the good feeling belongs to all. He hoped the Guard would tell the people of the South that the feeling of honor and citizenship should return, and then the country would march on to prosperity—North and South together.

Capt. Dolan of the Lawrence Light Infantry was glad to extend a fraternal greeting to the soldiers from the South.

Farmer Emery was introduced as a man who knew more agriculture to the square inch than any other man in the country. He made an amusing speech, narrating his experience in selling cabbages to Southern men in the war (prisoners) and said he should always be found in the front rank when cabbages were wanted (loud applause).

As a memento for the company, each was given an elegant horse-shoe in gold and silver, bearing the word "Luck," and "S. C. to G. C. G."

THE PARADE

After the banquet the guests, committee and military escort repaired to the Cadets' armory, where arms were taken, and the procession reformed and paraded through the important streets.

Some amusing references were made to this visit of the Guard to Lawrence, by a dialect writer in the Lawrence *Sentinel*, over the *nom de plume* of Maria Green. A few extracts are made available here to show the Georgians the New England dialect:

"Dear Mr. Editor:" said she, "Saturday mornin I got my beans on a soakin and a parbiline—Nathaniel (her husband) is proper fond of baked beans—when Lider Ann said she'd look after things ef me and Nathaniel wanted to go down street and see them Southern chaps come into town—them that everybody was a makin such a touse about. So we put on our best things and sailed down Essex Street. I declare it was a sight. All the malicious officers in town wus out. There was Major Merrill, and they said he had his staff, but he didn't have nothin in his hand when I see him; and there was Mr. Kelly—he sells catsup down by the Post Office—and lots more good looking men as you can commonly see, a horseback, with rubber boots on a goin through the streets lickety—when to meet the Southerners. Me and Nathaniel preambulated as fast as we could to the City Hall so's to get a front seat in the gallery where we could see all the revolutions. The hall was all harpooned with flags and streamers stretchin from side to side—cata-cornered, and eagles, and shields, and all sorts of hifalutin things strung up around.

"The Georgy men looked sweet and pretty as they come a marchin in with their handsome uniforms, and when the Cadets, and the Infuntry, and everybody had got sot down to the tables and the band struck up 'Dixie,' I thought the roof would come down, such a racket of cheers and hoorays—'twas lak bein on board of a man-o-war.

"But the vittles did make my mouth water—I aint seen sich a sight uv good eatin since our minister's darnation party last fall.   Tha gals that tended onto the tables and passes things looked mity tidy.

"The galleries wus full of women folks, I wore my new atheist set of jewelry—the one with the purple stones, and looked as well as any on 'em. After they had all et as much as they could manage, Major Merrill riz up and made a tidy speech, and then Capen Burke, he got up and answered him, and all the wummin in the galry waved ther hankerchers to him when he sot down, and then he got up, and made a perlite bow.   I was so flustrated, for he looked right at me, but I come to pretty quick, you better blive, for there was Nathaniel a standin up all by hisself, and a wavin his old bandanner with a big slit in it on one side, and a great knot in one corner whur he tied up ten coppers to pay his hoss-carfare, I caught hold onto him, and bounced him into his seat putty hard.   I declar I haint ben so decomposed sence I cum down the machine rapid last summer on the ordway party.   I do blieve Nathaniel would a made a speech if I hadn't grabbed him in time an hauled him into his seat.   I declar, what I've been through with that man would fill a vollum, and I know if I should write my life it would sound like a strange wered tail.

"Nathaniel said he wus a tryin to ketch Capen Noonan's eye, so as to have him get up and sing 'Marchin thro' Georgy,' as he thought it would be jest the thing fur the 'casion.   You kin see what a gump Nathaniel is to think the Southerners would like to be twitted like that—they would have been as mad as hatters, and I wouldn't blamed 'em nuther.   If Nathaniel hadn't a ben non compost he might a got Capen Noonan to sing 'Down in the old log hole,' fur that aint got nothin to do with pollyticks—or any other sort o' ticks.

"Then Capen Duchesney got up—he's as well apeared a man as you commonly see.   I fergit whur his text wus, and then Capen Simpson, and Mr. Tarbox, and Commander Noonan and Mr. Emery.   Nathaniel says Capen Dolan made the best speech, but give me Capen Burke—he wus right peart and funny.   MARIA GREEN."

(From the Lawrence *Daily Eagle*)

The visit of the Gate City Guard offered a most excellent opportunity for our local militia to make a display, which they did not fail to improve, as well as to pay proper respect to such distinguished visitors. And we mean by the word distinguished to use it in its broadest sense, that is, having distinction.

Since the war of the rebellion, a Southern militia organization under arms has not been witnessed in our streets 'til now, and to see such again, marching under the old flag, on a mission of patriotic fellowship, is certainly a distinguished sight, and our citizens and soldiery did just right to give them a hearty welcome. A better acquaintance with the people of the North will do great good, and though the magnanimity shown to them by us is unparalelled in history, it is an omen of our advanced civilization.

THE GUARD RECALLED TO HARTFORD

The appetite of the Charter Oak City for the society of the Southerners was only whetted by the first visit of the Guard and they insisted upon a second opportunity to do them honor. A special from Hartford to the Boston *Herald* said:

The announcement that the Gate City Guard would return to this city on their way back from Boston was hailed with general satisfaction. Meetings of the military officers and citizens were held on Saturday evening, and arrangements were perfected to give them welcome even more hearty than that of Thursday last, if that were possible. They arrived at half past one this morning, and were met at the depot of the consolidated railroad by delegations from every military organization in the city. They were escorted to the United States Hotel where they were left to a season of rest. Later in the day most of them attended divine service at the various churches.

This evening the Gate City Guard are being entertained at many of the residences of our citizens. Gen. W. H. Green, on behalf of the citizens, tendered the services of Colt's band to the visitors during their stay. To-morrow morning they will visit Colt's armory and witness the performance of the Gatling gun. They will also visit the new Capitol and other places of interest. In the afternoon there will be a parade, in which the Governors Foot Guard commanded by Maj. Geo. B. Fisher and the other military organizations of the city will take part. Then the Georgians will give an exhibition drill in Bushnell Park, at the request of the Governor's Foot Guard. They will leave for New York on the midnight train of Monday. The Guard are delighted with the city and its hospitalities. Capt. Burke said this evening that he regretted not being able to remain here longer.   Maj. Fisher and the Foot Guard were untiring in their efforts to entertain the Gate City Guard.   The company have greatly prepossessed the young men of the city, and friendships have been formed which it is hoped will last.   No company that ever visited the city has made such a favorable impression.

The *Sunday Journal, Courant, Times* and other Hartford papers contained flattering and voluminous accounts of the movements of Capt. Burke and the Guard during their second sojourn in that place.

From Hartford Back to New York City—Poughkeepsie Meets Them in the Metropolis and Carries Them Captive up the Romantic Hudson

That the patriotic mission of the Gate City Guard was appreciated and reciprocated was shown by many circumstances, but by none more forcibly than by the conduct of the people of Poughkeepsie, New York.   The spirit of that community was doubtless truthfully interpreted by the Poughkeepsie *Daily News*, which under appropriate headlines, in its issue of Oct. 10, 1879, said:

In a very few days, possibly the week after next, the Gate City Guard the crack military company of Atlanta, Ga., will be the guests of the Twenty-First Regiment, Col. A. T. Lindley, commanding, of this city.

Since the lamentable war which separated the country into two opposing and hostile sections, when brother was pitted against brother, and father against son, no means for healing the wounds engendered by this internecine strife have been found more conducive to a re-establishment of good feeling than a more intimate knowledge of each other.

The Southerners show their wisdom in making an extended trip through the North on their mission of peace.   They will carry back with them to their Southern home a record of the hospitality they have enjoyed, of the thrift they have witnessed, of the kind feelings expressed for the prosperity of the South, and of the great progress the North has made in commerce, agriculture and manufacturing since the war; and the refrain will be taken up by the Southern press, and in a month after the return home of the Gate City Guard, every fireside in the South will be recounting the glories of New York, Boston, Poughkeepsie and other cities, made familiar to them through a medium in whose recital they will repose implicit belief. Can it be said that such results are not to be desired?

That our citizens will not be found wanting in any effort for which they may be called upon to further Col. Lindsey's plans for a fitting reception to our Southern brothers goes without saying. In a short time, as soon as the date of the purposed visit can be fixed, a meeting of those interested in military matters, and of prominent citizens will be called, at which views will be exchanged, suggestions offered and plans perfected looking to a fitting reception of the Southerners, as the city will honor herself by honoring her visitors, who are to be our guests at the invitation of the Colonel of a Regiment which is the pride of this section of the State.

The Atlanta *Constitution* recently said:

While the visit of the Guard to the Northern and Eastern cities has no political significance, it has suddenly lost its local, and assumed a national character. From letters and telegrams received each day, it is evident that the Northern people are vieing with each other in offering the most flattering courtesies to our young soldiers. In the history of this country, there has never been a military organization that has undertaken such an extended tour in the interest of national fraternity, as that for which the Gate City Guard have prepared, and we doubt if there is a city in the Union, except Atlanta, that could show such a marked evidence of pluck and patriotic enterprise. In ante-bellum days it was customary for military organizations to visit each other where the distance was not great, but nothing approaching three thousand miles of travel was undertaken to clasp hands of former adversaries.

It was intended to leave New York by steamer for Boston and Lawrence, Mass., but arrangements are now being made to take the private car of the company on a boat from Jersey City and place it on the New York and New Haven track, and roll it through to Boston. This car will be the handsomest passenger coach that has ever left Atlanta, no pains being spared to provide every convenience combined with artistic effect.

On learning of the proposed trip of the Gate City Guard, continues the Poughkeepsie *News*, Col. Lindley sent them an invitation to make Poughkeepsie one of their tarrying places, and the following is Capt. Burke's acceptance, written hurriedly on the train as they were leaving Atlanta:

ON THE TRAIN, Oct. 7, 1879.

MY DEAR COLONEL: Please accept our thanks for your flattering invitation. We accept it with pleasure, and will go to your city on our return from Boston, by boat from New York. The day will be named several days before our arrival. Excuse this informal manner of acceptance.

Very truly,

J. F. BURKE, Captain,

Gate City Guard.

It is proposed that a committee will meet them at New York, and accompany them by boat up the Hudson, when they will have an opportunity of having all points of interest described to them. They will probably stop at West Point, and salutes will be fired at Newburgh and other points as the boat passes up.

Several companies of the Twenty-first will likely meet them at the dock and a parade, a ball, or banquet would bring the affair to a happy termination, and send the Southerners home to give a good account of the hospitality of Poughkeepsie.

The same paper published the following graphic account under display headlines which are too long for quotation. We extract as follows:

The Gate City Guard arrived in New York yesterday from Hartford, at 5:30 o'clock and were met in the Grand Central Depot by the reporter of the *News*. The Guardsmen were completely tired out by the series of receptions and entertainments to which they have been treated on their journeyings in Boston, Lawrence and Hartford, and they all expressed themselves as perfectly astonished at the hospitality of which they had been the recipients. The Putnam Phalanx of Hartford, and the Governor's Foot Guard gave them the grandest and most hearty reception yesterday, and the citizens vied with each other as to who should have the honor of entertaining the individual members of the Guard at their houses. At the invitation of Miss Maggie Mitchell, the Guard attended her performance in the Opera House, after which they retired for a much needed rest. Their car was attached to the two o'clock train, and reached New York as already stated at half past five.

After breakfasting the men were free to wander about and take a last look at the city until eleven o'clock, at which time they assembled in their car at the Grand Central Depot, and proceeded to the Sixth Avenue elevated road, accompanied by Capt. Beneway, of the Twenty-first.

By some misunderstanding they were ordered to the foot of Franklin Street instead of to the foot of Twenty-fourth Street, where the steamer "Miller" lay, awaiting their arrival. The boat dropped down the river, and the command came on board about two o'clock. At the foot of Franklin Street the Guard were met by the reception committee of the Twenty-first Regiment, Lt.-Col. Walcott, Capt. Haubennested, and Capt. Beneway, and also the civilians who accompanied them, E. White, Esq., Principal of Eastman College, and Messrs. W. G. Lathrope and F. Garmany, of Savannah; R. P. Morgan and S. D. Jones, of Macon, and H. G. Converse, of Palmer, Mass., were also present on behalf of Eastman College. As soon as the "Miller" got under good headway, the Guardsmen scattered over the boat, some on the hurricane deck to enjoy the breeze and the beautiful scenery of the Hudson, some too much fatigued, took possession of the lounges in the salon, and were soon dreaming of the loved ones in Atlanta. An excellent dinner was served to the guests on board, after which they mingled with the gentlemen of the reception committee, and all the places of interest along the river were pointed out and explained. * * * *

As the "Miller" passed West Point, a national salute of one gun for each State in the Union was fired, which was responded to by the steamer's whistle.

At Newburgh a salute was fired from Washington's headquarters, which was replied to by the discharge of musketry from the Gate City Guard, standing on the hurricane deck of the steamer. The dock was thronged with spectators who cheered vociferously on the arrival and departure of the boat. Col. A. F. Lindley of the Twenty-first Regiment and Col. Hayt, Mayor Tice, Quartermaster Weston and Lieut. Wells of the Seventeenth, together with a large delegation of the citizens of Poughkeepsie, came on board the "Miller" at Newburgh, and the boat proceeded on her upward trip, reaching this city at seven o'clock.

In a short time the Twenty-first Regiment and the Fire Department of the city proceeded to the dock and escorted the visiting militiamen through the principal streets. The route was a perfect ovation, for Poughkeepsians are not accustomed to do things by halves. The streets were densely crowded with citizens, who seemed to turn out en masse to give a grand welcome to the Southern boys. Bonfires, fire-works, red and blue lights, and transparencies made the line of procession as bright as day. A particularly fine display of pyrotechnics was made by the students of Eastman College as the column passed through Washington Street. At the armory the visitors were given a short rest, and were introduced to their brothers of the Twenty-first, to the Firemen, and to those citizens who had come in to make their acquaintance.

The officers of the Gate City Guard, the Brigade Staff, the officers of the Twenty-first Regiment, the invited military and civilian guests then proceeded to the Nelson House and took their places at the tables which had been prepared for the banquet. Soon after the Gate City Guard filed in and took their seats, when Col. A. F. Lindley, in a few appropriate remarks, bade them and their friends welcome to Poughkeepsie, and invited them to partake of the viands.

The beautiful menu card was interspersed with appropriate literary quotations, beginning with this:

GREETINGS

"To say you were welcome were superfluous;
As in a title-page, your worth in arms,
Since every worth in show commends itself,
Prepare for mirth, for mirth becomes a feast;
You are our guests,
        Take hold."
"Short stomachs make short graces."

Then follows an elaborate description of the details of the festive and genial occasion.

Maj. George H. Williams was toast-master.

"Our Guests," was responded to by Capt. Burke.

"The City of Poughkeepsie," by Mayor Harloe.

"The City of Atlanta," as usual, had a competent exponent in the person of Mayor Lowndes Calhoun.

"The National Guard," was answered for by Maj. Davis, of the Twenty-first.

Cyrus Macey, Esq., of the *Daily News*, spoke humorously to the sentiment, "The Press."

"The Fire Department," was responded to on behalf of Chief Howard by Mr. Edward Caldwell.

"Popular Education," by Gen. E. B. Smith, President of the Board of Education, and "The Ladies," by Mr. George W. Davis, city editor of the Poughkeepsie *Eagle*.

Next day, with splendid military accessories, the Guard was shown the many interesting places and institutions of the city, including Vassar College —that illustrious seat of learning which is responsible for the production of the altogether inimitable "Vassar Girl"—if newspaper wits are to be credited. Here they met President Caldwell, and Matthew Vassar, Jr.

On the way through the large dining room where the tables were set for dinner, said the *Daily Eagle*, in narrating the incidents of the day, Capt. Burke of the Guard spied a mysterious looking bottle, and, in obedience to an instinct which is popularly supposed to be characteristic of Southerners, seized it by the neck. "This," said he, hesitatingly, "is a— is a—." President Caldwell, "Bass Ale." Capt. Burke, "Ah! Do you—ah—that is to say—"

President Caldwell (laughing), "We give it occasionally to students in ill health."

This little incident, doubtless made a strong impression on the President of the College, and the escort, for the veracious *Eagle* reporter has recorded that the Gate City Guard was conducted at once to Vassar's Brewery, and had refreshments out of the North cellar.

The company was next taken to Eastman College, where Mr. E. White addressed them, followed by Capt. H. W. Johnstone, of the Guard, who mentioned the fact that Lieut. Sparks of the Guard had been a student of Eastman. Surprised to find himself thus so securely hooked, the Lieutenant floundered about in a manner that showed he was a game fish, but despite his splashing he was brought to the surface, and made a short talk in which he admitted his former connection with Eastman, and expressed the greatest affection for her memory, and highest admiration for her methods and achievements.

After the reception at Eastman, the Guard was escorted to the armory to prepare for the Street Parade. We now quote briefly from the *Eagle*:

Arriving at Eastman Park it was found that despite the threatening indications of rain, thousands had braved it, and were packed in dense masses in positions that would enable them to witness the maneuvers of the visitors. That they were amply repaid for any temporary discomfort, was manifested

HARRY MATRAVERS ASHE.

THOMAS J. FLEMING.

WILLIAM T. KUHNS.

ST. ELMO MASSENGALE.

in the hearty interest that they took in the drill, the like of which had never been their lot to witness before. Such perfect motions, made with a clock-like regularity, and the finished perfection that characterized each movement undertaken, has never before been displayed in this city, and would be difficult indeed to excel. In the manual of arms the movements were as one, while in the more difficult movements of loading and firing in the different positions of kneeling and lying down, the obliqueing of fours, and all the hard and intricate movements known in Upton's tactics, were performed with an ease and precision that was marvellous. Numerous and loud were the well-merited cheers that greeted each movement of the drill, amounting at the finish to an ovation.

After completing the drill the Guard was escorted to the Nelson House where they had supper. In the evening, at seven o'clock, Company D again took the visitors in escort, and marched to the landing, where the Guard embarked on the Hasbrouk en route home. Interchanges of friendly courtesies· were gone through with, kindly good wishes given, and amid the cheers of a large crowd on the dock, the Southward journey was commenced.

Arrived back in New York, the Gate City Guard, somewhat wearied, but in excellent health and spirits, embarked on their own car for the return journey to Georgia, and realizing strongly the truth that however eager we may be to seek change and pleasure in far-away places, we turn our faces homeward and with even keener enjoyment.

At Washington, D. C., the Washington Light Infantry, fearing the Guard would be worn out, had a bountiful luncheon awaiting them at the depot. At Charlotte, N. C., they were held up by the citizens and the military and feasted and complimented, and congratulated on the splendid record they had left as a memento among the Northern people.

The return of the Guard to Atlanta after an absence of nearly three weeks was an ovation by the military and the citizens who met them at the depot. Lieut. J. H. Lumpkin met them with the company of the Guard who could not go on the Northern tour.

And thus ended one of the most patriotic and successful military expeditions ever planned and executed in time of peace.

The movements of the Guard from place to place on its grand tour of reconciliation had been closely watched by the people and press of the South. Dixie reached every round of applause accorded to her representative sons, and felt pride in the general acclamations of welcome that greeted the Gate City Guard on Northern soil.

And this conciliatory movement proved the forerunner of a wave of fraternal feeling that swept over the Union, and culminated in the ever-memorable reunion of the Blue and the Gray on the tragic field of Gettysburg.

CHAPTER VI

PUBLIC AND PRIVATE OPINIONS VERY BRIEFLY EXPRESSED

WASHINGTON POST

THE brilliant display of fireworks that lighted up Pennsylvania Avenue as the Gate City Guard marched from the depot last night,
made a scene of wild enchantment. Thousands who joined in the
procession and those who witnessed it will never forget the beautiful sight.
The precision of the Guard is seldom equaled. No visiting company ever
met with such a welcome in this city."

BALTIMORE SUN

"Never in the history of Baltimore was there such a cordial, general
and enthusiastic welcome as that which greeted the Gate City Guard, of
Atlanta, yesterday. For miles the streets were crowded, and everywhere
the clapping of hands, and rounds of cheers from the immense crowds gave
token of generous and earnest feeling, and the admirable bearing and proficiency of the company captured every one."

WASHINGTON NATIONAL REPUBLICAN

"The execution of Upton's Tactics by the Gate City Guard, of Atlanta, is truly wonderful for precision and accuracy. It was only by special and earnest request that Capt. J. F. Burke consented to give a public drill, as it was the desire of the members, while on their tour, to avoid, if possible, the notoriety that would probably result. The continued cheers by the thousands who witnessed the drill, the waving of handkerchiefs by the hundreds of ladies from the balconies and windows, as each movement was faultlessly executed, must indeed have been appreciated by the Guard. Nothing has ever been seen like it in this city. The whole line was more like mechanical figures than human beings."

HOUSTON TELEGRAM

"THE TOUR OF THE GUARD—What a world of fraternity has been opened up by their visits to the North. In the light of history of the past fifteen years the conception of such a tour—and the spirit in which it has been met—make the undertaking sublime. Fanatics and demagogues may try to keep the people apart, but the visit of the Gate City Guard has covered the hideousness of fratricidal strife with the mantel of a common brotherhood."

TRAVELERS RECORD, HARTFORD, CONN.

"The Gate City Guard took possession of our city without firing a gun —but they conquered our hearts and we surrendered. Friends of the South, we can never quarrel again with those for whom Captain Burke so feelingly spoke in his address."

NEW YORK SUN

"The visit among us of the Gate City Guard will do more to bring about an understanding between North and South than the legislation of a century."

BALTIMORE DAILY NEWS

"As the Guard passed in parade along our streets their precision of step and soldierly bearing elicited general commendation, but whenever they performed any evolution or executed a command, all of which were done as by one man, the enthusiasm knew no bounds—the multitude broke into long-continued applause. One feature was especially noticeable, which was the gentlemanly appearance and deportment of the members."

THE PRESS, PHILADELPHIA, PA.

"The city had on its holiday garb yesterday in honor of the visit of the Gate City Guard, from Atlanta, Ga. Flags without number floated from private residences, public buildings and business houses, and the crowds cheered vociferously as the Guard passed on the line of march under the escort of perfection itself, while their maneuvers were admitted by military critics to be really astonishing."

PHILADELPHIA EVENING PAPER

"Maj. J. W. Ryan, of the State Fencibles, has the thanks of all public-spirited citizens for extending a cordial invitation to the Gate City Guard to visit Philadelphia. There is a ring of true statesmanship about that visit that politicians can not ignore. It was a happy thought, and we are glad that our people welcomed them so heartily. They are certainly a fine body of young gentlemen."

NEW YORK HERALD

"The reception of the Gate City Guard at the armory of the Seventh Regiment was one of those open, generous affairs that only soldiers can give, and which must be seen to be appreciated, and it was a happy and refreshing change from the vociferous and continued cheering that greeted the soldierly Georgians along three miles of Broadway, marching from the ferry to the armory. * * * *The drill that the Guard gave before going to their hotel was at the earnest request of the Seventh, and the drill certainly astonished every one present, and each evolution was cheered to the echo. The precision and accuracy of the strangers were certainly marvelous. The marching, counter-marching, in line, column and platoons—firing front, right and left, on knee and lying down—were beautiful, and the armory fairly rang with the plaudits of the Seventh."

On December 17, 1879, the Guard were given a magnificent reception at DeGive's Opera House by their friends. The members had been resting since their return from their "Tour of Reconstruction" and their friends desired to see them again. Long before the time for the doors of the Opera House to be opened, the invited guests filled the side-walks and main stair-case, and as each carriage arrived the police had to make space for the occupants to alight.

The following was the

PROGRAMME

PART FIRST

1. Overture. Four Hands, Piano, "Jubel" . . . . WEBER
   Mme. Van Der Hoya-Schultz, Mr. C. A. Capwell

2. Studies in the Manual . . . . UPTON
   Gate City Guard

3. Aria from Traviata, "Ah! Forse e lui" . . . . VERDI
   Mrs. C. A. Capwell

4. Fantasia for Violin, "Souvenir de L'Eclair" . . . SCHULTZ
   Prof. E. A. Schultz

5. "Sleep Well, Sweet Angel," Tenor Solo . . . . ABT
   Mr. J. H. Morgan

PART SECOND

6. Organ Solo . . . . IMPROVISATION
   Mr. C. A. Capwell

7. Armory Pastime . . . . IMPROMPTU
   Gate City Guard

8. Piano Solo, "Rhapsodie Hongroise," No. 2 . . . LISZT
   Mme. Von Der Hoya-Schultz

9. Ave Maria . . . . GOUNOD
   Mrs. C. A. Capwell, Soprano; Mme. Von Der Hoya-Schultz, Piano;
   Prof. E. A. Schultz, Violin; Mr. C. A. Capwell, Organ

10. Recreation (en silence) . . . . IMPROMPTU
    Gate City Guard

Owing to the limited size of the stage no regular field movements can be executed, and only a part of the company can appear.

At Rome Once More

In July, 1880, the Guard encamped at Rome again at the request of the citizens and participated in a review by Gov. Colquitt. The hospitality of the citizens maintained their reputation for unbounded generosity.

The Jonesboro Affair—The Gate City Guard Marches with Loaded Rifles

So went the Gate City Guard to Jonesboro, Georgia, July 31, 1880, under orders of Commander-in-Chief Governor Colquitt, who accompanied them.

A most atrocious outrage and murder had been committed on the family of old Joe Thompson, a colored man of Clayton County, by a crowd of white ruffians. Seven arrests had been made, and the prisoners were jailed by Sheriff Archer, who, two days afterward, was reliably informed that it was the purpose of the prisoners' friends to organize a mob, overpower the jail guard, and release the accused men. The sheriff then began a telegraphic correspondence with the Governor in which he asked for military assistance.

The affair created great excitement and furnished a newspaper sensation even in the leading Northern newspapers. This was particularly noticeable in certain partisan journals which made political capital out of the episode. It was a presidential year. Garfield and Hancock were opposing candidates.

The *Constitution* of July 31, 1880, contained the following:

A Call for Troops to Preserve Order in Jonesboro, etc., etc.

As might have been expected, the outrage on Joe Thompson and his family in Clayton County created an intense feeling there, which yesterday promised mischief. Three accused men had been arrested and jailed on Thursday. Yesterday three other arrests were made and the town was kept all day in a state of dangerous excitement. Crowds of negroes came in to hear the particulars of the horror and to gloomily discuss what they should do. The good people of the town have been untiring in their efforts to disclose everything in this disgraceful matter. Sheriff Archer has acted like a faithful, zealous officer, and has been backed by the sympathy of the entire community. Persons who came from Jonesboro yesterday reported that the town was in a most unhealthy excitement and that some trouble was apprehended. Last night Governor Colquitt received the following telegram:

"Send down a military company at once. The safety of the town demands it."

He at once telegraphed and asked for particulars of the trouble, and received in reply a brief message saying that there had been some demonstrations of resistance to legal authority, and it was deemed prudent to have sufficient force to carry out the law.

The *Constitution* received this telegram at 10 o'clock last night:

"Seven arrests made. Others to make. Town in great excitement. Trouble apprehended."

It appears that there were two sources of alarm. One was that the friends of those already arrested and of those suspected would attempt to rescue the prisoners from the custody of the law. Most of the parties accused are from Fayette County, and a raid of their friends upon the jail was mentioned in the telegrams as a probability. Another fear was that the negroes might cause some trouble. They were in town in great numbers, and seemed greatly outraged at the brutal treatment which their friends had received. At any rate the town was in a state of intense excitement, and a fatal outburst of popular passion seemed at least sufficiently probable to render it necessary to make proper preparation to preserve peace.

THE MILITARY ORDER

The same paper contained the following:

"The latest information received at midnight showed that the danger was that the friends of the prisoners would attempt to rescue them from jail."

The following is the correspondence between Governor Colquitt and the citizens of Jonesboro:

"Jonesboro, July 30, 7:45 P. M., Gov. A. H. Colquitt: Send a company of military here as quick as possible. It is necessary for the safety of the town. Answer.

W. S. ARCHER, Sheriff,
W. L. WATTERSON, County Judge,
JESSE ANTHONY, Justice Peace,
W. T. KINSEY, Mayor."

The Governor's Reply

"Atlanta, Ga., July 30.

"W. S. Archer, W. L. Watterson, Jesse Anthony, W. T. Kinsey, Jonesboro, Georgia: Telegraph immediately the circumstances that render a company necessary. It is better to get a posse of citizens, if possible. A company can not leave here until 12 o'clock tonight. Answer so that I can act promptly and intelligently.

A. H. Colquitt, Governor."

The following second message was received:

"Jonesboro, July 30, 10 P. M.

"Governor A. H. Colquitt: Demonstration by resistance and threats of violence. The citizens refuse to leave their families. The guard is insufficient. Ten prisoners are in custody, and several yet at large. The posse on duty are exhausted. The dread is fire. Answer.

W. S. Archer, Sheriff.
W. T. Kinsey, Mayor,
Jesse Anthony, Justice Peace,
W. L. Watterson, County Judge,

Reply

"Atlanta, Ga., July 30, 1880.

"W. S. Archer, W. T. Kinsey, Jesse Anthony, W. L. Watterson, Jonesboro: Telegraph me at half past eleven if the necessity still exists. In the meantime increase the citizens guard, if possible, and be firm.

A. H. Colquitt, Governor."

At half past eleven o'clock Governor Colquitt received the following message, which decided him as to what course was best.

"Jonesboro, July 30, 11:50 P. M.

"Governor Colquitt: Serious apprehensions still exist of an attempt to release the prisoners. The Guard is insufficient, if attacked. Answer at once.

W. S. Archer, Sheriff,
W. L. Kinsey, Mayor."

The Governor at once replied as follows:

"ATLANTA, July 30,

"W. S. Archer, W. L. Kinsey, Jonesboro: I leave on the train with the Gate City Guard.   Hold firmly.

A. H. COLQUITT, Governor."

Meantime Capt. Burke had been in consultation with the Governor, and had advised taking a strong force of men.   He argued that if only a very small force should go, it might act as an invitation to attack, if the mob were strong, and lead to bloodshed, while the appearance of a strong force of armed men at the point of danger accompanied by the Chief Magistrate would at once over-awe the lawless, and the prisoners could be readily removed beyond the reach and influence of the disaffected.   Governor Colquitt acquiesced.

The *Constitution's* article continued as follows:

Capt. J. F. Burke had been notified of the state of affairs at Jonesboro, and that his company might be needed.   He, accordingly, had 78 men in full uniform, under arms, and all ready for duty, when Gov. Colquitt at a quarter to twelve issued the following:

ORDER

"EXECUTIVE DEPARTMENT, STATE OF GEORGIA, ATLANTA, GEORGIA, July 30, 1880.

"Ordered, that Capt. Joseph F. Burke, commanding the Gate City Guard, proceed with his company to Jonesboro, Georgia, by the 12 o'clock night train, and give such aid as is necessary in preserving the peace, and protecting the officers of the law in arresting and holding parties under arrest whose violent release is threatened.

"Capt. Burke will also aid in protecting the town of Jonesboro from fire and violence.   He will report to the sheriff, and use every   discretion and good judgment in controlling his command, only resorting to force in the last extremity.   He will, by a firm, kind course, aid in quelling disorder.

By order of,

ALFRED H. COLQUITT,

Governor and Commander-in-Chief.

I. W. AVERY, Secretary and Acting Adjutant."

The Macon train waited until half past 12, when it left with Governor Colquitt and the gallant Guard under Capt. Burke, Lieutenants Sparks and J. H. Lumpkin, and Dr. E. W. Roach, Surgeon. It is hoped that the arrival of the company will prevent any disturbance. Governor Colquitt acted with great deliberation in the matter, and his course will, in all probability, prevent what might have been a serious breach of the peace.

"With the Governor and company aboard," said the Atlanta *Post* reporter, "the train pulled out, and at half past one A. M. the depot at Jonesboro was reached, where the military was formed and Capt. Burke reported to the sheriff, who immediately placed the town under his charge. Some apprehension had been felt lest an attempt should be made to wreck the train, or a fusilade be fired from the bushes that skirted the road on either side, but fortunately such fears proved groundless, and the Gate City Guard quietly assumed control of the town.

"The prisoners, ten in number, were confined in the court-house, the jail being considered insecure, and to this place the soldiers were marched, where arms were stacked, reliefs formed, guards mounted and pickets posted. Then began an investigation of the trouble by a *Daily Post* reporter, who accompanied the Guard."

(The details of the case are omitted—not being within the purview of this compilation.)

The reporter, after reviewing the revolting facts, says:

"This morning the sheriff held a consultation with Governor Colquitt, and determined to send the prisoners to Atlanta for safe-keeping, and when this information became circulated large crowds began to assemble around the temporary armory and here again trouble was anticipated, because it was thought that a rescue might be attempted, but Capt. Burke effectually demonstrated that such a proceeding would bring fatal results, and the prisoners were put aboard the train, and brought to the Fulton County jail (in Atlanta), where they now are, and will remain until taken back to Jonesboro for trial."

The late Henry W. Grady, of the Atlanta *Constitution*, of August 1, 1880, wrote the following editorial:

Making a Good Record

"All honor to Capt. Jos. F. Burke and the Gate City Guard! It is an honor to Atlanta that on a midnight call, in less than one hour, seventy-eight gallant young fellows, uniformed and equipped, cool and earnest, can be rallied for the preservation of order, the enforcement of law, and the protection of the home of even the humblest negro in the State.

"Friday night's work, and the horrors that were averted by Friday night's action, proves what we have always held, that a volunteer militia, well-disciplined and prompt, is more than a mere holiday pageant. It means security to property, safety for life, enforced order in an exigency, and organization amidst sudden confusion. Capt. Burke and the Gate City Guard are all this and more.

"The merchant and the banker who gives his clerks an occasional half holiday for the purpose of drill or parade need not think that he is wasting their time. One hour of firmness on some threatening night—such as may occur at any time—will recompense all the half-days that are lost in parade."

The Great Fair for the Benefit of the Gate City Guard

The fraternal tour of the Guard through the cities of the North and East in 1879 had made the company known to the reading public of the United States. The propriety and dignity of their conduct as individuals had won general admiration, and their patriotic object had elicited universal approbation.

But this was only the beginning of the great work which the untiring and efficient commander and his devoted followers had had in mind from the beginning. Having marched through the North under the old flag; having met the soldiers old and young, and the civilians, men, women and children of the North in their homes and on historic grounds; having clasped hands with the victors, and, without the sacrifice of dignity or principle, having pledged fealty to the restored Union, it remained to induce the military and civilians of the Northern section to visit Southern soil, and mingle as brethren with the veterans who upheld the Southern cause, and with their sons and daughters.

It was resolved to have a great fair for the benefit of the Gate City Guard. The special object being to raise funds for the erection of an ar-

FRANCIS MARION BERRY.

GEORGE HILLYER, JR.

JAMES S. FLOYD.

MAJ. CHAS. P. BYRD.

mory building in commemoration of the great pacificatory movement that had been inaugurated by the company.

It was further resolved to have a grand military reunion of Northern and Southern military organizations at Atlanta in the Fall (1880), during the progress of the fair, and make the laying of the corner-stone of the armory building one of the chief events of the occasion.

In order to give ample time for elaborate preparations the movement was begun in the Spring. One of the most impressive features of the project was the publishing of a paper by the Gate City Guard called *The Cartridge Box*. The title-head of the paper was composed of a cut showing a stack of muskets to which was suspended a cartridge box inscribed "G. C. G." A wreath encircled the box, and beneath was the motto of the company *"In bello pace que primus."* The national flag was displayed in the back-ground, and two soldiers—one in blue, and the other in gray—were clasping hands over the cartridge box.

The prospectus number of the *Cartridge Box** was dated May 9, 1880, and contained articles from which liberal quotations are made as showing the motives that moved the Guard at that time. First is introduced the

ADDRESS OF THE GATE CITY GUARD TO THE PEOPLE

The close of the late unfortunate war left our city studded with blackened walls and spectre chimneys, that recorded the fratricidal struggle that deluged our country in misfortune. The Gate City Guard, like other similar organizations in the South, acting according to the light before them, were the first to leave Atlanta for the seat of war. It is not necessary here to detail the results of that conflict. Let it suffice that the questions and conditions which produced it have been settled forever by the most powerful arbiter known to man. Being the first to leave Atlanta for the struggle, it was becoming that we should be as prompt to extend to those who gallantly opposed us the gloved hand of peace as we were in buckling on the armor of strife.

Acting on this conviction, we determined to test the temper of the North, and with the colors of our common country, penetrate the territory that united so powerfully against us.

"The Tour of the North" was made by the Gate City Guard in October last; and when the overtures that brought about harmony and fraternal fel-

* Lieut. J. H. Lumpkin, now Associate Justice of the Supreme Court, was editor of "The Cartridge Box," and Thos. C. Erwin, now cashier of the Third National Bank, was assistant editor.

lowship between the sections shall be written by future historians, this memorable tour of the Gate City Guard will have its place in the historical record. In every city that we visited the people, civil and military, received us with the most unmistakable demonstrations of welcome; and the thousands that lined the streets and greeted us with hearty and prolonged cheers, gave undeniable evidence that the people of this country are *one people*, separated only by the ambition of designing men who float on the waves of discord. It is our desire to commemorate this eventful tour by a

Memorial Armory

to be placed in the heart of our city—a lasting monument of our "Tour of Peace," and to commemorate the resurrection of Atlanta from the desolation of war—a memorial armory whose doors shall ever open to the North and South, East and West, and from whose turret shall float henceforth our emblem of unity and peace. Left to our own resources we are unable to build such a monument, and we ask you to assist us, and your assistance, be it great or small, will be warmly appreciated. It is the first time in the history of the organization that it has asked for public support in any of its enterprises. The company will hold a

Grand Fair

which will attract thousands of people to our city; and any donation of money, wares, or merchandise that you may be pleased to send, rest assured, will be thankfully received and promptly acknowledged by the committee.

An eight-page paper, *The Cartridge Box*, will be published daily in large editions. This will contain the advertisements of those who aid us, without charge to them.

Donations should be sent to E. W. Hewitt, Chairman Committee, P. O. Box 697, Atlanta, Ga., and will receive prompt acknowledgement. The committee feel confident in making this appeal to your generosity and patriotism that it will not be made in vain.

Very respectfully,

E. W. Hewitt, Chairman,   Dr. R. A. Holliday,
F. W. Hart, Jr.,   W. M. Camp,
C. E. Sciple,   Geo. W. Sciple, Jr.

FAIR COMMITTEE GATE CITY GUARD

HON. W. L. CALHOUN, Mayor,
PAUL ROMARE, ESQ.,
　　Cashier Atlanta National Bank,
B. B. CREW, ESQ.,
J. F. BURKE, Capt.,
　　Commanding Gate City Guard.

The initial number contained also the following letter from U. S. Senator David Davis, afterwards Associate Justice of the U. S. Supreme Court:

"U. S. SENATE CHAMBER,
WASHINGTON, D. C.

"DEAR SIR: The proposition to erect a monument at Atlanta to commemorate the reunion of the States and the return of peace should commend itself to every lover of his country, and is made doubly attractive by emanating from the heart of the South.

"Any movement which tends to rivet the bonds of union, and to make us all feel as one people with common aspirations for the growth and perpetuity of free institutions, with equal rights and equal protection for all who live under them, deserves to be welcomed cordially. This is the true way to silence sectional strife, and to make the republic what the fathers intended it should be—a blessing to mankind, and a refuge for the oppressed of all lands.
　　　　　　　　With great respect,
　　　　　　　　　　　　DAVID DAVIS."

FURTHER EXTRACTS FROM "THE CARTRIDGE BOX"—THE GATE CITY
　　GUARD—GREAT FAIR FOR THEIR MEMORIAL ARMORY—REUNION
　　OF THE CITIZEN SOLDIERY OF THE NORTH AND THE SOUTH TO
　　LAY THE CORNERSTONE—THE GRANDEST ENTERPRISE EVER UN-
　　DERTAKEN IN THE SOUTHERN STATES

The people of Atlanta, accustomed as they are to new enterprises, and to keeping time to the march of progressive events in our new-born city, hail with pleasure every new evidence of spirit and energy on the part of our merchants, manufacturers, organizations or corporate bodies, and willingly lend a helping hand to every measure calculated to correct false impressions about our people, and enhance the material and popular interests of our city.

It is true we have been unfortunate in having a few occurrences that have thrown a doubtful odor about our law-abiding citizens, and have created a wrong idea of the morals of our people. Notably, and an occurence that perhaps more than any other gave color to these misapprehensions, was the Alston tragedy, which not only paralyzed the citizens of Atlanta, but of the whole State, and the good people everywhere.

Then came the Simmon's murder, and the DeFoor murder in quick succession, each being taken up in turn by the press of the country and pictured in the most abhorring manner, and calculated to give us a character for lawlessness that would rival the brigands of the Middle Ages, or eclipse the criminal laurels of some other cities in our Union, which we have no desire to do. There are people foolish enough to believe that it is unsafe to come south of Washington, while in the West there are others who are fully convinced that a visitor to the South, should he be fortunate enough to escape the raw head and bloody bones of the Ku-Klux, who are supposed to parade Southern thoroughfares at all hours, would surely fall into the hands of that agent of Azrael, yellow fever. Though the Southern people have done much toward correcting these *false impressions*, which, to those who know better, must appear ludicrous, yet there is much yet to be accomplished in that direction.

The energy and spirit of the Gate City Guard that moved them to undertake their Northern tour, at their own private expense, can not be overestimated. There is no denying the fact that they did more to correct erroneous opinions of the Southern people during their visit to the different cities of the North than could have been accomplished by any other measure. There is nothing like personal contact in order to have a correct understanding one for another. It is conceded now that had the people of the two sections fully understood each other, the Civil War and all its disasters would have no place in our country's history.

Hence, many look upon the four years' struggle between the States as a *politicians' war*, fostered by an ignorance resulting from the want of an intimate communication between the people of the North and the South. It is now proposed, during the fair of the Gate City Guard next Fall, to lay the cornerstone of their new armory, and, as far as possible, have a reunion of the citizen soldiery of the North with those of the South, on this occasion, and thus promote a unity of national sentiment based on a common patriotism.   There is no city in the South that suffered more during the war than the city of Atlanta, and, consequently, there is no more appropriate place for this reunion of the citizen soldiery of the nation.   Preparations for this grand event have been active for the past three months, though it was deemed advisable not to make the details public until it was ascertained how far the effort would be successful.   The combined military of the two sections will visit Atlanta to lay the cornerstone of the memorial armory.

It will be seen at a glance how extensive are the preparations necessary for such a monster gathering, yet everything has been going on quietly for months.   Of the forty thousand inhabitants of Atlanta, probably there were thirty-eight thousand of them who knew nothing of the project until recently, and every citizen who has thus far been approached on the subject, has at once not only offered his aid, but endorsed the undertaking with warmth and emphasis.

Our citizens will give our visiting friends such a reception that will convince them that, in spite of the devastation of war, we have not forgotten our Southern hospitality.   When North and South last met on this historic spot, it was in the smoke and carnage of battle, when the shrieks of the wounded and dying penetrated deeper than the death hissing of flying shot and shell.   The next meeting will be with the dignity of brave men, softened by the fraternal fellowship of a love of country, and as possessors of a common heritage.

The building to be erected for holding the fair will measure about 200 by 300 feet, and will be divided into fifteen departments.   The corps of ladies who will have charge of the different departments will embrace the beauty and refinement of many Northern as well as Southern cities.

The Spring, Summer and early Autumn were consumed in almost incessant labor by the Captain and the various committees having in charge the preparations for the fair and the military reunion.   A great volume of correspondence was had with the commanders of organizations in the North and East, and with merchants, bankers, statesmen and generals who contributed money, merchandise, and words of cheer to the enterprise.   *The Cartridge Box* published columns of names of contributors—they were from the chief cities and towns of the North, South and East.

In the month of September the *Constitution* contained the following:

THE GREAT REUNION AND FAIR OF THE GATE CITY GUARD NEXT MONTH

A reporter strolled into the armory of the Gate City Guard last night and found the fair committee busily at work assorting papers, answering letters, etc., preparatory to the great event of next month. Mr. E. W. Hewitt, chairman of the committee, was at once approached for a few items as follows:

REPORTER—"Where, and when, will the company fair open?"

MR. HEWITT—"At the Markham House, on Monday, October 11th in order to have everything in proper working order before the arrival of the military, on the 17th. The large tent will be here in a few days from Boston, and after its erection workmen will begin at once to lay the floor, build the booths, lay gas pipes, etc., after which it will be turned over to the decorative committee. We are discussing the electric light and will have it, if not very expensive."

REPORTER—"Will the booths represent any particular designs?"

MR. HEWITT—"Each booth will be decorated by the ladies in charge of it to suit their taste, and will unite the names of a Northern and Southern State. For instance, the booth in charge of Mrs. T. G. Fry, will be named in honor of Pennsylvania and Tennessee, and half of the corps of young lady assistants at that booth will wear the Quaker costume, and I learn that the cigar booth in charge of Mrs. W. H. Venable, will be attended by ladies wearing Turkish costumes, while the Florida booth will be draped with open cotton bolls."

REPORTER—"Will the booths be side by side along the tent?"

MR. HEWITT—"No; they will occupy different parts of the floor so arranged that passage-ways eighteen feet wide will be between them. The center of the tent will be occupied by the band stand, under which will be the cloak room. The dancing platform will be at one end of the tent. The refreshment tables will be under a separate canvas, while the third tent will be reserved for the 'Smith Family,' from Cincinnati."

REPORTER—"The 'Smith family,' who are they?"

MR. HEWITT—"Old Bijah Smith is going to bring his 'gals' down to sing for us. They are well and favorably known in that city."

REPORTER—"Seems to me I heard that name before. The 'gals' will no doubt 'make a mash.' How many booths will there be and who has charge of them?"

MR. HEWITT—"The Washington, D. C., booth will be in charge of Mrs. John A. Bowie, Mrs. Ella Wright, and Mrs. S. J. Rodes, their assisting ladies being Mrs. Alexander, and the Misses Belle, Emma, Rosa, and Lillie Bowie, Misses Rodes, Bostick, Calhoun, Cohen, Whitner, Russell, and others not yet reported.

"The Massachusetts and South Carolina booth is in charge of Mrs. H. I. Kimball, with Mrs. George Winship, Mrs. R. A. Hemphill, Mrs. A. E. Buck, Mrs. Judge Woods, Mrs. H. Y. Snow, Mrs. Samuel Stocking, Mrs. E. A. Knight, Miss Fannie Winship, Miss Buck, Miss Woods, Miss Lowry, Miss Kimball, Miss Culpepper and others.

"The Connecticut and Alabama booth will be under the control of Mrs. M. H. Dooley, with Misses Mahoney, Flynn, Haynes, Loyd, Gardner, Allen, Bostick, Pickney and McOwen to assist.

"The Georgia booth will be in charge of Mrs. J. H. Morgan, and promises to be one of the most attractive at the fair. The assisting ladies have not yet been reported.

"The Ohio and Louisiana booth will be in charge of Mrs. Neal, assisted by Mrs. Eagan, Mrs. Toy, Misses Ellis, Force, Walker, Brown, Peters and other ladies.

"The New York and Mississippi booth will be in charge of Mrs. G. W. D. Cook, aided by Mrs. Dr. King, Mrs. Henry W. Grady, Mrs. J. W. Culpepper, Mrs. Dr. Wilson, Mrs. W. L. Peel and the Misses Inman, Redding, King, Harris and others.

"The Illinois and North Carolina booth will be in charge of Mrs. J. W. Fears, assisted by Mrs. Judge Jackson, Mrs. T. Johnson, Mrs. Castleman, Mrs. Poullain, Mrs. Dickson, Mrs. Morrow, Mrs. Decotts, Mrs. Butler, and the Misses Butler, Lewis, Tuller, Brown, Muse, Jackson, Westmoreland, Erwin, Hill, Morgan, Pittman, Freeman and others not yet named.

"The German booth will be in charge of Mrs. J. T. Eichberg, with the Misses Slaton, Mayer, Michie, Park, Benjamine, Silverman, Gunst, Castleberry, Eichberg, Shehane, Capwell and other ladies.

"The Virginia and Wisconsin booth will be in charge of Mrs. H. H. Colquitt, who is now in New York and will not report the names of her assistants until after her return.

"The Florida and Michigan booth will be under the management of Mrs. Wallace Rhodes, with Mrs. Blodgett, Mrs. Shropshire, Mrs. Mims, Mrs. Johnson, Mrs. Stewart, Mrs. Ray, Mrs. Sharman, Mrs. E. L. Hills, Mrs. L. Hall, Mrs. Dr. Pinson, and the Misses Holcombe, Peeples, Kellum, McLendon, Prather, Sargeant, Beattie, Mims, Jones, Shropshire and other names not reported.

"The United States booth will be under the control of Mrs. General H. J. Hunt, whose corps of assistant ladies is now being organized, and, it is stated, will be dressed in red, white and blue.

"The Pennsylvania and Tennessee booth will be in charge of Mrs. G. T. Fry, assisted by Mrs. Scott, Mrs. Abbott, Mrs. Trotti, and the Misses Rushton, Hammond, Coleman, Clayton, Hall, Shelby, Durham, Smilie, Duncan, Biers, Force, Cooper, Brown, Parlor, Waird, Howell, Aldrich and others.

"The flower booth will be one of the most striking places in the tent. It is in charge of Mrs. Walter Taylor, who will be assisted by a bevy of beauty, while 'Taylor's Cologne' will sprinkle spray to mingle with odorous blossoms. The confectionery and lemonade booth will be managed by Mrs. Alfred Ford, who will be assisted by a number of young ladies. Mrs. W. H. Venable will be the presiding spirit of the cigar stand, which, with the charming ladies she is calling to her aid, will be a rendezvous for gallants. The refreshment department is in the hands of a corps of excellent ladies, who will see that our Northern friends shall not lack for a taste of Southern dishes. Mrs. Dr. James M. Johnson is the chairman of all the booths, and constitutes an advisory committee. The above list is by no means correct, as it has not been revised, and consequently many names have been omitted."

REPORTER—"How many military organizations do you think will be here?"

MR. HEWITT—"About thirty-five or forty. The object is not to gather a large number of soldiers, but to have military representatives from different States. Some of the companies will have to travel twelve hundred miles to reach this city. The meeting is significant fact that it is the only military reunion of soldiers of different States that has occurred in the South."

REPORTER—"Where are the military organizations coming from?"

MR. HEWITT—"From Lawrence, Mass.; Eufaula, Ala.; New Orleans; Boston; Columbia, S. C.; New York; Mississippi; Detroit, Mich.; Fernandina, Fla; Charlotte, N. C.; Cincinnati, O.; Janesville, Wis.; Rockford, Ill.; Savannah; Charleston; Springfield, Ill.; Springfield, Mass.; Mobile, Ala.; Hartford, Conn.; Richmond, Va.; Chicago, Ill.; Augusta, Ga.; Philadelphia, Pa.; Greenville, Ala.; Greenville, S. C.; Washington, D. C.; Nashville, Tenn.; Memphis, Tenn.; St. Louis; Montgomery, Ala.; Waterbury, Conn.; Indianapolis, and other places that I can not recall at this moment."

REPORTER—"When will the programme be published?"

MR. HEWITT—"It is now in the hands of a committee and will probably not be published until the morning of each day on which the exercises and ceremonies for that day will take place. Our company paper, *The Cartridge Box*, will be issued daily, with the official programme which will occupy the whole of each day."

REPORTER—"Where will the camp be?"

MR. HEWITT—"Probably at the old camp ground of the 13th United States Infantry, near Peachtree Street. The soldiers can ramble over the Confederate rifle pits and earth works that witnessed the death struggle of many a brave man during the battles around the city a few years ago."

REPORTER—"A few political orators have asserted that the military of Georgia, assisted by the State, refuse to carry the United States flag."

MR. HEWITT—"Such an assertion is untrue. The Gate City Guard carried the national colors through the Northern States last October, and like all the volunteer soldiery of Georgia, it is their determination to 'stand by the old flag,' though the prospect of 'an appropriation' is exceedingly slim. Georgia does not appropriate a penny for the support of her volunteers. Organizations that have sustained the honor of the State and illumined her escutcheon in many hard fought battles during the Revolution, and the Indian, and Mexican Wars, to say nothing of their heroism in the late unfortunate conflict between the States, are denied an appropriation sufficient to buy a blank book in which to record their achievements."

REPORTER—"Is it possible that the citizen soldiery of the State are granted no privileges?"

MR. HEWITT—"I believe there are a few toll bridges scattered throughout the State. I don't know where they are; I have never seen but one, but we are not afraid of them, for the law of the State says that her volunteers, if they should find one, shall be allowed to march over them without charge. In addition to this, there are invaluable privileges—for instance, the volunteers are permitted to furnish their own uniforms, or go without any; hire their own armories and pay their gas bills. If they should damage or wear out their uniforms they are permitted to replace them at their own expense, and if they lose a bayonet they are required to pay for it."

REPORTER—"The volunteer soldiery of the State maintain their organizations without official assistance or encouragement?"

MR. HEWITT—"State pride and a hope of future encouragement on the part of the State, is all that holds the organizations together."

REPORTER—"Do the Northern soldiers expect to be welcomed by the Southern military and citizens?"

MR. HEWITT—"Assuredly they do, and it is the duty of every Southern organization to be here in time to join in their reception. I am satisfied that our citizens will do their part."

REPORTER—"The military fair will be the largest undertaking of the kind ever held in the South. Is there any chance for a dignified journalist to get a free ticket?"

MR. HEWITT—"Ne'er a ticket."

REPORTER—"Ta-ta, soldier."

MR. HEWITT—"Bye-bye, journalist."

(Extract from letter of Genl. W. T. Sherman.)

"HEADQUARTERS, ARMY OF THE UNITED STATES,
WASHINGTON, D. C., March 10, 1880.

CAPT. J. F. BURKE,
Gate City Guard, Atlanta, Ga.

"MY DEAR SIR: Your letter of March 6th, with enclosure of February 5, 1880, is received, and I assure you of my interest in the subject matter, and willingness to contribute to the execution of your plans to erect in the city of Atlanta a memorial hall of the revival of national unity and sentiment.

"Were I to do so, for the reasons set forth in your printed circular, I would be construed as endorsing two expressions which are erroneous, viz.: 'During the late unfortunate war, the City of Atlanta was destroyed by the forces of Genl. Sherman', and, 'A wilderness of blackened walls recorded the fratricidal struggle that deluged the country in misfortune.'

"Atlanta was not destroyed by the army of the United States commanded by Genl. Sherman. No private dwelling was destroyed by the U. S. Army—but some were by that commanded by Genl. Hood along his line of defenses.

"The court-house still stands, all the buildings on that side of the railroad, and all those along Peachtree Street, then the best street of the city, still remain. Nothing was destroyed by my orders but the depots, workshops, foundries, etc., close by the depot—and two blocks of mercantile stores, also close to the depot, took fire from the burning storehouse (or foundry), and our troops were prevented from checking the spread of fire by reason of concealed shells, loaded and exploding in that old building.

"The railroad cars and machine shops on the edge of town towards Decatur were burned before we entered Atlanta, by Genl. Hood's orders. I believe the expressions to which I take exceptions were used without real meaning, but you must see that I should be equally careful not to make admissions of statements which I know of my own knowledge to be erroneous."

To this letter Capt. Burke made a humorous response, that it would be somewhat difficult for him to convince the people that Genl. Sherman did not destroy Atlanta, because they had a confirmed impression that if the General had not come here, the city would not have been destroyed, and the General promptly sent a contribution to help build the armory.

In the early Fall of the same year the Guard began to receive favorable replys from military organizations in many of the States, accepting their invitation to attend the military reunion and fair for the erection of a memorial armory in Atlanta during the month of October, and it was necessary to obtain a large number of comfortable tents for the visiting troops from the quartermaster's department of the army, at Washington, D. C., so it was decided by the Guard and the citizens' committee, that Capt. Burke should go to Washington at once for an interview with Genl. Sherman.

When Capt. Burke was ushered into the General's office, he immediately left his chair and coming forward gave the Captain a hearty handshake, saying,

WILLIAM M. BURKE.

GEORGE ROBINSON DONOVAN.

SERGT. WM. A. HAYGOOD, JR.

WALTER HANCOCK.

"Captain, did you get that little contribution I sent you for the memorial hall?"

"Yes, General, and I am glad to thank you in person for it—"

"Now hold on, Captain, none of that; it is an excellent undertaking to build such a monument to the good work of your Gate City Guard—I regret that I was not in Washington when you came through—that idea of creating a national sentiment among the military and citizens, for the Union, was timely and successful. Is there anything that I can do for you?"

"General," said Capt. Burke, "in October we will have a large military reunion on the old battle-fields around Atlanta, and we have received official communications from military organizations from all parts of the Union accepting the Guard's invitation to be present. There are no places in Atlanta sufficient to shelter all the troops that will come, and I am here to ask your aid in procuring tents sufficient for the purpose."

"Humph," grunted the General, "it's serious, ain't it? The law will not permit me to allow the use of Government property except for public purposes, and it will be necessary for you to obtain a joint resolution of Congress directing the Quartermaster-General to send you the number of tents you will need."

"But, General, there are but three days remaining for this session of Congress. Suppose the resolution should not be reached?"

"Well," replied the General, emphatically, "in that case, I promise you now that the boys shall not be without shelter." And after some time spent in general conversation, with a cordial good-bye, Capt. Burke, his mind greatly relieved, parted from Genl. Sherman.

The Captain at once called on Hon. Alex. H. Stephens, ex-Vice-President of the Confederate States, now a member of Congress from Georgia, and explained the situation. Mr. Stephens instructed Capt. Burke to draw up the resolution and he would introduce it at once and see that it was adopted in time for the Senate's action. The part it played in the Senate was best told by Senator Joseph E. Brown, of Georgia, at a dinner given by Governor R. B. Bullock a few weeks afterward at his residence, Capt. Burke being present and hearing for the first time the precautious circumstances attending the effort to have the resolution passed.

"It was a close rub," said Senator Brown. "I had received a letter from Capt. Burke informing me of what he wanted done—and it was necessary that the tents should be in Atlanta to shelter the visiting soldiery. This was followed by an urgent telegram; there were but two days of the session left, and twelve hundred bills to be acted on before the reading of Burke's resolution; therefore, the slightest opposition on the part of any of the Senators, and nearly all of them were pressing their own bills, would prevent the passage of the resolution. There was but one man in the Senate," continued Senator Brown, "whom I feared, because he watched closely every bill and resolution read by the clerk, and I knew it would be impossible to conciliate him. When the session opened he was surprised to find me sitting beside him, and I at once engaged him in conversation about a measure in which he was deeply interested.

"I had previously seen the clerk, and as a special favor to me asked him to take Burke's resolution from the bottom of the large bundle and read it before he read any of the regular bills, and to hurry through it; fortunately it was not much over a half-page of legal cap. But as soon as the clerk began to read it my watchful friend, said excitedly, 'Hello! hello! Brown, what's all this,' and he jumped up and called out 'Mr. President, I object,' but I had him by the coat-tails in an instant, and jerked him down into his seat, and insisted on his listening to me if he wanted my aid. By that time the reading of the resolution was finished, the vote taken and Burke got the tents."

Capt. Burke received a dispatch from Senator Brown stating that the resolution had passed unanimously, and he at once made a personal bond for ten thousand dollars and forwarded it to the Quartermaster-General to secure the Government from loss. The Quartermaster was at once instructed to forward the tents on Capt. Burke's order.

The following from the commander of the Old Guard of New York is one of the scores of like epistles received from prominent members from all parts of the country:

A PATRIOTIC SENTIMENT

"In response to an invitation in behalf of the residents of Atlanta, the Old Guard of New York, to participate in the ceremony of laying the cornerstone of a memorial hall in Atlanta. Maj. George W. McLean addressed a letter to Capt. Burke of the Gate City Guard, which is a very patriotic one. The sentiments contained therein are manly, noble and just, and if other military men of the North were actuated and prompted by the same generous impulses as Major McLean, all dissensions would be healed and sectional bitterness ended."

The following is the letter:

"MY DEAR CAPTAIN: I have the honor to acknowledge receipt of your esteemed favor extending an invitation to the Old Guard to participate in the ceremonies under the auspices of the Gate City Guard on the 18th, inst. It gives me great pleasure to accept, on behalf of my command, the invitation so kindly offered and the white coats of the Old Guard will be seen at your patriotic gathering. The people are determined no longer to live in a war that ended fifteen years ago. Its issues are buried, and I am for burying its animosities in the same grave. As a united people we must realize that the Government of our fathers is not a failure; that the blessings of peace and national union are an inheritance as broad and deep as the land bequeathed to us.

"I am rejoiced that the gallant Gate City Guard and our fellow-citizens of the Empire State of the South have taken the lead in a great national reunion on Southern soil. The idea is a noble one, and will not be without the best results; and I sincerely hope that under the cornerstone of the memorial hall which you are about to erect, to commemorate the unity of all the States, may be buried forever the last vestige of sectional strife, while the fair daughters of the South (God bless them) chant an anthem of 'Peace and good will to men!'

"With sentiments of high regard, I remain,

Very truly,

GEO. W. McLEAN, Major."

CHAPTER VII

The Gate City Guard Fair in October, 1880—Fairyland with Beautiful Ladies and Flashing Uniforms Representing Nearly All the States—A Chapter of Names of Old Friends Who Conducted the Enterprise—Arrival of the Military by Every Train—Bands of Music Galore—The Barbecue—Enthusiasm of the Visiting Military—Departure of the Visitors—Two Weeks of Work and Excitement—Armory Building Purchased—Board of Trustees Chartered—The Company Badge—Visit to Nashville, Tenn., to Witness Prize Drill—Atlanta Cotton Exposition in 1881—The Rifle Tournament—The Guard at DeGive's Opera House Flag Presentation—The Privates Present Capt. Burke with a Handsome Gold-Mounted Cane

DESCRIPTION OF THE FAIR

(From the Atlanta *Post*, Oct. 21, 1880)

FOR many months the Gate City Guard have been preparing for a grand fair to be conducted by the ladies of the city for the benefit of the memorial fund. It was intended that it shall be the grandest affair the Guards ever held in Georgia.

Now that every arrangement has been perfected, and the doors of the canvas wherein the fair is being held have been thrown open to the public, it is only necessary for any person to visit the scene of the gay festivities in order to be substantially convinced of the magnitude of the undertaking and that it will result in a complete success.

Last night a "new *Post-Appeal*" man wended his way down Wall Street, which was brilliantly lighted by two rows of gas jets on the front porch of the Markham House, and turning slightly to the left, halted long enough at the gate entrance to the rear grounds of the Markham House to divest his exchequer of the sum of fifty cents and place it in the hands of the door-keeper, he passed on amidst swinging Chinese lanterns, placed there by Mr. Huff, proprietor of the Markham House, and soon entered the great

SCENES AT THE REUNION IN ATLANTA, GA., UNDER THE AUSPICES OF THE GATE CITY GUARD.
(From Frank Leslie's Illustrated Newspaper, Nov. 1880.)

Top—Review before Governor A. H. Colquitt. Left—Parade of the Putnam Phalanx, of Hartford, Conn.
Center—Boston Light Infantry in sham battle. Right—The visiting troops welcomed with fireworks.
Lower Left—Barbecue. Lower Center—Capt. Burke review off the Newborn soldiers with Confed

172

tent, which once stretched over the immense congregation that assembled to hear Moody & Sankey. The canvas is large enough for a full-grown circus—still it was very near crowded with people last night. It is nicely floored with planks and there are fifteen booths or stands, all elegantly decorated, and arranged in regular order. Each booth is presided over by some matronly lady, who makes it her special duty to look after the bevy of beautiful young ladies whom she has as assistants to sell the articles at her stand, and to take in the cash. The latter pleasing duty is performed with the same *sang froid* and ease as is the tender watchfulness she maintains over the heaven-sent angels in dresses.

The women of the South are beautiful, the women of Georgia are more beautiful, but in the language of our local sarcastic humorist, the women of Atlanta are beautifuller than all. But we must proceed with the fair—the show. The booths are decorated in various styles, all more or less expressive of the industries of the State, or the cause it represents. U. S. flags float freely from every frame and pole. The beauty of the scene is dazzling. The place is lighted with electric lights, located at different points under the great canvas. It resembles an enchanting fairy scene.

The Gate City Guard are ever on duty, and a lady has to only nod her head in indication that she desires something, and one of the "boys" is instantly at her command. The "Headquarters," at the south side of the canvas, are in charge of Chairman Eugene Hewitt, of the Committee of Arrangements, who has so laboriously devoted his whole soul and time to the success of the enterprise from its incipiency. Capt. Burke may also be found at these headquarters.

The first booth presented to the gaze on entering is the

UNITED STATES

It is in charge of Mrs. Wm. King, assisted by Mrs. Ed. Kendrick, Misses Mamie White, Mary Bell, Mattie Young, Ida Kendrick, Miss McCauley, Miss Haynie, Miss Jennings, Miss Willingham, Miss Rawson, Miss Matthews, and Miss Willbanks.

The largest enterprise, and the best chance to get the largest return for your money invested, is at this table in the memorial venture.

Chances are one dollar each, and among some of the articles at which you will have a chance may be mentioned a fine piano, two lots of land, one of 50 and the other 60 acres, a buggy, one U. S. bond, City of Atlanta bond, a magnificent diamond ring. Also at this table will be voted a large handsome silk flag to either Hancock or Garfield—the one who gets the most votes at 25 cents each.

LOUISIANA AND OHIO

Just here is the most charming array of young ladies to be found in all Georgia. The bevy of beauties are like bees—they do not remain idle at the tent all the time, but may be found skimming around the canvas in all directions, seeking the man-flower from whom to extract the honey—making money.

Mrs. J. C. Neal is in charge, and assisted by Mrs. Lois Morrow, Mrs. Mary Eagan, Mrs. R. B. Toy, Misses Minnie Force, Mattie and Eva Winter, Annie Ausley, Sallie Dick, Lillie Dozier, Nina Pinckney, Cora Brown, Kate Leyden, Sallie Camp, Lula Foster of Savannah, and Miss May Inman.

Next is the booth representing

WASHINGTON, D. C.

A man might linger here all night and never get fatigued. The eagle bird perched on top of the booth is guarded by the Goddess of Liberty.

Mrs. A. B. Bostwick has charge of this sylvan home, and is assisted by Mrs. Chas. W. Hubner, Mrs. C. C. Rhodes, Mrs. Wade, Misses Stella Bostwick, Emma Calhoun, of Mobile, Annie Murphy, Katie Murphy, Hattie Rhodes, Annie Powers, of Macon, and first, though last, Miss C. Wilson.

Further on is

PENNSYLVANIA AND TENNESSEE

This booth is admirably arranged and superintended by Mrs. Geo. T. Fry. The coat of arms of Tennessee and Pennsylvania are displayed and a miniature *fac-simile* of the old cracked bell of liberty swings from the cupola. The booth is decorated in national colors, and on one side is a large picture of the signing of the Declaration of Independence, and on another is a large picture of Old Hickory.

Mrs. Fry is assisted by Mrs. Crosby, Mrs. Trotti, Mrs. W. F. Abbott, Mrs. W. M. Scott, Misses Julia and Eva Rushton, Mary and Lula Hammond, Mamie Hall, Janie Durham, of Decatur, Eva Smilie, Ida Duncan,

Ava and Kate Clayton, of Greensboro, Florence Force, Marion and Farie Aldrich, Alice May Byers, Mary Wiard, Lillie Currie, Olie Buice, of Rome, Lillie Spalding, Lottie Parlor, and Willie Powell, of Charleston. The Pennsylvania contingent are dressed and speak as Quakers.

Next in line is

New York and Mississippi

Mrs. George W. D. Cook has charge here, assisted by Mrs. Dr. Henry L. Wilson, Mrs. Henry W. Grady, Mrs. Culpepper, Mrs. W. L. Peel, Miss Lucy Harris, Miss Mary Redding, Miss Emma Inman, and Miss G. King.

The Military Booth

Mrs. J. T. Eichberg is in charge of this splendid establishment. Little Marion Capwell, as the "Old Lady in the Shoe," is the sweetest thing in the tent. The assistants are Mrs. C. A. Capwell, Misses Ida and Bertha Wiseburg, Bertha Silverman, Pearl Munday, Lula Edwards, Jennie Benjamin, Minnie Park, Ida Hirschfield, Ida Mayer, Jennie Michel, Hannah Gunter, Annie Hancock, Miss Ozburn, Misses Ella and Florence Talleson, Mrs. Geo. Drummond, and Mr. H. Silverman. All these young ladies wear blue trimmed with canary-colored cloth, with white belts and military fatigue caps, being the colors of the Gate City Guard uniform.

Georgia

The Empire State of the South stands alone and is presided over by Mrs. Maj. J. H. Morgan, assisted by Mrs. Fred Bell, Mrs. Genl. Wm. H. Walker, Mrs. D. W. Appler, Mrs. W. F. Beck, Mrs. M. B. Torbett, Mrs. P. H. Snook, Mrs. J. W. Slappy, Mrs. Frank Hancock, Mrs. Wm. Scott, Mrs. Sam Bradley, Mrs. W. S. Bassinger of Savannah, Mrs. Edgar Thompson, Mrs. J. C. Courtney, Misses Nita Black, Dollie Bell, Ellie Peck, Lula Snook, Bessie Alston, Mollie Courtney, Helen Prescott, Nettie Williams and Mattie Mason of Columbus. Maj. Morgan, Fred Bell, D. W. Appler and L. Laboitoux, of the Guard, assist at these places.

The Cigar Stand

is in charge of Mrs. W. H. Venable and Mrs. W. B. Lowe, assisted by Misses Hattie Irwin, Libbie Tuller, Blanch Glenn, Mary Tomlinson, Fannie Peeples, Irene Lovejoy and Messrs. Fred and Will Hart, all in Turkish costumes.

NORTH CAROLINA AND ILLINOIS

Mrs. John W. Fears in charge. Her assistants are Mrs. Tobe Johnson, Mrs. W. M. Dickson, Mrs. J. F. Burke, Mrs. Er. Lawshe, Miss Fannie Freeman, Miss Mary Pittman, Miss Carrie Westmoreland, Miss Mabel Cumming, Miss Addie Jackson, Miss Brown, Miss Lizzie Butler, Miss Libbie Tuller, and Miss Lelia Austell.

CONNECTICUT AND ALABAMA

Under management of Mrs. Martin S. Dooly, assisted by Mrs. James Loyd, Mrs. John Loyd, Mrs. Dr. R. D. Spalding, and Mrs. Ella Myers; also by Misses Hannah and Mary Mahoney, Mary Flynn, Effie and Mabel Haynes, Lillie Loyd, Kate and Clara Gardner, Gertrude Allen, Lena Pinckney, Lillie McOwen, and Miss Ida Johnson.

The flag painted and presented by the Putnam Phalanx of Hartford to the Gate City Guard is suspended over this booth.

FLORIDA AND MICHIGAN

are joined together. The booth representing these two States is beautifully decorated. Mrs. L. C. Jones presides, assisted by Mrs. J. F. Blodgett, Mrs. E. F. Shropshire, Mrs. R. C. Johnson, Mrs. C. G. Ray, Mrs. A. P. Stewart, Mrs. C. B. Sherman, Mrs. T. Hall, Mrs. E. L. Hill, Mrs. Dr. Pinson, Mrs. Wm. Mims; also Misses Eva and Emma Prather, Ida Sargeant, Mary Peeples, Helen Holcomb, Mattie Kellum, Lethia McLendon, Minnie Walker, Nettie and Louis Sargeant, Miss Beattie, Misses J. Sims and L. McLin.

VIRGINIA AND WISCONSIN

Conducted by Mrs. Hugh H. Colquitt, assisted by Misses Lizzie Colquitt, Lizzie Morgan, Kate Myrant, Hattie Warren, Gussie King, Jennie Fowler, Kate Bleckley, Kate Carter, of Dalton, Annie Pace, of Covington, Mrs. Wm. P. Crawford, Miss Lou Casey, of Augusta, Miss Myrtis McCarty, of Jackson County, and Miss Mabel Hillyer, of Rome.

CALIFORNIA

In charge of Mrs. Alf. Ford. Her assistants are Mrs. Dr. H. V. M. Miller, Mrs. Oliver, Mrs. Dr. A. W. Calhoun, Mrs. George Harrison, Mrs. Lewis H. Clark, Mrs. John F. Simmons, Misses Zurie and Fannie Berry, Misses Julia Hayden, Jennie Towns, Minnie Bellamy, Cora and Susie Wellborn, Misses McKinney, Estelle Wheelan, Sallie Woodson and Sallie Span.

NORTH CAROLINA AND MASSACHUSETTS

Mrs. H. I. Kimball, with assistance of Mrs. George Winship, Mrs. R. A. Hemphill, Mrs. A. E. Buck, Mrs. Henry Snow, Mrs. Sam'l Stocking, Misses Fannie Winship, Laura Kimball, Mary Harris, Jessie Culpepper, Florence Woods, and Miss E. Buck.

MILITARY ARRIVALS

One of the Atlanta papers begins a long descriptive account of the arrivals of military organizations as follows:

"Although yesterday was the Sabbath day, military necessity, which like other necessities knows no law, compelled the Gate City Guard and friends to be on active duty from dawn to dawn again this morning. The arrivals of the visiting military were constant on every train, and a hundred other duties at camp, fair and armory demanded attention.

"Capt. Burke, with true soldierly fortitude and devotion stuck to the work, and with a coolness commendable, directed the complicated movements of his men and aids. His officers and privates were alert and ready, and every request or command met with ready compliance.

THE DECORATIONS

"Visible throughout the city are uniquely and handsomely displayed. They are increased liberally this morning, and before sundown it is possible that the city will be more generally and elaborately draped than ever before in its history.

"Yesterday's arrivals were met at each train, either by the Guard in full, or in detachments, assisted by the Atlanta Grays Battalion and visiting military. The companies thus far arrived are: Montgomery Greys, Mobile Rifles, Eufaula Rifles, Old Guard of New York, Governor's Guard of Columbia, S. C., Richland Rifles, of Columbia, S. C.; Washington Light Infantry of Washington, D. C., and Sherman Cadets of Lawrence, Mass."

Chas. W. Hubner, Esq., of Atlanta, wrote especially for the occasion of the laying of the corner-stone of the memorial armory, a memorial hymn, which was set to music by Prof. Henry Schoeller, of Atlanta, and was a very effective feature of the reunion. It was dedicated to the soldiers of the North and South.

The following are the names of some of the military organizations that participated in the reunion:

HILL CITY CADETS, ROME, GA.

Capt. John C. Printup, First Lieut. John B. F. Lumpkin, Second Lieut. A. A. Burnett, Second Jr. Lieut. J. M. Dempsey, Orderly Sergt. Ed. Quinn.

ROCKFORD RIFLES, ROCKFORD, ILL.

Company B, 3rd Regiment, Illionis National Guards. Capt. T. G. Lawler, First Lieut. Geo. J. Manny, Second Lieut. A. C. Gray, First Sergt. G. Will Fish.

GOVERNOR'S GUARDS, COLUMBIA, S. C.

Capt. Wiley Jones, First Lieut. W. G. Childs, Second Lieut. W. A. Metts, Third Lt. C. E. Calvo, Ensign G. P. Miller, First Sgt. R. C. Wright.

MONTGOMERY GREYS, ALABAMA

Capt. E. A. Graham, First Lt. J. P. Saffold, First Sgt. H. D. Herron.

SOUTHERN RIFLES, TALBOTTON, GEORGIA

Capt. W. E. Ragland, First Lieut. J. H. Worrell, Second Lieut. J. H. Harvey, Third Lieut. W. A. Daniels, Jr., First Sgt. B. A. Richards.

GOVERNOR'S GUARDS, SPRINGFIELD, ILLINOIS

Company C, 5th Regiment, Illinois National Guards. Capt. John J. Brinkerhoff, First Lieut. Wm. Wickersham, Second Lieut. Thomas C. Kimber, First Sgt. Isaac N. Ransom.

Sherman Cadets, Co. M, 8th Regiment, Massachusetts Infantry, of Lawrence, Mass. Capt. L. N. Duchesney, First Lieut. Geo. W. Dow, Second Lieut. Geo. L. Huntoon, First Sgt. Joseph C. Duchesney.

PUTNAM PHALANX, HARTFORD, CONNECTICUT

Maj. F. M. Brown. Staff: Herman A. Tyler, Adjutant; R. P. Kenyon, Sergt.-Major; Alvin Squires, Quartermaster; H. P. Harris, Quartermaster-Sergt; J. S. Hussey, Inspector; C. M. Joslyn, Judge Advocate; O. H. Blanchard, Paymaster; P. D. Peltier, U. D. Surgeon; Rev. W. L. Gage, Chaplain; J. M. Riggs, Engineer; Jas. P. Moore, Commissary, and others.

Officers First Company—Capt. Thomas Dowd, First Lieut. W. P. Chamberlain, Second Lieut. Joseph Warner, Ensign W. R. Hurd, First Sergt. E. A. Perry.

Officers Second Company—C. H. Chase, Capt.; E. D. Dexter, First Lieut.; A. P. Moore, Second Lieut.; H. M. Burnham, Ensign; Martin Taylor, First Sergeant.

The famous Phalanx was organized during the Revolutionary War, and is peculiar and picturesque among military organizations because of its adoption of the old Continental uniforms and drill of the days of Washington. Its name commemorates that sturdy old hero, Israel Putnam. This body, it will be remembered, entertained the Gate City Guard in royal style during their visit to Hartford in 1879, and the Georgia boys rejoice now at the opportunity to pay the debt with usurious interest.

OLD GUARD BATTALION, NEW YORK CITY

Maj. Geo. W. McLean, Capt. G. A. Fuller, Capt. H. L. Farris, First Lieut. James Haniel, Second Lieut. L. C. Bruce, Second Lieut. Walter K. Page, First Lieut. E. S. Ballin.

"ATLANTA GRAYS" BATTALION

Lieut.-Col. W. J. Heyward. Staff: Adjutant J. E. Mann, Sergt-Maj. T. F. Monroe, Quartermaster J. T. Cooper, Paymaster J. L. Crenshaw, Surgeon M. C. Surgeon.

Company "A" Officers

Capt. Joseph Smith, First Lieut. W. M. Mickleberry, Second Lieut. L. S. Morris, First Sergt. W. F. Bass.

Company "B" Officers

Capt. J. M. Hunnicutt, First Lieut. H. T. Gatchell, Second Lieut. M. M. Turner, First Sergt. C. G. Loeffler.

Richland Dragoons, Columbia, South Carolina. An old company that boasts the name of Wade Hampton among its captains. Officers at time of the reunion: Capt. A. Chas. Laughlin, First Lieut. A. M. Boazer, Orderly Sergt. J. G. Mobley.

German Hussars, Charleston, S. C.

Capt. C. Reike, First Lieut. A. F. Stelling, Second Lieut. E. J. Hesse, Third Lieut. G. C. Seeber, Orderly Sergt. J. H. Harken.

Sedgwick Guards

Company G, 2nd Regiment, First Brigade, Waterbury, Connecticut. Capt. C. R. Bannon, First Lieut. Thomas White, Second Lieut. Jas. Hanigan, First Sergt. J. C. Downey.

Cherokee Artillery, Rome, Georgia

Capt. J. G. Yeiser, Sr. Lieut. J. J. Seay, First Jr. Lieut. Jack King, Second Jr. Lieut. W. M. Towers, First Sergeant S. C. Caldwell.

Eufaula Light Infantry, Alabama

C. C. Shorter, Capt.; W. C. Hart, Second Lieut.; W. J. Ross, First Sgt.

Richland Volunteer Rifle Company, Columbia, S. C.

R. A. Keenan, Capt.; R. W. Richbourg, First Lieut.; E. R. Arthur, Second Lieut.; L. D. Childs, Third Lieut.; J. R. Scott, First Sergt.

Nashville Light Dragoons

Capt. Geo. L. Cowan, First Lieut. S. W. Edwards, Second Lieut. A. K. Ward, Surgeon M. S. Hawkins, Second Sergt. C. J. Meriwether.

FLOYD RIFLES, MACON, GA.

J. L. Hardeman, Capt.; W. N. Arnold, First Lieut.; W. M. McFils, Second Lieut.; H. L. Davis, First Sergeant.

MOBILE RIFLE COMPANY, ALA.

Capt. Price Williams, Jr., First Lieut. Dick Roper, Second Lieut. Murry Wheeler, First Sergeant Geo. A. Layet.

JANESVILLE, WISCONSIN, GUARDS

Capt. H. H. Smith, First Lieut. M. A. Newman, Second Lieut. C. F. Glass, First Sergeant J. B. Doe, Jr.

HORNET'S NEST RIFLES, CHARLOTTE, N. C.

Capt. Geo. H. Brockenbrough, First Lieut. W. E. Pegram.

ILLINOIS NATIONAL GUARD, COMPANY B, SECOND REGT., CHICAGO, ILL.

Capt. P. P. O'Connor, First Lieut. J. Ford.

HOWELL'S ARTILLERY COMPANY, SANDERSVILLE, GEORGIA

Organized at the outbreak of the Civil War and commanded by E. P. Howell, now editor of the Atlanta *Constitution*. Capt. J. Herman, First Lieut. W. H. Hines, Second Lieut. J. F. Shephard, Second Jr. Lieut. A. P. Heath, First Sergeant S. G. Jordan.

DETROIT LIGHT INFANTRY, MICHIGAN

Capt. Chas. Dupont, First Lieut. Harry Milward, Second Lieut. Chas. L. Sian, First Sergeant Geo. W. Corus.

WASHINGTON LIGHT INFANTRY BATTALION, WASHINGTON, D. C.

Col. Wm. G. Moore, Comdg. First Company: Lieut. W. N. Dalton, Second Lieut. M. Goddard. Second Company: Lieut. J. S. Miller and Lieut. S. T. Linn, Sergeant G. C. Thomas.

Military organizations and visitors are arriving by every train.

TORCHLIGHT PROCESSION

One of the striking features of the fair and reunion, was a great torchlight procession in which the citizens and all the soldiers participated. The

CAPT. GEORGE MELVILLE HOPE.

J. D. RHODES.

RANSOME HOGUE COMER.

GEORGE F. EUBANKS.

line was headed by the Washington Light Infantry, of Washington, D. C. The march was made resplendent by illuminations, Roman candles and rockets, and when the Markham House was reached, a speech of welcome was made by Governor Colquitt, followed by Mayor Calhoun.

Capt. Burke then introduced Col. Jones (afterwards Governor of Alabama) of the Second Alabama, who responded in felicitous style.

He was succeeded by Capt. Duchesney, of the Lawrence, Mass., Sherman Cadets, who forcefully expressed warm thanks for the royal entertainment accorded the New Englanders.

THE MEMORIAL ARMORY—THE CORNERSTONE LAID WITH IMPRESSIVE CEREMONIES

The site originally selected for the armory building was the vacant lot on the corner of Wheat and Pryor Streets, and the cornerstone ceremony was had there, but the plans of the company were afterwards changed, and another building purchased and refitted as an armory. This will be remarked upon more fully in subsequent pages. Of the ceremonies of the laying of the cornerstone the *Constitution* published the following on the 22d of October, 1880:

"Yesterday at 11 o'clock the various military companies assembled around the site of the armory of the Gate City Guard, at the corner of Wheat and Pryor Streets to attend the ceremony of laying the cornerstone.

"There was no speechmaking. Everything was done in silence except the music by the bands attending the soldiers, and the following memorial hymn written for the occasion by Mr. Charles W. Hubner:

I

Upon this ever-hallowed spot,
The dead past's hate and harm forgot,
Our hands stretched forth in kindly greeting,
Our hearts with pride and rapture beating;

Refrain

Columbia, thy sons behold!
Columbia, thy sons behold!
Columbia, thy sons behold!
United brothers as of old!

II

O star-crowned goddess of the Free!
An altar we would raise to thee
That holy hands have dedicated,
That patriotic prayers have consecrated;

Refrain

Columbia, thy sons behold!
Columbia, thy sons behold!
And by the sacred name we swear
No flame but thine shall kindle there!

III

Rise, emblem of the night of peace!
Until the tide of time shall cease
Shine forth in undiminished glory,
And tell to coming years the story!

Refrain

Columbia, thy sons behold!
Columbia, thy sons behold!
Lo! here, on this auspicious day
For age were wed the 'Blue and Gray!'

"The masons had the stone in readiness, and soon it was put into place and the receptacle filled with relics.

"There was but little parade over it. The articles were quickly deposited and sealed up, and the companies took up the line of march to their quarters to attend

THE BARBECUE

"Yesterday," continued the *Constitution*, "was a red letter day at the encampment. It was the day set apart by the citizens' committee for the grand old-fashioned Georgia barbecue, given in honor of the visiting military. At the hour of ten that prince of barbecuers, Mr. Patrick Henry Primrose, who had supreme control of the cooking department, had the carcasses properly pierced and placed in the pit, which had been dug and fired at the foot of the old fortification, just back of the huge dining tent. There were forty carcasses in all—twenty of pork, and twenty of lamb. The feast over, the Detroit Light Infantry Band struck up 'Dixie' at the foot of the tent, at which the Blue and the Gray rose to their feet and shouted until the very tables trembled. Then the 'Star Spangled Banner' was played with fine effect. It was received with great enthusiasm, many singing it—all cheering lustily. Then the band played 'Yankee Doodle,' and it seemed as if the citizens and soldiers would go wild with enthusiasm. Suddenly the great confusion subsided, and loud calls were made for Capt. Burke. He arose amid tremendous applauding, and after three cheers were given him with hearty good will, he spoke somewhat as follows:

CAPT. BURKE'S SPEECH

" 'My Countrymen—I rejoice today that I have an opportunity to speak to Massachusetts and South Carolina, Alabama, Wisconsin, Georgia and Illinois, and to the people of the other States, who but a few years ago were arrayed against each other in fratricidal strife, and from this historic spot send a greeting to our countrymen of every State in this Union, and tell them that we here pledged our faith to protect the legacy of our forefathers; to guard a common heritage, and cement the bond of a national brotherhood. Surrounded as we are by rifle-pits that bear witness of many a deadly struggle, standing on ground that drank the life-blood of many a brave soldier, who sealed his convictions by the sacrifice of his life, we gather around the glowing camp-fire to smoke the pipe of peace.

" 'We do not ask you here that we may obliterate your memories of the past, for they are dear to you; nor will you ask us to forget recollections that are sacred to us; but we have brought you here, that hand in hand we may cast a retrospective glance at our past misfortunes while we press forward in the bonds of a fraternal union to keep pace with the giant strides of progress and an advanced state of civilization, in which the emblem of our great republic is destined to be enshrined.

" 'Speaking for the citizen soldiery of the South—the element that does not make, but sustains war—speaking for the law-abiding people of the South, I ask you of the North to believe me when I say that the Southern people will never permit the flag of this country to float over the bonds of a Southern slave (cheers). Do you believe us? (Cries—'We do! We do!') And will you join with us in pledging united faith to uphold the Constitution as it is and an impartial administration of the laws? (Cries of 'We will! We will!') Will you enter into a bond with us on this hallowed spot, sacred alike to Blue and Gray, to regard that man an enemy who attempts in the future to sever this Union of States? ('We will! We will!' and cheers.)

" 'Here then on this bullet-sown field, we make the pledge of a National Brotherhood, invoking that sacred peace which comes from on high to bless our Union of States, and lead us in patriotic love to a glorious future!' " (Prolonged cheers.)

Capt. Lawler, of the Rockford Rifles; Mayor Calhoun; Col. Britain, of Wisconsin (who led the "Old Eagle Regiment" in the war between the States); Dr. H. B. Lee; Capt. Duchesney, of the Sherman Cadets; Capt. E. P. Howell, of the *Constitution;* Wm. Markham; W. D. Ellis; Patrick Walsh, of the Augusta *Chronicle,* and Capt. Smith, of the Janesville (Wis.) Guards, each made entertaining remarks, and so ended the long-to-be-remembered barbecue.

CAPT. LAWLER AND THE SWORDS

(From *The Cartridge Box*)

On Friday last the two swords voted to Capt. Lawler, of the Rockford Rifles, as the most popular of the visiting officers competing, were presented by Mr. Henry Jackson, of this city, at the fair tent in the presence of the company and a number of ladies and gentlemen who had assembled to witness the ceremony. Mr. Jackson made a happy and appropriate speech.

Capt. Lawler responded that he endorsed every sentiment that had been enunciated by Mr. Jackson, and would pledge himself that the swords should never be drawn in war except against a foreign foe. That the visit of his company to the South had been most enjoyable and gratifying to them all; that they had been overwhelmed with kindness.

Capt. Lawler having won two swords by vote, he generously presented one of them to Capt. Dupont of the Detroit Light Infantry who was his next and very close competitor for popular favor.

The publication of the "Cartridge Box" ended with the fair. The staff of the paper, as published in the concluding number, was composed as follows: Lieut. Joseph H. Lumpkin, managing editor (now Judge of the Supreme Court); Private Thos. C. Erwin (now Cashier of the Third National Bank); Private Geo. W. Sciple, Jr., Advertising Agent. Reporters: Private Ed. White, Jr., Private T. A. White, Private Martin F. Amorous (afterwards one of Atlanta's Aldermen).

Files of this interesting publication are preserved by various members of the Guard as highly prized souvenirs.

The fair and reunion was a success at all points. After fraternizing in the most enthusiastic manner with our people and citizen soldiery, the Northern visitors returned to their homes to antagonize sectionalism to the end of their days. Each became a zealous missionary in the cause of a common country, and their influence has permeated the mass of the Northern people. When demagogues for campaign purposes have waved the bloody shirt, our late guests have been living witnesses of the loyalty of the South, and to their testimony in no small degree we are indebted for the inability of Congress to enact the force bills, and other unjust sectional measures.

And now, Capt. Burke, and his patriotic followers, having triumphantly carried out their great designs of visiting the North, and of entertaining the Northerners in return, rested from their long-protracted and exhaustive labors, and absorbed at leisure the applause that greeted them from all parts of the country.

Notwithstanding the very great expense of the fair, enough remained to purchase an armory site, and this was a most delightful surprise to the company. The weather during the first week was rainy, and the streets and side-walks correspondingly unpleasant. Hence disaster, financially, was naturally apprehended. So that when Chairman Hewitt, at a company meeting in the armory hall, made his report showing the extraordinary success of the fair, the members manifested their gratification by repeated rounds of applause. And as a more formal and endearing expression, a vote of thanks to the Captain and Committeemen was unanimously adopted, ordered engrossed and framed, and hung in the armory.

ARMORY BUILDING PURCHASED

In the winter of 1880 the Guard purchased a two-story brick building situated on Peachtree and James Streets (Atlanta) running through to Forsyth. The width was 27 feet on Peachtree, and the depth to Forsyth was about 120 feet. The purchase price was $7,000. Afterward an additional lot adjoining, and fronting 25 feet on Forsyth and running back toward Peachtree about 80 feet was purchased for $1,100. All the purchase money was paid in cash except $3,400 for which notes were given running three years. This building became the armory of the Gate City Guard, and plans were made under Capt. Burke's instructions for enlargement as soon as it should be found practicable. Mr. Thos. H. Morgan, a member of the company, drew the plans and specifications.

The company, as before mentioned, was incorporated by Act of the Legislature, December 14, 1859, and on the 18th of June, 1881, the following order incorporating a Board of Trustees of the company was passed by the Fulton County Superior Court:

CHARTER OF THE BOARD OF TRUSTEES OF THE GATE CITY GUARD

Georgia, Fulton County.
        Spring Term, 1881.

To the Honorable Superior Court of said County:

The petition of Joseph F. Burke, William C. Sparks, Joseph H. Lumpkin, Eugene W. Hewitt, Thomas H. Morgan and Charles E. Sciple respectfully shows, that they desire a charter incorporating them, and their successors, under the name of "The Board of Trustees of the Gate City Guard." The object of their incorporation is to purchase property and erect or prepare an Armory for said Gate City Guard, and to protect and keep and manage the same, and the other property or funds which may come into their hands as such trustees. They desire power to use a corporate seal, sue and be sued, make contracts, to buy, take title, sell and convey property for the purpose of furthering the objects aforesaid, to give entertainments or exhibitions, issue negotiable securities, and in general to do such acts as may seem best to them in furtherance of the objects of their incorporation. Their principal place of doing business will be in Atlanta, said State and County. They will have no shares or paid-in capital, but will receive such property or funds as may come to them from time to time from any source, and will keep, manage or dispose of the same as they may deem best for the object aforesaid. The said trustees are to serve for the time and in the manner now provided for by the Constitution and by-laws of said Gate City Guard. Wherefore they pray that they and their successors may be incorporated for the full period of twenty years, with privilege of renewal, with the powers and rights above stated.

J. H. LUMPKIN,
Petitioner's Att'y.

Georgia, Fulton County.
Spring Term, 1881.

It appearing to the Court, that on the 9th of May, 1881, during the Spring Term, 1881, of Fulton Superior Court, a petition was filed by Joseph F. Burke, Wm. C. Sparks, Joseph H. Lumpkin, Eugene W. Hewitt, Thomas H. Morgan and Charles E. Sciple, for themselves and their successors, asking to be incorporated under the name and style of "The Board of Trustees of the Gate City Guard," upon terms, and with the powers therein recited; that the same was in accordance with the requirements of law, and was entered on the minutes of said Court, in Book P., page 481; that the same has been published once a week for four weeks, as by law provided, and all the requirements of law have been complied with, it is ordered that said parties and their successors be and are hereby incorporated under the name of "The Board of Trustees of the Gate City Guard," for the full term of twenty years, with power of renewal thereafter, with the powers, rights and privileges in said petition set forth.

J. H. LUMPKIN,
Petitioner's Att'y.

In open court, this June 18, 1881.
By the Court,
George Hillyer, Judge.

THE COMPANY BADGE

A committee was appointed in August, 1880, to select a design and motto for a company badge. Capt. Burke, Lieut. Lumpkin and Sgt. Hewitt were the committee, and after several conferences, they selected a design.

For sometime it was not determined what would be the most appropriate motto—Lieut. Lumpkin submitted the following: "First in Peace and War," in Latin, Capt. Burke submitting substantially the same in French—but the Latin being more condensed it was accepted, and in October following the badges were made for the members.

Nashville Interstate Drill

In 1881, on invitation of the managers of an interstate drill at Nashville, Tenn., Capt. Burke took a detachment of the Guard to that city. Gov. Colquitt was also of the party. The object being to witness the contest for a large prize offered to the most proficient military company.

Atlanta Cotton Exposition

Upon the occasion of the celebrated Cotton Exposition at Atlanta this year (1881) the Gate City Guard had the place of honor at the opening.

A great feature of the Exposition was

The Rifle Tournament

given under the auspices of the Gate City Guard. The matches were at distances of from 200 to 1,000 yards. Several members of the Guard won prizes, but their names are not recalled, except that of Capt. Burke, who made a clean score at 1,000 yards, winning the first prize.

The Atlanta *Post-Appeal* contained an interesting article on the Rifle Tournament, from which we make some extracts.

"How many citizens whose early days have been spent on the plantations of Georgia," said the paper, "can recall the time when they have shouldered their long-barrelled rifles, filled their pockets with round bullets, and their homely cowhorns with powder and wended their way to the designated crossroads to meet their neighbors and have a 'shoot for beef'? What a world of incident this sport brings to mind, and what a cloud of doubts, hopes and anxieties clustered around the rude paper target, with its black cross marks as each 'shooter' in turn advanced to his place, and prostrating himself on the ground, rested his trusty rifle on a stump of convenient height, set his hair-trigger, and with many doubts took dead aim at the little cross about sixty yards distant. How carefully each shot was scrutinized and measured from the centre, and how eagerly the unfortunate ones explained why they made a bad shot, alway remembering the cause after the shot was fired, but never before it was too late to recall it. It seemed like sacrilege to interrupt this old pastime by scientific marksmanship, which intrudes its improved appliances that enable a rifleman to calculate with wonderful certainty the force of wind that carries a bullet wide of its mark, and directs him how to provide against it. How many persons are there in this city who believe that any one of the many riflemen who were here last week could stand on the top of the City Hall and shoot a man standing on the top of the Atlanta Cotton Factory? Yet that would be easier to do than to strike a 'bull's eye' nearly three quarters of a mile away on the rifle range.

"The tournament last week occupied five days, and was one of the most enjoyable contests of the kind that ever occurred in Georgia. Riflemen from different cities in the North and East began to arrive on Sunday week, and the first match was called on the following morning at eleven o'clock. There were seventeen matches in all, some of them at 200 yards, being the shortest range, and others at 500 and 1,000 yards distance. The interest centered in the 1,000 yard matches, because the distance was so great that the best judgment and skill of each rifleman was brought to bear in calculating elevation, force of wind, and other important considerations before each shot was fired. It seems almost incredible, but it is true, that when Capt. J. F. Burke shot his score at 1,000 yards, the wind was so strong across the range that he had to aim nine and a half feet to the right of the bull's eye in many of his shots in order to strike the centre black spot, and other members of the Gate City Guard, and visiting teams, owing to increasing wind, were obliged to aim thirteen feet from the centre in order to strike it. This is done by a wind-gauge attached to the muzzle, but the best judgment is required to calculate accurately. The ball in traversing a thousand yards describes a parabola, the highest point of which is about forty feet from the ground, and a very strong wind across its path will carry it fully THIRTY FEET OFF OF THE TARGET.

"During three days of the tournament the wind was very strong and irregular, what is known as 'puffy,' and is a difficult wind to calculate, particularly so to those who have never shot at long range.

"The tournament was conducted by the Gate City Guard Committee according to the rules of the National Rifle Association, and Lieut. A. H. Weston, the treasurer of the National Rifle Association, came from New York to advise with Mr. Geo. E. Moser, of the Gate City Guard, who was appointed by Capt. Burke to act as executive officer, the intricate duties of which position he filled with great credit to himself and entire satisfaction to those who entered the contests. The whole affair was under the management of the Gate City Guard, and that public-spirited organization have in this enterprise again demonstrated the determination and progress that characterize all their undertakings.

"With the exception of one muzzle-loading rifle, all the rifles used were breach-loaders. The position of the marksmen while shooting at long range was lying on the ground with feet to the target, though the position of the feet and hands varied according to the habits of each rifleman."

Thus the credit of introducing long-range rifle-shooting in Georgia belongs to the Gate City Guard.

The Guard at DeGive's Opera House

In September, 1881, the company gave a reception to their friends at DeGive's Opera House, which was mentioned by the *Constitution* as follows:

"Each appearance of the Gate City Guard was the signal for the most enthusiastic applause from all parts of the house, and this marked evidence of their popularity seemed to urge them to their best efforts. Their 'Manual Studies' in Upton's tactics, were executed with a precision and finish that makes one wonder how so many plumes, eyes, hands, fingers, heads and guns can be made to move exactly the same distance in the same second of time. The 'fix' and 'unfix bayonets,' 'stack arms,' loadings and firings direct, oblique, kneeling and lying down were remarkable for accuracy, and beyond criticism. It was a beautiful sight, and army officers present were demonstrative in their approbation. But the movement that completely captivated tacticians was the 'fire by file' given in response to an *encore*. This is one of the most difficult movements in the school of the company, and was executed in a manner peculiar to this company alone. The movement was compared to a monster engine, each piece performing its own part, while the regular 'ticking' and 'clicking' as guns were cocked or chambers closed betrayed the most consummate system.

"The third appearance of the company brought out their new white bearskin hats for the first time, and entirely changed their appearance. The marching consisted of movements adapted to the size of the stage, common, quick and double time, flank, halt and reverse movements by file, twos and fours, followed by other movements so intricate and rapid that the eye could not follow them, but which charmed the audience and brought forth continued applause, while Capt. Burke stood in the centre of the stage, calm and soldierly, and by a word brought order out of what a moment before ap-

COL. LOUIS GHOLSTIN.

FRANK SMILEY.

MACON SHARP.

GOODLOE H. YANCEY, JR.

peared to be irretrievable confusion around him without a step lost or a motion out of time. The size of the stage prevented any regular field movements, but gave evidence of the remarkable proficiency of the company.

THE SILENT DRILL

"On their next appearance they executed all their movements without command. They went through the whole manual of arms according to Upton's tactics. There was no music, or other indication of time, yet the drill went on easy, graceful and in perfect cadence, many of the audience looking around expecting to fathom the secret by the discovery of some hidden director, but there was none. Still it went on to the end, which left the men standing like statues, while the applause that followed gave ample evidence of warmest appreciation."

FLAG PRESENTATION

In December, 1881, the Guard won great applause at another entertainment at DeGive's. The *Constitution* thus related an episode of the evening which was highly flattering to the company:

"The intermission was occupied by a pleasing incident not on the programme, but which added greatly to the exercises.

"Friends of the company in Philadelphia, through Mr. W. A. Camp, presented the Gate City Guard with a magnificent silk company flag. Gov. R. B. Bullock was selected to make the presentation address, which was as follows:

" 'Capt. Burke, the Gate City Guard, Ladies and Gentlemen: I accept the duty which has been placed upon me with a special pleasure, because not only myself, but I believe every other citizen of Atlanta finds satisfaction in doing all in our power to honor these gallant gentlemen and their generous commander.

" 'Now that we are on the high tide of the International Cotton Exposition's success and our streets are filled with people from the North, East, the West and the South, we must not forget, sirs, that it was your courage, your perseverance and your courtesy which opened the way and made this great event possible. While public men hesitated and the two sections stood apart, you, gentlemen, bearing the banner of the Gate City, with muskets in your hands, and love in your hearts, marched on the North, and conquered a Union—a union of hearts, and a union of hands.

" 'That brilliant tour of the Gate City Guard through the North two years ago reflected credit upon Atlanta, and lighted a fraternal feeling between the sections, the good effects of which can not be overestimated, and shall never be forgotten. To this benign influence, gentlemen, is to be credited the return visit of the citizen soldiers of the North to fraternize around your campfires and to toast the Blue and the Gray; and from that interchange of personal courtesies grew the brotherly feeling that has made our great industrial gathering and exposition possible.

" 'You are now, gentlemen, in the presence of another Camp, and are about to receive through it a recognition of your well-earned fame. I am commissioned by Mr. W. A. Camp, representing your friends in Philadelphia, to present to you this beautiful emblem, combining at once the glorious colors of our common country, and the ingenuity of inventive industry. It is especially meet and fit, sir, that this American flag should come to you from the City of Brotherly Love. I am aware, gentlemen, that an occasion like this is expected to call forth the well-rounded periods of glowing sentiment. But, sir, I prefer the more material vein. The tenderest sentiments of our hearts are furled, and we march on in the present and the future. You, gentlemen, are the leaders in the victories of peace. You have overthrown the barriers of prejudice, and captured the flags of industry, and I deem it a proud privilege to have been selected to make this surrender.' " * * * *

Capt. Burke, as usual, made a very happy response.

Of the flag the *Constitution* said:

"The flag is of finest silk with alternate blue and white stripes—the union being of red silk triangular shaped, with the letters G. C. G. embroidered in the centre. It is the design adopted some years ago as the special company flag."

A Foreigner's Opinion—Best Drilled Company in the World

Mr. S. E. Kelsey, an English gentleman, sojourning in Atlanta, published the following in the Atlanta *Constitution* of January 10, 1882:

Honor to Whom Honor is Due

"Atlanta, January 7, 1882.   Editor *Constitution*: It was my intention to have written an article with the above caption some time ago, but owing to my being very busy, I have postponed it.

"Being one of the exhibitors here at the Atlanta International Cotton Exposition, it was my good fortune to receive an invitation with the rest of the exhibitors, to an entertainment gotten up by the Gate City Guard of Atlanta at DeGive's Opera House on Thursday afternoon of December the 8th. I am not disposed to flatter in the least, and far be it from me to do so, but the good old motto 'Honor to whom honor is due,' corresponds precisely with my idea of what I saw at that entertainment.   It has been my good fortune to visit nearly all of the great countries of Europe, and in so doing I have had numerous chances to see many of their best military organizations, who were announced as not only the very flower of their nation's army, but were looked upon as akin to a miracle, so perfect were they in their drilling, and in field movements, and we had come to look on the drilled soldiers of many parts of the old country as far superior to those of any other, and especially so to any in a new and young country like the United States of America.   But great indeed was our surprise on witnessing what we did in the way of perfect army drill by the famed Gate City Guard on that memorable occasion. Never before, in any part of this or any other country, have we seen anything to compare at all with the difficult feats we saw executed there.   In fact, should any one have told us that it were possible for any body or company of soldiers to go through such a difficult and wonderful drill, and all in such exact and precise time, notwithstanding all the extreme counter-changes, we could not have believed it possible until we saw it actually done in the masterly and faultless manner with which every command was executed.

"On the 9th of last July I was present at the royal review of Her Majesty, Queen Victoria's volunteers of the Army and Navy at Windsor Park, in England, in which 62,000 men were in line, and it certainly did great credit to the people and nation.   I saw the flower of the English Army in the two large regiments called Her Majesty's Foot Guards, and saw them go through the whole manual of arms, which they executed with astonishing precision; but I can say, and say boldly, that they did not compare at all with the ease and precision with which the commands were executed by the

Gate City Guard and the whole country are to be congratulated on possessing *the best drilled company in the world today.* * * * *

S. E. KELSEY."

PRESENTATION OF A GOLD-MOUNTED CANE

The *Constitution* of June 23, 1881, contained the following interesting article:

THE GATE CITY GUARD

"One of the most pleasing incidents in the history of this splendid organization occurred at their armory last evening. In response to 'Company Order No. 9,' the members assembled in fatigue uniform for the purpose of electing a first lieutenant, that position having been vacant for nearly two years. Second Lieut. W. C. Sparks was the choice of the company, and as the members in column of files passed the ballot box in charge of Judge Pitchford, each one dropping a ballot as he passed, it was believed by all that a just tribute was being offered to a faithful and untiring officer.

"When the ballots had all been deposited the company was formed in a hollow square faced inward, at the request of Private S. R. Johnston.

"Capt. Burke, after complying with this request, announced to the members that he had been requested to give command of the company to Private Johnston for a few minutes for some purpose which he could not divine, but shrewdly suspected it was a ruse of Private Johnston's to march company and officers to a repast prepared in compliment to Lieut. Sparks, but whatever the object was, he announced Private Johnston in command, and for the time being to be obeyed and respected accordingly.

"Private Johnston, who it appears, was chairman of a committee representing the privates of the company, advanced to the centre and in an appropriate address presented a handsome gold-headed cane to Capt. Burke, as a token of appreciation from the privates of the company. The matter was kept so secret, that the commissioned and non-commissioned officers looked with astonishment when the beautiful present was made visible.

"Mr. Johnston closed his remarks as follows:

" 'To you, Capt. Burke, representing the privates of this company, I desire to accord our success as a military organization. You have by your untiring energy made for us a reputation that is enviable and national. It gratifies me beyond expression to show to you that all the members of the company appreciate what you have done for them, and in behalf of the privates of the company I ask you to accept this cane as a slight testimonial of affection and friendship, as well as our appreciation of your valuable services, and in closing, let me add that your uniform kindness to us is recorded on memory's tablet so indelibly that time can never remove its impress. Accept this from us and be assured that it is the heartfelt pleasure of each and every member of this company to wish for you and yours a long life of happiness and prosperity.

"The surprise was complete. The whole affair could not have been more adroitly managed. Capt. Burke was taken entirely off his guard, and, dropping his head on his hand, remained for several moments, unable to utter a word. Recovering himself, he delivered one of the most tender and beautiful speeches ever heard in the armory. It was prolific in pathos, choice in diction, and faultless in delivery. We can give but a synopsis of it here, which reveals the object of the organization under its present commander and the secrets of its success. Capt. Burke began somewhat as follows:

" 'My friends, I know you will excuse my momentary embarrassment. I never thought I could suffer embarrassment in addressing my command to whom I have so frequently spoken. But I am overcome by this manifestation of your attachment to me as your commander, and expressions of gratitude swell up from my heart so rapidly, and so weight my tongue, that I dare not trust myself to give them utterance lest the effort might result in incoherency. The appropriate words of your chairman recall to me the history of the organization whose name you bear, with all its struggles and vicissitudes.

" 'Three years ago when I took command, chaos reigned over the military of this city; one good organization after another fell under the powerful attacks of discord. Personal and organized competitive contests planted and fostered the seeds that afterward blossomed in disintegration and destruction. Patriotism and true soldierly bearing were sacrificed often for a contested prize, until wearied by fruitless attempts at harmony, disruption prevailed and gloated over the fragments. It was at this period that you called me to command you. I now confess that I consented much against my inclination. Four years of war's hardships in my boyhood had severed, as I had determined, my connection with military service.

" 'Beginning my military career in 1861 as a boy of sixteen years of age in a cadet corps of South Carolina, a stripling but little higher than the rifle I was given to shoot, sacrificing the comforts of home to gratify a boyish patriotism and sense of duty to my State; bearing the exposure, the hunger, thirst and fatigue of a soldier's life; witnessing the harrowing scenes of devastating war, I had but little fancy to resume again the garb that recalled these fearful scenes so vividly to my mind.   But despite these discouraging thoughts, I saw that with the trappings of war there were fields yet to conquer—battles yet to be fought—victories yet to be achieved—not by the clash of arms, but in the realms of blissful peace, clasping the hands of our fellowmen in the embrace of a patriotic and fraternal brotherhood.   I saw those who led the stirring movements that plunged us into the unfortunate struggle, one by one passing from earth, their theories swept away by the resistless pressure of progress.   I saw that those who came after them must govern this country, and they must be taught that we are of one family, with a common birthright and an equal heritage.

" 'Here then was the field, and a purpose higher, nobler, grander than the bloodiest victory ever won, and with many a 'God-speed' we left our city on this peaceful mission, taking with us the flag of our common country, to penetrate the North in the interest of unity and national brotherhood, and proclaimed to our Northern countrymen that Georgia and the whole South extended the hand of fellowship and decreed that there should be but one flag, one country and one destiny.'

"Referring to absent friends, and to the friendship that exists between members of the company, Capt. Burke said:

" 'There is a halo of sadness which surrounds the word "absence" when we speak of absent friends, for we feel that the genial sunshine of friendship has been penetrated by darkening shadows, and their vacant chairs silently and suggestively awaken within us the pleasing recollections of happy intercourse.   "When we look abroad upon this beautiful world—a world of living actions and endurances—it is not possible to estimate the influence which is being exercised upon it by acts of friendship.   They penetrate the mass of mankind like the delicate network of veins and arteries of the human body."   They prompt numberless good actions while they hinder the harsh consequences of numberless evil ones.   There is far more suffering than joy in this world, and a consideration of this fact alone should stimulate us to foster those tender feelings toward each other, which, when nurtured, grow to be such consolation in the declining years of life. We are fortunate in the spirit of friendship that pervades our organization. So long as harmony shall characterize our intercourse, success shall signalize our efforts. As the glowing sunlight develops the beautiful flowers of the fields, tinting them with variegated hues, so may our acts of friendship touch the tender chords of nature, and inflame us with fraternal charity. To the absent brotherhood in Massachusetts, Connecticut, New York, Baltimore, Washington, Philadelphia, Virginia, North Carolina, Michigan, Illinois, Wisconsin, South Carolina, Alabama, and Georgia, we waft a kindly greeting in the cherished memories of Auld Lang Syne.

" 'Your elegant gift, my comrades, will be preserved as one of my most cherished possessions.'

"During the serving of refreshments Lieut. Jos. H. Lumpkin and others made appropriate and happy remarks.

"The members say that one of the secrets of the success of the company is that discipline and proficiency in drill are maintained without a cross or unkind word ever being spoken by the Captain.

"At the closing of the polls it was found that W. C. Sparks had received the unanimous vote of the company for the vacant Lieutenancy."

CHAPTER VIII

RESIGNATION OF CAPT. BURKE

INCREASING business demands and frequent absence from the city, prompted Capt. Burke to resign the Captaincy of the Guard, and on the 29th of July, 1882, he addressed to Governor A. H. Colquitt the following letter:

"ATLANTA, GA., July 29,

"*To His Excellency, Alfred H. Colquitt, Governor, etc.,*

"SIR: I hereby respectfully tender my resignation as Captain of the Gate City Guard, and beg your acceptance. I find that I must yield to the demands of personal business interests, which require my time to such an extent that it is impossible for me to give that attention to the command which is essential to its success.

"Permit me to express the warm sentiments of personal regard I entertain for yourself, and assure you of my appreciation of your uniform courtesy in all our official intercourse.   I have the honor to be your obedient servant,

J. F. BURKE."

The Atlanta *Post* published the following flattering article:

THE GATE CITY GUARD—CAPT. BURKE'S RESIGNATION—A HISTORY OF THE ORGANIZATION

The resignation of Capt. J. F. Burke, of the Gate City Guard, deprives that famous company of a commanding officer whose fidelity, zeal, and rare abilities have commanded universal recognition.   Our citizens generally, including many who were not supposed to take much interest in military affairs, speak of Capt. Burke's resignation in terms of regret, mingled with many complimentary expressions concerning the efficiency of the retiring officer.

Few military companies in the country are better known than the Gate City Guard.   When called to its command, about five years ago, the company was a rather languid organization, with apparently little military spirit, and with but little promise of any marked improvement.

Under the new Captain a rapid and remarkable change took place. The soldierly spirit was revived, the interest of the members was engaged in their work, and very soon there was a general determination on the part of all to push the company forward into the front rank of the voluntary military of the country.

In 1878 the company made a tour through South Carolina, Governor Colquitt accompanying them. At Columbia their reception was exceedingly enthusiastic, and Governor Hampton joining them at that point they carried the two Governors with them to Charleston, where they were received with a hearty welcome.

The results of this trip were so beneficial that Capt. Burke planned another excursion of broader and deeper import, which became an event of national significance and is still frequently referred to by the press, and by the orators of the day, both North and South.   This excursion carried the gallant Guard through the principal cities of the Middle and Northern States, and everywhere their soldierly bearing, perfect drilling and other characteristics, commanded applause and admiration. In the New England States they were received with the most cordial greetings, and every possible honor was heaped upon them. This peaceful mission drew forth an expression of national feeling from the North, which was promptly echoed at the South, and perhaps did more to bring the two sections together than anything that has occurred since the war.

In 1880, under the auspices of the Guard, a military reunion took place in Atlanta, which brought together the crack companies of the North and South to fraternize on the very battlefields where they had illustrated their respective sections a few years before. The reunion was a magnificent success. Massachusetts and South Carolina fell into each others' embrace and swore eternal friendship, and all united in acknowledging their debt of gratitude to the gallant Georgia soldiers whose patriotic thoughtfulness had rendered such a reunion possible.

Such events would have made any military organization in the land conspicuous, and the country rang with the praise of the Gate City Guard. And it is due to the officers and soldiers to say that they put forth every effort to deserve the enconiums which they received. Their esprit du corps, proficiency in drill and thorough discipline reached a high standard.

To resign the command of such a company is naturally done with reluctance and regret by Capt. Burke, but the character of his business enterprises is such as to demand his entire attention for some time to come. He has assumed the personal management of his mills in this city, and is making arrangements for the erection of a larger building better suited to his increasing business. All this compels him to devote more time than heretofore to his affairs, but he will retain his membership with the Guard, and his interest in its progress and welfare will be as warm as ever. The Captain entertains the highest regard for his late fellow-officers and his many friends in the company, and they will always find in him a comrade as true as steel. Capt. Burke is a splendid type of a true gentleman, patriotic citizen and volunteer soldier, and the Guard will find it exceedingly difficult to replace him. At his request it is stated that a meeting will soon be held to decide upon his successor, and in common with the citizens generally, the *Post-Appeal* trusts that the company will make a judicious and fortunate selection.

MAJOR ARCHIBALD HUNT DAVIS.

CHAS. C. THOMAS.

FREDERICK GEISSLER.

BEN LEE CREW.

HENRY JACKSON, CAPTAIN

In September of the same year, 1882, Henry Jackson was elected Captain to fill the vacancy occasioned by Capt. Burke's resignation. Capt. Jackson was a practicing lawyer and an excellent military man. He entered into the work before him with earnestness and zeal, and continued to keep the company up to its reputation. He devoted much of his time to the company's interests. His natural military taste suggested many ideas which were carried out successfully.

Soon after Capt. Burke resigned the command of his old company, Gov. Alex. H. Stephens, who was Vice-President of the Southern Confederacy, invited him to become a member of his staff, and assume command of that body and reorganize it. Consenting, he was accordingly appointed and proceeded to execute the Governor's wishes.

Previous to this time the staff had been accustomed to wear civilian dress. Capt. Burke introduced the military staff uniform of gray.

The duty of chief of staff occupied but little of Col. Burke's time, and with but small effort the Governor's staff was fully organized.

THE FUNERAL OF ALEX. H. STEPHENS—THE GATE CITY GUARD PROMINENT IN THE CEREMONIES

In March, 1883, occurred the death of the Governor of Georgia, the beloved and illustrious Alexander H. Stephens, Vice-President of the late Southern Confederacy.

A description of the lying in state, the multitude of people present at the funeral ceremonies, the military display, the speeches of leading men, with Gen. Robert Toombs at the head; the sermon of Rev. John Jones, and the prayer of Rev. Thomas DeWitt Talmadge, would occupy many pages. Suffice it, as to these points, to say, that the State of Georgia wept over the coffin of the great Commoner.

The Gate City Guard participated prominently and with credit, of course, in the obsequies. President of the Senate, James S. Boynton, having succeeded to the office of Chief Executive, invited Capt. J. F. Burke, of the late Governor's staff, to assume the direction of affairs. The following is the text of the executive order:

STATE OF GEORGIA, EXECUTIVE DEPARTMENT,
ATLANTA, March 7th, 1883.

WHEREAS, Col. John A. Stephens, Adjutant-General of the State, is not able to perform his official duties on the present occasion; it is therefore ORDERED, That Lieut.-Col. J. F. Burke is hereby placed in command, and will act as Adjutant-General with the rank of Colonel, on the Governor's staff, during the continuance of the present services.

JAS. S. BOYNTON, Governor.

BY THE GOVERNOR, CHAS. W. SEIDELL,
    Sec'y Ex. Dept.

Col. Burke accepted and assumed command at once, and issued the following:

EXECUTIVE DEPARTMENT, ATLANTA, GA., March 7th.

IT IS ORDERED, That from 12 M. to 1 P. M., March 8th, be set apart for the purpose of enabling visiting delegations to view the remains of the late Governor Stephens. Members of the staff will govern themselves accordingly.

All local and visiting civic and military organizations and bodies, foreign consuls and delegations that desire to visit the remains of the late Governor are requested to report at the representative chamber in the Capitol Building at 12 o'clock M. precisely.

J. F. BURKE, Colonel and A. A. Gen.

Capt. Henry Jackson, of the Gate City Guard, was appointed Chief Marshal of the occasion, and the company was commanded by Lieut. Sparks.

These facts are related here to show the Gate City Guard's connection with great public events and the part their members took in them.

Governor Stephens' remains were placed by Col. J. F. Burke in his family vault, where they remained for about a year. A monument was erected to his memory at his old home, Crawfordville, Ga., and his remains were taken there on its completion.

MOREHEAD CITY AND THE SHIPWRECK

In July, 1883, the Guard, under command of Capt. Henry Jackson and Lieuts. E. W. Hewitt and C. E. Sciple, visited Morehead, North Carolina, for a summer outing. The chief event of this expedition was the capsizing on the Atlantic of a boat containing thirteen members of the company. An Atlanta paper, after the Guards returned home, published the following reference to it:

The shipwreck story, as told by some of the boys, is thrilling. Messrs. White, Weinar, Fletcher, Fleming, Thompson, Camp, Kiser, Selby, Kuhn, Penson, Moore, Culberson and Elsas hired a boat of a negro man. They went out to fish and were about ten miles from land when they were capsized. As the boat went over each man thought he saw death, but when each of the thirteen had grappled the boat they began to feel better. The captain of their boat was a negro and he told them to hold on. They were in water up to their necks, and for five hours they lived thinking each moment would be their last. Several boats were out hunting for them. The boys tried to attract their attention, but failed, and as they observed the boats receding from sight their hearts sank within them. Mr. Elsas offered one of the negro men $175 to swim ashore and secure aid, but as they were then twenty miles out the darky thought his hold on the boat the safest place. The waves rolled over the boys and the boat, and when they came up again they instantly counted their number to see if all were present. After long waiting a boat came in sight and the crew sent up their cheers. The rescue was accidental; the boat that found them was returning to land. The capsized boat was towed to land fifteen miles from Morehead, and some of the boys wanted to walk, but they were carried by water in safety. The thirteen now call themselves the "shipwrecked crew."

The news of this perilous adventure, of course, preceded the company's return home, and upon their arrival they were treated to a highly flattering welcome. The vessel that accomplished the rescue was called the "Julia Bell," and the capsizing incident afterwards became the basis for organizing the "Julia Bell Thirteen Club," which consisted of the men who had been wrecked. This club finally disbanded, but it gave a banquet on the first anniversary of the adventure, and Mr. W. M. Camp, of the company, made a capital speech in which he graphically pictured the perilous episode.

Armory Enlarged

About three years after the purchase of the armory in the Spring of 1884, it was enlarged. The company, commanded by Capt. Jackson, borrowed thirteen thousand dollars by mortgage on the original armory for this purpose, and the building was extended and completed according to the plan given to Capt. Jackson by Capt. Burke. The old debt of $3,400 was paid this year also. The money for this latter purpose was raised by contribution from friends of the company, and the work was accomplished by personal efforts of Capt. Jackson and the building committee.

Proposed Sale of Armory—An Impending Crisis Averted

An assessment for street improvements having been levied on the property of the company, it was found difficult to meet the tax demand, and at the same time pay interest on the bonded debt. Capt. Jackson had advanced some hundreds of dollars to pay off coupons that had fallen due, on the bonded debt, and he conceived the idea that it would be better for the company to relieve itself of the indebtedness by deeding the armory property to the City of Atlanta, conditioned that the Council should pay the debt and become the owners, and that the Guard should continue to have the right to use the drill-room for company purposes. The interest in military affairs had been waning for some time past and it was difficult to create enthusiasm among the members, hence Capt. Jackson thought his new plan was the best for the company.

The matter was discussed by the members of the company, and at the next meeting the difficulties under which the company were laboring were fully explained by Capt. Jackson, and he advised that his plan of deeding the armory property to the City should be adopted, as it would relieve the company from debt, and give them the use of the armory without expense; and he presented a deed that he had prepared for the trustees to sign.

But this project met with such unanimous and determined opposition from the officers and members, that it was abandoned. Then at the suggestion of Lieut. Sparks, a subscription was at once begun among the members, and sufficient money raised to pay the amount due the City. The idea prevailing that as the armory was built by contributions from Northern and Southern friends to be a memorial armory commemorating the Guards' "Tour of Reconciliation" through the North, in 1879, it should be maintained.

The Fair in 1883

In October, 1883, a fair was held for the company's benefit, during Capt. Jackson's captaincy, and about $2,500 was realized, of which sum about $2,000.00 was appropriated to reducing the company's bonded indebtedness.

OLD CORNERSTONE RELAID

This month and year, the Guard under Capt. Jackson, laid the cornerstone of the old armory building on Peachtree, James and Forsyth Streets, which had been enlarged. The same cornerstone was used that was laid in 1880 under Capt. J. F. Burke's administration, when it was afterwards discovered that a necessary delay would occur in obtaining title to the property then selected for the armory, and the site was changed to the location above named.

GENERAL GRANT'S FUNERAL IN 1885

About forty members of the Guard, under command of First Lieut. W. M. Camp, visited New York, and participated in the funeral ceremonies of Gen. U. S. Grant. Capt. Burke, who was visiting in New York State at that time, went to the city to meet and welcome Lieut. Camp and the company and arrange for their entertainment.

THE FIFTH MARYLAND REGIMENT

During the year 1885, the Fifth Maryland Regiment was heartily and handsomely entertained by the Guard. The Fifth was on its way to New Orleans, and accepted the invitation of the Gate City Guard to stop off in Atlanta. The Guard was only too glad to have opportunity of returning the civilities they had enjoyed in Baltimore in 1879, at the hands of the "Fifth Maryland."

SERGEANT J. L. JACKSON

In October, 1885, Sergeant J. L. Jackson died and was buried with military honors. His sister, Mrs. Ed. Wood, executed a fine crayon portrait of the deceased and presented it to the Gate City Guard. The *Constitution* of November 11, 1885, contained the following account of the presentation:

THE LATE SERGEANT JACKSON—PRESENTATION OF HIS PORTRAIT TO THE GATE CITY GUARD LAST NIGHT

At the armory of the Gate City Guard last evening occurred the presentation to the company of a splendid crayon portrait of the late Sergeant

GATE CITY GUARD AT HOME IN THEIR ARMORY, 1884.

J. L. Jackson, recently deceased. The portrait was the handiwork of Mrs. Ed. Wood, one of the devoted sisters of the deceased. It was enclosed in a massive gilt frame and was pronounced a most faithful likeness. Mrs. Wood executed the portrait as a testimonial of her esteem for the soldier-companions who so loved and so affectionately ministered to her brother in his last illness and guarded his grave after his death.

In the unavoidable absence of Rev. Sam Jones, the presentation was made in a brief address by Mr. Sam W. Small. His remarks were well-timed and feelingly uttered. The portrait was received by Capt. Henry Jackson, in a short and touching response, eulogistic of the qualities and graces of manhood that had so endeared the deceased to his comrades.

The occasion was one of peculiar interest to all concerned, and was graced by the presence of a number of the friends of Sergeant Jackson and the company.

THE SAVANNAH VISIT

In May, 1886, Captain Henry Jackson resigned command of the Guard, and was succeeded by Lieut. A. C. Sneed, who was elected to succeed him.

Under command of Capt. Sneed, the Guard visited Savannah in June of this year. In July of this same year, Capt. Sneed resigned.

J. F. BURKE RE-ELECTED CAPTAIN

On the 23rd of July, 1886, the company unanimously determined to request Capt. Burke to again take command of the company. Capt. Jackson and Private P. F. Clarke had called upon Capt. Burke and obtained his consent, and on the 28th an enthusiastic reunion occurred at the armory in honor of the event. The *Constitution* published the following account of the affair:

The Gate City Guard armory was crowded with the members and friends of the organization last night, the object of the assembly being a welcome to Capt. Burke, who was re-elected to the command last Friday night. The evening was one of the pleasantest in the history of the company, though it was known to the company that he could not hold the position long, owing to the business demands on his time.

When Capt. Burke arrived he was greeted with wild cheers and round after round followed, making the solid walls of the building tremble with its echoes. It was a reception as sincere as it was enthusiastic, and was warmly appreciated by Capt. Burke, who sustained an ordeal of hand-shaking and flattering compliments on every side. The manifestation of good feeling was not confined to one part of the room, but became infectious. As the memories of old times, awakened by Capt. Burke's presence, came fresh to mind, many of the members embraced each other in their enthusiasm and a general rally around their old commander ensued. It seemed to inspire the members with a future for their organization that will surpass all their former achievements. Capt. Burke was loudly called for, but in a few words excused himself saying that he would be heard from later. The quartermaster had provided an abundance of refreshments, and the boys enjoyed themselves discussing the prospects, while the captain was being attended by his officers. The talk among the boys was refreshing and shows the esteem in which Capt. Burke is held by the company.

While everyone felt happy, an old member of the company was asked when Capt. Burke first took command of the company.

"Oh! Let's see," he answered, "in the year 1878, and he remained in command about five years, during which time he made the memorable tour with the company through the Eastern and Northern States, which was followed the next year by the reunion of the Northern and Southern military on the battle-fields of Atlanta. Capt. Burke resigned about four years ago and was appointed by the late Governor Alex. H. Stephens on his staff, where he served until Governor Stephens died."

"The members appear much elated to have him at the head of the company again."

"Yes; ever since he retired from command there has been a hope that he would be prevailed on to direct the company again, and he was re-elected by unanimous vote. The brilliant achievements that make up the company's history are due to Capt. Burke and center around him. He has the faculty of commanding without harshness, and giving dash, brilliancy and success to every undertaking. Besides he has a remarkable gift of imparting in-instruction to the men without fatiguing them, and there is a graceful polish in the execution of every movement when he is in command that I never saw displayed by any other company. The

PERSONNEL OF THE COMPANY

has undergone a complete change in the past two weeks, and the old members are applying to be placed on the active list again, and applications for membership are received at every meeting from the best young men in the city."

"Has Capt. Burke intimated any plans for the future?"

"Only in a remote way, but you may rest assured that he will have something to propose before long. In everything he has heretofore done he has kept Atlanta before the country. The destruction of this city during the war brought it prominently before the people as part of the history of the war, but Capt. Burke has kept the new Atlanta, with its enterprise and recuperative spirit before the whole country through the achievements of the Gate City Guard, who entered into his plans and enthusiastically followed his leadership. There is a general desire on the part of the friends of the company to see them once more in one of their entertainments at the opera house, and they will probably comply with this request when the weather grows cooler."

"It is said that Capt. Burke is opposed to prize drilling at fairs and other places."

"He does not favor that kind of notoriety. He has a higher and more patriotic work for the company than visiting military contests at public fairs, besides it interferes with business, and he disapproves of useless parades or any interference with business except in case of necessity."

"But suppose some organization should challenge the Gate City Guard for a contest?"

"Capt. Burke would accept the challenge so quick that it would give the tactics a fit of ague. There is no doubt about that, provided the invitation came from a reputable company and the men could be spared from business."

A SPLENDID GIFT

The company in August, 1886, by unanimous vote, presented to Capt. Burke, personally, the diamond badge which had been bestowed upon the Gate City Guard in Boston, Mass., in 1879, by the Boston Light Infantry and their Veteran Association jointly with the active company of that name. The commander expressed, as well as words could do it, his profound thanks for this high testimonial of confidence and friendship, and prizes the beautiful ornament as among the most precious of his possessions.

Afterward, at the solicitation of the members, and as a very slight return for the many honors and courtesies received at their hands, Capt. Burke presented to the Guard, an oil portrait of himself to be hung in the rooms of the armory.

In September of the same year the Guard gave a reception to their friends at DeGive's Opera House. The admission was by card, and long before the opening of the theatre the street was lined with carriages and the side-walk crowded until the hour of opening. The advance was in camp costume and the appearance of the Guard was greeted with an ovation that revived memories of former years.

A CHRISTMAS GIFT

December 25, 1886, the company gave to Capt. Burke as a Christmas present, a costly gold military decoration mounted with diamonds in clusters and solitaires. It is one of the most elaborate military decorations ever made in this country, and appropriate in emblems made with precious stones and varied-colored gold. It was a generous token of the Guards' attachment to their old commander, and the ceremony of presentation was elaborate and highly enjoyed.

FUNERAL OF JEFFERSON DAVIS

The most celebrated of the Confederate chieftains passed from life in New Orleans, La., on the 6th of December, 1889, and the Gate City Guard took a prominent and creditable part in the imposing funeral ceremonies.

The Gate City Guard was the first military organization in Atlanta to respond to the call of Jefferson Davis, President of the Confederate States, in 1861, and it was the melancholy duty of the same organization to guard him in his sleep of death in 1889.

The frequent absence from the city of Capt. J. F. Burke prevented him from giving the time to the company that was necessary, and in June, 1887, he resigned the Captaincy and Clifford L. Anderson was elected to fill the vacancy. Capt. Anderson was subsequently made Brig.-Genl. of the State troops. Capt. Anderson was elected August 5th, 1887, and on June 29th, 1888, he resigned. Capt. Lyman Hall followed Capt. Anderson, being elected July 5th, 1888. He held the Captaincy until May, 1890.

Capt. A. C. Sneed was elected Captain July 4, 1890, following Capt. Lyman Hall. The State Fair was held in Atlanta in October, 1890, and offered a prize of $2,500 for the best drilled infantry company. The Gate City Guard, under Capt. Sneed, won the prize.

Nothing of an eventful nature occurred in the history of the company from 1890 to 1893, from which date the "Chronicles" are continued by Prof. J. T. Derry, who was a member of the First Regt. of Ga. Volunteers, C. S. A., of which the Gate City Guard formed a part. He prefaces his part of the work by a history of the First Regiment in the early part of the Civil War, and goes over briefly the questions that were warmly discussed by members of the regiment and the people throughout the separated sections of the Union.

THE GATE CITY GUARD

(By Prof. Jos. T. Derry, of the First Regt., Georgia Volunteers)

In the winter of 1860-61 there was great anxiety in the Southern States on the question of war or peace.

When the national election of the Fall of 1860 resulted in the choice of Abraham Lincoln to the Presidency of the United States, there was genuine alarm throughout the South Atlantic and Gulf States of the Union.

Mr. Lincoln had· been elected without a single electoral vote from the South. He represented not only the free-soil or Republican party, which declared its purpose to allow no new State, in which slavery existed, to enter the Union, but also the extreme Abolitionists who had for years insisted upon the immediate abolition of slavery without any compensation to the master for the loss of their species of property, and regardless of the danger to the South of such a policy. The emissaries of the Abolitionists had more than once sought to incite the negroes to insurrection. Mr. Lincoln was not an Abolitionist, but he and his party had accepted the alliance of the Abolitionists, and many of the Republican leaders did not lag behind those aliens in bitter speeches about the South.

All Southerners agreed that their States were in imminent peril and disagreed only as to the remedy. Many believed that the best defense of the South was in the courts and congress of the republic, while a majority in the more Southern States could see no safety other than in secession and a united front of a solid South. In fact they regarded this as the only hope for peace.

By February 1st, seven States had seceded and formed a new Union under the title of the Confederate States of America.

Although efforts were still being made to secure a peaceful settlement of all differences, troops were being concentrated at Charleston, S. C., and Pensacola, Fla., as the possible centre of the war.

During the first week in April, Georgia companies, that had offered their services and had been ordered into camp, assembled at Macon. Among these were the Gate City Guard, of Atlanta, who with nine other companies gathered from every section of the State, were formed into a command styled The First Regiment of Georgia Volunteers. Of this Regiment Harvey Thompson, Captain of the Gate City Guard, was elected Major.

The great majority of these patriotic volunteers, so eager to defend their native South, were young men, many under 21 years of age and many others who had either voted against secession, or for it with great regret, because they believed there was no other remedy.

It was at Montgomery, Ala., that the news of firing on Fort Sumter reached them, and at Garland, Ala., the story of the surrender of the Fort to Genl. Beauregard was confirmed.

After several weeks spent at Pensacola, building fortifications, doing guard duty and drilling, the First Georgia was ordered to Virginia, which State, as well as Alabama and North Carolina, had now joined the Confederacy, to be followed soon after by Tennessee.

The four States had preferred to remain in the Union, but when it became evident that coercion was to be the policy of the government, they resolved to fight against any such policy, which they regarded as perversive of the principles on which the government of the Union had been founded.

While the First Georgia was in camp at Richmond, occurred the battle of Big Bethel. This small affair, in which the Confederates were successful, was hailed as a great victory.

From Richmond the First Georgia went by rail to Staunton and there camped for several days. All the way from Pensacola, Fla., their journey had been an ovation. Cheering throngs had greeted them at every station. At Waynesboro, Va., a splendid dinner had been served them.

When they began their northward march from Staunton, they went but a few miles before they were halted to partake of a bounteous meal. There they quenched their thirst with water, almost ice-cold, that gushed from a spring in the side of a rocky hill.

That night they bivouaced in the rain at Buffalo Gap, because their wagon train had not kept with them. For the rest of the several days march they had their tents and cooking utensils and suffered no inconvenience beyond the fatigue of the tramp over mountains or through charming valleys. The glorious scenery was ample compensation for all inconveniences.

The night at Beverly was a disagreeable exception by reason of a pouring rain accompanied by furious gales of wind, that blew down tents as fast as they could be put up.

At last the First Georgia reached Laurel Hill, an outpost beyond the Shenandoah, Alleghany and Cheat ranges, where was gathered a little army of gallant Virginians under the command of Brig.-Genl. Selden Garnett. The First Georgia with full ranks proved a welcome accession to this little host upon the frontier.

After several days of guard duty, picketing and scouting, tidings came one day of the advance of a large Union Army under Genl. B. McClellan.

Garnett's command, at Laurel Hill and at Rice Mountain, stood little chance for victory against 20,000 under McClellan.

But the brave Georgians and Virginians under Garnett marched out from their camp at Laurel Hill and at Belington, making a swift charge up a hill, drove from it some of the advance regiments of McClellan's host. With exultant feelings they returned that evening to their camp. But shells from McClellan's batteries began to fall into the Confederate camp, just before darkness descended and stopped further proceedings.

It was a day or two before the hostile guns got the range and began to make things uncomfortable.

All day of July 11th, 1861, McClellan's shells were falling in Garnett's camp and by afternoon the steady dropping became a furious shower. Meanwhile, at Rice Mountain, Col. Wm. S. Rosecrans (later a Maj.-Genl.) was fighting Pegram's command. Just at dark he carried the position, taking guns and provisions.

A courier reached Genl. Garnett with the news; Laurel Hill, was by Pegram's defeat, untenable. So about midnight Garnett's command began to retire, while a pouring rain greatly impeded his wagon train and artillery.

As the morning dawned and the sun was just breaking through the parting clouds, Garnett's wearied men saw just before them the little town of

Beverly, and beyond rose Cheat Mountain, from whose crest the Confederates could easily repel five times their number.

Hope that they might yet crown the campaign with victory was beginning to cheer them, when a courier dashed up to Garnett with the news that the Federals already occupied Beverly in force.

The courier was mistaken; but Garnett believed his statement and sorrowfully countermarched almost to his abandoned camp; then, turning sharply northeastward, moved as rapidly as the dreadful roads would permit, in the forlorn hope of turning the mountains and regaining his communications.

On the 13th of July, Brig.-Genl. Morris, with half of McClellan's Army, overtook the Confederates, who by their steady bearing, held back their pursuers at ford after ford of the Cheat River. A part of the wagon train, stalled in the mud, was abandoned by the teamsters, who rode off on the horses. In one of these wagons was a flag that had been presented to the Gate City Guard in Atlanta.

Just beyond Carrick's Ford, Genl. Garnett, after holding the enemy in check until the greater part of the wagon train and artillery were safe, ordered a retreat from their last position and, while posting skirmishers behind some drift-wood, was shot by a sharp-shooter and instantly killed. The pursuit, however, was pressed no further, and Garnett's little command, now led by Cols. James Ramsey, of the First Georgia, and Wm. Talliaferro, of the Twenty-third Virginia, on the morning of the 14th, passed safely Red House, on the edge of Maryland. A force that had been sent to intercept them had moved out of the way, then allowing the fulfillment of Garnett's forlorn hope of turning the mountain and rescuing his army from its perilous position.

But the gallant Garnett, who was the first General on either side to be killed in battle, had given his noble life for the safety of his army.

But on the day of the battle at this ford six companies of the First Georgia, with whom were the Gate City Guard, having been posted on the flank of the advancing Federals and on the same side of the ford with them, receiving no order to retire and finding themselves without support of any kind, instead of surrendering, crouched behind the thick laurel bushes, until the Federal Army had moved out of their way, then began to climb the pathless mountain, hoping in some way to escape and rejoin their comrades.

Col. Pegram, retreating from Rice Mountain, had tried to find his way to safety, but failed and surrendered his six hundred Confederates on July 13th, the day of Garnett's death and the same day that the six companies of Georgians began their almost hopeless tramp over the mountains.

For two days the Georgians wandered through the dense laurels, eating nothing but the inside of the bark which they stripped from the birch trees. On the third day a mountaineer named Parsons, who had heard of their wanderings, found them, led them to the home of himself and other friends, and killing some beeves, fed them bountifully. Then, filling their haversacks, he led them over the mountains safe to the camp at Monterey, where their comrades had safely arrived and mid laughter and tears greeted them with hearty hand-shakes or embraces.

After passing Red House, the troops, under Ramsey and Talliaferro, had moved by easy marches and at "little" Petersburg, in West Virginia, had been splendidly fed by men, women and children from the little town and the surrounding country. They had splendid news to tell the men of the Gate City Guard and the other five companies who had been lost, but were found.

The glad tidings had come from the glorious field of Manassas, where, on July 21st, the first great battle of the war had been fought and won by assembled heroes of every Southern State, led by Genl. Joe Johnston, of Virginia, and P. G. T. Beauregard, of Louisiana. The story of the firm stand of "Stonewall Jackson" and of how Bee and Barton had fallen, as they led their commands in a victorious charge, was already thrilling every Southern heart.

The shouts of Manassas were re-echoed from Monterey, where reinforcements from Virginia, Georgia, Arkansas and Tennessee aroused the hope that the next campaign in the Virginia mountains would be more successful.

During the latter part of August and the first days of September a considerable Confederate force was assembled in West Virginia. Genl. Floyd had routed a Federal force at Cross Lanes and repulsed Rosecrans at Caccrifax Ferry on the Gauley. Genl. Wise was operating in the Valley of the Kanawha. Genl. Loring, with his division, was at or near Huttonsville, and Brig.-Genl. H. R. Jackson had a division at Camp Barton on the north side of the Alleghanies at the head of a little valley that lay between the Green-brier and Cheat Rivers, the latter of which flowed around the base of Cheat Mountain, upon whose summit was a Federal garrison.

Genl. Robert E. Lee, who had taken command of all these forces and had his headquarters with Loring's division, planned an attack upon the Federal fortified camp on Cheat Mountain. Lee, with Loring's division, was to advance from the north and Jackson's division from the south and Col. Rust, of the Third Arkansas, was to move along the mountain upon an unprotected side of the Union camp. All were to be in position at dawn of the 12th of September, and at the sound of Rust's guns advance to the attack. Henry R. Jackson's division was preceded by an advance guard of one hundred men, consisting of detail from each company of the First and Twelfth Georgia Regiments under Lieut. Dawson, of Americus, Ga.

The Gate City Guard furnished one of the details for the advance guard, while the majority of the company were with the main body.

The advance under Dawson marched up the turnpike to Slaver's Cabin, where under the guidance of a mountaineer they turned into a dark ravine and drenched by a pouring rain groped their way around Cheat Mountain to a point near the fortified camp of the Union Army. Fixing bayonets they climbed the steep ascent, made slippery by the heavy rains. They would plunge their bayonets into the ground and, holding their guns firmly draw themselves up and continue that method of ascent until they reached the summit. There stood Lieut. Dawson, who spoke to each soldier, as he came up, and pointing to a clump of trees, directed him to go there and lie down behind some logs. The enemy's pickets were in full view, a half mile down the road up which Henry R. Jackson's Confederate division was advancing and would soon come into view.

The movement of Dawson's men was concealed from the view of the Federal pickets by a thick growth of broom straw which covered the wide field. As the Georgians lay concealed behind the logs they could hear the sentinels in the camp call out: "Six o'clock, and all is well!" Then distinctly the voices of the soldiers in the camp were heard, which were not drowned by the beating of the morning drums.

It was a thrilling moment. On one side of them was the Federal garrison, on the other and between them and Jackson's division were the Union pickets. The plan was to meet those pickets as the Confederate division drove them back and force their surrender.

GEORGE HARRINGTON.

WM. GRAHAM.

G. H. MORROW.

SAMUEL BOYKIN TURMAN.

But suddenly there rang out the sound of a musket, fired by a man in Dawson's party who had fallen asleep and in a dream gave the alarm.

Fortunately the Federal pickets were already falling back before Jackson's advance. Dawson's men, who had to be quick, charged upon them from their ambuscade. Several of the Federals were shot, but the majority left the road and darted down a path which soon took them out of view.

Dawson's party were mistaken for enemies by the row of Jackson's division, who fired upon them. The fire was returned by Dawson's party, who amid a hot fire suffered no loss, while two of the men in the main line were killed and a few others wounded, before the mistake was discovered and the firing ceased.

By the appointed time all the troops were in position ready to begin the assault. Until ten o'clock they waited for the sound of Col. Rust's guns. But that officer, fearing that the other commands might not be up did not assault as expected.

Since success depended upon prompt action, Lee, after inquiring into the cause of the delay that had thwarted his plan, ordered that no attack be made and that the various commands return to their respective camps. There had been no battle, and only a little skirmishing at different points.

After their fatiguing marches and bivouacs mid drenching rains, the tents of Camp Barton presented a cheering sight to the Georgians, and never in the history of that locality did its name, "Travelers' Repose," seem so appropriate.

Soon after this, Gen. Lee, taking Loring's division, marched away from the vicinity of Cheat Mountain, to reinforce Wise and Floyd in the valleys of the Kanawha and Gauley Rivers. He left the division under Brig.-Gen. Henry R. Jackson, with Colonel (later Maj.-Genl.) Edward Johnson as second in command, at Camp Barton, to keep back any force that might attempt to march toward Staunton.

Jackson's division, reduced greatly by sickness, brought on by necessary exposure to an unusually inclement season, numbered barely 2,000 men fit for any kind of service.

On the morning of October 3rd, 1861, the soldiers at Camp Barton were aroused by heavy firing at the foot of Cheat Mountain, where Brig.-Gen. J. J. Reynolds, at the head of 5,000 men, was crossing Cheat River. The pickets numbering one hundred men, rallied to those at the extreme outpost and under the lead of Edward Johnson, taking advantage of trees and boulders along the road, so delayed the Federal advance that by the time Reynolds had deployed his men for the attack, the works behind the Greenbrier were manned by Jackson's division.

Col. Johnson complimented the gallant conduct of the pickets and made special mention of Private J. W. Brown, of the Gate City Guard, who was killed while ramming down his 29th cartridge.

A spirited battle of several hours occurred during which the Third Arkansas repulsed a Federal charge and in the pursuit of the discomfited troops opposed to them, captured a large and beautiful United States flag. Being thus repulsed in the only charge of the day, and finding it impossible to climb the banks of the Greenbrier to attack the position occupied by the Georgia and Virginia regiments, Genl. Reynolds withdrew from the field, leaving a dismounted cannon as a trophy to the Confederates. The absence of cavalry prevented any effective pursuit.

This was the first battle the Georgians of the West Virginia Army had been engaged in since Laurel Hill and Carrick's Ford. Those in the advance guard at Cheat Mountain had shared in the skirmish near the enemy's camp. There was nothing but skirmishing at a few points on Cheat Mountain. The so-called battle of Cheat Mountain is a myth. Lee made no attack and hence met with no repulse.

For two months longer the Gate City Guard at Camp Barton shared in arduous picket duty, scouting expeditions and skirmishes, suffering great hardships amid the snow and ice of that bleak Fall amid the West Virginia mountains. In December the First Georgia, the Third Arkansas and the Twenty-third Virginia were ordered to Winchester to reinforce "Stonewall Jackson." The Twelfth Georgia and two Virginia regiments under Col. Edward Johnson marched to the summit of the Alleghanies and there fortified Camp Alleghany.

Genl. Robert E. Lee had marched against Rosecrans, who declined battle and retreated. Finding it impossible to continue an active campaign in weather so terrible that it rendered all further movements by either army impossible, Lee sent Loring's division also to reinforce "Stonewall Jackson."

As the Georgians marched through the lovely Shenandoah, their souls were cheered by kind words of the patriotic people of the Valley, and the bright glances from beauty's eyes set all their hearts aglow.

Several pleasant weeks they spent in the camp near the charming little city of Winchester. Good news also came to them from Edward Johnson's brigade at Camp Alleghany. The Federal General, Milroy, coming from Cheat Mountain, tried on December 13th, 1861, to surprise the Confederate camp. But he met with a warm reception and a stunning defeat.

The morning of January 1st, 1862, was as balmy as May and it seemed to be the right kind of weather for "Stonewall Jackson" to carry out his plan of a campaign that would clear his district of the enemy.

Accordingly, he set out from Winchester at the head of ten thousand men, in which each arm of the service had its proper representation.

Before night a furious storm from the northwest began, which grew in intensity until roads were rendered almost impassible and streams were frozen over. Great were the sufferings of the soldiers. But when they charged into Bath and drove the Union soldiers through that town and across the Potomac, they were in jolly mood and shouted to each other: "Who would not be a soldier?" Then as again the remembrance of how on the first afternoon of their march from Winchester ladies and children met them with bread, butter-milk, cakes and pies, came back to them and they witnessed the meetings so fraught with joy and pain, as Virginia soldiers on the rush through the little town of Bath paused for a moment to clasp loved ones in a fond embrace, there could be heard on every side: "God bless the women of the South! Who would not fight for them?"

On the banks of the Potomac, opposite Hancock, they waited three days, shelling the enemy and being shelled in turn, while Jackson led his own men and the Federals also to think that he was about to cross into Maryland. The result was that reinforcements were rushed to the Federal garrison at Hancock. Then having destroyed the Baltimore and Ohio Railroad bridge over the Big Cacapan, Jackson, leaving a force of cavalry to picket the river bank and convey the impression that he was still there, moved away with his little army. Although delayed in his movements by the horrible condition of the frozen roads, he seized Romney, which the enemy had hastily aban-doned. Throughout all these trying movements the brave lads of the Gate City Guard were noted for soldierly and cheerful spirits, notwithstanding their heavy losses. There he placed Loring's division of three brigades (including the First Georgia, Twenty-third Virginia and Third Arkansas); his picket posts extended eastward to Bath and the Potomac, and westward until they joined the advanced pickets from Ed. Johnson's troops at Camp Alleghany.

Then, with the troops of the "Stonewall brigade," he moved back to Winchester, while his outposts watched against any Federal advance from Martinsburg.

The citizens of Winchester, in obedience to his request, opened their homes to the many hundreds of his soldiers, who, by the order of his surgeon, had been pronounced unable to stand out any longer against the hardships of that terrible winter campaign.

The soldiers from other Southern States, who, under Jackson's orders, thus found rest in Winchester, never ceased to love the people of that grand Virginia town, whose hearts throbbed so loyally for the Southern cause. Men, ladies, children and even the slaves seemed never to grow weary in deeds of kindness and words of cheer.

But Loring, at Romney, made such loud complaint to the War Department at Richmond, that his command was ordered back to Winchester without consulting Jackson. At this Jackson was so indignant that he tendered his resignation. The Richmond government was already so impressed with his ability that it promised never to interfere again with his orders except in the recognized proper manner. Thereupon Jackson withdrew his resignation.

Loring's insubordination on this occasion doubtless had much to do with the fact that he never reached any higher rank in the Confederate Army than he then had, that of Brigadier-General.

But there is this excuse for his conduct. He and his division had suffered such hardship in the mountains of West Virginia, that they thought it was then due that some other troops take their place for a while in the vigorous climate of the far frontier.

The First Georgia Regiment had, like all other Confederate regiments at that time, enlisted for twelve months. Accordingly, they were sent to Augusta, Ga., and on March 18th, 1862, were mustered out of service. Four of the companies re-enlisted in a body and formed the Twelfth Georgia Battalion of Artillery, which served as infantry most of the time.

Owing to these depleted ranks, the Gate City Guard did not re-enlist as a company. But many of them enlisted in the Ninth Battalion of Artillery under Maj. Leyden, who had served in 1861 as Lieutenant in the Gate City Guard, and other members served in different commands. The Ninth Battalion served a while in southeast Kentucky and southwest Virginia. It served with distinction around Chattanooga in September and October 1863, and with Longstreet at Knoxville. A part of the battalion served in southwest Virginia and a part in the defense of Richmond in the Winter of 1864-65 and during the final campaign in the Spring of 1865.

At the termination of hostilities, the Southern soldiers, following the example of their great chieftain, Robert E. Lee, accepted the decision of arms as final, gave in their allegiance to the new order of things and went to work to repair the desolation of war.

They did not even dream of such a reconstruction as followed; for the government of the United States had declared at the beginning of the war, that it would be prosecuted only for the purpose of maintaining the supremacy of the Constitution and of preserving the Union with all the dignity, equality and rights of the several States unimpaired.

They therefore believed that President Johnson's plan of reconstruction would be carried out. They knew that Horace Greely, at the beginning of the secession movement, had declared in the New York *Tribune*, a leading organ of the Abolitionists, that "if the cotton States wished to withdraw from the Union, they should be allowed to do so, that any attempt to compel them to remain by force would be contrary to the principles of the Declaration of Independence and to the fundamental ideas upon which human liberty is based" and that "if the Declaration of Independence justified the secession from the British Empire of three millions of subjects in 1776, it was not seen why it would not justify the secession of five millions of Southerners from the Union in 1861."

Again at New Bedford, Mass., in 1861, Wendell Phillips said: "Here are a series of States girding the Gulf who think their peculiar institutions require that they should have a separate government. They have a right to decide that question without appealing to you or to me."

In view of these declarations and of the fact that more than once the New England States had threatened secession and, through the withholding of troops, and their Hartford Convention in 1814, had so paralyzed the arm of the Federal government, that President Madison concluded an unfavorable peace with Great Britain in order to save the Union, the Southern people could not believe that oppressive terms would be required of them.

Expressions like those just quoted had not been confined to New England, for as late as 1859, at a convention held in Cleveland, Ohio, in which Joshua Geddings, Senator Ben Wade, Governor Salmon P. Chase and ex-Governor Dennison participated, resolutions were adopted using the language of the Virginia and Kentucky resolutions and advocating their most extreme declarations of State sovereignty.

But during the years that had passed since the establishment of the government of the United States under the Constitution, millions of people, consisting of emigrants from Europe who had crossed the ocean to become citizens of the United States and their descendants, had built up States in the West, which they considered as subordinate in all things to the government of the Union. These people were Nationalists. They had looked upon the institution of slavery as standing in the way of their settling in all the territories of the Union. They had declared that they had no desire to interfere with slavery where it already existed but were fixed in the resolve that there should be no more slave States.

These Nationalists had made a close alliance with the Abolitionists, who had been advocates of State sovereignty so long as that policy would serve their ends. The views expressed by Greely and Phillips had given moral support to secession in the South. But, when, in obedience to their demands, Mr. Lincoln, by his emancipation proclamation, had made the purpose of the war not only the maintenance of the Union but also the abolition of slavery, they abandoned their State sovereignty ideas, and favored the most radical measures. Men of the most extreme ideas, for whom Mr. Lincoln had never been radical enough, now repudiated President Johnson's reconstruction policy, which coincided with Mr. Lincoln's views. There were enough of these men to control and direct the policy of the government toward the South, carrying their measures over the President's veto.

The States that had seceded had complied with the terms required by President Johnson, had repealed their ordinances of secession, had ratified the thirteenth amendment abolishing slavery and elected senators and representatives. They were now required, as a condition for readmission to all their former rights as States, to ratify a fourteenth amendment to the Constitution, which not only made citizens of the negroes, but placed political disabilities upon the men who had led them during the war.

Feeling that if they were States to ratify, they could also reject a proposed amendment, they did reject. For this they were declared to be in a state of rebellion and the whole South was divided into military districts, ruled by generals of the United State Army.

Under the reconstruction laws, now passed over the President's veto, thousands of white men were disfranchised and unlimited suffrage was conferred upon negro men of 21 years and over. Conventions were called and the State governments thus created ratified the fourteenth amendment. The fifteenth amendment was carried through in a similar manner.

The one relieving incident of these dark years was the release of President Davis on bail, his principal bondsmen being two notable Abolitionists—Horace Greely and Gerritt Smith. Mr. Davis was later unconditionally released without trial.

The State governments established under the reconstruction measures were notoriously corrupt. The white people of the South determined to turn the rascals out, and one State after another was redeemed.

The Congressional election of 1874 changed a two-thirds Republican majority in the House of Representatives to a Democratic majority nearly as large. The Presidential election of 1876 showed on the face of the returns a majority for Samuel J. Tilden, the Democratic candidate. But by unfair means Tilden was counted out and his Republican rival, Rutherford B. Hayes, was declared elected. But the Democrats were in a position to extort from him the removal of the troops from the capitals of the Southern States. Then the last Southern State was redeemed and restored to the absolute control of the whites.

The last vestige of reconstruction tyranny was wiped out and the Southern States began again the career of progress upon all industrial lines that had been interrupted by war and reconstruction.

But mutual distrust between North and South still remained. The Southern people believed that it was Northern distrust of them that led to the counting out of Tilden and the seating of Hayes by the decision of the electoral commission on which the Republicans had a majority.

John B. Gordon, Wade B. Hampton, Benjamin Hill, Henry Grady and others were doing great things toward the breaking down of Northern prejudice.

Many of the old military companies of the South had been reorganized. Among these the Gate City Guard, of Atlanta, under the command of Capt. Joseph F. Burke, had attained great reputation for drill and discipline. They determined to add their mite to the promotion of brotherly love between the sections and the upbuilding of a strong sentiment that should weld our great republic into an indestructible Union of indestructible States.

This they did by a tour through the North, which has been well described in the "Chronicles of the Gate City Guard," by H. C. Fairman, in this book.

MARION LUTHER BRITTAIN.

WILLIAM V. McMILLAN.

MAJ. THOMAS S. LANARD,
Comd. Infantry Battalion State Fencibles,
Philadelphia, Pa., 1913.

WM. B. STOVALL.

CHAPTER IX

The Guard Discusses the New Military Laws—Danger to Property Owned by Military Organizations—Capt. J. F. Burke Again in Command—L. D. White Elected Captain of the Younger Company—The Old Members Enrolling—The Old Guard Battalion Formed—Presentation of Silver Urn to the Guard—The Active Company Decline to Reinlist under the New State Law—The Guard at the Columbian Exposition at Chicago, 1893—The Veterans Given a Home in the Guard's Armory—Visit of the Burgesses Corps of Albany, N. Y.—Banquet at the Kimball House—Memorial Day, April 26, 1894—No Change in the Guards' Relations to the State in 1895—Anniversary Day, July 19, 1895—Memorial Day, April 28, 1895—The International Cotton Exposition, October, 1895—The Old Guard to the Rescue President's Day—The Younger Members Reinlist—Maj. W. H. Hulsey Elected to Command the Old Guard

THE year of 1893 was one of important events for the Gate City Guard, and presented new conditions that the company had to meet. The memorial armory that had been purchased and enlarged, in commemoration of the tour of reconciliation through the Northeastern States in 1879, was now valued at fifty thousand dollars. The property is now (1914) valued at $500,000.00. Owing to the growth of the city and the increased price of property, the Georgia Legislature for the past few years had materially changed the military laws of the State, requiring many duties of the military organizations not previously demanded, one part of the new law being particularly dangerous, as the Guard saw it, to the preservation of their property.

This law gave the Governor the right, whenever he deemed necessary, to take possession of any armory in the State for military purposes without the consent of the owners of it, and quarter troops, whites or negroes, in it,

for military purposes.   This law was considered by the Guard not only unjust, but as over-riding the rights granted to them when chartered in 1858,
which charter was yet in force, authorizing them to purchase and own property for their own use and benefit.   It was argued that the Guard, under
their charter, had a right to preserve their property and maintain their corporate company a separate organization, except in times of war when they
could be attached to a battalion or regiment for the protection of the State;
it was also argued that if the Governor had the right to deprive them of the
use of their property, and put it in charge of other troops, that the members
of the Guard would be required to pay for repairs, and if burned down
while in possession of other organizations the Guard would lose the insurance,
as no insurance company would take a risk under such a provision of the
law.   These and many other reasons were urged, which finally resulted in
the Guard declining to re-enlist in the State troops under the new laws, prefer-
ring to maintain their organization under their charter and preserve their
property.

Capt. J. F. Burke Called to Command for the Third Time

In April, 1893, a committee appointed from the company, Lieut. L. D.
White being in command, called on Capt. J. F. Burke and requested him
to again take command of the Guard; at this time the committee talked over
the situation and Capt. Burke took the same view of the danger to the company's property that was held by the members.   He stated to the committee
that he could not take charge of the Guard at that time, but owing to the new
conditions under the military law, he thought it would be best to get all the
old members to join the organization again, and form the "Old Guard," and
all together stand for their rights under their charter.   Accordingly, on May
4, 1893, a circular letter of invitation was sent by the Guard to the old
members, requesting them to renew their membership, and about sixty of them
responded favorably, and a battalion was formed consisting of the active company and the Old Guard.

The following extract from the Atlanta *Constitution* of August 1st, describes the meeting of the Guard:

It is Done—The Gate City Guard Has Completed its Organiza-
tion and is Now at Work—The Company Had a Rousing
Meeting (July 31, 1893) in the Armory Last Night—Col.
Burke Again at the Head of the Organization—Lieut.
White Elected Captain of the Younger Company

The Gate City Guard launched upon the military seas anew last night.
And if the troops' voyage is always as pleasant as was its launching, the company will forever have smooth sailing.

The armory was packed with the members of the company when the
meeting was called to order last night, and for more than three hours there
was a friendly communion among those who have enlisted under the company's flag.

Not only were those who are now active members of the company present,
but there were those who were with the company years ago when it was in
its zenith, and those who were with it when it was enlisted in the Confederate
Army; all alike devoted to the company and the history it has made in the
military work of the State.

Conspicuous among those present was Col. J. F. Burke, who led the
company through the North soon after the war, where it was received by the
best people and in the most flattering manner, and under whose leadership
it became the best drilled company in the country. Col. Burke has not been
active in military affairs lately, though a member of the Guard, as his business
affairs required his frequent absence from the city. But in his heart there
has always been a warm spot for the Gate City Guard, and more than once
he has been importuned to take charge of the company again, but he always
declined for the reasons above stated. When he entered the armory last
night he was given a rousing reception by those who had been drilled by
him and by those who later entered the ranks.

After the meeting was called to order, an organization, which had been
contemplated for some months, was undertaken. The work of the organization, however, was not completed, and will not be for some time. It was
like this, however.

The members of the Gate City Guard, present and past, will be combined in one organization, named the Old Guard Battalion of the Gate City
Guard, and that organization will be under the command of Col. Burke,

who was elected President of the association, with L. D. White Vice-President, which two officers are required by the charter. The body will be divided into the Old Guard and the Active Guard, and the Active Guard will have for its Captain L. D. White, who has been Lieutenant of the company for a long time, and who has been acting Captain for quite a while; Capt. White was elected last night, but the election of his Lieutenants and the further organization of the Active Guard was completed at a subsignment meeting. The meeting elected officers of the organization as follows:

President and Battalion Commander—Col. Joseph F. Burke.

Vice-President—Capt. L. D. White.

Second Vice-President—Lieut. C. E. Sciple.

Directors—R. Schmidt, Jr., W. C. Sparks, Dr. George Brown, George McKenzie, A. L. Delkin.

Secretary—B. F. Bennett.

Trustees—W. C. Sparks, C. E. Sciple, E. W. Hewitt, S. R. Johnson and Thomas H. Morgan.

Of the Old Guard the officers elected are:

Commander—Col. Joseph F. Burke.

First Lieut.—W. C. Sparks.

Second Lieut.—J. B. Hollis.

The new by-laws of the association were presented and adopted and went into effect last night, and it is hoped that the organization will preserve their corporate capacity and property under their new conditions.

The Guard had a pleasant meeting on May 23, 1893, as appears from the Atlanta *Journal*:

THE PRESENTATION WHICH THE GATE CITY GUARD CELEBRATED LAST NIGHT

The armory of the Gate City Guard presented a lively picture last night. The occasion of the large gathering of old members of the Guard and other invited guests, and the company in uniform, was the presentation of a handsome silver urn to the Guard by the "Davy Crockett Fire Company," of Poughkeepsie, N. Y.

Judge Robert L. Rodgers was the spokesman for the "Crocketts," and when the large company assembled and were comfortably seated, Lieut. L. D. White, in command of the Guard, in a short and appropriate speech stated the object of the meeting, and introduced Judge Rodgers, who made an interesting address on behalf of the donors and uncovered the handsome gift to the gaze of those present. Judge Rodgers spoke for about fifteen minutes, and was frequently applauded, particularly his generous references and compliments to "Crocketts." The present having been delivered, he called on Capt. J. F. Burke to respond for the Guard. Capt. Burke never made a happier effort. He held the interest of the audience during the whole speech; set the veterans to musing and the old G. C. G. to thinking of the past. The occasion was an enjoyable one for all present, and refreshments were served until the company dispersed.

May, 1893: "From grave to gay, from lively to severe," are conditions that follow military life as well as that of the quiet citizen. In 1861, on the call of President Jefferson Davis, of the Southern Confederacy, the Gate City Guard was the first to respond from Atlanta and marched to the seat of war. In 1879, the Guard, under the patriotic inspiration of Capt. Burke, was the first military organization to visit our late adversaries who met them on the battle-fields of war between the States, on a mission of peace and reconciliation. Now there comes another duty for the Guard to perform. Jefferson Davis has passed away, and the Guard in mourning badges, under command of Lieut. H. F. Ellis, boarded the train for New Orleans to pay tribute to his memory more than thirty years after he had called them to battle. It was a fitting tribute for the Guard to offer to their dead Chieftain.

During this year the Columbian Exposition at Chicago was opened, and during the summer the Guard concluded to visit the great display. Without arms and in their neat-fitting fatigue dress, under command of Capt. L. D. White, about fifty-five members went to the Exposition, accompanied by Col. Burke, and remained five days. But the relations of the Guard to the State remained unchanged, and a committee from the organization called on Governor Northen to lay their claim before him to continue as a military organization under their charter. After going over the ground the Governor stated that unless there was some provision in the law to the contrary, he would consider the company's position tenable, but later, on September 12, 1893, he

HENRY L. SCHLESSINGER.

CAPT. JOHN POWELL, M. D.
Surgeon.

MAJ. BOLLING H. JONES.

HARRALSON BLECKLEY.

issued an order disbanding the Guard, as required by the statute, because they did not re-enlist.

This action was not unlooked for by the Guard, and they determined to make their argument before the military committee at the next meeting of the Legislature. But the Guard sent their arms and equipments to the Adjutant-General with a letter of explanation.

The war veterans of the Gate City Guard and other commands had formed a Confederate Camp, and were sorely in need of a place of meeting; one place after another was rented, but none of them were comfortable nor in other respects satisfactory.

The Gate City Guard learned of the difficulties under which the veterans were laboring and determined to come to their assistance. A meeting was called, and after discussing the matter the members unanimously voted to tender them the large club room in their memorial armory for their use, without charge of any kind whatever, and appointed the evening of September 2, 1893, for a meeting of the veterans of the Guard, and to install the veterans in their new quarters. Many excellent speeches were made, Col. J. F. Burke, on behalf of the Guard, welcoming the veterans, and Gen. C. A. Evans eloquently responding.

On February 7, 1894, true to the patriotic inspiration engendered by their "tour of reconciliation," in 1879, they gave the "Burgesses Corps," an old military organization of Albany, N. Y., a magnificent welcome to Atlanta in their memorial armory, and our prominent citizens joined the Guard in extending courtesies to the corps and the friends who accompanied them.

ENTHUSIASM AT THE BANQUET TO THE VISITING NEW YORKERS—RE-
    CEPTION OF THE BURGESSES CORPS COMMANDED BY MAJ. J. O.
    WOODWARD—THEY PROMISE TO RETURN TO ATLANTA'S GREAT
    EXPOSITION—GEN. CARR PROMISES THAT THE GRAND ARMY WILL
    MEET HERE NEXT YEAR—GATE CITY GUARD AS HOSTS

Through the instrumentality of that sterling organization, the Gate City Guard Battalion, Atlanta won about one hundred and fifty influential friends from New York last night, and at the same time put in some splendid work for the Cotton States Exposition (held in 1895).

Probably the most significant utterance heard at the great banquet tendered the members of the Albany Burgesses Corps and their guests was that of Gen. Joseph Carr, a gray-haired Federal veteran, former Lieutenant-Governor of New York.

"I am a delegate to the Pittsburg meeting of the Grand Army of the Republic this Fall, and I pledge myself to go there and insist that Atlanta be chosen as the meeting-place in 1895."

This declaration, coming from such a distinguished member of the Grand Army, is fraught with meaning and full of glorious promise.

Those who witnessed and took part in the enthusiasm which characterized the reception of the New Yorkers last night will never forget it.

ARRIVAL OF THE VISITORS

On their way to the Mardi Gras festivities in New Orleans, the Burgesses Corps and its guests left Atlanta at 1 o'clock yesterday morning. They were detained in Montgomery three hours at noon to enjoy the hospitality of the military organizations of Alabama's capital city. The splendid special train in which they are making the tour reached Atlanta shortly after 6 o'clock. The Gate City Guard, forming in two companies, and together with hundreds of citizens, met the visitors at the train. They were escorted to the Guard's armory, on Peachtree Street, and made to feel thoroughly at home.

Besides the members of the command were General Joseph Carr, the youngest General to serve in the Union Army; several members of the Old Guard of New York, and quite a number of visitors made up of prominent citizens of Albany, New York.

AT THE BANQUET

At 8 o'clock the Guard accompanied their guests to the Kimball House. The visitors wore bright red uniforms trimmed in gold with heavy black bear skin shakos. They were headed by a splendid band. The active company of the Gate City Guard wore their white uniforms and the other company, the Old Guard, wore blue, the double line making a splendid appearance of red, white and blue.

Shortly before 9 o'clock the guests, the members of the Guard and several prominent Atlantans were invited into the main dining hall. There were five long tables, the speaker's table extending across the breadth of the hall and the other four placed at right angles to it, extending the entire length of the dining room. Nearly four hundred people were seated at these tables.

The great mantelpiece was handsomely decorated with flags of the Gate City Guard and the tables were tastefully set.

When the collation had been served, Toastmaster S. R. Johnson introduced Capt. Joseph F. Burke, President and Commander of the Old Guard, of the Gate City Guard, who made the opening address, extending a most generous welcome to the visitors, who acknowledged it by continued applause.

At its conclusion the Burgesses Corps gave three "A. B. C." cheers for Capt. Burke and the Gate City Guard, their band played "Dixie," then "Yankee Doodle," and the utmost enthusiasm prevailed.

THEIR NEXT GOVERNOR

The next speaker introduced was Hon. Elliott Danforth, whom Toastmaster Johnson said would be the next Governor of the Empire State of the North.

He said that of all splendid receptions which they had been the recipients of on their present tour the one they were then enjoying was the best. He said that five years ago he met Henry W. Grady in New York, and then paid a beautiful tribute to Grady's oratory.

Hon. James F. O'Neill, former member of the Legislature and a member of the Gate City Guard, was called upon to welcome the guests on behalf of the State. He said that he took Governor Northen's place with much reluctance for he was not so well versed in military tactics by any manner of means as was Georgia's Governor just now. This thrust brought forth laughter and applause.

He spoke for the younger generation of the Southerners a feeling of perfect loyalty to their country and of love for their brethren of the North. "Forget that there was a Gettysburg or a Petersburg, and think only of Yorktown and Saratoga." He was loudly applauded.

GENERAL CARR SPEAKS

Genl. Joseph Carr was introduced as the youngest and one of the bravest of Federal Generals.

His speech elicited wild enthusiasm. He said that he had hoped to meet his brave friend, Genl. Gordon, in Atlanta. This was loudly applauded.

"The troops of Georgia, Louisiana and Alabama were always found in the front of the battle," he declared, "and I shall always esteem it an honor to clasp the hands of those who opposed me in that conflict (applause). I tried to come to Atlanta in 1864, but couldn't get any further than Richmond. But I am coming again. I'm coming next year, in 1895, with the Grand Army of the Republic (applause). We are coming to show you gentlemen that we love you as brothers (loud applause). I am a delegate to the Pittsburg meeting of the Grand Army this Fall and I shall go there to urge Atlanta as the meeting-place in 1895. I know no North, no South, no East, no West, but only our common country."

A scene followed. The band played "Hail, Columbia," and the air was white with waving napkins, while the applause and shouts of enthusiasm were deafening.

Mr. E. P. Chamberlin acted for Mayor Goodwin in welcoming the guests on behalf of the City of Atlanta. "We have a population of over 100,000," he said, "and there's plenty of room for more." He spoke of the great Exposition which Atlanta will hold next year and invited the visitors to return to it.

Governor Bullock Heard From

Ex-Governor Rufus B. Bullock was next introduced. "No word of welcome is necessary from me," he said. "These distinguished gentlemen in their brilliant scarlet uniforms are all kinsfolk of mine and they are at home here. I was born in Albany County, New York, comparatively a few years ago (laughter) and this is an occasion of peculiar satisfaction to me, a native of the capital county of the Empire State of the North, to welcome you, gentlemen, to the capital city of the Empire State of the South.

"I can give you in evidence my nearly forty years of residence in this, my adopted State, that your welcome here is sincere and hearty. You are as sure of it here as anywhere in your own county of Albany.

"It is the earnest hope of us all that you will have a safe and pleasant journey to your home, and when you slip on the ice as you climb old State Street hill we know you will wish yourselves back in the warm end of this great republic."

Capt. L. Frank Barry responded for the Old Guard of New York City, and Major Kincaid for the Citizens Corps of Utica, New York.

He Shook Hands

Hon. W. A. Hemphill welcomed the guests in behalf of the Confederate veterans. His words were eloquently spoken and he seemed to feel them. When he said the South was willing to accept the result of the war, General Carr arose and the two clasped hands, amid a perfect storm of applause. It was a thrilling scene.

For the Exposition

Toastmaster Johnson then introduced the "liveliest director-general that ever trod the earth," Hon. H. E. W. Palmer.

Judge Palmer, after paying a compliment to New England hospitality spoke in the most enthusiastic terms of the Cotton States and International Exposition. "It will be worthy of the South," he assured the guests, "and worthy of your presence. Don't be afraid to come and make a showing. Go back home and tell your mothers, and wives, and sisters that there is no longer a bloody chasm, and that the next decade will be one of splendid industrial development alone. We want you to visit us next year, and we'll be disappointed if you don't come." His speech created much enthusiasm.

For the Press

Mr. H. H. Cabaniss was called upon to respond for the press.

He said that it ought, indeed, to be a happy occasion when the press and the military came together. They were two factors, he said that made and unmade nations and dethroned rulers. They are the two great powers of the age. After dealing in bright witticisms for the moment, he concluded in an eloquent comparison of the power of the press in comparison of the power of England's great warlike forces.

Judge Palmer presented, on behalf of the Gate City Guard, a beautiful little souvenir to the Burgesses Corps in the shape of a silken flag of the Gate City Guard. The band played "Dixie," and the enthusiasm was again at a high pitch.

Commandant J. O. Woodward received the token in a graceful speech, and concluded by proposing that a seldom granted and distinguished honor be conferred upon Capt. Joseph F. Burke, of the Gate City Guard, by electing him a life member of the Burgesses Corps, and a handsome badge given him. The motion was put by Mr. Danforth and carried with a will. Capt. Burke responded feelingly, and Major Woodward pinned on the breast of Captain Burke the beautiful gold badge of the Corps.

The visitors were then escorted to their train which left at 12:15 o'clock.

On Memorial Day, April 26, 1894, the Guards' Battalion turned out in force dressed in full uniforms, without arms. They were warmly received by the crowds along the thoroughfares leading to the cemetery. The following is from the Atlanta *Journal*, April 27, 1894:

THE GUARDS' MARCH

The Gate City Guard made a striking feature in the procession yesterday. They were divided into four companies, commanded by Captains Sparks and White, and Lieutenants Beck and Schmidt. The battalion was under command of Col. J. F. Burke, with Capt. Johnston as aid, and formed the special escort of the Confederate veterans commanded by Col. Thomas, A magnificent floral cross, eight feet high, was carried on the shoulders of four colored men in fatigue uniform, with a placard inscribed as follows:

"Tribute from the Gate City Guard to the Confederate Dead."

As the Guard, in their handsome uniforms, preceded by the United States Artillery band, appeared in sight, with their light swinging step, they were applauded all along the line by the people.

At the cemetery they opened ranks and the veterans passed between their lines while the Guard saluted them by raising their right hands to their hats. The large floral cross was placed in front of the Lion of Lucerne, after it was unveiled.

The year 1895 opened without change in the relations existing between the State and the Gate City Guard. The company still declined to re-enlist in the State service unless provision could be made by law placing their memorial armory beyond danger of eventually passing from the possession of the Guard by future Legislative enactment under the claim of military necessity. It appears that the people generally, in Atlanta and elsewhere, having no special affiliation with the military of the State, believed the Guard to be right in their contention, and this opinion was greatly strengthened from the fact that in many other States special provision was made by law for "Separate" military organizations existing under charters granted by Legislatures.

On January 19th, of this year, the organization celebrated its anniver-

J. H. BEUSSE.

MARVIN L. THROWER.

ANDREW M. WEEMS.

WM. B. CUMMINGS.

sary, and old friends were not forgotten. Toasts were offered to their friends in the cities that welcomed them on their "Mission of Peace" throughout the North and East.

The popular sentiment in favor of the Guard found ample expression on Memorial Day, April 28th, as will be seen from the following notices:

HAPPY SOLDIER BOYS—THE GATE CITY GUARD CELEBRATES ITS ANNI-
VERSARY—DRANK TOASTS TO ITS FRIENDS—A JOLLY GATHERING
OF MEMBERS OF THIS COMPANY PASS A DELIGHTFUL EVENING IN
CELEBRATING THE EVENT

There was an enthusiastic meeting of the members of the Gate City Guard at their armory Saturday night to celebrate the anniversary of the company. This company was organized in 1858, and embraced a member-ship of 100. Among its members at that time were many well-known citizens. Among them were Col. R. F. Maddox, Mr. Thomas Clarke, Col. Albert Howell, Sr., James Chisholm, George Winship, A. J. Orme, Harry Krouse, Joseph Thompson and many others.

In 1859 the company was chartered by the Legislature of the State as an independent volunteer military organization, and granted certain privileges and immunities which it has ever since enjoyed.

At the outbreak of the war between the States, the company was the first to leave Atlanta and engage in hostilities. A hundred men were in the ranks. Many of those who went to battle with the company have long since passed over the river and joined the great majority. The few who are now alive continue their interest in the welfare of the organization, rejoicing in its successes and aiding the company's efforts in all patriotic purposes. The corps is now stronger than ever before. Its membership numbers 140, rank and file, a large number of whom were present last night. Refreshments were served, and there was a display of oratory and eloquence that awakened the enthusiasm of the members to the highest pitch, and recalled memories and associations which make the history of this company one of interest and patriotism.

Among the organizations that were the recipients of the complimentary toasts, though far away, were the following:

The Old Guard, of New York; Seventh Regiment, of New York; Boston Light Infantry; Sherman Cadets, of Lawrence, Mass.; Fifth Regiment, of Baltimore, Md.; First Regiment, of Virginia; City Council, of New York; Twenty-first Regiment, Poughkeepsie, N. Y.; Davy Crockett Hook and Ladder Company, Poughkeepsie, N. Y.; Vassar College, Poughkeepsie, N. Y.; Putnam Phalanx, Hartford, Conn.; Governor's Foot Guard, Hartford, Conn.; State Fencibles, Philadelphia, Pa.; Washington Light Infantry Corps, Washington, D. C.; Detroit Light Infantry; Janesville Guards, Wisconsin; Rockford Rifles, Illinois; Richmond Rifles, South Carolina; Governor's Guards, South Carolina; Hornet's Nest Rifles, Charlotte, N. C.; Mobile Rifles, Mobile, Ala.; Company B, of Chicago; Fourth Brigade, of Charleston, S. C.; Irish Volunteers, of Charleston, S. C.; Sumter Guards, of Charleston; Carolina Rifle Battalion, of Charleston; Washington Light Infantry, of Charleston; Capt. Bannon and command, of Waterbury, Conn.; Evergreen Rifles, Alabama; Montgomery Grays, Montgomery, Ala.; Seventeenth Separate Company, Flushing, N. Y.; Fourth New Jersey Regiment, of Jersey City; Burgesses Corps, Albany, N. Y.; National Fencibles, Washington, D. C., and others.

Each of the above organizations found an eloquent spokesman to represent it, and many were the compliments paid to their absent friends, which were most heartily endorsed by the members of the Gate City Guard.

Taken altogether, the anniversary meeting of the corps was a memorable one. There is no other organization in this part of the State that enjoys the national reputation and the influence which forty-five years of existence and many old friends from all parts of the country bring them.

The corps is now operating as in the past, under their charter, and is destined to continue to be a part of the history of this commonwealth, and will continue on its patriotic mission, ready, as in the past, to serve the State when called upon, with promptness and efficiency, characteristic of the soldierly discipline that has always been a feature of this organization.

THE GATE CITY GUARD—THREE GENERATIONS REPRESENTED IN THE COMPANY'S RANKS—A GREAT DISPLAY MADE YESTERDAY—A FEW BITS OF HISTORY ABOUT THE CRACK MILITARY ORGANIZATION—FIRST IN WAR AND FIRST IN PEACE

(April 29th, 1895)

The Gate City Guard presented an appearance when it marched out from its magnificent armory yesterday afternoon, into Peachtree Street, that gave every member of the organization and every citizen of Atlanta, for that matter, a just cause for feeling proud. For years the Gate City Guard has held a reputation, both at home and abroad, that few military companies have ever enjoyed. For years it has stood in the front rank of the crack military companies of the country, and yesterday's appearance added fresh laurels to a record filled with honorable conquests.

The companies of the Guard practically represented three generations of military men. The Old Guard is composed of men who went to battle when the first call was made for men who were willing to march into the face of cannon and stand the rain of shot and shell. These men have grown gray since they left home and friends and faced the enemy. They are the men who formed the backbone of the Old Guard. With them a number of men were active in perfecting the reorganization of the Gate City Guard after peace had been declared and the smoke of battle had cleared away. When this work was started many of the brave fellows who had left Atlanta with the first company had perished on the field of battle.

These men have served years in the ranks of the company and are now at that age where business or health will not admit of active service and now they wear the uniform of the old company.

The active company is composed of young men, in whom the military fire has really just been kindled. They are the men who, in ten years from to-day, will form another branch of the organization. They are perfectly drilled and are in every sense active military men. The third division of the organization is the color company, which is composed of young men, who wear a uniform different from that of the other companies.

One of the most pleasant bits of history connected with the Gate City Guard is its invasion of the principal cities of the North and East in 1879. This trip did much towards making the Guard famous the country over. The Guard entered cities unresisted that Southern generals had fought for four years to invade. This was because the mission of the company was one of peace and instead of being armed with leaden messengers of death the company was the bearer of messages of friendship and prosperity.

The company today is a much larger and stronger organization than the one that made this famous trip. The years that have passed since then have brought to it additional strength, which was proved by yesterday's display.

THE "OLD GUARD," MEMORIAL DAY, APRIL 26, 1895.
The Color Guard are Wearing White Uniforms.

The Gate City Guard Arrives

The Gate City Guard did not arrive at the place selected for the formation of the procession until after all of the other organizations were in line. Just at three o'clock the company marched down Peachtree Street and halted in front of the other military on Marietta Street.

There were four companies in line and following them were the Confederate veterans.

The Fifth Regiment band from Fort McPherson headed the procession formed by the Guard, and following it was the Veteran Company, then came the color guard, and the active company came last. There were just 135 men and officers who wore the uniform of the company. Marching with the band was the bugle corps of the Guard, composed of ten men.

To Our Confederate Dead

One of the most beautiful features of the entire parade was the floral tribute of the Gate City Guard. The design was fashioned after the Confederate monument at Oakland, and was ten feet high. It was built of immortelles, and was perfectly white, except the monogram of the company on one side and an inscription, which read: "To Our Confederate Dead."

This tribute was placed in a carriage, drawn by four gray horses, and when the procession moved, was placed ahead of the company.

When the company passed into Marietta Street it was loudly cheered and so great was the crowd that gathered around it that the police had considerable difficulty in keeping the street opened. A veteran, who was anxious to see the company pass, was unable to stand the heat and fainted.

All along the line of march to the cemetery the company was loudly cheered.

The Procession at the Cemetery

The procession moved out Hunter Street to the cemetery and then divided, marching down the different avenues until the Confederate monument was completely surrounded.

The International Cotton Exposition, which was the largest ever held in Georgia, was to be opened in October of this year (1895) and continue for three months. The Government lent its aid in money and an interesting exhibit—the merchants, manufacturers, professional men and the citizens generally became enthused with the project and gave liberally for its success. But of the many stubborn conditions that met the Board of Managers, none was so complicated as the military problem. It was known that the Governors who came to the Exposition would, in most cases, be accompanied by their staff officers, and in some cases by military organizations, and it was the desire of the managers to have an extensive military display when the President of the United States and his Cabinet visited the Exposition—but what to do with the troops, how to meet and where to shelter them—and how they were to be provided with food—every hotel, boarding house, and private home that could take boarders, would be filled to overflowing, but no provision could be made for the visiting military organizations.

In this dilemma the Gate City Guard, with their old-time spirit, solved the problem, as the following extract from the Atlanta *Constitution* of July 13th, 1895, shows:

THE GALLANT GUARDS—CAPT. BURKE MAKES A PROPOSITION TO THE EXPOSITION EXECUTIVE COMMITTEE—WILL CARE FOR ALL THE TROOPS THAT COME—AS THEY ARRIVE, THE GATE CITY GUARD WILL TAKE THEM IN CHARGE AND HOUSE THEM

That patriotic company, the Gate City Guard, made a ten-strike yesterday afternoon.

In a body the executive officers of the Exposition arose and extended to the company and to Capt. J. F. Burke, the heartiest thanks of the Exposition company. Then the directors took their seats and in the midst of enthusiastic applause Capt. Burke was elected an honorary Vice-President of the Exposition.

The cause of this unbounded enthusiasm was a proposition made by the Guard through Capt. Burke that the company would take charge of all military organizations that came to Atlanta during the Exposition. It is the purpose of this patriotic company to care for all the military, to prepare tents, receive them and see that they are provided with meals. It is a responsibility of no little weight and the company has, through its action, relieved the Exposition company of what would have been a serious question.

Several days ago at a meeting of the company, Capt. Burke informed his men that there would be a serious problem before the Exposition company in the way of looking out for all of the military organizations that would come during the fair. He thought that it was the duty of his company, as they had previously had experience in this, to relieve the directors of the Exposition as much as possible. The members of the company gave him to understand that all of them would be glad to share in the duties which such an undertaking would involve.

CAPT. BURKE APPEARS

So it was that Capt. Burke came before the directors yesterday afternoon. His talk was short but earnest. He said that his company realized that the question of housing the mass of military men who would come here during the 100 days of the Exposition had caused uneasiness in Exposition circles. He said that he knew, and all who were familiar with the subject knew, that bodies of military could not be housed like the crowds of civilians. Military bodies it was necessary to keep together. Once scattered in different parts of the city and the soldiers would get beyond reach of the orders of their commanding officers. Hence it was necessary that a way be provided to keep them together solidly and to comfortably shelter them.

Capt. Burke said that he and his company realized the great labor that would come to the Exposition directors and the additional expense that would result in providing, arranging and guarding the large camp, escorting them on their departure from the city, meeting them when they arrived. Realizing this, he said that it was the purpose of the Guard, if it was the pleasure of the Exposition company, to meet all expenses—in fact, shoulder the whole responsibility.

MET WITH LOUD APPLAUSE

When Capt. Burke had finished there was a round of loud applause. In a moment they had extended a rising vote to the company and its officers, and by motion Capt. Burke was elected honorary Vice-President.

This is a great undertaking and means much work and responsibility for the Guard.

"I think that we can meet the demand and come up to all that is required," said Capt. Burke yesterday afternoon. The company has had experience in this line of work and is fully able financially and otherwise to care for all the military companies that come.

Col. Albert Howell says that the Gate City Guard undertakes the work, knowing what they have to accomplish, and that the work will be taken up as a duty.

The next day Capt. Burke was on the road to Washington City to procure tents for the troops that were expected to come. Invitations were issued by the Guard to their old friends in the other States of the Union to come to the great Exposition and the Guard would take care of them. For about six weeks they were on duty night and day. Visiting troops that were scheduled to arrive in Atlanta at 3 P. M. would not arrive until 11 P. M., and military organizations that should have reached the city at 1 A. M. would not arrive until 6 and 7 A. M., nevertheless they found the Guard waiting with refreshments and a warm welcome to escort them to their quarters. It was a severe trial, interferring with the business and domestic affairs of the members, but none of them flinched and the work was carried through successfully.

But the brilliant culmination of the military feature of the Exposition took place on President's Day, October 23, 1895—every one who could leave their homes—everyone who could reach Atlanta by rail, horse, mule or balloon conveyance was at the Exposition ground—business was entirely suspended, the city was profusely festooned and gorgeously bedecked with the State and National colors.

From the Atlanta *Journal*:

ORDERS FROM MARSHAL J. F. BURKE

The following orders were this morning issued by the marshal of the day, Col. Joseph F. Burke:

GENERAL ORDERS

The following instructions for the formation of the column for the parade on President's Day, October 23, 1895, are published for the information of officers of the military organizations that will participate. The hour for the assembly at the places designated below is 9 o'clock A. M. The column will move at 9:30 promptly.

Aides to the marshal will assemble on the northeast corner of Whitehall and Mitchell Streets.

The Fifth Regiment of Infantry, United States Army, will go direct

FRANK COKER.

CHAS. BOWEN.

CAPT. JOHN W. MURRELL.
Adjutant.

THOMAS H. PITT.

to the Exposition grounds from Fort McPherson by railway. They will remain at the station on the grounds until the arrival of the other commands.

The Battalion of Cadets, Virginia Military Institute, with Gov. O'Ferrall and staff, will form on the south side of Trinity Avenue, right resting on Whitehall Street. The Fourth Regiment of Infantry, Virginia Volunteers, will form on the east side of Whitehall Street, right resting on Trinity Avenue.

Grimes' Battery, Portsmouth, Va., will form on the left of the Fourth Va. Regiment. The Asheville, N. C., Light Infantry will form on the north side of Trinity Avenue, right resting on Whitehall Street.

Military organizations not yet arrived will form on Mitchell Street, between Whitehall and Pryor Streets, and will be assigned position in the column.

The Gate City Guard Battalion will form on the south side of Mitchell Street, right resting on Whitehall Street.

The First Company, Governor's Foot Guard, Hartford, Conn., with Governor Coffin and staff, will form on left of the Gate City Guard Battalion.

The Second Company, Governor's Foot Guard, New Haven, Conn., will form on the north side of Mitchell St., right resting on Whitehall St.

The Atlanta Artillery will form on the left of the Second Company, Governor's Foot Guard.

Each command will take position in the column in the following order:
Marshal J. F. Burke.
Aides, Colonel Clifford Anderson, Gate City Guard.
Colonel, W. H. Hulsey, Gate City Guard.
Colonel, Albert Howell, Gate City Guard.
Major, John Clem, United States Army.
Major, W. C. Smythe, Fourth N. C. Infantry.
Fifth Regiment Infantry, U. S. A., Col. W. H. Kellogg, Commanding.
Captain, L. H. Kennan, Georgia Volunteers.
Governor Charles T. O'Ferrall and staff, Va.
Battalion Va. Military Institute Cadets, Maj. Shipp, Commanding.
Fourth Regiment Infantry, Va. Volunteers, Col. C. A. Nash, Com'dg.
Grimes' Battery, Va., Capt. C. R. Warren, Commanding.
Asheville, N. C., Light Infantry, Capt. Bookehart, Commanding.

Gate City Guard Battalion, Maj. W. C. Sparks, Commanding.
Governor Coffin and staff.
First Company Governor's Foot Guard, Maj. Hyde, Commanding.
Second Company Governor's Foot Guard, Maj. Brown, Commanding.
Atlanta Artillery, Capt. J. F. Kempton, Commanding.
Later arrivals to be assigned.

The column will move at 9:30 A. M. promptly for the Exposition railway station adjoining the Markham House.

Trains will be waiting to take the troops to the Exposition grounds where the parade and review by the President of the United States will take place. On arrival at the Exposition grounds Capt. Hollis, of the Gate City Guard, will station the battalion markers at the place where President Cleveland will review the column. When the head of the column shall have reached the Markham House, Governor Coffin and staff, Governor O'Ferrall and staff and all mounted officers, the Atlanta Artillery and mounted police will immediately leave the column and join the marshal and aides in front of the Kimball House and ride to the Exposition grounds.

J. F. BURKE, Marshal.

CLIFFORD L. ANDERSON,
      Chief of Staff.

After the parade all the military were massed on the three sides of the large auditorium to witness the presentation to the Old Guard, of the Gate City Guard, a large silk flag of the blue and white stripes with triangular union of dark red silk, with the embroidered letters "O. G.—G. C. G." Without delay the ladies appeared on the large balcony and Mrs. Loulie M. Gordon was brought forward and introduced to the assembled military below by Maj. E. Henry Hyde, Jr., of the First Company Governor's Foot Guard, of Hartford, Conn., in an excellent impromptu speech. Mrs. Gordon's speech of presentation was eloquent and appropriate but can not be printed here owing to the loss of the manuscript.

Col. J. F. Burke, for the Gate City Guard, sustained his reputation as a public speaker.

The Atlanta *Constitution* speaks editorially of the management of the extensive military display on President's Day as follows:

THE GATE CITY GUARD

The splendid military display on President's Day was mainly due to Capt. J. F. Burke, who had the matter in charge, and his gallant battalion, the Gate City Guard.

The Guard never fails to come to time when it is important for Atlanta to make a good showing.

It was a notable factor in the ceremonies on President's Day, and but for public spirit of its members and the masterly leadership of Capt. Burke, the military demonstration would have been a tame affair.

These big-hearted soldier boys have shown how much they appreciate Atlanta, and it is now Atlanta's turn to show how much she appreciates them. There is not a finer organization in the South than this historic command—not one that is more devoted to its home people and their interests, and it deserves to be honored and encouraged.

COL. J. F. BURKE RETIRES FROM COMMAND
ATLANTA, GA., Jan. 6th, 1896.

To the Officers and Members of the Gate City Guard.

Gentlemen: On next Tuesday (January 14th) the terms of all the officers of your organization will, by operation of our by-laws, expire, and new officers for the ensuing year should at once be elected. The reports of the officers for the closing year will be read and plans for the future will be discussed.

For nearly three years I have been in command of the Old Guard by unanimous desire of the members. In that period, nearly all the available old members (about eighty-five) have returned to the fold, and about sixty of them are uniformed in the dress of the Old Guard.

The active company has increased their membership, arms and equipments have been purchased by the company, thus supplying themselves without aid from the State.

The large drill room in the armory, that for the past eleven years has been in an unfurnished and unsightly condition, has been completed and the whole room repaired and painted.

The company's relations with the State, under their charter, having been magnanimously left, by the members, to the Governor, for him to determine the company's rights under the law, have been amicably settled by the decision of the Attorney-General and acquiesced in by the company.

The offer made to the Exposition directors, by the company, to relieve them of the onerous and expensive duty of caring for the large number of troops that would visit the Exposition, has been faithfully fulfilled, and forms an epoch in the military history of the country that commands the admiration of the people.

For nine consecutive weeks the company, in detachments, were on duty receiving visiting military organizations, many of them arriving at unseasonable hours—escorting them to quarters previously arranged for them—accompanying them on parades—holding receptions at the armory—theatre parties and other social functions in their honor, making a protracted, arduous and expensive undertaking that was handsomely carried out to the end of the Exposition, to the credit of the Guard and the honor of the people of the city and the State.

I suggest that the first business of the New Year be the issuance of certificates of indebtedness, bearing one per cent interest, and to run for fifteen years, unless sooner cancelled, and that the proceeds of these certificates be used to pay off the present indebtedness on the armory, and be called in by drawing, one or two each month, as the funds of the trustees may warrant. I suggested this plan to the trustees about eight months ago, but I now suggest that the company recommend that the plan be adopted by the trustees without further delay.

As too much weight can not be given to the importance of selecting proper officers for the incoming year, I think a meeting of all the members should be held next Friday evening at the armory for the purpose of counselling together on this important matter, and that the President be requested to call such a meeting.

In terminating my official connection with the Old Guard, I return thanks to all the members of the organization for the many courtesies I have received from them in the past, and I assure them that in the future I will always feel the warmest interest in the welfare of the command.

I have the honor to be,

Yours respectfully,

J. F. BURKE.

LIEUT. ERNEST LAMAR BERGSTROM.

WALTER P. ANDREWS.

A. H. BANCKER.

WM. A. FULLER.

The following is from the Atlanta *Constitution*, Jan. 8, 1896:

THE COMMANDANT OF THE GATE CITY GUARD WILL RESIGN IN A FEW DAYS—REFUSES PLEA OF FRIENDS TO CONTINUE IN OFFICE—DID GOOD WORK DURING THE EXPOSITION

Major J. F. Burke, of the Gate City Guard, will resign.

This announcement will cause a stir in the military circles of the State and arouse much interest among local organizations as the action will rob the service of one of its most efficient officers and tacticians.

In a few days the term of Maj. Burke, as commandant of the Guard, will expire and he has written a letter to a number of friends who have urged him to stand for re-election, declaring that he would prefer to be a private in the ranks.

For years there has been no more conspicuous military figure in the State than Major Burke. As head of the pluckiest and best-known organization of the South he has steered the affairs of his corps in such a way as to bring compliments from all. Major Burke was the head and front of the fight against State enlistment under the new law. He was true to his colors. When the Governor expressed his view that the Gate City Guard should enlist, according to the decision of the Attorney-General, Major Burke did not continue his opposition, but told the command that time would bring about, in effect, the position under the charter for which he contended. He claimed that the Gate City Guard could maintain its organization under the terms of its charter, and as such was entitled to all of the rights of the State militia, and right to carry arms and be subject to the call of the Governor for service within the State.

The part played by Major Burke and the Gate City Guard during the Exposition and the visits of the military companies from other cities has received the highest commendation. It was long before the opening of the Exposition that Major Burke went before the board of Exposition directors and offered the services of the Gate City Guard to entertain all the companies that came during the fair. This offer was accepted with a rising vote.

Then opened the Exposition. The visiting regiments came. Major Burke threw open the doors of the armory. He had things well organized and all of the men volunteered to act on the committees of entertainment. The Gate City Guard did a good work. That the visiting organizations appreciated their services was shown by the profuse thanks and resolutions passed upon their return home.

Major Burke and his gallant men were on duty night and day. As senior officer of the Guard he was in command upon various occasions and acted as marshal of the day on various important events.

Several days ago Major Burke decided that he would not accept the office of Commander again. He informed several of the members of the Guard of the fact. Since then there has been an organized effort to obtain his consent to remain in office, but he prefers to be a private, and at the annual meeting in January, 1896, Major W. H. Hulsey, an old war member of the Guard, was elected to command the Old Guard.

At the next annual meeting, in January, 1897, Col. J. F. Burke was again placed at the head of the Old Guard by the unanimous wishes of the members.

CHAPTER X

THE ANNIVERSARY DINNER

ON January 30th, 1909, on the occasion of the fifty-second anniversary of the Gate City Guard, there was held at the Kimball House a banquet long to be remembered. The handsomely decorated table was made brilliant by electric lights, which, with the fragrant flowers, added to the inspiration of those who in song or story recited amusing or thrilling incidents of the company's history.

The enthusiastic gathering determined by a unanimous vote to place the names of honorary members on the invitation lists for all future occasions. To this end a committee was appointed to ascertain names and addresses.

Associate Justice J. H. Lumpkin was re-elected President, Col. J. F. Burke re-elected Vice-President and Commander, and John F. Bates, Secretary and Treasurer.

At the anniversary dinner it was suggested that a monument be erected in the city, commemorating their "Mission of Peace" through the Northern and Eastern States in October, 1879. The suggestion was warmly approved by the members, and a committee was appointed to ascertain all necessary information and to carry out the project.

The first meeting of the committee was at the residence of Col. J. F. Burke. It was at this and subsequent meetings that the soul of the movement was quickened into life. Col. Burke was dispatched to see our old friends through the North and East, and invite them to visit Atlanta at the unveiling. Col. Burke made four visits to New York and other places conferring with sculptors and bronze founders, and the work went on, as appears on the following pages.

A charter for the Old Guard was applied for April 15th, 1910, and the corporators were F. J. Cooledge, Thomas M. Clarke, J. F. Burke, Geo. Winship, Jos. Thompson, Chas. P. Byrd, Samuel Meyer, Jr., Thos. H. Morgan, S. R. Johnson, all of Fulton County, Ga., and Joseph F. Gatins, of New York.

August 25th, 1910, witnessed a gathering of the members of the Old Guard at the New Kimball House for the purpose of accepting the charter and hearing reports concerning the preparations for erecting an "Old Guard Peace Monument" in Piedmont Park some time in 1911.

GEORGIA, FULTON COUNTY.

To the Superior Court of said County:

The petition of F. J. Cooledge, Thomas M. Clarke, J. F. Burke, Geo. Winship, T. H. Morgan, S. R. Johnson, Joseph Thompson, C. P. Byrd, Samuel Meyer, Jr., of Fulton County, and Jos. F. Gatins, of New York respectfully shows:

1. Petitioners desire for themselves and such other ex-members of the Gate City Guard as may hereafter become associated with them to be incorporated as a social organization for the purposes hereinafter specified.

2. The name which they desire for the corporation is

"OLD GUARD OF THE GATE CITY GUARD"

3. The object of their association is not individual pecuniary gain, but is the preservation of the memory of the services and past record of the military organization heretofore known as the Gate City Guard.

4. The corporation will have no capital stock and no place of doing business.

5. Petitioners desire to be incorporated for twenty years.

Wherefore the petitioners pray the Court to pass an order declaring this, their application, granted and incorporating petitioners and their successors for and during the term of twenty years with the privilege of renewal as provided by law, and with all the rights and powers usually appertaining to such organizations.

A. H. DAVIS,
Attorney for Petitioners.

Filed in office April 15, 1910. Arnold Broyles, Clerk.

No. 3408.

In re:

F. J. Cooledge, Thomas M. Clarke, et al. Application for charter.

IN THE SUPERIOR COURT OF FULTON COUNTY:

Upon hearing the petition in the foregoing application, the Court being satisfied that the application is legitimately within the purview and intention of the Code, it is hereby ordered that the said application is granted, and the petitioners and their successors are incorporated for and during a term not exceeding twenty years, with the privilege of renewal at the expiration of that time, according to the provisions of the Code and laws amendatory thereof, and with all the rights, powers and privileges usually appertaining to such organizations.

This May 27, 1910.

J. T. PENDLETON,
Judge S. C. A. C.

STATE OF GEORGIA,
COUNTY OF FULTON,

I, Arnold Broyles, Clerk of the Superior Court of Fulton County, Georgia, do hereby certify that the within and foregoing is a true and correct copy of the application for charter, and the order of Court granting same of

"OLD GUARD OF THE GATE CITY GUARD,"

as appears of file and record in this office.

Witness my hand and official seal,

this, the 7th day of June, 1910.

ARNOLD BROYLES,

Clerk Superior Court, Fulton County, Ga.

The committee, that had been appointed the previous year for carrying out the plan for the Peace Monument, reported the hearty approval of the plan by not only the members of the Old Guard, but by many other citizens also. This was evinced by the fact that a large part of the sum needed had been already subscribed. Col. Burke mentioned as evidence of the popularity of the proposed monument that the money had been raised without solicitation.

A resolution was unanimously adopted, requesting the Atlanta Chamber of Commerce to send a committee, with members of the Old Guard, to Washington to invite President Taft to make the unveiling speech.

In September, 1910, Col. J. F. Burke, with whom as Captain the Gate City Guard had made its famous tour of the North in 1879, now as Commander of the Old Guard, made a trip through the North and East to invite representatives from many cities in that section and old friends and organizations that approved of their Northern Mission in 1879.

The following clippings from newspapers of the cities visited show the spirit in which Col. Burke's visit and invitations were received.

ALDERMEN MEET—BACK TO WORK AFTER SUMMER VACATION

(New York *Evening Sun*, Sept. 20, 1910)

New York City is not fatherless any more. The City Fathers, some seventy odd of them got together in the Aldermanic Chamber at the City Hall this afternoon for their first regular meeting since the vacation adjournment. Some of the members straggled in late, but most of them got there.

The first thing off the bat they received an invitation to another vacation. Capt. J. F. Burke, of the Old Gate City Guard, of Atlanta, Ga., was granted the privilege of the floor and extended an invitation to the Board of Aldermen to be present in a body at the unveiling of a monument to com-

LUCIEN J. HARRIS.

CAPT. T. ARDELL KEMP.

MAJ. FREDERICK JEROME COOLEDGE.

JAMES TOMPKINS SCOTT.

memorate the peaceful mission of that organization to New York in 1879, in Atlanta, on October 8, 1911. There will be a celebration lasting a week. President Taft has been invited to unveil the memorial. The Board accepted the invitation unanimously.

Vice-Chairman Bent took the gavel at the reassembling of the Board today. President Mitchel being kept away by his duties in the Mayor's office, owing to the absence of Mayor Gaynor.

The Old Guard, of the Gate City Guard, respectfully invites you to participate in the dedication of the monument commemorating their "Mission of Peace" to the Eastern States after the Civil War. The ceremonies will be held on the ninth, tenth and eleventh of October, nineteen hundred and eleven, at Atlanta, Georgia.

J. F. BURKE,
Commanding Old Guard

HOKE SMITH,
  Governor

FREDERIC J. PAXON,
President Chamber of Commerce

COURTLAND S. WINN,
  Mayor

LOUIS GHOLSTIN,
Chairman Citizens Committee

OLD GUARD MONUMENT COMMITTEE

Jos. F. Burke, T. C. Erwin, Geo. Winship, F. J. Cooledge, Jno. S. Owens, Chas. P. Byrd, Peter F. Clarke, Archibald H. Davis, Samuel Meyer, Jr., Thos. H. Morgan, Geo. M. McKenzie, J. F. Gatins.

CITIZENS' COMMITTEE

Louis Gholstin, W. M. Crumley, W. S. Elkin, Wm. Hurd Hillyer, Milton N. Armstrong, James R. Gray, Benjamin B. Crew, W. W. White, Wm. S. Witham, Joseph Jacobs, Herbert L. Wiggs, W. T. Ashford, S. H. Phelan, Jno. A. Perdue.

CHAMBER OF COMMERCE COMMITTEE

Frederic J. Paxon, Asa G. Candler, J. K. Orr, Sam D. Jones, Alex. W. Smith, J. M. Terrell, Robert J. Lowry, David Woodward, John E. Murphy, Mell R. Wilkinson, J. H. Nunnally, Edward H. Inman, W. W. Orr, Victor Lamar Smith, John M. Slaton, Jno. W. Grant, S. M. Inman, H. S. Johnson, Hilmer R. Morris, Brooks Morgan, Clark Howell, J. T. Holleman, F. T. Seely, W. G. Cooper, V. H. Kriegshaber, J. T. Orme.

SOUTHERN VETERAN GUEST OF HONOR—COL. J. F. BURKE, OF ATLANTA, IN THIS CITY—BRINGS INVITATIONS TO LOCAL MILITARY ORGANIZATIONS TO UNVEILING OF MON- UMENT—"WAR AND PEACE"

(Hartford *Courant*, Sept. 22, 1910)

Nearly forty years ago, the Gate City Guard, of Atlanta, Ga., was entertained in Hartford by the First Company, Governor's Foot Guard and the Putnam Phalanx. Then a member of the Gate City Guard and now its commander, Col. J. F. Burke is the guest here of Major Frank L. Wilcox, of the Foot Guard. His mission North at this time is one of honor. At meetings this evening of the Foot Guard and the Putnam Phalanx, Col. Burke will extend an invitation to these military organizations, in recogni- tion of their hospitality forty years ago, to attend the unveiling of a monument now being erected in Atlanta, commemorating their peaceful mission in Octo- ber, 1879. This will be in October of next year. Col. Burke will address the Foot Guard at the armory at 8 o'clock, and Putnam Phalanx at 9:30 o'clock.

Following the Civil War, at the time of the Reconstruction period, in the Seventies, there were many Confederates who came North into the ene- my's country, not knowing how cordially, or otherwise, they might be re- ceived. Among the numbers were the then members of the Gate City Guard, of which Col. Burke was a member. Hartford was among the Northern cities visited by the Gate City Guard, and so cordial was their greeting by the local Foot Guard and the Putnam Phalanx, that the spirit of friendship then shown, still lingers in the memory of those men, nearly forty years later. From this city the Gate City Guard visited other New England cities, and several cities in other Northern States, before returning to their Georgia

The Old Guard
of the
Gate City Guard
respectfully invites you to participate in
the dedication of the
monument commemorating their

"Mission of Peace"

to the Eastern States after the Civil War
The ceremonies will be held
on the ninth, tenth and eleventh of October
nineteen hundred and eleven
at Atlanta, Georgia

Hoke Smith,
Governor

Courtland S. Winn,
Mayor

J. F. Burke,
Commanding Old Guard

Frederic J. Paxon,
President Chamber of Commerce

Louis Gholstin,
Chairman Citizens Committee

Old Guard Monument Committee

Jos. F. Burke — [signature] — Geo Winship

H. J. Coolidge — Jno. S. Owens — Chas. P. Byrd

Peter F. Clarke — Archibald H. Davis — Saml. Meyer Jr.

Thos. H. Morgan — Geo. W. M. McKenzie — Jeff J. Atkins

Citizens Committee

Louis Gholstin — W. M. Crumley — W. S. Erskin

Wm. Hurd Hillyer — Milton N. Armstrong — James R. Gray

Benjamin B. Crew — [signature] — [signature]

Wm. S. Witham — Joseph Jacobs — Herbert L. Wiggs

W. T. Ashford — S. H. Phelan — Mrs. A. Perdue

Chamber of Commerce Committee

Frederick J. Paxon — Asa G. Candler — J. K. Orr

Sam D. Jones — Aley W. Smith

J. M. Sewell — Robert J. Lowry — David Woodward

John E. Murphy — Mell R. Wilkinson

J. K. Kennedy — Edward H. Inman — W. W. Pitt

Victor Lamar Smith — John M. Slaton — Jno W. Grant

S. M. Inman — H. S. Johnson — Hilmer L. Moore

Rouss Morgan — Clark Howell — J. K. Hallman — F. L. Seely

C. W. G. Cooper — T. H. Kriegshaber — J. T. Morris

homes. The spirit of peace and friendship shown by the North for the South during those years has never been forgotten, and now comes the desire to return, in a way, the hospitality then shown. To every Northern company that entertained the Gate City Guard at the time of its first Northern visit, will be extended an invitation at this time to be present upon the occasion of the unveiling of the monument.

In 1896, the First Company, Governor's Foot Guard, under the command of Major E. Henry Hyde, visited Atlanta, as escort of Governor O. Vincent Coffin on the occasion of his visit to deliver the address on Connecticut Day at the Atlanta Exposition. At that time the Gate City Guard handsomely entertained the local company, as well as welcoming the company upon its arrival at the railroad station, and being the escort to Governor Coffin and the Foot Guard in the Connecticut Day parade. Later the Gate City Guard gave the Governor and Foot Guard a reception in the armory, before royally sending them off on the third day of their visit. Col. Burke was then in command of the Gate City Guard.

The Putnam Phalanx, under Major Henry Bickford, also visited Atlanta two weeks following the Foot Guard's visit, and were entertained by the Gate City Guard. All of those who visited Atlanta from this city cherish fond memories of hospitality shown them and have great respect for Col. Burke. From this city Col. Burke will go to Boston to invite the members of a military organization of that city, the celebrated Ancients and Honorables. Upon the conclusion of his visit to the Hub City he will go to New York to invite the Seventh Regiment; from there to Philadelphia and Richmond, and then back to Atlanta.

Although apparently young in speech and action, Col. Burke is now a man in the sixties. He will remain here until Saturday to renew old acquaintances and discuss the events of other days.

MEMORIES OF VISITS TO ATLANTA FIFTEEN YEARS AGO—FOOT GUARD
AND PUTNAM PHALANX ENTERTAINED BY GATE CITY
GUARD EXPOSITION YEAR—COL. BURKE'S INVITATION

(Hartford *Evening Daily Times*, Sept. 23, 1910)

Special meetings of the First Company, Governor's Foot Guard, and the Putnam Phalanx will be held tonight, to discuss the invitation of Col.

J. F. Burke, commander of the Gate City Guard, of Atlanta, Ga., for the commands to participate in the ceremonies of dedication of the Old Guard (G. C. G.) Monument in October, next year. The Foot Guard will be addressed by Col. Burke at 8 o'clock and the Putnam Phalanx at 9:30.

The friendly relations of the Gate City Guard and the Foot Guard and the Phalanx are of long standing. The crack Southern command has been the guest of the two battalions, and the "Feeters" (Foot Guard) and the "Puts" (Putnams) have been entertained by the Old Gate City Guard. Both were entertained on the occasion of their visits to the Atlanta Exposition in 1895.

The Foot Guard, under Maj. E. Henry Hyde, was the body guard of O. Vincent Coffin, who attended the Connecticut Day exercises, with his staff, and was the principal speaker. The Hon. Frank B. Weeks, now Governor of the State, was the president of the Connecticut commission, and had charge of the arrangements for Connecticut Day, Monday, October 21. The staff correspondent of the *Times*, who accompanied the Connecticut party made several references in his dispatches to the entertainment of the Foot Guard by the Gate City Guard. In the report of the arrival at Atlanta, Sunday evening, October 20, the *Times* correspondent said:

"As the Governor and Maj. Hyde alighted they were greeted by Maj. J. F. Burke and the Gate City Guard, old friends in Hartford, and Capt. J. L. Kempton, of the Atlanta Artillery, who extended an offer of escort to the Jackson House, the headquarters of the Guard. Governor Coffin courteously expressed his wish to go to his hotel without pomp. But the Guard accepted the escort, and after a short march arrived at the hotel, where supper was waiting."

Of the parade on Connecticut Day, the correspondent said:

"The First Company, Governor's Foot Guard, Maj. Hyde, was escorted by the Gate City Guard, a high honor when it is considered that this crack command has been the prime mover in arranging the program. Maj. Burke was the grand marshal of the parade. The company formed with the Gate City Guard at 9 o'clock."

On President's Day, Wednesday, 23rd, when President Grover Cleveland and Cabinet officers were the guests of the Exposition management, the Gate City Guard tendered a reception to the Foot Guard at their handsome armory. Colt's band played a concert program and the Foot Guard Glee

Club sang with the band accompaniment. The correspondent concluded his dispatch with this sentence: "The 'Feeters' are more than pleased with their welcome to the Gate City."

Two weeks later the Putnam Phalanx, under Maj. Henry Bickford, visited the Exposition and were royally entertained by the Gate City Guard.

In October, 1879, the Gate City Guard was at Hartford, the guests of the Putnam Phalanx. The command was on the way to Boston. On the return of the Guard, it was entertained by the Foot Guard. The command was invited to the home of Governor Marshall Jewell, visited Colt's armory and the capitol, then new, and in the afternoon gave an exhibition drill on the West Park. At the close of the drill each soldier was presented with a handsome bouquet.

From this city Col. Burke will go to Boston to invite the celebrated Ancient and Honorables, the Boston Light Infantry and the Veteran Corps, to visit Atlanta. Upon the conclusion of his visit to the Hub City he will go to New York to invite the Seventh Regiment; from there to Philadelphia and Richmond, and then back to Atlanta.

FOOT GUARD WILL GO TO ATLANTA—ACCEPTS INVITATION OF GATE CITY GUARD—TO MAKE TRIP IN OCTOBER OF NEXT YEAR—THE OLD GUARD MONUMENT OF "PEACE" TO BE DEDICATED

(Hartford *Daily Courant*, Sept. 24, 1910)

The members of the First Company, Governor's Foot Guard, last evening unanimously and with great enthusiasm accepted the invitation of the Old Gate City Guard of Atlanta, Ga., and of various committees of that city, to be present at the dedication of their statue of "Peace" in that city during the second week of October, 1911. The invitation was delivered to the company in a speech by Col. J. F. Burke, of the Gate City Guard, who was the commanding officer of that organization when it was entertained in this city, in 1879, while making their "Mission of Peace" through the Northern States. It is in recognition of the hospitality extended to the members of the company at that time that the invitation has been given to the Foot Guard to attend the unveiling of the monument in the city park in Atlanta, which is to commemorate the visit of the Atlanta company.

COL. E. L. CONNALLY, M. D.

PERRY LYNNFIELD BLACKSHEAR.

V. H. KRIEGSHABER.

JAMES MARSHALL FULLER.

Col. Burke spoke in the dining room at Foot Guard Hall, following a meeting of the company. Maj. Frank L. Wilcox presided, and Col. Burke was escorted into the room by Capt. Ralph W. Cutler, Capt. P. H. Ingalls, former Major Fred R. Bill, former Maj. E. Henry Hyde, and Quartermaster Edward W. Hooker. Major Wilcox introduced Major Hyde as the man best suited to present Col. Burke to the meeting, Maj. Hyde having commanded the Foot Guard in 1895, when the company visited Atlanta as an escort to Governor O. Vincent Coffin when he delivered the address on Connecticut Day at the Atlanta Exposition. At that time the company was entertained by the Gate City Guard.

Mr. Hyde said that it was only because thirty-one years had passed since Col. Burke had visited Hartford that he needed any introduction. He spoke of the fact that many people had recognized Col. Burke on the street, having remembered him since 1879. He also recalled the events of the trip of the Foot Guard to Atlanta in 1896, and of the warm welcome it had received.

Col. Burke was greeted with great applause when he began to speak. He said that he did not feel like a stranger so long as he was under the roof of the First Company, Governor's Foot Guard, although it had been a generation since he had been there. The Old Gate City Guard, he said, was the first company that left Atlanta for the front in the Civil War. After the war was over he became its Captain. One night, he said, in the armory, he advanced the idea that it would be a wise plan for the members of the company to make a trip to the North and test the feelings of the Northerners toward their former adversaries. The bitterest part of the war, he said, had been the period of reconstruction.

Dreadful as had been the cruel ravages of the war itself, the period that immediately followed was much more bitter and humiliating. Men would come home to find they had no homes, their families scattered they knew not where. Then, as they wandered about in their old uniforms, the only clothing they had, the U. S. Court hangers-on would come up to them in the streets and cut the buttons from their coats. This, said Col. Burke, was but an instance of the prevailing conditions.

The suggestion that the trip be made was met by the men with enthusiasm. There were eighty men in the company at the time and it was found that fifty would go. The news once abroad aroused opposition in many quarters. Letters came every day to Col. Burke advising him to give up the idea. Many of his friends said the same thing. They feared the time was too soon after the war. The Governor of the State, however, as well as many other prominent men, favored the plan.

Then, said Col. Burke, the news reached the North, and the Northern papers, almost without exception, both editorially and in their news columns, favored the plan. The first invitation came from Col. Clark, of the Seventh New York Regiment. The second, characterized as the most patriotic letter he had ever received, came from Maj. Brown, of the Putnam Phalanx. "We would be going yet, I think," said Col. Burke, "had we accepted all the invitations which we received."

The trip was made, and returning from Boston the company spent nearly two days in Hartford as the guests of the Foot Guard. "I don't think," said Col. Burke, "that in all the places where we stopped in our efforts to heal the wounds that the war had caused, there was any place where the reception was more whole-souled, more public-spirited and more patriotic, than that given us in your city."

These things, he said, were not and could not be forgotten. It was to commemorate the visit that the monument, to cost about $20,000 or more, was to be erected. President Taft was to be asked to make the dedication speech, and the organizations that had entertained the Gate City Guard on the visit thirty-one years ago were all to be invited. The House of Governors would be present, and it was expected there would be a tournament by the U. S. troops that would last three days. There would be other features to make the occasion one well worth attending.

With great feeling Col. Burke urged the members of the Foot Guard to attend. He said there would be a large bronze tablet at the base of the statue on which would be the names of the companies attending. "When the First Company, Governor's Foot Guard, is called, will they answer 'Present?' Or will the name fall with the silence of the grave?" he asked. In concluding he said: "I may not have made myself clear or even interesting, but I know that if there is one spark of the spirit in the members of the First Company, Governor's Foot Guard, today, that there was thirty-one years ago, I need not doubt your presence in Atlanta."

When the cheering subsided Capt. P. H. Ingalls moved that the company accept the invitation. About twenty persons seconded the motion, and after Maj. Fred H. Bill and Capt. Chas. W. Newton had spoken in favor of the motion, it was unanimously carried. A telegram was ordered sent to the Atlanta *Constitution* and to Col. F. J. Paxon, the president of the Atlanta Chamber of Commerce, announcing the fact.

PHALANX RECEIVES COL. J. F. BURKE—"WAR AND PEACE" WILL BE MEMORIAL UNVEILED

The first Fall indoor shoot by Putnam Phalanx came off last evening in the armory with twelve prizes won, and with the acceptance of an invitation in person from Col. J. F. Burke, of the Gate City Guard, Atlanta, Ga., in behalf of several committees to attend the unveiling of a statue "War and Peace," by President William H. Taft, at that city during the second week in October.

The Colonel then shot on the range and won a solid silver match safe, subsequently engraved with "Major J. F. Burke, P. P. Target Shoot, 1910," upon it.

COUNCIL GRANT RARE PRIVILEGE—GIVE FLOOR TO GEORGIAN COLONEL AT REQUEST OF MAYOR REYBURN—SOUTHERNER ASKS CITY TO SEND DELEGATION TO PEACE MONUMENT UNVEILING

(Philadelphia *Enquirer*, October 7, 1910)

City Councils met in joint session yesterday afternoon and, by special request of the Mayor, granted the privileges of the floor to Col. J. F. Burke, of Atlanta, Ga., who has come to this city to ask that Philadelphia be officially represented at the unveiling of the Peace Monument to be erected in Atlanta by the Old Guard, of the Gate City Guard, on October 10, 1911.

The movement will commemorate a visit made to the Northern cities by the Guard just after the Civil War in an effort to cement the ties of friendship between the North and South. Col. Burke related the history of the monument to Councils. He said:

"At the conclusion of the Civil War, the Gate City Guard, of which I was commander, and who were the first to enlist in the Confederate Army, determined that the break still existing between the North and the South should be cemented. So we determined to make a tour of the North in furtherance of this idea.

"Many people in the South warned us not to go. They said we would be snubbed; but we were not deterred, and we made the visit. We came to Philadelphia somewhat doubtful of the reception we were to get. To our surprise and joy we were dined and feted and treated like princes. At the Union League, which had the reputation in the South of being the hotbed of animosity against the Southern States, we were given one of the most gratifying receptions in our whole tour.

Never Forgot Visit

"The Gate City Guard never forgot that reception. Atlanta was then ruined by the war, but she soon recovered and now we are on the high tide of prosperity. Now we are able to show our appreciation of the cordiality shown us many years ago. We have decided to erect a monument to commemorate our tour of fraternity. We have also decided to ask representatives of all the cities that received us to take part in its dedication.

"That is the reason why I am here today. I want to ask the Councils of this big city to send a delegation to Atlanta on October 10, 1911. I ask you on behalf of the Old Guard, of the Gate City Guard, the city of Atlanta, the Board of Trade, and other organizations of citizens.

"The President of the United States will be invited to dedicate the monument. On its base will be inscribed the names of the cities who are represented there. I want, and all Atlanta wants, Philadelphia's name to occupy a prominent place on that memorial."

At the conclusion of Col. Burke's address, Select Councilman Edward W. Patton moved that a resolution be prepared and presented to Councils, in proper form, accepting the invitation. It was carried amid cheers.

Seventh New York Accepts Invitation

(The Atlanta *Georgian and News*, Oct, 4, 1910)

News has been received in this city that the celebrated Seventh Regiment of New York has accepted the invitation of Capt. J. F. Burke, of the Old Guard, of the Gate City Guard, of Atlanta, in October, 1911, at the time of the unveiling of the monument of the Gate City Guard. A committee was appointed from the board of officers of the Seventh New York Regiment to make the necessary arrangements for the trip.

The Seventh Regiment is considered the leading organization in the National Guard on account of its wealth and personnel. The monument to be erected is in commemoration of the peaceful mission of the Gate City Guard to the Northern and Eastern cities after the Civil War.

THE CHAMBER OF COMMERCE DINNER

The following clipping from the Atlanta *Georgian and News* gives the report made by Col. Burke at the great dinner of the Chamber of Commerce, of the city of Atlanta, on the evening of November 8th, 1910.

G. A. R. COMPANIES COMING

Col. Joseph F. Burke told of the great plan for having many of the companies of the Grand Army of the Republic to visit Atlanta at the unveiling of the monument next Fall to the Old Gate City Guard, the Confederate company that visited the North after the Civil War, carrying the Union flag and in great measure healing the wound caused by the war of secession.

Major Burke recounted the reception given that company on its memorable trip. The sequel to that visit was his recent visit to many Northern cities and the extending of an invitation to the surviving companies of the Federals to visit Atlanta next October at the unveiling of the monument in Piedmont Park, commemorating that fraternal event.

"There was great enthusiasm in the acceptance of that invitation by those organizations. It promises one of the greatest events in the history of our city. Will we extend as enthusiastic a welcome as they have an acceptance?" he asked.

E. C. Callaway then introduced a resolution pledging the hearty support of the Chamber of Commerce and Atlanta in welcoming the soldiers of the North.

THE GREAT PARADE

The grand climax came on October 10th, 1911, when Atlanta witnessed the greatest military parade since the day when Sherman and his hosts entered the captured city. "But this," said the Atlanta *Constitution*, of October 11th, 1911, "was the only similarity in the two events. The advent of the blue-coated men of the Federal General was greeted with a silent hate, more expressive than the most fiery phillipic of Demosthenes.

"Yesterday the invasion of the visiting hosts was greeted with cheers of love, more telling than a mother's lullaby.

"When the Old Guard of the Nation, and the younger and active members of the citizen soldiery paraded through the streets of Atlanta in commemoration of the 'mission of peace' of the Gate City Guard, Atlanta grasped the idea and rendered its tribute to the men who had traveled from afar to bear testimony to the North of Atlanta's reconstruction, way back in the seventies."

Parade Was Magnificent

The parade in itself was a startlingly beautiful and impressive one. Even the downpour added to its excellence. For as the rain fell, the faces of the men in march became brighter and the enthusiasm of the crowd that watched them grew to bounds beyond the power of description.

It was witnessed by a throng no less remarkable than the pageant itself. For two days Atlanta patriotism had been worked to a boiling point. The people recognized that Tuesday's parade would be the climax. It was eager for it. Long before the mobilization of the troops the people had crowded the line of march, which was several miles long.

From every building banners and bunting were flung to the breezes. Every vantage point of view was crowded with humanity. The parade was not scheduled to move until 10 o'clock. At 9 o'clock, passage along the sidewalks of Whitehall and Peachtree Streets was impossible.

The crowd was good natured, but was eager for the arrival of the troops. They moved with rare promptness. The commands were mobilized at the Auditorium-Armory. At 10 o'clock they moved. At 11 o'clock they were in the heart of the city.

Loud Greetings for Troops

Enthusiasm grew as each command passed. First came the police escort, followed by Colonel J. F. Burke, the grand marshal, and his staff. Behind him, mounted and uniformed, came the veterans of Little Joe Wheeler's Cavalry, and the grizzled old Confederates received cheer after cheer.

Then cadet contingent, gay in their gray uniforms, their white belts, and bell buttons. After the Georgia guardsmen had passed the Old Guard organizations came, resplendent in their uniforms showing their historic commands of a hundred years ago, and more.

They marched with firm, quick steps, although the wear and tear of age were on many faces. Each of the Old Guard organizations was preceded by a military band or a fife and drum corps, either of which could provoke unlimited cheers from the viewing thousands.

But the troops were not all. There were cheers for the old Confederates on foot. There were cheers for Mrs. Matthew Scott, the president-general of the D. A. R., for Governor Simeon Baldwin, of Connecticut, for the Atlanta Old Guard, Mayor Reyburn, of Philadelphia, Mayor Edw. L. Smith, of Hartford, and Mayor James H. Preston, of Baltimore, and for every military corps in the parade. Many distant organizations were represented by detachments.

The Commands in Line

The following commands participated in the pageant:

Fifth Georgia Infantry, National Guard, Col. E. E. Pomeroy, Com'dg.

Fourth Battalion Infantry, Ga. National Guard, Maj. Abram Levy, Commanding.

Georgia Military Academy Cadets, Col. J. Q. Nash, Commanding.

Waleski Cadets, Maj. A. T. Hind, Commanding.

Milledgeville Cadet Corps, Capt. Chas M. Maigne, Commanding.

Fifth Maryland Infantry, National Guard, Col. Evins Murray Rawlins, Commanding, and band of sixty musicians.

Fifth Maryland Infantry Veterans.

Red Men's Drum Corps and Band.

Old Gate City Guard, Atlanta, Lieut. Wm. M. Camp, Commanding.

(Col. Burke, Gate City Guard, Commander, acted as chief marshal of the day.)

Ancient and Honorable Artillery, of Boston, Col. Everett C. Benton, Commanding.

Boston Light Infantry, Capt. Conrad M. Gerlach, Commanding.

Boston Light Infantry Veterans, Col. Wm. H. Jackson, Commanding.

Putnam Phalanx, of Hartford, Maj. Bigelow, Commanding.

Old Guard, of New York, Maj. S. Ellis Briggs, Commanding.

First Company, Governor's Foot Guards, of Hartford, Maj. Frank L. Wilcox, Commanding.

FIFTH REGIMENT, MARYLAND NATIONAL GUARD OF BALTIMORE,
Col. Louis M. Rawlings, Comd., attending the dedication of the Old Guard Monument,
October 10, 1911.

Battalion State Fencibles of Penn., Maj. Thurman T. Brazer, Com'dg.

State Fencibles Veterans of Phila., Capt. Emanuel Furth, Com'dg.

Richmond Light Infantry Blues, National Guard of Virginia, Col. J. Edgar Bowles, Commanding.

Second Squadron Cavalry, National Guard of Ga., Capt. J. O. Seamans, Commanding.

Battery B, Atlanta Artillery, Capt. J. Ed Eubanks, Commanding.

The United States Army was represented by Brigadier-General Albert L. Mills and staff of the Department of the Gulf.

RAIN FALLS

When the Old Guard Peace Monument was unveiled Tuesday, the rain was falling heavily. From every direction pedestrians and automobilists were proceeding townward, and to a casual onlooker it seemed that the Park would be deserted in a short time, but the heavy rain did not last. Down near the lake, Lake Clara Mere, however, several shelters were standing around which sentries were posted, and from under which smoke was sailing skyward.

"What's that?" asked a private of the Fifth Maryland, pointing to the shelters. "Why, that's just another sample of the good time these Atlanta people have been showing us since we arrived," said a comrade. "That's the barbecue for us all. Won't it be swell to be waited upon by millionaires?"

Many there, of course, knew that the barbecue was to be held, but few expected to witness the spectacle of staid old Atlanta business men, a number of whose fortunes run up into the hundred thousands, waiting on the humble private and the lordly drum-major as well as did ever an imported French waiter attend to the wants of an epicure of the old school.

Crowds gathered 'round the line of sentries posted all around the barbecue pits, endeavoring to pass, joshing the dripping men on post, and having a general good time in spite of the many hours which had passed since breakfast and the discomfort of the drizzling rain. The long tables, covered with wooden platters and shining forks, were an alluring sight to the hungry privates, not to speak of a number of civilians in automobiles, and it was all the sentries could do to hold back the crowd until the meal was served.

THEN CAME GREAT RUSH

When the welcome news came, to let in all the military men and members of the reception committee, the rush was almost greater than the man at the steps could handle. Even then, in spite of the gnawing hunger and enticing cooling beverages, the Northern soldiers stopped to stare and wonder at the sight of barbecue pits, in which no fire was burning and nothing but ashes to be seen. They couldn't understand how ashes could cook a big sheep or hog, and it was not until a practical demonstration of the heat arising from the ashes was given them that they really believed the food was cooked there.

Others did not wait to investigate the mysteries of cooking. They made a rush for the tables, caught up a platter and a cup, made a dash for the welcome drinks and the pans of meat, then retired to a satisfied seclusion, until word of the merits of brunswick stew was immediately in order, and it was not long before every man had his platter heaped high with the typically Southern dish.

There were no speeches nor preliminaries. All there was to it was eating—but such eating! And it was a credit to Atlanta to say that not only food in plenty was provided, but that much was left over and carried away. As one private expressed it: "I don't see why they don't give us another dinner tomorrow."

It was late in the afternoon when the last of the companies, their ranks depleted, formed up and marched back to town, all uniting in their praise of Atlanta and the meal which had been served. The rain had been forgotten, and there is no doubt but that in many of the homes on Fifth Avenue, Chestnut Street and Beacon Hill, as well as on the New York Riverside Drive and the Baltimore water front the barbecue served yesterday will long be remembered with longing sighs and with hopes that this will not be the last visit ever made southward.

We quote again from the Atlanta *Constitution* of October 11th, 1911, the description of the unveiling of the Peace Monument and the speeches that followed:

"While veterans of the gray and veterans of the blue, united in a common cause, stood with bared heads in the rain, the magnificent Old Guard Peace Monument was unveiled at Piedmont Park yesterday afternoon.

"The unveiling of the monument came as a fitting climax to the spectacu-

YOUNG LADIES WHO UNVEILED THE OLD GUARD MONUMENT.

Top Row—Alice Orme, Eloise Robinson, Gladys Byrd, Francis Winship, Miriam Clarke.
Bottom Row—Dorothy Arkwright, Catherine Erwin, Nina Hansell.

lar parade through the streets of the city, in which military organizations from every section of the country participated.

"The parade, which was one of the largest and longest ever witnessed in Atlanta, left the center of the city at 11 o'clock, and shortly after noon the head of the first division arrived at Piedmont Park and passed the reviewing stand, where were located Genl. Albert L. Mills, and staff, of the Department of the Gulf; Governor Baldwin, and staff, of Connecticut; Governor Smith's staff; Mayor Courtland S. Winn, and members of the City Council; Mayor Jno. E. Reyburn; Mayor Preston, of Baltimore; Mayor Smith, of Hartford; Adjutant-General O'Bear, of Georgia; members of the Atlanta Chamber of Commerce; several ladies of the various patriotic organizations, and others.

"Governor Smith was not present on account of a death in his family.

"After the parade had passed in review, Governor Baldwin and the visiting delegations were escorted to the speakers' stand at the entrance of the park. Hardly had the speakers taken their seats before a very heavy rain began to fall and the actual unveiling took place in a downpour of rain.

"While the crowds were assembling, G. DiMatteo, a member of the Ninth New York band, rendered a cornet solo, 'My Old Kentucky Home.'

Signal Gun is Fired

"At the conclusion of the solo, the bands ceased to play, the signal gun was fired, and, amid perfect silence, eight young ladies, who were selected for the occasion, tugged at the cords which held the veil about the monument. As it fell, a mighty cheer rent the air, the bands struck up 'America,' the cannon boomed the national salute, and the handsome bronze Monument of Peace, the handiwork of Allen G. Newman, of New York, stood unveiled.

"The young ladies who drew the cords which unveiled the monument were Misses Gladys Byrd, Catherine Irwin, Dorothy Arkwright, Antonia Hansell, Alice Orme, Eloise Robinson, Frances Winship, and Miriam Clarke.

"On account of the rain, the other exercises at the monument, including a number of speeches by local and visiting gentlemen, were called off.

"In spite of the threatening weather, the unveiling was witnessed by perhaps the largest assemblage ever seen in Atlanta. Lowering clouds and even rain failed to dim the ardor of those who were assembled to view the exercises and it is safe to say that had the speeches not been called off, they too, would have been heard by a tremendous gathering that would have braved the rain and defied the elements.

"The review of the troops and the unveiling was witnessed by several thousand persons, who were massed on the hills overlooking the inclosure to the old race track, where the reviewing stand was located, and where the troops were massed after passing in review. Hundreds of automobiles and carriages were also parked around the entrance to the Park.

"The exercises at the unveiling were in charge of Col. J. F. Burke, commander of the Old Guard of the Gate City Guard, and marshal of the day, and Gen. Clifford L. Anderson, commander of the Georgia National Guard.

COL. BURKE'S ADDRESS

"Col. Burke's address, in part, as prepared for the occasion, was as follows:

" 'The South was just emerging from those dark days of reconstruction, when the Gate City Guard, holding sacred the memories of the past, and accepting, as all patriotic people of the South accepted, in good faith, the result of the war between the States, ignoring partisan strife and sectional animosity, went forth on a peaceful mission to their former antagonists in war in the Northeastern States, carrying the Stars and Stripes of a reunited nation and offering the hand of national fellowship in pledge for a brighter and prosperous future for our country.

" 'Thirty-two years have passed since that historic visit was made, and we meet again to ratify that pledge on ground hallowed by deeds of heroism and suffering. A short distance from where we are now assembled the brave Gen. McPherson led his Union troops against the war-worn Confederates, falling to his death in the struggle. A short distance to the south of us the gallant Confederate Gen. Walker gave up his life in defending his works. A few steps farther out Peachtree Street, Capt. Howell, the father of Clark Howell, editor of the *Constitution*, fought his artillery to a frazzle before yielding his position to the overwhelming force investing the city, and where we are now assembled, bullets flew like a storm of hail from every direction, while exploding shells tore the earth with deafening reverberation.

A DAY OF REJUVENATION

" 'And now, in the day of our rejuvenation, we look through the passing years and see our Confederate Generals in the blue uniforms of our reunited States. Wheeler, Dickinson and Fitzhugh Lee, who when he returned from Cuba, doffed his blue uniform and laid it across a chair as his wife entered the room. She said, "Fitz, what will I do with this blue uniform?" and he replied: "Well, wife, I think you had better lock it up where I can't see it, for I might forget and shoot at it." We are now in the position of the old Rebel who summed up a war argument with a maimed Union soldier when he said: "Now, Yank, we spent the first two years of that 'ere war a-runnin after you-uns, and you-uns spent the last two years of it a-runnin after we-uns. We fit, you whipped us; let's take a drink and drap it."

" 'Forty-six years have passed since that period of carnage, suffering and misfortune, and to you, friends from the North and from the South, here on this historic ground we have erected a monument to transmit to posterity the story of your enthusiastic endorsement of our peaceful mission of national fraternity a generation ago, and it has fallen to me to deliver it into the keeping of the people of Atlanta through our esteemed mayor, Courtland S. Winn.

" 'Therefore, on your behalf, and speaking for the Old Guard, of the Gate City Guard, I present it to you, Mr. Mayor, hoping it will be guarded and cherished for its intimate association with our city's history and for the story that it tells. Accept it, therefore, for the people of Atlanta, that they may preserve it for future generations who will learn from it to emulate the patriotic motives that inspired it, and as the generations roll onward, may the bright rays of each morning's sun illuminate it into life, and its lesson of fraternal peace, and may the dews from the silent stars keep fresh the memory of its dead.'

Mayor Preston Speaks

"James H. Preston, Mayor of Baltimore, said in part:

" 'Upon this notable occasion, I esteem it a great honor to be privileged to visit you as the official representative of the largest city of the South.

" 'When the Gate City Guard, on their memorable visit on October 9, 1879, visited the city of Baltimore, the program of their entertainment included a parade through some of the principal streets of Baltimore, escorted by Company B, Maryland Fifth Regiment; a public reception at the City Hall; a military banquet in the afternoon, and a theater party at the Academy of Music to see Maurice Barrymore and Lester Wallack and their company in a military drama, and the hospitality of our city extended by all classes of our citizens.

" 'In thirty-two years of peace and fraternal feeling that have elapsed since that visit, our whole country has gone forward by leaps and bounds in the pursuit of prosperity, happiness and good government, and the cultivation of the refinements and blessings of civilization.

PHENOMENAL GROWTH

" 'Your own fair city has made wonderful strides. Your growth and development, especially during the past twenty years, have been almost phenomenal. Situated as she is in the heart of this great Southland, her railroads stretching out to the cotton fields on every hand, carrying away the products of your mines, fields and mills, and pouring into your treasury the returns from their sale, guarantee her the brightest future that can be in store for any people or municipality.

" 'Baltimore took great delight in welcoming you and giving you Godspeed on your mission of peace thirty years ago; and she has sent some of her soldier boys and city officials to rejoice with you at the unveiling of this beautiful monument to the Old Gate City Guard and their memorable effort in behalf of the restoration of friendship and fraternity between the North and South.

" 'That effort deserves to be commemorated by a monument. Such a mission of peace, having for its purpose the banishment of sectional feeling and accomplishing to a high degree the beneficent end, should be perpetuated in enduring bronze, as this is, so that future generations shall see and remember the great march to the North. "Peace hath her victories no less renowned than war." You, my friends of the Old Gate City Guard, may point to this monument of your peaceful march to the North when the warlike march to the sea shall have long been forgotten.

" 'At a time when bitterness, engendered by the horrors of war and inflamed by the atrocities of reconstruction, had but little subsided, only brave, patriotic and great-hearted men who could have put aside that feeling and journeyed to the North to hold out the olive branch and ask for friendship. The Old Gate City Guard did that; and this great gathering, representative of the whole people, North and South, attests the appreciation of your good work by your fellow-citizens of our united country. And among those who

HENRY F. SMITH,
Captain and Adjutant Putnam Phalanx,
Hartford, Conn., 1911.

MAJ. E. C. BIGELOW,
Commanding Putnam Phalanx, Hartford,
Conn., in Atlanta, Oct. 10, 1911.

MAJ. FRANK L. WILCOX,
Comd. Governor's Foot Guard of Hartford,
Conn., in Atlanta, Ga., Oct. 10, 1911.

MAJ. THURBER T. BRAZER,
Comdg. State Fencible Battalion of Philadelph
Pa., in Atlanta, Georgia, Oct. 10, 1911.

have come to take part in these ceremonies which honor you with double crown given for renown in war and fame in peace, there are none who rejoice with you more sincerely than the representatives of Baltimore, the Queen City of the South—the Gateway to the North.'

GOVERNOR BALDWIN'S ADDRESS

" 'The soldiery of the North and South are uniting today upon this spot to pay worship to the angel of peace. Here she rises before us in the simple majesty of that compelling power by which peace, sooner or later, ever stays the hand of war. But war leaves wounds that are sometimes hard to heal, and happy are they who can help to brush away the last lingering bitterness and restore the good understanding of former days. Such help the Old Gate City Guard of Atlanta rendered in 1879 in their Northern tour.

" 'This imposing gathering is an assembly of the soldiery of the States of the American Union, which have been longest acquainted with each other. Each company here comes from one of the thirteen which joined in the Declaration of Independence—between those thirteen States, the close association of colonial days has drawn a peculiar bond of union.

" 'I come from an ancient, historic commonwealth that was long a British colony. I come to an ancient, historic commonwealth that also had such a colonial life.

" 'A governor of any of the old thirteen States has a certain home feeling in any of them. Each of those States was brought very close to each other in the days of the Revolution. A good deal has happened since that struggle closed.

" 'The history of every country, that is worth talking about, divides itself into two. There is its ancient history—and it may not be so very ancient—and there is its modern history.

" 'The history of the United States is thus divided. No one doubts where the division line runs.

" 'Our forefathers bequeathed to us a hard problem to solve. It was so hard that they could not solve it themselves. It was a problem of Constitutional law. Did the Constitution of the United States create a government by the whole people, ordained by the whole people; or did it set up a government obtained by the States, each speaking for its own people, and for nobody else? That was the problem. It meant: Can a State rightfully and lawfully secede from the Union?

" 'It was a fair question for debate. The lawyers debated it for 70 years and could not convince each other. The lawyers on both sides of a controversy seldom agree.

PASSED IT OVER

" 'Then they passed it over to their clients—to the people, or to the States—call it as you will. Then came the closing chapter of our ancient history. If it could not be argued out, it had to be fought out. Those were terrible years that came then. Years of civil war and then years of civil wreck. Peace came at last, such as it was. Order came at last. Our modern history opened, and one of the opening pages tells the story of the fraternal visit to the North of the Old Gate City Guard of Atlanta.

" 'Thank heaven for our modern history. Thank heaven for real peace, real order, real brotherhood restored. Thank the men who brought all this about, and among them we do not, at the North, you do not at the South, forget the mission of peace that this day commemorates.'

MAYOR SMITH OF HARTFORD

"The speech of Mayor Edwin L. Smith, of Hartford, paid a splendid tribute to the significance of the Peace Monument. He said:

" 'The city of Atlanta and the city of Hartford are separated almost by the whole Atlantic seaboard of the United States. But great though the geographical separation may be, their life as cities is a part of the greater life of the nation, whose future is made more secure every time such a function as this is performed.

" 'The Old Guard, of the Gate City Guard, of Atlanta, came to the North and stopped at Hartford in 1879, by its very visit proving that it was endeavoring to follow the advice of him who told us to bind up the nation's wounds. We were proud and happy then to be the host, as now we are happy and proud to be the guest.

" 'The problem of governing an enormous country, made up of sovereign States, under the form of a federation, must in part be solved by each member of the federation adopting an attitude of mind that is unmarked by jealousy, and in which historical agreements rather than disagreements are emphasized. We, in the North, in the city of Hartford, believe that the Old Gate City Guard, with an honorable history behind it, is making its present and its future history even more notably honorable in the high service of peace and good will.

HISTORICAL PARALLELS

" 'There are, I believe, in this assemblage, some 400 men from the city of Hartford. The Governor's Foot Guard was organized at a time when Georgia and Connecticut were His Majesty's colonies, far back in 1771. It is dressed in the uniform of the British grenadier of that period, and its very appearance will bring you back 140 years to the time when the thirteen colonies were a fringe of settlements. The Putnam Phalanx wears the uniform of the Revolutionary Continental. Each is a picture from the history of Hartford.

" 'There are some hundreds of citizens of Hartford in this gathering today. The Governor's Foot Guard is here with its British grenadier uniform that marks its origin in 1771. The Putnam Phalanx is here, a marching company of continentals in blue and buff. Hartford is proud of both commands. Through me today they express their deep appreciation of the good will and hospitality extended to them.

" 'Fervently the city of Hartford prays that this mounment, unveiled here today, may speak to future generations of men of Atlanta and Hartford the same sweet words of peace and good will that it speaks to us who are privileged to be here.'

CAPT. WM. H. JACKSON'S SPEECH

"The speech of Capt. William H. Jackson, of Boston, commander of the Boston Light Infantry Veteran Corps, was as follows:

" 'I am pleased to be with you as your guest at the unveiling of this beautiful and appropriate monument.

" 'I come from sturdy New England, situated in the far northeast corner of our land. We are called cold and stern as our rock-bound coast, upon which the furious storms of the Atlantic unavailingly beat. I think that we have outgrown that severe reputation, which we inherited from our Pilgrim forefathers. However, Col. Burke has been amongst us, and I think he can

OFFICERS OF BATTALION STATE FENCIBLES, PHILADELPHIA, PA.,
In front of Old Guard Monument, Piedmont Park, Atlanta, Georgia, the day of the dedication,
Oct. 11, 1911.   J. F. Burke in center of group not in uniform.

tell you, if he will, that he found the cold sternness only the outward shell, covering a warm, loving heart for our Southern friends.

" 'We have long forgotten the troublesome times of 1861 and 1865; they are only brought to mind once a year, when the Veterans turn out to decorate the graves of their fallen comrades.

" 'We are looking forward, not backward. The North, the South, the East, and the West all join as one people, living together in unity and peace, in this our country, the noblest and best country in the world. We all love our United States, and we love our emblem of our prosperity, fidelity and unity, the dear old flag that floats from yonder staff, the Star Spangled Banner. Long may it wave!' "

From the Atlanta *Journal* of the same date we take the following account of another interesting feature of this memorable occasion:

Several score of the South's most beautiful young women, tastefully gowned and wearing American Beauty roses, Wednesday morning pinned bronze souvenirs of the unveiling exercises of the Peace Monument upon the breasts of the Northern military men—some of them grizzled warriors who fought the South in the sixties, others debonair young officers in new uniforms, with gold braid and polished sabers.

The ceremonies, which formed a beautiful climax to the unveiling exercises, took place the following day on the flowered terrace of the Piedmont Driving Club beneath the diffused rays of a Southern sun, softened by a screen of thin clouds. Charming Atlanta young ladies and matrons, with their typical winning grace, flitted from officer to private, pinning roses and badges on their breasts while an orchestra from the far North played Southern airs.

The medals were presented by the "Ladies of the Decoration" in behalf of the Old Guard of the Gate City Guard. As each medal was presented the ladies gave the military men envelopes containing cards on which were words expressive of the sentiment of the occasion.

The message of the ladies of the decoration to the visitors was: "We hope that you will preserve your medal as a souvenir of your visit to Atlanta. Keep it bright in memory of your Atlanta friends who wish you happiness and blessings without number."

The medals were of bronze and were exact replicas of the medal on the Peace Monument. The bronze medal was suspended from a bronze bar by ribbon in the national colors.   Engraved on the badges was the Latin inscription, "*In Bello Paceque Primus*"—"First in War and Peace."

The decoration ceremonies followed a breakfast at the Driving Club, given by the Richmond Blues, in compliment to the ladies of the decoration. Chaperoned by charming matrons, Atlanta's most beautiful young ladies presented the badges.

Over 100 members of the Fifth Maryland Regiment were present.   The Richmond Blues were largely represented, as were the Philadelphia Fencibles, the Ancient and Honorable Artillery of Massachusetts, the Old Guard of New York, and other organizations.   Half a dozen Northern newspaper correspondents, dubbed "war correspondents," were present.

Following the decoration an informal dance was held at the Driving Club. After this the entire company visited the chapter house of the Atlanta Chapter of the Daughters of the American Revolution, which was beautifully decorated for the occasion with flowers and patriotic colors.   They held an open house to the visitors, serving dainty refreshments.   Mrs. E. L. Connally was chairman of the D. A. R. committee.   The vice-chairmen were Mrs. A. J. Smith, Mrs. Frank Rice, Mrs. A. McD. Wilson, Mrs. E. H. Barnes, and Misses Sally and Cora Brown.   Mrs. Jos. H. Morgan, regent, and Mrs. Geo. Hope, vice-regent.

The Old Guard of New York were entertained at luncheon at the Driving Club by Messrs. George and Charles Sciple.

The idea of presenting the visiting military men with souvenirs of their visit to Atlanta originated with Capt. J. F. Burke.   Mrs. John Hill was chairman of the "Ladies of the Decoration," with Mrs. J. Frank Meador as vice-chairman.   The chaperons were Mrs. Harry Stearns, Mrs. Willis Westmoreland, Mrs. Edwin Johnson, Mrs. Ulric Atkinson, Mrs. Wyckliffe Goldsmith, Mrs. Howard Bucknell, Mrs. A. D. Adair, Jr., Mrs. J. T. Williams, Mrs. E. P. Lawson, Mrs. J. L. Dickey, Jr., Mrs. Mitchell King, Mrs. Henry Johnson, Jr., Mrs. Gordon Kiser, Mrs. Phinizy Calhoun, Mrs. C. S. Northen, and Mrs. W. C. Jernigan.

The committee included Misses Aurelia Speer, Virginia McCarty, Bessie Jones, Isabel Kuhrt, Margaret Thomas, Clifford West, Elizabeth Morgan, Alice May Freeman, Annie Lee McKenzie, Helen Thorn, Fort, Harriet Cole, Kathryn Gordon, Margaret Northen, Laura Cole, Katherine Wylie, Marjorie Brown, Mary Traylor, Passie May Ottley, Harriet Calhoun, Mary Allgood Jones, Marion Goldsmith, Caroline Muse, Maxel Sonn, Carrie Dallis, Janet Lowndes, Louise Riley, Roslyn Benjamin, Isolen Campbell, Mary Helen Moody, Marie Pappenheimer, Helen Dobbs, Lucy Hoke Smith, Hattie Orr, Emma Kate Amorous, Penelope Clarke, Sarah Dorsey, Bess Richardson, Edith Kirkpatrick, Antoinette Kirkpatrick, Sallie Cobb Johnson, Bessie Woodward, Emmie Willingham, Edith Dunson, Louise Dooly, Agnes Ladson, Ida Hightower, Harrie Fumade, Nellie Hightower, Marie Ridley, Bessie Brady, Harrie Stockdell, Alline Gentry, Margaret Dissosway, Frances Nunnally, Carolyn King, Adeline Thomas, Lula Dean Jones, Gladys Levin, Callie Smith, Frances Akin, Jennie D. Harris, Lyda Brown, Annie Sykes Rice, Mary Hopkins, Helen Hawkins, Sarah Carter, Marion Foster, Emily Winship, Ruth Wing, Adrienne Battey, Leone Ladson, Julia Meador, Cobbie Vaughan, Elizabeth Adair, Nan DuBignon, M. A. Phelan, Elanor Raoul, Jane Thornton, Elizabeth Rawson, Sarah Rawson, Charles Owens, Hattie May Holland, Helen Payne, Edna McCandless, Lottie Wylie, Frances Connally, Courtney Harrison, Nellie Stewart, Jennie Mobley, Eloise Oliver, Martha Francis, Nina Gentry, Lillian Logan.

We continue selections from the Atlanta *Constitution*:

PENCIL SNAPSHOTS OF THE BIG PARADE THROUGH THE STREETS

Georgia's cadet contingent in the parade Tuesday was the subject of unbounded enthusiasm all along the line of march. The boys from the Georgia Military Academy and the Marist College were in gray dress uniforms, while the Riverside Battalion also called for cheers despite the fact that they wore their fatigue uniforms. It was noticeable that the cadet contingent followed the Confederate veterans. For once it was a condition of December coming before May.

SMALL BOYS' GRAND STAND

The railings of the Whitehall viaduct formed an excellent grandstand for the small boys who couldn't horn their way into an office building. On each side the bridge was lined to capacity with youthful sightseers. They cheered lustily for anything, everything and everybody, though most of the time a switch engine below was coughing smoke in immense volumes right into their lungs.

Improvised Confetti Used

An appearance of carnival was given before the parade passed through the downtown district by persons perched in windows of the tall office buildings. They amused themselves by tearing up paper and scattering it on the heads of their less fortunate fellows, who were compelled to be jostled around and to crane their necks on the side-walks below. The paper fall soon began to be as thick as confetti in the air of New Orleans on Mardi Gras day.

Where the Crowd was Thickest

At Whitehall and Alabama and Hunter Streets the crowd reached its greatest density. For anyone to gain a position near the curbing after 9:30 seemed impossible. A boy, about as big as a peanut and as formidable as a flea, did it, though, after dozens of strong, husky men had failed.

He relied on Southern chivalry to obtain for him the point of vantage he could not gain by physical force. Just as the parade approached, a small voice far back on the sidewalk piped out, "Let the lady through—she's fainting!" Room was promptly made. The spectators looked for the fainting form. They didn't see it. What they saw was a youngster slip through to the curbstone and begin yelling as the first band hove in sight.

A Jap Commanded Company

Capt. Richmond Pearson Hobson would have been decidedly shocked if he had beheld the Old Guard parade. The gallant hero of the Merrimac is in constant fear that Japan is about to wipe the United States off the map. Yesterday, in one of the cadet battalions, the commander of a company was an almond-eyed son of Nippon. He was marching under the Stars and Stripes of Uncle Sam and was giving his commands in perfectly good English. The gallant Captain would probably have seen a scheme of the Mikado to learn the inner secrets of cadet life in America in the incident.

Foot Guards a Merry Lot

The Governor's Foot Guard, of Connecticut, made merry all along the route. Whenever they were halted they proceeded to amuse the populace with songs, varied with college yells, despite the fact that their magnificent shakos and brilliant uniforms and glittering swords made them as utterly unlike the chorus man or a rah-rah boy as could be conceived in the brain of the most learned man in all the universe.

LOCAL OLD GUARD

Atlanta's Old Guard of the Gate City Guard appeared in the martial costume of frock coats, top hats and walking sticks. They kept step as in days of yore, though, and swung their canes jauntily. When the rain came there was unanimous sympathy expressed for the top hats, but the Old Guardsmen didn't seem to mind it.

In these prosaic days of things military, when boards of strategy deem it the part of prudence to dress the soldiers in a cloth colored considerably like Mother Earth rather than have the entire armed forces attired in rainbow raiment, the spectacle of yesterday, to the minds of many of the present generation smacked but slightly of the martial. "It looks like a combination of the male choruses of every comic opera and musical comedy in the world," said a cynic as gay uniform after gay uniform passed, representing the military dress of years gone by.

BORE THE ANCIENT RELICS

At the head of the Ancient and Honorable Artillery of Boston marched Col. E. C. Benton, its present commander. He bore with him as a badge of office an espontoon, which weapon, a combination of a pike and a battle axe, was considered as formidable as a magazine Springfield rifle in its day. The espontoon was carried by the first commander back in the Seventeenth century and the Ancient and Honorables never appear without the commander bearing it. He also wears a gorget of silver that was worn by the first commander.

OLD CONFEDS GIVEN AN OVATION

The Confederate veterans were given ovations every foot of the way. Both the Wheeler Cavalry and the dismounted old warriors were cheered constantly, and they returned the cheers vigorously. They continued in the line of march after the downpour began, despite the danger of rheumatism from the cold rain to the aged limbs.

AMONG THE VISITORS

Dr. John Morrissey, widely known medical practitioner, George Lacy, an extensive and successful contractor, and James McBride, a secret service

CAPT. A. McD. WILSON.

SAMUEL MEYER, JR.

C. W. TIDWELL.

H. M. BEUTELL.

man, all of Baltimore, are among the military visitors to Atlanta. They are all members of the famous Fifth Maryland Regiment and clad in the regulation gray uniform of that military organization they are being given a warm welcome by Atlantans, both civilian and military. Dr. Morrissey and Messrs. Lacy and McBride have apartments at the Kimball and are keeping unlocked doors to their many friends from the Monumental City, as well as the many friends they have made in Atlanta since their arrival Sunday night. Happy and timely songs, the catchy airs known along the shores of the Chesapeake Bay and down to Annapolis, they are singing from the arcade and balconies of the Kimball when they are not on dress parade or in line of march.

GOSSIP FROM HARTFORD OF INTEREST TO ATLANTA

Conspicuous among the distinguished visitors to the city is Mayor Edwin Smith, of Hartford, Conn. Mayor Smith is a democrat and the youngest mayor Hartford has ever had—possibly the youngest mayor of a large city in the country. He is just thirty-five years of age, and this is his first political office of importance. A rather peculiar thing is the fact that he is of the law firm of Henry & Smith. Judge Henry is an ex-mayor of Hartford, and a republican.

In the same party is ex-mayor Hooker, of Hartford, also a republican. Hartford, it appears, has a large independent vote and this vote controls the municipal elections.

We democrats of Hartford and Connecticut have high hopes of victory in the next presidential election. All over New England there is a feeling of unrest over republican abuses. Connecticut is almost certain to go democratic in the next election, as it did in the last gubernatorial election.

Governor Baldwin is a democrat and one of our strongest men. He is doing a great work for the State in correcting corporation abuses. For some years it has had corporations with a small paid-in capital to issue bales of watered stock and Gov. Baldwin has put the screws on this pretty effectually.

"I have often wondered why a Greek paper, which I subscribe for in Hartford on account of its fruit and produce news came from Atlanta," said Theo. H. Goodrich, of Hartford, a well-known merchant of that city. "I can understand it now. In no city in the North have I seen so many Greeks. All of them seem to be prosperous. Little as you may think it, that Greek paper is doing much to advertise Atlanta and keep the city's name before the country."

Judge P. Waldo Marvin, of the probate court, of Hartford, is one of the distinguished legal visitors with the Hartford party. He expressed surprise to see Atlanta such a metropolitan city.

"One would never imagine this was the dreamy South that we of the North have read so much of. I don't see how you can find time to sleep here, much less dream."

Lieut. Theodore H. Goodrich, historian of the Putnam Phalanx, is one of the three members of the company who were with it when the Old Gate City Guard visited Hartford on that memorable occasion. Up to the time of the reception of the University Club last night he had been so busy that he had not met any of the Old Guard whom he met in the Seventies.

GEORGIA SOLDIERS MAKE FINE SHOWING IN PARADE

Georgia troops were not so imposingly dressed as were other organizations in the parade yesterday, nor had they bright red or white uniforms nor enormous hats, but they attracted just as much attention as did the others, and were just as well drilled.

The Fourth Battalion Infantry, National Guard of Georgia, arrived yesterday morning from Columbus, Ga., commanded by Major Abram Levy. They immediately made friends with the men from the north of the Mason and Dixon line, and when marching along to Piedmont Park, were repeatedly greeted with cheers. They will leave Atlanta tonight.

The boys from the Georgia Military College, at Milledgeville, commanded by Lieut. Charles W. Maigne, arrived late Monday night. They made an excellent showing in the parade.

Major A. Levy, who commands the First Battalion of the Second Georgia, arriving Tuesday morning, thinks his men are about the best going. Their behavior during Tuesday was exceptionally good, a thing remarkable in the usual private out for a good time, and while marching his men showed the results of much drill.

Though the Reinhardt College Cadets, from Waleska, Ga., Maj. A. T. Hind, commander, could stay in Atlanta but one day, they made many friends who were sorry to see them go. The boys were not even able to stay to the barbecue. They arrived on a special L. & N. train from Canton, Ga., Tuesday morning.

The Walton Guards, Capt. A. R. Nunnally, from Monroe, Ga., have been in Atlanta since Monday morning and can be seen everywhere. They were among the jolliest of the crowd at the Auditorium-Armory Monday night. They're jolly good fellows and are liked by all.

Gov. Baldwin Entertains for Major of Foot Guard

A formal reception was tendered Major Wilcox, of the Foot Guards of Connecticut last night by Gov. Baldwin in the latter's private car, at the Terminal Station.

The event was given as a farewell recognition of courtesies, and was brilliant in every respect. Three up-to-date dining cars were thrown together to compose a buffet, in which the reception was given. About thirty guests were present. Those who enjoyed the reception were the staff of Gov. Baldwin, Maj. Wilcox and his staff, President F. J. Paxon and Walter G. Cooper, of the Atlanta Chamber of Commerce.

Immediately following the reception, those in attendance went in a body to the Piedmont Driving Club, where they were present at the affair given there.

Moving Pictures of Big Parade

Within the next two weeks, the big Atlanta Peace celebration will be vividly presented for the benefit of the moving picture show patrons of the United States, thus affording an excellent advertisement for the city.

In Atlanta, on Tuesday, ranged along the route of the parade and at the monument at Piedmont Park, were the moving picture outfits of the Imp Company, which manufactures an independent film, and of the Pathe service. The pictures were fine, it is stated, the operators being greatly pleased with results. The pictures will be shown in Atlanta in about ten days, it is said.

Mrs. John M. Slaton, wife of Gov. Slaton, was hostess yesterday at afternoon tea at her home on Peachtree Road, the occasion a compliment to Mrs. Matthew Scott and one of the happiest expressions of hospitality during the feted visit of the distinguished president-general of the D. A. R.

Assembled to meet Mrs. Scott were the members of the Atlanta Chapter, the officers of the Piedmont Continental and Joseph Habersham Chapters, the State officers, visiting D. A. R.'s and the ladies accompanying the visiting military companies.

Mrs. Slaton's beautiful home was artistically decorated with palms and ferns, and a profusion of pink roses, and in the dining room the tea table was picturesque in pink, the centerpiece a silver loving cup of roses.

The stately hostess wore a black lace gown over black satin, and Mrs. Scott wore black lace with an embroidery in pearls. Mrs. Joseph Morgan, regent of the Atlanta Chapter, receiving with them, was one of the handsomest women present, wearing a black lace gown. Mrs. W. D. Grant wore black Olga crepe and lace.

MR. GEORGE B. FISHER,
Son of a former Commander of the
Governor's Foot Guard.

COL. EVERETT C. BENTON,
Comd. Ancient and Honorable Artillery of
Boston, Mass., in Atlanta, Ga., with the
Ancient and Honorables at the dedication of
the Old Guard Monument, Oct. 10, 1911.

CHAPTER XI

INCIDENTS OF THE GUARD PARADE—HOSPITALITY AND ENTHUSIASTIC
WELCOME EVERYWHERE—MRS. M. T. SCOTT, PRESIDENT OF THE
DAUGHTERS OF THE AMERICAN REVOLUTION, WARMLY RECEIVED
—LUNCHEON AT THE DRIVING CLUB—RECEPTION BY THE AT-
LANTA CHAPTER OF THE D. A. R. AND UNIVERSITY CLUB—BRIL-
LIANT RECEPTION AT THE DRIVING CLUB—THE ANCIENT AND
HONORABLE ARTILLERY, OF BOSTON, GIVE A RECEPTION AT THE
PIEDMONT HOTEL—DINNER TO THE OLD GUARD OF NEW YORK—
"WE KNOW EACH OTHER NOW"—INSCRIPTIONS ON THE MONU-
MENT—THE PUTNAM AND FOOT GUARD AT CHARLESTON, S. C.—
A PRESENT FROM THE BOSTON LIGHT INFANTRY—OLD GUARD
RECEPTION AT THE AUDITORIUM—MONUMENT DAY, 1913, AT THE
CAPITAL CITY CLUB—OFF TO SEE OLD FRIENDS—A REUNION ON
NORTHERN SOIL—THE GUARDS' ITINERARY—RECEPTION BY PRES-
IDENT AND MRS. WILSON AT WASHINGTON, D. C.—WELCOME TO
BALTIMORE—DEMONSTRATION AT PHILADELPHIA— RECALLING
OLD FRIENDS AT THE SEVENTH REGIMENT ARMORY, NEW YORK—
OLD GUARD OF NEW YORK GIVE A DINNER TO THE OLD GUARD OF
ATLANTA—THE NEW HAVEN GRAYS—ENTHUSIASM IN BOSTON

LADIES OF PUTNAM PHALANX ARE SHOWN
MANY ATTENTIONS

THE Ladies' Auxiliary, of the Putnam Phalanx, who have been in the
city with that old and distinguished military organization, have been
among the many being entertained by the Atlanta Chapter, D. A. R.
Mrs. Rice, the President of the Auxiliary, who is also a prominent
member of the Hartford Chapter, D. A. R., tells an interesting story of the
pleasures shared by the members of the Phalanx with the ladies. At certain
times during the year brilliant entertainments are given, at which both ladies
and gentlemen are present. These are held in the spacious armory of the

company; the ladies looking after the decorations and the refreshments, while the gentlemen look after the other features of pleasure.

The ladies have a sewing society, when they meet to sew for the poor, and their Auxiliary has also a benevolent feature.

The Connecticut ladies witnessed the parade from the balcony of the Georgian Terrace, and were interested spectators, but when the Hartford companies appeared their pride was enthusiastically expressed, and many of them left their chairs and went down to the side-walk to wave their handkerchiefs to their soldiers.

With the Hartford ladies were a number of the Daughters of the American Revolution, here to meet Mrs. Matthew T. Scott.

MRS. SCOTT IN THE PARADE

She occupied an automobile in the rear of the procession and was accompanied by Mrs. Joseph Morgan, Mrs. John M. Graham, Miss Anna Benning, Mrs. George Hope, and Mrs. Foster. As she passed the Terrace. the other ladies of the visiting party followed in machines and were parked back of the reviewing stand. Mrs. Scott, Col W. L. Peel, and Governor Baldwin, representing Connecticut and the North, placed a wreath on the Old Guard Monument.

AT THE DRIVING CLUB

The inclemency of the weather made it advisable for the ladies of the visiting party to go to the Driving Club after the unveiling exercises, where they were delightfully entertained. A number of Atlanta's prominent people were there, and an informal luncheon was served. Delicious barbecue and brunswick stew were sent up from the 'cue, and the occasion afforded one of the first opportunities for the visiting people to meet Atlanta people socially. In the afternoon, the reception given by Mrs. John Marshall Slaton, was the bright social event.

HOSPITALITY ON THE LINE

When the parade reached the corner of Peachtree and Fourteenth Streets, there was a moment of rest, when a group of Atlanta ladies gave the "strangers within the gate" a cup of cold water. Mrs. John Murphy had a party of friends with her; also Mrs. J. K. Orr, Mrs. Charles Gately and Mrs.

Alex. Smith. Soon trays with glasses and pitchers of ice water and other refreshing delicacies were passed among the soldiers, who, though working in times of peace, were suffering for refreshment after the long march from town.

OPEN HOUSE TODAY

The Atlanta Chapter, D. A. R., will keep open house today between the hours of 11 and 2 o'clock. They will be at home at Craigie House, and the entire Chapter will act as an entertaining party. The State officers, Mrs. Graham, Mrs. Hope, and Miss Benning, will also be in the party. All visiting ladies are invited to call.

BRILLIANT ENTERTAINMENTS AT PIEDMONT DRIVING CLUB AND AT UNIVERSITY CLUB

The University Club entertained at a brilliant reception last night in honor of Governor Baldwin, of Connecticut, when distinguished guests from all the visiting parties in the city were present.

The reception was at 9 o'clock, and Governor Baldwin, at the head of the receiving line, was introduced by Hon. John Marshall Slaton. Next in line stood Mrs. Slaton, and the officers of the club and their wives, including Mr. H. M. Atkinson, Messrs. S. S. Wallace, Burton Smith, Mr. and Mrs. J. R. A. Hobson, Dr. Jas. N. Ellis, Mrs. Ellis, Mr. and Mrs. Ben Lee Crew, Mr. Hal F. Hentz, Mr. and Mrs. H. C. Peeples, Mr. and Mrs. Ten Ecyk Brown, Mr. and Mrs. P. S. Arkwright, Mr. and Mrs. Jas. L. Floyd, Mr. and Mrs. Alex King, and Mr. and Mrs. A. M. Schoen.

The club sought to do honor to Governor Baldwin, not because of his political position, but for the fact that he is a Yale graduate, and has for forty years given two evenings a week to the college lecturing on constitutional law and private international law. The scholarly attainments of Governor Baldwin, rather than his political attainments, was what the club sought to recognize in this way. Among the other notable visitors invited to the reception were Mayor Edwin L. Smith, of Hartford, Conn., Mayor John E. Reyburn, of Philadelphia, Mayor John F. Fitzgerald, of Boston, ex-Governor Joseph Warfield, of Maryland, and Mayor J. H. Preston, of Baltimore.

Every Yale man in the city of Atlanta was invited to meet Governor Baldwin, as were the graduates of the State University, Emory College, Mercer University, and the Georgia School of Technology.

The club-house was radiant in decorations which showed the red, white and blue with a back-ground in luxurious palms and cut flowers. American Beauty roses were the flowers used with fern and smilax. Delicious refreshments were served, and the entire club-house was thrown open for the entertainment of the guests. An orchestra of music rendered bright music, the patriotic airs winning enthusiastic appreciation, and there was a spirit of good comradeship, which, combined with that of hospitality, made of the occasion a charming success.

AT THE DRIVING CLUB

Following the entertainment at the University Club, many of the guests went to the Piedmont Driving Club, where the visitors from New York were the hosts at a concert, when the famous New York Old Guard band played, and there were refreshments and an informal dance. The entire club-house was decorated in red, white and blue, and there were brilliant illuminations and flowers.

Mrs. James H. Nunnally, President of the Club, the officers of the Club, and other prominent Atlanta people assisted the New York hosts in the entertainment of the guests. There were several hundred present.

ARTILLERY TO ENTERTAIN

The Ancient and Honorable Artillery, of Boston, will give a reception tonight at the Piedmont Hotel in compliment to the D. A. R. in Atlanta, the guests to include also the visiting D. A. R.'s.

The compliment is peculiarly appropriate, since Craigie House, the former home of the Atlanta Chapter, D. A. R., was the gift of the State of Massachusetts, and the new Chapter House counts as its most valued feature, the table commemorating that gift and explaining its part in the present new home.

TO THE OLD GUARD

Messrs. George and Charles Sciple, of the Atlanta Old Guard, will be the hosts at a luncheon to be given the Old Guard of New York and their party today at 1 o'clock, at the Piedmont Driving Club, the occasion to be one of the happiest of the many during the Peace exercises.

The following editorial is a fitting close to the Atlanta *Constitution's* accounts of the great parade of October 10, 1911.

THE SECTIONS KNOW EACH OTHER

Some years ago Joel Chandler Harris wrote an editorial on "Neighbor Knowledge." It was a masterful treatment, in his quiet but incisive way, of the obligations and advantages that flowed from neighbor to neighbor, and of the manner almost magical, in which fancied or real differences took wings as the men who had held them came into closer and more understanding relations.

The philosophy may aptly be applied on the day following the unveiling of the Peace Monument, erected by the Old Guard of the Gate City Guard, and the day also that brings finale to the celebration so long in planning and contemplation.

The sections now know each other thoroughly. The process has been made possible by such events as those of this week, as it was given perceptible impetus by the far-away invasion of the North by the Gate City Guard in 1879, and the fraternal reception accorded them by the prominent Northerners whom it is the privilege of Atlanta to entertain.

The reconstruction immediately following the war was not a reconstruction at all. Time only can obliterate misunderstandings, kindle generosity, engender toleration and rebuild the conceptions and practices of a national citizenship.

And time, aided by such mutual interchanges as we have this week witnessed, has accomplished the task. In the stress of the war's aftermath, Benjamin Harvey Hill told the United States Senate, "We are back in the house of our fathers, and we are here to stay, thank God." But the genuine renationalization of the South came only with later years. Imaginary and genuine divergences, political and economic factors, and influences that now seem bogies, for a considerable interval kept the South more or less isolated from the nation, and the nation from the South.

The bonds of common interests, the forces of mutual standards, the marvelous growth of the whole country as a factor in international counsels have broken the barriers, and today the nation rejoices in that destiny which the South faces and which her own people hardly comprehend in its vastness.

Our distinguished visitors of this week have seen everywhere evidences of a new and an electrical South. But it is merely a dim forecast of the South of tomorrow, and of its looming importance to the country-at-large. Many experts of national and international vision have told us that material empire is to swing southward of Mason and Dixon's line. America as a whole nation will be sharer in the rich development of that day. And the factor most strongly contributory to its dawning is the welding of the sections by the amalgam of mutual knowledge and fraternity. Posterity will hold in due gratitude the men on both sides who have facilitated the process.

We complete the story of the memorable parade in Atlanta and incidents connected with it by the following clippings from the Atlanta *Journal* of October 11, 1911:

RECEPTION TO GOVERNOR BALDWIN AT UNIVERSITY CLUB

The beautiful reception at the University Club last evening in honor of Governor Simeon Eben Baldwin, of Connecticut, added another to the delightful entertainments for which the new club is making itself famous.

The new club-house, which was opened for the first time, formally, last evening, was beautifully decorated on the outside with flags and bunting, and within there were great vases of American Beauty roses and effective groups of palms and ferns.

In the receiving line with Governor Baldwin were the President, Mr. John M. Slaton, and his wife, and a number of the officers of the club and their wives. The officers are H. M. Atkinson, S. S. Wallace, J. H. Porter, vice-presidents; executive committee, Burton Smith, chairman, J. R. A. Hobson, Dr. Jas. N. Ellis, Ben Lee Crew, Hal F. Hentz; members of the council, H. C. Peeples, A. Ten Ecyk Brown, P. S. Arkwright, James S. Floyd, Alex. C. King, A. M. Schoen.

Bright music was played during the evening and the scene was made brilliant by the uniforms of the members of visiting troops, the Old Guard, the Fencibles, the Ancient and Honorables, the Fifth Maryland, Boston Light Infantry, Putnam Phalanx, Governor's Foot Guard, of Connecticut, and our own officers of the Department of the Gulf, and Atlanta and Georgia Regiments.

Delicious punch and refreshments were served during the evening.

GAYETIES AT THE PIEDMONT DRIVING CLUB

Following the reception at the University Club a number of the guests went to the Driving Club, where the Old Guard, of New York, entertained at a concert and informal dance, music being furnished by the Old Guard band of New York.

The club, which had been the scene of continued gayeties throughout the entire day, was filled, the ladies in lovely evening gowns and the bright uniforms of the visiting military who were the hosts of the occasion making a brilliant picture.

The club was beautifully decorated, the red, white and blue of the Stars and Stripes forming festoons in the ball room, where several great flags were draped above the mantel of the fire-place and the musician's balcony was screened with bunting and palms.

The buff and blue of the colonial uniforms of the Putnam Phalanx were a picturesque addition to the gay crowd, many of whom had been entertained at dinner at the club prior to the concert.

Among the dinners was that at which Mr. James L. Dickey entertained in honor of a number of distinguished visitors, his guests including Colonel Everett C. Benton, commander of the Ancient and Honorable Artillery Company, of Boston, Lieut. Harry Hamilton, Col. S. M. Hedges, Col. A. M. Ferris, Col. Rodney MacDonough, Maj. J. F. Burke, Mr. Robt. Maddox, Mr. Carroll Payne and Mr. Morris Brandon.

To Richmond Blues

A beautiful breakfast was given this morning at the Piedmont Driving Club in honor of the Richmond Blues, one of the interesting groups of visiting military who have a great many friends in the city and who made a great many more during their stay.

The long table in the dining room at which the young troopers and about twenty young ladies were seated had for its decoration quantities of red and white roses, in tall silver vases, and flags, and at intervals silver candelabra holding red-shaded candles. A delicious breakfast was served, the dishes being decorated with tiny red, white and blue flags.

The party was chaperoned by Mrs. J. R. A. Hobson, Mrs. John Hill, Mrs. Ben Lee Crew, Mrs. Emil Laurson.

Many Visit Peace Monument on Day After Dedication

Scores of visitors and Atlantans flocked to Piedmont Park Wednesday to see the Old Guard Peace Monument which was unveiled Tuesday. Many brought pencils and pads to copy the inscriptions on the monument, groups of soldiers stood about throughout the morning and dozens of photographers took snapshots as souvenirs. Hardly a person who went to the park or the Driving Club failed to go by the monument for a close inspection. The following are the inscriptions on the monument:

COLOR SERGEANT BEN LEE CREW.

"CEASE FIRING—PEACE IS PROCLAIMED"

Bronze figures on the Old Guard Monument in Piedmont Park, Atlanta, Ga.   The
Angel of Peace holding an olive branch, suddenly appears to the Confederate
Soldier who is about to fire, and announces that Peace is proclaimed.

SOUTH TABLET

CITIZENS' COMMITTEE

Louis Gholstin, Wm. M. Crumley, Wm. S. Elkin, J. Epps Brown, Wm. Hurd Hillyer, Milton M. Armstrong, Jas. R. Gray, W. W. Orr, Benj. B. Crew, W. Woods White, Wm. S. Whitham, Joseph Jacobs, Herbert L. Wiggs, W. T. Ashford, Sidney H. Phelan, Jno. A. Perdue, Jas. T. Orme, Victor Lamar Smith.

CHAMBER OF COMMERCE COMMITTEE

Fred J. Paxon, Asa G. Candler, J. K. Orr, Saml. D. Jones, Robt. J. Lowry, Jos. M. Terrell, Jno. E. Murphy, Mel. R. Wilkinson, David Woodward, J. H. Nunnally, Edward H. Inman, John M. Slaton, Jno. W. Grant, Saml. M. Inman, Henry S. Johnson, Alex. W. Smith, Wilmer L. Moore, Brooks Morgan, Clark Howell, J. T. Holleman, F. L. Seely, Walter G. Cooper, V. H. Kriegshaber.

NORTH TABLET

OLD GUARD MONUMENT COMMITTEE

Joseph F. Burke, F. J. Cooledge, John S. Owens, P. F. Clarke, George Winship, George McKenzie, Thomas C. Erwin, Chas. P. Byrd, Arch H. Davis, Saml. Meyer, Jr., Thos. H. Morgan, Jos. F. Gatins.

"OLD GUARD GENERAL COMMITTEE"

Thomas M. Clarke, Clifford L. Anderson, J. J. Haverty, W. H. Franklin, H. P. Hall, Henry C. Beerman, J. Charles Gavan, W. V. McMillan, Macon C. Sharp, T. J. Hightower, Jr., E. L. Bergstrom, W. L. Hancock, Floyd C. Fenn, G. C. Rogers, F. T. Ridge, H. A. Daniels, Paul Burkert, Frank M. Berry, H. L. Collier, W. B. Cummings, W. A. Graham. H. F. Scott, R. H. Comer, Frank C. Smillie, W. T. Kuhns, J. Van Holt Nash, J. P. Selby, Chas. E. Sciple, W. E. Hancock.

FRONT TABLET

THE GATE CITY GUARD

Captain G. Harvey Thompson

In the conscientious conviction of their duty to uphold the cause of the Southern Confederacy, offered their services to the Governor of Georgia, and were enrolled in the Confederate Army April 3rd, 1861.

Inspired with the same sincerity of purpose, and accepting in good faith the result of that heroic struggle,

THE GATE CITY GUARD

Under the Command of

Captain Joseph F. Burke

Desiring to restore fraternal sentiment among the people of all sections of our country, and ignoring sectional animosity, on October 6th, 1879, went forth to greet their former adversaries in the Northern and Eastern States, inviting them to unite with the people of the South to heal the nation's wounds in a peaceful and prosperous reunion of the States. This "Mission of Peace" was enthusiastically endorsed by the military and citizens in every part of the Union, and this Monument is erected as an enduring testimonial to their patriotic contribution to the cause of national fraternity.

DEDICATED OCTOBER 10, 1911

by

HOKE SMITH, and SIMEON E. BALDWIN,

Governor of Georgia. Governor of Connecticut.

EAST TABLET

This Monument is a Memorial to the Governors, Mayor and Councils, and Military Organizations that endorsed the Guards' "Mission" A. D. 1879, and which they ratified thirty-two years afterwards, by their presence at its dedication, Oct. 10, 1911.

State of Georgia. Alfred H. Colquitt, Gov., 1879; Hoke Smith, Gov., 1911.

National Guard of Georgia, City of Atlanta. W. L. Calhoun, Mayor, 1879; Courtland S. Winn, Mayor, 1911.

State of Maryland. John Lee Carroll, Gov., 1879; Austin L. Crothers, Gov., 1911.

City of Baltimore. F. C. Latrobe, Mayor, 1879; James H. Preston, Mayor, 1911.

Fifth Regiment Infantry, Maryland. Wm. P. Zollinger, Col., 1879; Louis Murray Rawlins, Col., 1911.

City of Philadelphia. W. S. Stokeley, Mayor, 1879; John E. Reyburn, Mayor, 1911.

Battalion of State Fencibles, Philadelphia. J. W. Ryan, Major, 1879; Thurber T. Brazer, Major, 1911.

Veteran Corps, State Fencibles, Philadelphia. Emanuel Furth, Comd., 1911.

State of New York. Lucius Robinson, Gov., 1879; John Alden Dix, Gov., 1911.

City of New York. Edward Cooper, Mayor, 1879; Wm. L. Gaynor, Mayor, 1911.

Seventh Regiment Infantry, N. G., N. Y. Emmons Clarke, Col., 1879; Daniel Appleton, Col., 1911; Geo. P. Barrett, Capt., 1879; Geo. B. Rhoads, Lieut., 1879.

Old Guard of New York. G. W. McLean, Major, 1879; S. Ellis Briggs, Major, 1911.

Twenty-First Infantry, N. G., N. Y. Alfred Lindley, Col., 1879.

State of Connecticut. Chas. B. Andrews, Gov., 1879; Simeon E. Baldwin, Gov., 1911.

City of Hartford. Geo. C. Sumner, Mayor, 1879; Edward L. Smith, Mayor, 1911.

Putnam Phalanx, Hartford. F. M. Brown, Major, 1879; E. C. Bigelow, Major, 1911.

First Company, Governor's Footguard, Hartford. Geo. B. Fisher, Major, 1879; Frank L. Wilcox, Major, 1911.

Sedgwick Guard, Waterbury. C. R. Bannon, Capt., 1879.

State of Massachusetts. Thomas Tolbert, Gov., 1879; Eugene M. Foss, Gov., 1911.

City of Boston. Frederick O. Prince, Mayor, 1879; Jno. F. Fitzgerald, Mayor, 1911.

Ancient and Honorable Artillery Company, Boston. Chas. W. Wilder, Comd., 1879; Everett C. Benton, Comd., 1911.

Boston Light Infantry. Wm. H. Thomes, Capt., 1879; Conrad M. Gerlach, Capt., 1911.

Boston Light Infantry, Veteran Corps. John K. Hall, Comd., 1879; Wm. H. Jackson, Comd., 1911.

Sherman Cadets, Lawrence, Mass. L. N. Duchesney, Capt., 1879; Louis S. Cox, Capt., 1911.

Lawrence Light Infantry, Mass. D. F. Dolan, Capt., 1879.

Richmond Light Infantry Blues, Virginia. John S. Wise, Capt., 1879; Edgar W. Bowles, Maj., 1911.

Richmond Howitzers, Virginia. R. C. Wortham, Capt., 1879; Wm. M. Meyers, Capt., 1911.

Washington Light Infantry, District of Columbia. Wm. G. Moore, Col., 1879.

Indianapolis Light Infantry, Indiana. Nicholas R. Ruckle, Capt., 1879; Geo. S. Greene, Capt., 1911.

Rockford Rifles, Illinois. Thos. C. Lawler, Capt., 1879; W. S. Woodburn, Capt., 1911.

Fifth Regiment, Maryland, Veteran Corps. G. W. Hyde, Comdr.

Company B, Second Infantry, Illinois. E. P. O'Connor, Capt., 1879.

Detroit Light Infantry, Michigan, Chas. DuPont, Capt., 1879; J. Edw. Dupont, 1911.

Janesville Guards, Wisconsin. H. M. Smith, Capt., 1879.

Governor's Guards, Columbia, S. C. Willie Jones, Capt., 1879; Dibert Jackson, Capt., 1911.

Richland Volunteer Rifle Company, Columbia, S. C. R. A. Keenan, Capt., 1879; Jas. H. Hammond, Capt., 1911.

Richland Dragoons, Columbia, S. C. Charles A. Laughton, Capt., 1879.

German Huzzars, Charleston, S. C. C. Keike, Capt., 1879.

Mobile Cadets, Alabama. Wm. S. Brainard, Capt., 1879; John W. Rutherford, Capt., 1911.

Mobile Rifle Company, Alabama. Price Williams, Jr., Capt., 1879; John A. Mahon, Capt., 1911.

Montgomery True Blues, Alabama. Jno. G. Winter, Capt., 1879; P. O. Franson, Capt., 1911.

Montgomery Greys, Alabama, E. A. Graham, Capt., 1879; J. A. Davidson, Capt., 1911.

Eufaula Light Infantry, Alabama. C. C. Shorter, Capt., 1879.

Governor's Guard, Springfield, Ill. John J. Brinkerhoff, Capt., 1879.

Washington Artillery, New Orleans, La. W. Miller Owen, Major, 1879; Allison Owen, Major, 1911.

Nashville Light Dragoons, Tennessee. George L. Cowan, Capt., 1879.

Hornet's Nest Rifles, Charlotte, N. C. C. A. Brockenbrough, Capt., 1879.

Military Companies Guests of Charleston

"Charleston, S. C., Oct. 11.—Gov. Simeon E. Baldwin, his staff and the First Company, Governor's Foot Guard, of Hartford, Conn., arrived this morning from Atlanta, where they have been attending the ceremonies incident to the unveiling of the Peace Monument.

"The New Englanders were greeted at the Union Station by a committee headed by Mayor Rhett. An escort from the National Guard was present.

"A program of entertainment was at once taken up. The Putnam Phalanx, of Hartford, also spent the day in Charleston, coming separately. The historic Foot Guard has been in Charleston before. The old continental uniform of the Putnam Phalanx enthused the Charlestonians."

These two incidents clipped from the *Georgian* have also an appropriate place in the story of the visit of our brothers from the North:

"Col. Joseph F. Burke wore Tuesday a handsome gold medal that was presented him thirty-two years ago, when he commanded the Old Guard on their Northern tour in 1879. He was entertained in Boston by the Light Infantry and was given this medal by them.

"His appreciation of it and the fact that he had kept it to wear on the day when the men of the North came South to return that visit went to the hearts of the Tigers, and they all crowded around him to look at the medal and congratulate the wearer."

The Boston Light Infantry Give Old Guard Unique Souvenir of Visit

"As a 'peace offering' to the Old Guard of Atlanta, the Boston Light Infantry presented Col. J. F. Burke Tuesday afternoon with a handsome projectile which was made specially for the occasion and appropriately engraved.

"The projectile is an exact model of the regulation six-inch shell used by the United States artillerymen and is made of German pewter, silver-plated. Surmounting the shell is an American eagle and below that the coat of arms of Massachusetts and the crest of the Boston Light Infantry.

"Deeply engraved on the face of the offering appear the words, 'To the Old Guard of the Gate City Guard, Atlanta, Ga., from the Boston Light Infantry, October 9, 1911.'

"The presentation was made by Major Gerlach and his staff, who stated that when their company found it impossible to bring a large number of men to Atlanta, they determined to show in some way their appreciation of the Old Guard and the invitation to take part in the exercises.

"In addition to the projectile, the Light Infantry brought with them hundreds of bronze badges, bearing the tiger head and with 'Tigers' across the bar on which the pin was fastened. They decorated every member of the Old Guard they could find and placed them on the coats of prominent Atlantans who were on the receiving committee."

The following incidents are gathered from the *Georgian*, published after the departure of the visitors from the North:

THE SOLDIERS ARE GONE, BUT NOT FORGOTTEN

In the soldiers of the North and the South Tuesday the spirit of the true American was shown. To every one who took part in the parade and dedication exercises, from the oldest member of the Confederate veteran corps or the Putnam Phalanx, to the youngest cadet in the college division, the affair was a hardship. Five miles were marched through the rain. Then followed a stand of an hour or so in the mud with rain pouring down upon them, after which came another five-mile march back to quarters. But not one faltered.

Notwithstanding the rain, the men stood in ranks until the call of the barbecue was heard. Then at commands from officers, they broke ranks and devoured with a will the many pounds of meat and brunswick stew that the committee had prepared.

After that came the march back to quarters through the rain, but arriving there with hearts as light as ever, the soldiers slipped into dry uniforms and were shortly afterward again on the streets, having the time of their lives.

For many of the Northern soldiers, Tuesday's barbecue was the first they had ever attended. They knew what to expect in the meat line, but when brunswick stew came on the table they were purely perplexed. Three steaming pans of the Southern dish were placed on one of the tables. The soldiers gazed wonderingly at it for a moment.

"What is it?" asked one.

"Don't know," said another, "but I'll try anything once."

"Fine!" he exclaimed, as he smacked his lips after the first taste.

And a minute or two later three bowls of brunswick stew had been rapidly emptied.

Not one of the visitors but will be sorry to leave Atlanta. The people of Atlanta and the military of the State have been untiring in their efforts to make the soldiers from the North feel at home, and their efforts are appreciated. But for the rain Tuesday the affair would have been one grand success from start to finish.

Taft Hall, Auditorium-Armory, was Tuesday night the scene of a smoker tendered to the visiting troops and the local soldiers by a special committee of the Old Guard reception committee.

The smoker began at 8 o'clock and lasted until 10 o'clock and was attended by fully 2,000 soldiers, the spacious hall being packed to its capacity, practically everyone remaining until the last song was sung and the final handshake given.

The Old Guard of New York. When they formed and how did they ever get to be called "old?" is the question that is on the lips of hundreds of Atlantans who want to know something of the splendid New York Company.

The Old Guard came into existence as the result of the union of two crack military companies in the City of New York. Way back in 1826 the Light Guards were formed. In 1833 the City Guards came into being. Both companies numbered the leading men of their city in their ranks and there was much rivalry in military affairs between the pair.

After the war was over the survivors of the two companies met again at home. There were not enough men to make up two companies and so, softened by the struggles together on the field of battle, the two companies became one and called themseleves the "Old Guard."

"Well, there's one thing going to happen as the result of my trip South," said Major Francis H. Hessels, of the New York Old Guard. "My boy is now about 28 years old and has determined to sell out his business and go West. A former school-mate of his is out there and has written again and again for him to come out. We discussed the matter and I told him to make up his own mind about it. Now, I've been here and seen the South and Atlanta and talked to a number of your prominent men, and if I've got anything to do with it, that boy of mine is coming right down here and go into business."

Major Hessels and J. E. McClelland, of Atlanta, got to talking about business conditions in the South, and Atlanta, in particular, and the Northern veteran was so pleased with accounts he heard of the city, that he made up his mind to persuade his son to come here.

Maj. Hessels is quite proud of a badge which he possesses. He was asked about it Tuesday night and told how he came by it. The State of New York presents to its National Guardsmen a badge for 10, 20 and 25 years faithful service. Last May the Major had completed 20 years and was given the beautiful gold and bronze medal, with a handsomely engraved certificate to accompany it.

The medal given at the end of 25 years is of gold, and the Major says he will certainly stay in the company long enough to earn one of them.

Robert Gwaltney Merritt, member of the Seventh Regiment of New York, was present during the Old Guard celebration. He accepted the invitation of Col. Joseph F. Burke to become a member of his staff.

Mr. Merritt is a brother of Dr. Simon Wickes Merritt, superintendent of the Atlanta Tuberculosis Sanitarium.

One of the prettiest incidents of the Old Guard celebration in Atlanta was the meeting between D. A. O'Mara, of the Fifty-ninth New York, and Dr. E. G. Jensen, of the Forty-eighth Georgia. The New Yorker had come South with the Old Guard and the Southerner had traveled over 100 miles from his home in Allentown to greet him. Together they stood at the capitol under the banner of the Forty-eighth Georgia, which Dr. Jensen had dropped at Gettysburg nearly 50 years ago.

The two men had never met before and their acquaintance started through the efforts of Dr. Jensen to locate the flag of his regiment. When a number of Confederate flags were returned to the South several years ago Dr. Jensen was incorrectly informed that the flag of the Forty-eighth was not one of those returned. He at once set out to find it and wrote a number of letters to various officials in the North. He was referred to Mr. O'Mara, as one of the survivors of the regiment that captured the banner. Through his efforts he found the flag to be here in the State capitol.

The correspondence started between the two veterans in finding the flag was kept up and when Dr. Jensen learned that Mr. O'Mara was a member of the New York Old Guard and would come to Atlanta, he also came here.

Tuesday morning the two veterans met for the first time in their lives and went to the capitol, where they got permission to take the battle-scarred flag out of its case and together they stood under its folds and shook hands on eternal friendship as men and as veterans of the Blue and Gray.

Dr. Jensen left Tuesday afternoon, after urging his friend to accompany him to his home and stay with him. Mr. O'Mara said that he could not do so at this time, but promises that if ever he gets in the South again he is going to visit Dr. Jensen.

The story of the capture of the flag of the Forty-eighth Georgia by the Fifty-ninth New York troops is an interesting one and brings out the bravery of the men who wore the Gray. The Forty-eighth was ordered to charge up a steep hill, on the top of which the Fifty-ninth Regiment was entrenched. Going up the hill the Southern banner fell four times and as many men were shot down. Dr. Jensen was the fifth man to bear the flag in that short dash and as he reached the Federal breastworks a shot tore into his thigh and he fell also. The flag was taken by the Northern troops and sent to Washington, from whence nearly 50 years later its return was to bring about the meeting of the two men who had faced each other across the raking fire of opposing armies.

The Boston Light Infantry, or Boston Tigers, as they are better known, paraded Tuesday in the uniform of artillerymen. The men who were the representatives of their regiment in Atlanta belong also to the crack artillery company of the Massachusetts National Guard, and hold the record for proficiency in shooting with service charges, and so when they came to Atlanta they wore the artillery uniform of which they are so justly proud.

"I met a splendid example of real Southern hospitality Tuesday," said Capt. William H. Jackson, commander of the veteran organization of the Boston Tigers.

"When the parade was over I crawled into an empty automobile to escape the rain. A few minutes later the owner came up, and I started to get out, but he would not hear of it, and introduced himself. He was Judge —oh, Judge somebody or other. I would give anything to recall his name. You know he would not hear of anything but that he must take me back to my hotel, and on the way we picked up about four other Northerners, and piled them in the car, and took the whole crowd back to town.

"Now that is what I call personal hospitality, and I want space enough

JOS. A. McCORD.

DR. E. J. SPRATLING.

JNO. S. OWENS.

J. D. CLOUDMAN.

in your paper to say that I appreciate it and feel like it is worth while coming South to learn how you folks do carry out your ideas of hospitality."

"Say," said one of the Tigers, "I don't know what you fellows put in that brunswick stew you gave us at the barbecue, but that is the best stuff I ever ate in my life, and, believe me, I ate it, too," he added, with a reminiscent smack of his lips. The Boston infantrymen took in the barbecue and say they enjoyed it, even if the weather did try to keep them away.

Col. J. F. Burke wore Tuesday a handsome gold diamond mounted medal that was presented him 32 years ago, when he commanded the Old Guard on their tour. He was entertained in Boston by the Light Infantry and was given this medal by them. His appreciation of it and the fact that he had kept it to wear on the day when the men of the North came South to return that visit, went to the hearts of the Tigers, and they all crowded around him to look at the medal and to congratulate the wearer.

Major Gerlach, who is commanding the Boston Light Infantry, brought his wife and mother to Atlanta with him. They will not return to Boston with the Major and his company Wednesday, but expect to spend the winter in Florida. Major Gerlach, who is stopping with his company at the Imperial Hotel, was loud in his praise of the Atlanta hotel service.

"Why, let me tell you," he said, "I've traveled a great deal, and I want to say that you fellows have got some of the best and most up-to-date hotels right here in Atlanta that I've ever been in."

In an incredibly short time after these events the people of Atlanta crowded the Savoy to witness again the march of the Northern and Southern veterans through the rain, reproduced with wonderful accuracy by the moving pictures. These were seen and admired in many other cities and towns of the Union.

As the first anniversary of the unveiling of the Old Guard Monument drew near, the Old Guard members, who had provided a handsome new uniform, made ready for a grand reception at the Auditorium, on October 10, 1912. A large number of artistically engraved invitations were sent to friends of the Old Guard at home and abroad for the reception.

Sponsors and maids of honor were chosen from among the most prominent ladies of the city. The Governor and his staff, and Genl. A. K. Evans, commanding the Department of the Gulf, and staff received invitations, as did also representatives of the Georgia National Guard.

Atlanta young ladies, styled the "Invincibles" Battalion of the Old Guard, were especially drilled for the occasion.

The exercises of the evening began with the entrance of the Old Guard in their fatigue uniforms, a grand march and a drill by a company of the G. M. A. Cadets, who did guard duty that night.

There was dancing of the old-time minuet, gracefully executed by Atlanta girls and matrons in colonial costumes, and with coiffures of powdered hair. Another favorite of ante-bellum days, the old Virginia reel, was danced by Atlanta debutantes.

The grand and most spectacular feature of the occasion occurred when the Old Guard Battalion entered the vast auditorium, preceded by their band. At once the audience of more than three thousand arose from their seats, the gentlemen applauding and the ladies waving handkerchiefs. The Guards' rythmic step and dignified carriage captured the audience at once, and the salute of the young ladies' battalion of "Invincibles" to the Guard was gracefully done and as promptly returned by the battalion. The "Invincibles" wore the coat of arms of the Old Guard on their breasts, and white and blue sashes over their evening costumes.

The presentation to the Guard of two large silk flags was another interesting feature of the evening. Governor Brown, accompanied by Adj.-Gen. J. Van Holt Nash, and Col. Joseph Brown Connally, and flanked on the right side by Miss Bessie Brady and her three maids of honor, Miss Marian Goldsmith, Miss Ruth Reed, and Miss Katie Sturdivan, carrying the National flag, and on the left by Mrs. J. Powers Pace, and her maids, Miss Sarah Coats, Miss Mignon McCarty and Miss Theo Prioleau, carrying the beautiful white battalion flag. The presentation was made by Governor Brown, and the colors were received by Col. J. F. Burke, who responded to Governor Brown's speech. At a late hour the Old Guards' reception and ball came to an end and hosts and guests went their respective ways, feeling that the recollections of that delightful evening would long abide and be a source of lasting pleasure.

Scarcely had the Old Guard completed one pleasant entertainment before its various committees began to plan other schemes, combining pleasure with patriotic sentiment. It was decided to visit again the cities of the Middle and Eastern States.

The first stop was to be Richmond, the home of the South's finest mili-

tary organization; thence to Washington to greet the first Southerner, who in
many years, had filled the Presidential chair; from thence to Baltimore;
thence crossing the old Mason and Dixon's line, the next stop was to be at
Philadelphia, the home of the Fencibles. Then they were to go to New York
where they would meet the Seventh Regiment and the Old Guard of New
York. At Hartford, Connecticut, the Governor's Foot Guard and the Putnam Phalanx waited to do them honor. At Boston, the Ancient and Honorable Artillery, the Boston Light Infantry and the Veteran Corps were waiting
to give them the glad hand. Thence the plan was to return by sea to Savannah, and after a day or two in the lovely Forest City, by invitation of
the Georgia Hussars, Capt. Frank McIntyre; then to return home to Atlanta.

The following is the Guards' itinerary:

Leave Atlanta, 11:30 A. M., Monday, May 19th, Southern Ry.
Arrive Washington, 7:00 A. M., Tuesday, May 20th, Southern Ry.
Leave Washington, Midnight, Tuesday, May 20th, Penna. R. R.
Arrive Baltimore, 8:00 A. M., Wednesday, May 21st, Penna. R. R.
Leave Baltimore, Midnight, Wednesday, May 21st, Penna. R. R.
Arrive Philadelphia, 7:00 A. M., Thursday, May 22nd, Penna. R. R.
Leave Philadelphia, 10:00 A. M., Saturday, May 24th, Penna. R. R.
Arrive New York, 12:30 Noon, Saturday, May 24th, Penna. R. R.
Leave New York, 3:00 P. M., Wed., May 28th, N. Y., N. H. & H.
Arrive Boston, 8:30 P. M., Wed., May 28th, N. Y., N. H. & H.
Leave Boston, 6:00 P. M., Friday, May 30th, Fall River Line.
Arrive New York, 7:00 A. M., Saturday, May 31st, Fall River Line.
Leave New York, 3:00 P. M. Saturday, May 31st, O. S. S. Company.
Arrive Savannah, 6:00 A. M., Tuesday, June 3rd, O. S. S. Company.
Leave Savannah, 8:00 P. M., Tuesday, June 3rd, C. of Ga. Ry.
Arrive Atlanta, 6:25 A. M., Wednesday, June 4th, C. of Ga. Ry.

Thirty-four years had passed since the Guard had made their patriotic
tour of national reconciliation to the Northern and Eastern cities, and the
friendly associations then formed continued through the intervening years as
was amply evidenced by the large number of military organizations and civic
bodies that responded to the Guards' invitation to visit Atlanta and dedicate
the monument that commemorated that peaceful mission of years ago, when
the Guard, carrying the National flag, went forth to extend the hand of pa-

triotic fellowship to their former adversaries in the war between the States. Many friendly letters had been received from Northern friends when it became known through the press that the Old Guard contemplated another visit over their former route of travel. Editorially, the Atlanta *Constitution* comments as follows:

THE OLD GUARDS' INVASION

Carrying the blended greetings of the old and the new South to their friends of the North, the Old Guard, of the Gate City Guard, of Atlanta, will shortly embark on a peaceful invasion of the North.

The present year of Civil War semi-centennial anniversaries offers an especially appropriate occasion for a return of the visit paid Atlanta by prominent Eastern military organizations upon the occasion of the dedication of the Old Guard Peace Monument. At that time many of the most historic and picturesque military aggregations in the country were the guests of Atlanta. Now, the Old Guard, under the command of Col. J. F. Burke, are going to tour the North, visiting Washington, Philadelphia, Baltimore, New York and other cities. In each place they will be the guests of the men to whom they played host in Atlanta, and in Washington they will be tendered a brilliant reception by President Wilson.

At Boston will come, from the historic stand-point, the crowning event of the trip. Concurrently with the presence in that city of the Old Guard, the local command of the Grand Army of the Republic is to decorate a monument to the Federal survivors of the Civil War. The occasion will be one of notable military display participated in by all Boston. To the Old Guard, of Atlanta, representatives at once of the old and the new South, is to be given the high honor of heading the parade, which will traverse the city before reaching the monument. Arriving there the Old Guard will place a large wreath of flowers from Atlanta on the shaft on Boston Common.

No more conclusive or poetically fitting evidence could be given of the complete disappearance of sectional animosity, the final bridging of the sectional gulf, than is supplied by this incident. In its way it will be a spectacle as dramatic and fitting as was the first invasion of the North by the Old Guard, made when wounds from the Civil War were freshly rankling. It will indicate that we are, indeed, "back in the house of our fathers," thrice welcome, and there without condition or qualification.

The battalion met at the Piedmont Hotel in accordance with the orders issued by Col. Burke, at 10 A. M., May 19, 1913, and preceded by the band, and the escort of officers of the Fifth Regiment, Georgia National Guard, they marched to the Terminal Station, applauded by the people along the line of march. A great crowd had gathered at the station to bid the Guard *bon voyage*, and without loss of time, they boarded the special train that was to take them to Washington, D. C.

On the morning of their arrival, May 20th, in that city, they were met by Congressman Schley Howard and military officers, and preparations were made to visit President Wilson and Mrs. Wilson at the White House. It was the intention of the Guard to take a huge floral design to Mrs. Wilson, made of flowers grown in her native city, Rome, Ga., but the long drought made that impossible, and a large bouquet of Georgia roses were presented to her. The President had named half past two o'clock to receive the Old Guard. The Washington *Herald* gives the following account of the visit to President and Mrs. Wilson:

That time heals all wounds was demonstrated yesterday by the triumphant march of the Old Guard, of the Gate City Guard, of Atlanta, Ga., down historic Pennsylvania Avenue to the White House, where they were received in the East Room by President and Mrs. Wilson.

Just thirty-five years ago this same famous organization of warriors, with the battles of the Civil War still fresh in their memory, made an extended tour of "Yankee Land," for the sole purpose of bringing to an end the intense sectional feeling then existing between the North and the South.

The enthusiastic cheering which was accorded the Old Guard yesterday on its march to the Executive Manison was in keeping with the reception accorded them thirty-four years ago. Yesterday thousands of persons on the Avenue paused on their way to give cordial welcome to the veterans from Dixie Land.

The Old Guard is one of the most famous military organizations in the South. On its roster are members of the best Southern families of the South. The right to serve in the Old Guard is handed down from father to son. Many of the gray-haired veterans who marched down the Avenue yesterday recalled the march of thirty-four years ago. Marching next to some white-haired veteran would be the youthful descendant of the original member of

CORPORAL E. L. BERGSTROM.   SERGT. W. A. HAYGOOD, JR.

COLORS OF THE OLD GUARD BATTALION.

the Guard who marched in that identical place in the line during the early days of its organization.

The Old Guard were escorted to the White House by a battalion of the District National Guard, with Major W. A. McCathran, Capt. W. H. Chase, Capt. W. A. Renmeyer, Lieut. and Adj. Geo. A. Monajan, Lieut. and O. M. W. A. Wall, and the National Guard band. The Old Guard wore their dress uniforms and made a picturesque sight. Their huge black fur shakos made them look like giants. The yards of gold lace on their white dress coats with collars of dark blue made their uniforms rival those of a German Hussar. At the head of the column marched their old-time commander, Colonel J. F. Burke.

President Wilson received the Old Guard in the East Room. Senator Hoke Smith presented each of the members of the Guard to President and Mrs. Wilson. Representatives Howard, Hardwick and Burnett were also present at the White House reception. A most enjoyable automobile ride around the suburbs of Washington was given by the military officers of the local troops, which terminated in an elaborate dinner.

On the arrival of the Old Guard in Baltimore, Wednesday, May 21, they were met at the train by Col. Jno. Hinkly and officers of the Fifth Regiment of Maryland, who accompanied them to their hotel. A delightful visit to Annapolis was planned by the officers of the regiment for the Old Guard and their ladies for the afternoon, and in the evening there was a full dress reception at the armory of the regiment. A most creditable drill by a battalion of our companies in full dress uniform, commanded by Lieut.-Col. Washington Bowie, brought flattering applause from the Old Guard. Delightful music by the regiment band, refreshments and dancing until midnight, while old friends and memories were the toasts of the evening.

The arrival of the Old Guard in Philadelphia on the morning of May 22, was an event of general public interest, as was demonstrated by the cheers of the people as they marched from the Broad Street Station escorted by the State Fencibles. It was the one hundredth anniversary of the organization of the Fencible Battalion, and it was thirty-four years since the Old Guard, of the Gate City Guard, visited them in the "Quaker City," when they came on the fraternal mission to heal the old wounds of the Civil War. Soon after their arrival the Old Guard, with the ladies accompanying them, were taken by steamer to League Island, which was an enjoyable sea voyage, and given a delightful planked shad dinner on arrival. Returning to their hotel, the ladies found an invitation to attend a dinner given by a committee of ladies, while the members of the Guard were escorted to the Belleview-Stratford Hotel, for an extensive display of, and indulgence in, buffet delicacies, and tempting liquid nectars fit for the gods of old, all of which was followed by an artistic vaudeville performance in the theatre of the hotel.

The next day, May 23, was the culmination of the anniversary ceremonies in one of the most spectacular and largest parades ever seen in Philadelphia. A number of visiting military organizations from New Haven, Boston, New York and other cities, arrived in time to take part in the parade. The Old Guard of Georgia traveled the longest distance to greet their old friends. The sidewalks were crowded with people and the different organizations received generous applause as they passed, while the Old Guard of Georgia, in their white coats, and black bear-skin shakos, their beautiful battalion flags, memories of the Civil War and their "mission of peace" to Philadelphia thirty-four years ago when they were the guests of the Fencibles, brought from the crowds continued applause along the line of march. The next day, with many good-byes and good wishes, the Guard entrained for New York.

At two thirty P. M., on Saturday, May 24, they arrived at New York and went to their hotel to rest and recuperate from the strenuous activities of the week. But friends soon began to call and the theatres entertained most of the Old Guard during the evening.

On Monday the Old Guard of New York, Maj. S. Ellis Briggs, were the hosts at an elaborate dinner in honor of the Old Guard of Georgia. This function was a most interesting one, where wit and wisdom mingled with oratory until near midnight and old friendships were recalled and renewed.

The following day the officers of the Seventh Regiment, New York National Guard, held a reception for the Georgians at their large and beautiful armory on Madison Avenue. The officers met the Old Guard at the main entrance and the introductions being soon over, Col. Daniel Appleton, accompanied by his staff escorted the Old Guard through the armory. Every company room, the large drill hall, the officers' rooms, the stair-cases, all gave evidence of the most scrupulous care, while portraits of the officers in the rooms called to the minds of the Old Guard members the officers who greeted them thirty-four years ago when on their "tour of peace." Then came an elaborate luncheon when toasts and old friends of former years were brought vividly to mind. Col. Appleton read from the regimental record of the visit of the Old Guard to New York in October, 1879, when they were the guests of the regiment, then commanded by Col. Emmons Clark.

CLARK'S HISTORY OF THE SEVENTH REGIMENT (October, 1879).

Page 273:

The Gate City Guard, of Atlanta, Ga., Capt. Burke commanding, arrived in New York on the 11th of October, and was received by the Fifth and Ninth Companies. The drill and discipline of the company was excellent; its officers and men were agreeable and intelligent gentlemen, and it was welcomed with generous hospitality. The march up Broadway, after passing the mayor and common council in review at the City Hall, was an ovation, and the Southern soldiers were handsomely entertained at the Seventh Regiment armory. On the 13th of October the Gate City Guard visited the public institutions at Blackwell's Island under escort of the Third Company, and the pleasures of the day terminated with a steamboat excursion on the Hudson River. The Fourth and Eighth Companies were the escort of the company on its departure for Boston.

Page 282, regarding Seventh Regiment Fair in 1880.

It is, perhaps, not invidious to mention the contribution of a valuable bale of cotton by the Gate City Guard of Atlanta, Ga. The cotton was grown in the city of Atlanta.

Col. Danl. Appleton, then in a short speech, extended a warm welcome to the Old Guard in the spirit of fraternity in which the two commands were brought together in 1879. Major Charles E. Lydecker, for thirty-five years a member and retired major of the regiment, made a very thoughtful and impressive speech on the same line. Col. J. F. Burke spoke feelingly of the friendly relations that have existed for so many years between the two commands, referring also to the long roll of officers of both organizations who have passed to the beyond.

The officers of the regiment had provided for the transportation of the Guard to their hotel, and with many farewells one of the most pleasant incidents of the Guards' tour terminated.

As the Old Guard expected to meet the Putnam Phalanx and the Foot Guard, both of Hartford, Connecticut, at Philadelphia, there was no stop to be made at that place, and instead the Old Guard accepted a very cordial invitation from the New Haven Grays, of Connecticut, to spend a few hours with them while on the road to Boston, which they did, and for which the Guard were well repaid. The Grays were the most generous of hosts. Capt. Harry C. Ward, their commander, was untiring in his attentions and it was with regret that the Guard could not lengthen their visit.

The Old Guard battalion reached Boston on the evening of May 28, and was welcomed by the officers of the Edw. W. Kingsley Post 113, Col. Alex. M. Ferriss, commander. Capt. Chas. H. Lake, of the Boston Light Infantry, Lieut. Chas. A. Lyman, of the Boston Light Infantry veterans, Col. Francis H. Appleton, commanding the Ancient and Honorable Artillery, of Massachusetts, and others.

The Boston *Post* editorially says:

THE DAY OF REMEMBERING

Memorial Day in Boston this year is made more suggestive and, perhaps, impressive, than usual, by the presence, as visitors here, of the men of the famous Gate City Old Guard, of Atlanta, Ga. When these Southerners, many of whom fought for the Confederacy, march into Boston Common and decorate the Soldiers' Monument there, a new precedent of fraternity and devotion to the flag will be set for other years to come.

The Boston papers were profusely illustrated with pictures of the Old Guard, Col. Burke, the commander, Col. Alex. M. Ferriss, of the Kingsley Post, G. A. R., Col. E. C. Benton, ex-commander of the Ancient and Honorables, Hon. Wm. C. Morse, orator of the day, and others, and outlined the program arranged for the Old Guard for their two days sojourn in Boston.

CHAPTER XII

The Boston *Globe* had the following editorial entitled "The Blue and the Gray."

OLD GUARD, OF THE GATE CITY GUARD, OF ATLANTA, GA.—THE BLUE AND THE GRAY

THE men who fought against members of the G. A. R. have come all the way from Atlanta, Ga., to show to the people of the North that all has been forgotten, and that there is only one country, the United States of America.

The Old Guard arrived here last night, having been ten days in coming as they had made stops at Washington, Baltimore, Philadelphia, New York and New Haven, where they had been wined and dined by Northern comrades. Wherever they went the right hand of fellowship was extended and their trip has been one round of pleasure since they left home.

Last night they were met by committees of the Ancient and Honorable Artillery Company, of Edward Kingsley Post No. 113, and the Boston

THE OLD GUARD ON BOSTON COMMON,

Returning from the decoration of the Monument of the Soldiers and Sailors who died in the Union Army and Navy during the "War between the States," 1861-1865.

Old Guard of the Gate City Guard of Atlanta, Ga., on Boston Common, May 30, 1915. Decoration of monument erected by Grand Army Post No. 113. (Edward F. Kingsley Post) Col. Alex. M. Ferris, Comd.

Light Infantry (Tigers) Veteran Corps. They were escorted to the hotel Brunswick and given a hearty welcome.

This morning the visitors were taken by the committee and business men of the city to places of historic interest and to the financial and shopping sections of the city.

At twelve thirty the members of the Ancients took a hand. Capt. Francis Hawkes Appleton, with some two score automobiles and as many members as guides, rode up to the hotel and took the visitors in tow. The objective point of the excursion was the beautiful estate at Belmont of Col. Everett C. Benton, past commander of the Ancients, and it was there that he tried to repay them for the many courtesies the Ancients received in Atlanta two years ago, when he commanded the delegation that went to assist the Old Guard in dedicating their Peace Monument in that city.

To reach Col. Benton's a circuitous route was taken. The first stop was at the base of the Bunker Hill Monument, where Col. Willis W. Stover made a short address, and the hosts and guests continued to Cambridge, where, under the Washington elm, Mayor Barry and several members of the city government were awaiting them.

The Mayor welcomed the visitors, wishing them a pleasant time and a safe return.

The next place visited was the monument on Lexington Green, and the town officials and a detail of the Minute Men, under command of Major Pierce, gave the Southerners a warm welcome, very different from that given the Britishers over a century ago.

Concord was next visited, and on their way back to Boston a long stay was made with Col. and Mrs. Benton. A bountiful luncheon had been prepared for the visitors and their hosts, and the ladies of the party were entertained by the Daughters of the Revolution.

They will return to Boston about 6 P. M. Before going to Faneuil Hall for the banquet which has been prepared by the Ancients, short exercises will be held at the head of State Street, in front of the old State House.

The ladies of the party will be taken to Point Shirley Club for tea, being the guests of Capt. and Mrs. J. Stearns Cushing. The program of the visitors tomorrow is to parade as escort to Edward W. Kingsley Post No. 113, participate in all the Post's exercises, and in the afternoon be the guests of honor at the banquet of the Post at the American House. They leave by Fall River boat train in the evening for New York, thence to Savannah, Ga., where they will be generously entertained.

The feature of the Memorial Day exercises in Boston tomorrow will be the presence of men who fought as soldiers of the Southern Confederacy, opposed to those who will tomorrow honor their deceased comrades by placing wreaths and bouquets of flowers on their graves and at the base of monuments dedicated to their memory.

From the Boston *Herald*:

ANCIENTS FETE GEORGIA CORPS—GATE CITY GUARD OF ATLANTA HERE—CORDIAL SENTIMENTS EXCHANGED

The Old Guard, of the Gate City Guard, of Atlanta, Ga., were the guests of the Ancient and Honorable Artillery Company last night at a banquet in the Ancient's armory, Faneuil Hall. While the forty members of the Old Guard of the South were being entertained by the Ancients, their wives were the guests at a reception given by the Woman's Relief Corps, of Edward W. Kingsley Post No. 113, G. A. R., at the Hotel Lenox.

The banquet at Faneuil Hall followed a day of entertainment, during which the visitors were taken in automobiles by the Ancients' committee to points of historic interest in Charlestown, Cambridge, Lexington and Concord. Col. F. H. Appleton, commander of the Ancients, presided at the banquet. Addresses typifying "the oneness of the North and South of today," and prophecies that "all future wars of this country will be fought under the Stars and Stripes" were made by speakers representing the visitors and their hosts.

The visitors were officially welcomed by Col. Appleton, and other Ancients who spoke were Col. Everett C. Benton, who entertained the visitors earlier in the day at his home in Belmont, and Col. Sidney M. Hedges. In the absence of Commander Col. J. F. Burke, of the Gate City Guard, remarks were made by Capt. F. J. Cooledge, J. R. Smith, Woods White, Lieut. Davis and First Sergeant Harrison Jones.

Memorial Day opened by the march of the Old Guard from their hotel, under the escort of the Boston Light Infantry, now the Second Coast Artillery, commanded by Capt. Hart, to join the Edward W. Kingsley Post No. 113, of the G. A. R., commanded by Col. Alex. M. Ferriss. The usual military salutes were given with old-time promptness and uniformity

AT THE SOLDIERS AND SAILORS MONUMENT ON BOSTON COMMON,
The Edward W. Kingsley Post No. 113, G. A. R. and Old Guard of Atlanta, Georgia,
October 30, 1913.

that might be a lesson to some of our younger militia men. The line of march was at once begun for the State Capitol. The common was crowded with people who were most generous in their applause as the column approached. The appropriate services in the flag room of the Capitol were impressive.

It was a short march from the Capitol to the Soldiers' and Sailors' Monument, on the common, where the crowd was greatest. The Old Guard and their escort halted about one hundred feet in front of the monument, Col. J. F. Burke, carrying a large wreath, with a broad ribbon across the center on which were the words: "From the Old Guard, of the Gate City Guard, Atlanta, Ga.", approached Col. Ferriss, and, saluting, placed the wreath at the base of the monument. Then followed the Old Guard in column of twos, each member carrying a small wreath, which were placed on each side of the large one. It was a beautiful and impressive sight which will not soon be forgotten by those who witnessed it.

Thirty-four years ago, the Old Guard were the guests of the city of Boston, and drilled on the common, not far from the location of the monu-

ment, which was not then erected.   They were here on a fraternal mission
to those who were their adversaries in the Civil War.   When the Ancient
and Honorable Artillery visited Atlanta in October, 1911, to participate in
the dedication of the Old Guard Monument, commemorating that visit to
Boston, Col. E. C. Benton and the Ancients quietly went to the cemetery
in Atlanta and placed flowers at the base of the Confederate Monument.   It
was not known who did this graceful act until after his departure for Boston.

After the decoration of the Soldiers' and Sailors' Monument, the Guard
were conducted to Tremont Temple which was crowded to its fullest capacity.
All along the line of march they were enthused by the plaudits of the people,
which were renewed as they entered the Temple.   On the stage were Col.
Alex. M. Ferriss, Hon. Wm. A. Morse, the orator of the day, Col. J. F.
Burke, of the Old Guard, and other gentlemen.   The stage was made beautiful with the large silk flags of the Old Guard and the Edw. W. Kingsley
Post, while the national red, white and blue hung from the balconies and
walls in great profusion.   The speech of the orator of the day was most appropriate in sentiment and forecasting a happy future for our united country,
in which the Old Guard led the way thirty-four years ago, when sectional
feeling prevailed to such an extent as to discourage all attempts to bring the
North and South together in a fraternal union.

The musical part of the program was carefully arranged so as to bring
out exquisite effects from organ, orchestra and the trained voices of one thousand children which blended in delightful harmony that charmed the great
audience into an almost breathless silence.   All this was most notable in the
crescendos and diminuendos during the rendering of the old song "Tenting
on the Old Camp Ground," which found its way to many a tender heart in
that great audience.

The day closed with a banquet to the Old Guard which measured
fully up to the congeniality of New England's proverbial hospitality.   The
band played "Dixie," the "Star-Spangled Banner," and "Maryland, My
Maryland," and patriotic enthusiasm poured out of all pores under which a
warm heart throbbed.

Col. Ferriss presided at the feast with Col. Burke on his left and Lieut.
Governor David I. Walsh* on his right, with representatives from the Mayor
and Council and other departments of State and city government.   Ex-Con-

*Mr. Walsh was elected Governor of Massachusetts in 1913.

gressman Samuel L. Powers was the Toastmaster. Governor Walsh spoke briefly, offering a flattering compliment to Georgia and the public work of the Old Guard in cementing the States in a stronger union, political and fraternal. All the speeches were impromptu and enjoyable. Col. Burke made the longest address, which was listened to with marked interest to the end, of which a few extracts are given below. Just as he was about to begin his speech, Hon. Wm. A. Morse approached him and pinned on his breast a handsome badge of the Edw. W. Kingsley Post No. 113, and announced that he was now an associate member of that Post. The pleasing incident was unanticipated and loudly applauded. Col. Burke in expressing his thanks addressed the hosts as "Fellow Colonels." Capt. W. M. Crumley, of the Confederate Army, was made an active member of the Post.

SPEECH AT BOSTON

Referring to the visit of the Gate City Guard, commanded by Capt. Burke, soon after the Civil War, he said:

"At that time there were 'carpers' and those who doubted our sincerity, and who sought to find a selfish motive underlying our presence in your city. Why was it that we came here thirty-four years ago? Was it with cringing flattery to the visitor, or to crook the pregnant hinges of the knee that thrift might come fawning? *No*, a thousand times *NO!* We came to meet you as man to man, heart to heart, and hand to hand in a fraternal bond of friendship for a closer union of all sections of our common country."

Referring to the "dark days" of the reconstruction period, he said: "There was, following the close of the war, a period of suffering for the Southern people more humiliating than the disasters resulting from the four years of strife and bloodshed, and I would not refer to it now were not this a day of memories. When the war closed, every city, village and hamlet throughout your great Eastern, Northern and Western country joined in grateful praise of your returning armies for the courage they displayed, and the suffering they had borne for the cause of the Union. Night was turned into day by illuminations; the air was rent with the reverberations of booming cannon, while waving flags and banners spoke the joy of the people for the return of peace. While these manifestations gladdened the hearts of the returning soldiers of your armies, the Confederate soldier, weary and foot-sore, trudged the rugged miles towards his home to find it destroyed and his family scattered among neighbors in not much better condition than himself. No joyous crowds shouted a welcome; no illuminations lighted his lonely pathway; no belching cannon said, 'Well done, thou good and faithful servant'; no banners nor flags waved him a joyous home-coming. The people bore his sufferings with him, and having fought in a cause that he sincerely believed to be right, he surrendered in good faith without mental preservation; to him the war was over, and the States again in the Union as they were before the conflict."

The speaker then gave a graphic history of the effect on the Southern people by the adverse legislation of Congress, that disfranchised 200,000 of the best men in the South and bestowed the right to vote on every negro over twenty-one years of age; how the camp-followers rode into office, and assessed taxes that could not then be paid by the white people because the negroes had deserted the plantations, expecting the government to give each one of them forty acres of land with a mule to work it; all of which conditions were not dreamed of when the Confederates surrendered at Appomatox, after an heroic struggle of 5,000,000 population against 20,000,000.

The prevailing sentiment in the speech is voiced in the following extracts: "The friends of Pericles, standing 'round his couch during his last illness, discussed his past life to find what public act of his would preserve his fame to posterity, when he said to them, 'Friends, the cornerstone of my fame is that in my long public career, I have done no act that caused a citizen of Athens to put on mourning.' Men, as they gather in their coming years, are apt to look back to learn what act of theirs brought to them the greatest consolation or satisfaction, and no doubt it will be so with me when I reach my final illness. I, too, will look through my past years to find some act of mine that will bring happiness in my closing hours, and, marshaling all my life's work before me as my memory may serve, there will be one act that will far over-shadow all the others, and that will be the inspiration that led me to your city thirty-four years ago, on a mission of peace and national brotherhood."

The speaker's closing words were as follows:

"It is no uncommon circumstance in the brain-wearying hurry and noise of this great city to read in the newspapers a notice to your veterans announcing the loss of a comrade by death, and as we read on we learn the funeral hour—a few names follow of those who may be detailed to escort his remains to the tomb. Thus, one by one, obeying an inscrutable decree of an all-wise Providence, we pay nature's penalty. One by one, like petals of the hillside blossoms, they droop and pass from sight to Mother Earth. The day of the recruiting officer is past, and the decree has gone forth that the gaps in the ranks shall never be filled.

'Leaf by leaf the roses fall,
    Drop by drop the springs run dry;
One by one—beyond recall—
    One by one they'll droop and die.'

"And as we journey along the pathway of life, one by one dropping by the wayside, the saddest moment in all your history will arrive, and it will be the death of a comrade, but there will be no announcement to the veterans —there will be no detail from them to escort the remains to the grave—there will be no officer to name the hour for the funeral, for the remains of that comrade will be all that is left.

"He was the last. One by one his comrades failed to answer roll-call; one by one they left him and crossed the dark, mysterious river until he, too, weary of solitude, weary of waiting, weary for the companionship of those who went before, laid himself down for his final rest. But in that hour it will fall to younger hands to care for his remains, and there will be a detail to guard his casket, who will tenderly place a pall over his bier, while bugle notes above his grave awaken the echoes of the silent forest in their call to rest.

"The Good Book tells us of two disciples on their way to Emmaus on the evening of the day of the crucifixion, who were overtaken by the Saviour, who walked with them and discussed, and their hearts warmed toward Him, though they knew Him not, and having reached the place of their destination, He made as if He would go further, but they stayed Him and said: 'Abide with us, for the day is far spent and the night cometh.' To you, men, who wore the Blue, who stood on field and battlement and braved the tempest of shot and shell, to you I bring a message of peace and brotherhood from those men of the South whose courage and determination called forth your best and most heroic efforts in battle, and their message is, 'Abide with us, for the day is far spent and the night cometh.' "

After the banquet the Old Guard were escorted to the railway depot by the Edw. W. Kingsley Post No. 113 and the Second Coast Artillery

JESSE E. MERCER.

GEORGE ALDEN WIGHT.

JOHN CLEVES SYMMES.

WILLIAM S. WITHAM.

(Boston Light Infantry) amid crowds of people along the route, who enlivened the march by the clapping of hands and waving of handkerchiefs.

(For the Boston *Transcript*, May 28, 1913)

THE ATLANTA OLD GUARD

We bid you a welcome, brave sons of the nation;
  Fraternal the spirit that unites us as one.
Inspiring the thought of a kindred relation—
  Lo! the angel of peace has gloriously won.

As the sun sheds its rays o'er the hills and the meadows,
  And nature rejoices in gem-golden light,
So the friendship of comrades dispels the dark shadows,
  As the cloud, like a raven, wings away in swift flight.

You have come with the hearts of heroes, in meeting
  With us to commune as we mourn for our dead;
The seraphs above bless this brotherly greeting,
  As the wreath you lay on their earth-hallowed bed.

Glad welcome we give to the lovely companions,
  Whose presence is ever like beams of the sun.
Our world is inspired by light of the fair ones,
  Who ever applaud what brave men have done.

How grand is the thought that we all are united
  In bonds that fast bind in oneness fraternal;
Again are the vows of affection here plighted
  With comrades enrolled in the legions eternal.

DARIUS COBB.

The following named ladies were the guests of the Old Guard during the tour and were delightfully entertained by ladies of the different cities on the tour: Mrs. Frank M. Berry, Mrs. A. McD. Wilson, Mrs. Henry F. Scott, Mrs. Henry C. Beerman, Miss Julia Evers Beerman, Mrs. and Miss Alice

Earle Harrington, Mrs. William A. Graham, Miss Bessie Burke Brady, the poetess of the Guard.

The trip was carried out as planned, the most noted event of which was a big parade in Boston on May 31st, the Memorial Day of the North. The Old Guard, of Atlanta, marched with the soldiery of the North and laid a beautiful wreath at the base of the Soldiers' and Sailors' Monument.

Soon after the return of the Old Guard to Atlanta, Commander Alexander M. Ferriss, of Edward Kingsley Post, G. A. R., Boston, sent the following communication to Col. J. F. Burke, Commander of the Old Guard, giving expression to the great significance which Bostonians attached to the visit of the famous Southern organization.

COMMANDER FERRISS

"Before this inspiration can grow dull, and the honor and gladness your visit brought to our city and the Edward W. Kingsley Post No. 113, G. A. R., has been dimmed by time, I desire to express to you and each individual member of the Old Guard, and with your approval, most particularly to those who could not be present with us on that memorable reunion, who we must believe would have been with us if possible, our great appreciation of the distinguished honor you have conferred upon us.

"As youngsters, guided by the principles inspired by our home environment, we quarreled, fought, and both of us got whipped good and plenty; as men we are reconciled to the fiat of a Divine Providence which doeth all things well.

"The photos you sent me of yourself and three comrades I desire to keep. They will be framed and grace the walls of our headquarters.

"Remember, dear Colonel, the words of Miles O'Reilley:

'But there's never a bond, old friend, like this—
We have drunk from the same canteen.'

"We did it Memorial Day, 1913."

A pleasing episode occurred on the steamer from Boston to New York that was a surprise to some of the officers and members of the Guard. Just before leaving Boston, it "leaked out" among the members that Capt. Harrison Jones, of the Guard, would have an anniversary birthday while on shipboard, and a handsome officer's gold-mounted sword was quietly purchased in Boston and appropriately engraved and presented to him before the assembled members and passengers. The surprise was complete and the popular recipient, who is always ready for a short speech, gave up the attempt amid the laughter of those present, who enjoyed his discomfiture.

After a delightful sea voyage to Savannah, Ga., they were met on arrival by the Georgia Hussars, Capt. Frank McIntyre. The Old Guard, with the ladies of their party, were provided with automobiles and the procession, led by the mounted Hussars, went to the hotel. At eleven A. M. the Hussars held an informal reception, which continued all day. In the afternoon, the Old Guard enjoyed an automobile ride to Thunderbolt, and the many interesting and historical places around Savannah, returning to the Hussars' armory, where an elaborate luncheon was served by the ladies of the corps, which was a pleasing finale to the day's enjoyment. Early the following morning, June 4, the Old Guard arrived in Atlanta, having completed a most enjoyable tour to see their old friends of years ago, and living again in old memories and renewing old ties of friendship that give zest to life and bind in bonds of sympathy through the light of other days.

The Atlanta *Constitution* in the following article gives the sequel of the Old Guards' visit to the North:

"Stay-at-Homes" Feast Old Guard—Recent Visit to East and Reception in Northern Cities Described at Banquet on Saturday Evening

Those members of the Old Guard Battalion of Atlanta who went on the recent patriotic journey to the large cities of the East to visit many of the most notable military organizations on this continent, were highly delighted during the past week to receive invitations from the "Stay-at-Homes" of the Old Guard, to attend a reception to be given in honor of those who went away, at the Cafe Durand last evening at 7 o'clock.

In addition to the guests of the commands, a number of prominent men were invited to the reception and supper. Among these were Governor Joseph M. Brown, Governor-elect John M. Slaton, Supreme Court Judge Joseph H. Lumpkin, a former member of the Old Gate City Guard, General R. K. Evans, United States Army, commanding the Department of the Gulf, and his aide, Colonel C. N. Barth, Colonel J. T. VanOrsdale, commanding Seventeenth Regiment, United States Army, Gen. J. Van Holt

Nash, Adj.-Genl. of Georgia, Col. E. E. Pomeroy, commanding Fifth Infantry National Guard, Clark Howell, editor *Constitution*, J. R. Gray, editor *Journal*, and Foster Coates, editor *Georgian*.

THE BANQUET

At seven o'clock the members of the Old Guard and their guests sat down to a sumptuous spread at the Cafe Durand, and began an evening of rare jollification and pleasure. Col. George M. Napier, who was selected by the committee as Toastmaster, presided.

Col. F. J. Paxon, being called upon, delivered a delightful welcome to the assembled guests, and stated that the evening had been planned to show the hearty appreciation of those of the command who could not go on the recent tour for their comrades who had been able to go, and who had illustrated the reputation of Atlanta and of the South in making a visit to the independent military organizations of the East.

A number of short speeches were made, and all who did not go on the recent peaceful tour to the East enjoyed interesting bits of report of the hospitality and entertainment accorded the members of the command which represented the city of Atlanta on the tour.

Among those who spoke were Col. J. F. Burke, commander of the Old Guard; J. R. Smith, one of Georgia's most famous business men and political managers, who, on the trip to Boston, won the sobriquet of "Reverend;" Col. J. T. VanOrsdale, U. S. A., and Col. Pomeroy, of the Fifth Regiment.

PRAISE FOR HOSPITALITY

In discussing the many delightful and long-to-be-remembered incidents of their recent trip, the members of the Old Guard who went on that happy journey, were loud in their praises of the lavish hospitality of the commands which entertained them; indeed, they fairly toasted their military friends of the East who rendered their tour such a complete success in point of entertainment and enjoyment, that happily culminated at Savannah, Ga.

A letter of regret was read from Judge Joseph H. Lumpkin, at one time a lieutenant in the Gate City Guard, who "proposed the health of the Corps." Eloquent toasts were offered to all the Old Guard.

Occasion a Happy One

It was an informal evening, the members of the Old Guard appearing in fatigue uniforms and without side arms, and the reception and spread were marked by entire unconventionality. Everyone was made to feel at ease, and the whole evening was spent in the fullest enjoyment by all present.

All the guests, including the favored members of the Old Guard, voted the occasion a most happy one, and the idea of having the members of the command meet in good fellowship, in order to talk over the recent visit of the Old Guard to the military of the East, was praised by all as a fitting conclusion to the recent journey, which was so highly enjoyed.

October 10th of each year is known as "Monument Day" by the Guard, because on October 10, 1911, the Old Guards' Monument was dedicated in Piedmont Park, by Governor Simeon E. Baldwin, of Connecticut, and Hoke Smith, Governor of Georgia, commemorating the Old Guards' mission to their former adversaries of the Civil War in the Northern and Eastern States.

Flags and Gold Lace at Old Guard Reception

Flags and flowers and the Old Guard in all their panoply of gorgeous full dress; the presence of beautiful women, with a gay sprinkling of girls, and the music of a large orchestra will be factors in the brilliance of the annual ball to be given by the Old Guard tonight at the Capital City Club.

This organization is one of the most note-worthy social institutions in the country, keeping their membership intact to preserve memories and achievements since 1858; admitting "new blood" only to perpetuate the men, the times and the deeds of the Old Guard in their most vital days and making it one of their chief aims to quicken the revival of a universal national spirit to soften the memory of sectionalism.

Their life is purely social, and tonight's hospitality will be the climax of this year, combining the happy spirit of reunion with that of a gracious hospitality to their friends.

The club-house is handsomely decorated with that effective combination —foliage plants and flags. Bay trees guard all the doors, and palms are massed effectively in their ball-room and salon. Swirls of bunting, draped flags and insignia are a brilliant array of color against the gray of the one large apartment, the yellow of the other, and pyramids of palms will form backgrounds for the punch bowls.

The receiving party will include the commander and his wife, Col. and Mrs. Joseph F. Burke; Governor and Mrs. Slaton, General and Mrs. Evans, Colonel and Mrs. VanOrsdale, and the members of their staffs with Colonel F. J. Paxon, will be present, as well as the governing board of the club and a large representative company. Dancing will be a feature of the evening.

CHATTER OF SOCIETY BY POLLY PEACHTREE

Well, the season has started off with a rush, hasn't it? I predict that this day many people will observe the "day of rest" with more than the usual appreciation, because of last week's excessive gayety. I wonder how much the pedometer—is that the right name?—would record if some of the girls who danced at the Old Guards' ball had worn the little measuring instrument.

The dazzle of color and brilliancy, the hundreds of people present, and the untiring way in which the fun was kept up made the Old Guards' ball a record-breaker. I grew dizzy just watching all the fun, very quietly and unobtrusively, and I can't imagine how some of the guests kept up the pace. I never saw an affair for which the oft-used expression, "brilliant occasion," was more appropriate than at this one.

The Old Guard were resplendent in gold braid and glittering uniforms, the officers from the post and the Department of the Gulf also wearing their full dress uniforms, not so glittering, but just as effective. Of course, all the women wore their most becoming gowns, and everything was "just too lovely."

During the evening the bugle notes suddenly called the guests together, and in the midst of the gay assembly, Capt. F. J. Cooledge, of the Old Guard, was led to the center and addressed by Governor Slaton, who in an appropriate speech, presented him with a gold medal from the members of the battalion and pinned it on his breast. Capt. Cooledge was acting quartermaster of the battalion on their recent visit to the Eastern States and so well did he discharge his duties that not a piece of baggage was lost or delayed during the whole line of travel. Capt. Cooledge made a very happy response to the Governor and to the members for their gift. It was a surprise to him.

CHAPTER XIII

THE OLD GUARD ERECT A MONUMENT TO ALEX. H. STEPHENS—CERE-
MONIES AND SPEECHES—MRS. MYRTA LOCKETT AVARY'S LETTER—
COL. J. F. BURKE RETIRES FROM ACTIVE COMMAND—BEAUTIFUL
LOVING CUP PRESENTED TO HIM—MADE HONORARY COLONEL
WITH A SPECIAL STAFF—A MEDAL FOR MRS. JNO. W. MURRELL—
ANNUAL ELECTION, JANUARY 28, 1915—ANOTHER MONUMENT
TO BE ERECTED—THE OLD GUARD'S TRIBUTE TO THE ANTE-BEL-
LUM NEGROES—CONCLUSION.

ON October 19, 1913, the Old Guard performed one of its greatest
and most lasting services. This was the dedication of the massive
double tablet of silver gray granite to mark the resting place of Georgia's great statesman, Alexander H. Stephens, at Crawfordville. The Daughters of the Confederacy, of that town, had already placed around the sacred
spot a granite coping with an iron fence, and some forty feet away there stands
a stone figure of Mr. Stephens.

TABLET UNVEILED TO A. H. STEPHENS—OLD GUARD, OF
THE GATE CITY GUARD, CONDUCT IMPRESSIVE
CEREMONIES IN CRAWFORDVILLE, GA.

Crawfordville, Ga., Oct. 19. (Special)—With beautiful and impres-
sive ceremonies the Old Guard, of the Gate City Guard, of Atlanta, on
Sunday afternoon unveiled their marble tablet over the grave of Alexander
Hamilton Stephens, at his old home "Liberty Hall," in Crawfordville, Ga.

Under the command of Col. J. F. Burke, whose idea it was to dedicate
these tablets to the memory of the great patriot and statesman, the Old Guard
and Company L, of the Fifth Regiment, which is the active company of the
Old Guard, commanded by Capt. P. F. Clarke, and the drum and bugle
corps, went to Crawfordville by special train Sunday morning.

They were met by a large delegation of Crawfordville citizens at the
train and escorted to the school building, which is next door to "Liberty
Hall," where a fine country dinner was served them by the ladies of the town.

TALES OF STEPHENS TOLD

During the dinner hour many a tale of the kind acts of Alexander Stephens was related—stories of how "Liberty Hall" was always open to any wayfarer, stranger or friend, rich or poor. The big dinner bell was always rung on the front porch and anyone within earshot was welcome to sit at the table.

An extremely interesting personage and beloved of all at "Liberty Hall," Sunday, was Aunt Liza Stephens, the old negro mammy of Alexander Stephens. No one was prouder of the honor paid "Marster Aleck" than she. Immediately after the luncheon the ceremonies began.

DRIZZLING RAIN INTERFERES

A drizzling rain interfered with the plans to have the speeches in the open. And so, with muffled drum, the Old Guardsmen, many of whom were personal friends and had been intimately associated with Alexander Stephens in his brilliant career, marched up the long front walk to "Liberty Hall," circled the tomb and statue which stands beside it, and entered the auditorium of the school building.

After an invocation by Professor Gibson, the Guardsmen were welcomed to "Liberty Hall" by Judge N. C. Andrews in behalf of the citizens of Crawfordville, the Daughters of the Confederacy and the Stephens Memorial Association.

Col. George M. Napier, of the Old Guard, presided at the meeting and introduced the speakers. He stated that Col. J. F. Burke requested to be excused from speaking, and his requests heretofore were always granted, but this time he was obliged to over-rule his commanding officer, and introduced him to the audience.

The following members of the Old Guard were on the stage: Col. Ed. L. Wight, who served with Col. Burke on Gov. Stephens' staff; Hon. M. L. Brittain, State Superintendent of Education; Hon. Lucian L. Knight, official Compiler of Georgia Records; Hon. Jos. A. McCord; Hon. J. R. Smith, and General A. J. West.

Col. Burke spoke in part as follows:

"On the morning of January 9, 1861, a lad, wearing the gray uniform of the Cadet Corps of which he was a member, on duty on Morris Island, in Charleston Harbor, was suddenly summoned, with his companions, by the drum's 'long roll,' to hasten to a sand battery on which two 24-pound guns had been mounted a few days before. Looking to seaward they saw a vessel approaching the harbor. This steamer, as the authorities had previously learned, had sailed from New York to reinforce Fort Sumter with provisions and seven hundred men. When she came within range a ball was fired across her bow, which warning being disregarded, the gunners struck her four times, when she lowered the United States flag and sailed out of the harbor. At this time the Southern Confederacy was composed of the single State of South Carolina, and the first gun of the war was fired on that day.

"A few weeks after this important incident in our history, there stood around a palmetto tree, in front of the office of the Charleston *Mercury*, about fifty persons, among whom was the lad in gray. A bulletin board hung on the tree and on it were dispatches from Montgomery, Alabama, where the representatives of the few States that had joined the Southern Confederacy at that time had formed a provisional Congress, and the dispatches stated that they had elected Jefferson Davis President, and Alexander H. Stephens, of Georgia, Vice-President.

"Beside the lad stood an old gentleman who was evidently a man of culture and wide political knowledge, conversing with those around him. Raising his gold-mounted walking-stick, he touched the name of Mr. Stephens with it, and spoke of his political life, his rugged honesty, consistency and sturdy manhood that deeply interested those around him, and made a stereotyped impression on the memory of the young cadet, that influenced and guided him through his boyhood and in later years. It was the first time that he had heard of Mr. Stephens, and soon afterward, being ordered again on active service, he crowded three school-books into his knap-sack and wrestled with Latin roots and French verbs when out of range of the guns of our adversaries, and when other sterner duties permitted, little dreaming of the close relationship that would exist between himself and Mr. Stephens in after years. That young cadet, impressed with the lesson that he had learned on that bright Sabbath morning under the palmetto tree, is still in life, having gathered the intervening years, and stands before you to pay tribute to his departed friend."

JAMES T. WRIGHT.

JOHN JUSTICE DISOSWAY.

GEN. A. J. WEST.

COL. FREDERIC J. PAXON.

Colonel Burke then narrated how Alexander Stephens, when in Congress, first became the great friend of the Old Guard. It was after the Old Guard had returned from its famous "mission of peace," through the North and East, and the soldiers of the North had promised to return the visit. The Old Guard was confronted with the problem of finding quarters for their visitors, and with more than 1,000 bills to be considered in the three remaining days of the Congress then in session, Congressman Stephens brought his influence to bear and had a resolution unanimously passed by the House, and Senator Jos. E. Brown, by the Senate, extending the Old Guard the use of United States army tents for the shelter of their guests.

Col. Burke, being on Mr. Stephens' staff, told dramatically of the death of Mr. Stephens, who on his death-bed sent Dr. Raines, his physician, for him. But his message arrived too late, and as a fitting finale of his friendship for his friend, Col. Burke placed his remains in his family vault where they remained for more than a year, when they were taken to Crawfordville. Then he told of how the old Stephens' homestead had been bought and preserved, of how the beautiful statue had been erected through the efforts of Miss Gay, and the Daughters of the Confederacy at Crawfordville.

Hon. Lucian L. Knight closed his speech, comparing Robert Toombs and Governor Stephens as follows:

"Both men were tenacious of conviction, but Mr. Stephens was the more tolerant; and while he was not disposed to temporize in any sense which implied surrender or compromise of principle, he was more disposed to treat with his adversary in the hope of finding some common basis of agreement. Both men were industrious workers, but Mr. Toombs, with tempermental impatience, worked spasmodically, while Mr. Stephens, with steady stroke, worked continuously. The one, like the woodman hewing down the forest, the other, like the oarsman plowing up the stream. Robert Toombs with the vigor of mountain granite in his frame, produced little or no literature, while delicate Stephens, with insistent and steady toil, wrote volume after volume. Both were princely givers and royal entertainers; but Toombs, by wise investment, accumulated two fortunes and died rich, while Mr. Stephens lived narrowly within his income, and died poor. On political issues Toombs was at one time a democrat, and Stephens a Whig. Equally loyal to the South, Stephens opposed, while Toombs advocated secession; and when the war was over Toombs resisted, while Stephens tolerated reconstruction.

Such differences as these appear to leave little room for friendship, but differences sometimes face each other in the friendly smile of supplements, rather than in the hostile frown of contradictions. At the Provisional Congress of the Confederate States, at Montgomery, in 1861, it was Mr. Toombs who advocated the election of Mr. Stephens to the chair of Vice-President. Though an uncompromising secessionist, it was Mr. Toombs who arose at the close of his friend's great speech before the Legislature, and said: 'Fellow-Citizens: We have just listened to a speech from one of the brightest intellects and one of the purest patriots alive. I move that we now adjourn with three cheers for Alex. H. Stephens.' Frequently, when Mr. Stephens was ill, it was Mr. Toombs who represented him in court. But the last tribute which the kingly Georgian ever paid his cherished friend was when he bent like the shade of an old forest giant over the mortal ashes of the Great Commoner. The trembling figure of the old man as he sobbed his simple eulogy in the plaintive accents of the dying swan, was one never to be forgotten. It was the last appearance in public of the veteran Mirabeau. Two lonesome years followed and then two glorious Georgians were again united. Mr. Stephens felt for Mr. Toombs, the same rapt and tender admiration which Mr. Toombs felt for him, and his eloquent estimate of the great Touchstone's genius has long been famous. Said he of Toombs: 'His was the greatest mind I ever came in contact with; and its operations, even in its errors, reminded me of some mighty waste of waters.'

"Both died in the faith of an 'undiscovered country from whose bourn no traveler returns.' There let us think of them today, with the dews of the morning land upon them. Under the boughs of the overhanging oaks of 'Liberty Hall,' they often held sweet converse in the old days; and now 'life's fitful fever o'er,' may they have met again in a green country, where boundless horizons stretch before them in an infinite expanse of beauty, and where, no longer fettered by the limitations of time and flesh, these masterminds can commune in unbroken fellowship at the eternal Fount of Truth."

The Old Guard, of the Gate City Guard, has emulated the honorable career of its predecessors.

It is a noble organization, representing the old and the new in the history of Atlanta and Georgia. The Gate City Guard was one of the first to respond to Georgia's call to arms. In the foremost rank of the sons of the South, whose chief aim has been to promote peace and brotherly love throughout the great republic, and to preserve also the sacred memories of the past, stand the members of the Old Guard, of the Gate City Guard.

STEPHENS, THE GREAT COMMONER

Outline of the address delivered by Hon. M. L. Brittain, at Crawfordville, Georgia.

"The people of his native State called the statesman, whose memory we revere today, the Great Commoner of Georgia. He saw the inward significance and value of the title and took pride in its claim.

"There are three classes of people in this world. The first, we might term that which calls itself Society, with a large S. Its members are prone to flatter themselves unduly as the leaders in their respective communities. They feel above and too good to take part in labor; are consumers instead of producers, leaners always instead of lifters in the struggle for existence. In reality, they count for little in the progress of humanity, being merely the foam and froth, or syllabub if you please, in life's cup.

"At the other extreme we have the Criminal Class, the mud-sills or submerged. From them we can expect nothing towards human betterment, merely protection and safety from these human wild beasts, is the main end desired.

"Midway between these two stands the great Middle Class. From it have come the leaders in science, art, letters, invention and progress of all kind, as well as those who feed and clothe the world. They are for the most part dazed by the superior pretentions of the society folk and suffer them to live in luxury from the products of their labor, and content themselves with the scant receipts from their daily toil. When pressed too hard, however, as in the scarlet days of the French Revolution, they inevitably learn their own strength, rise in their might, and dash tyrants from their tinsel thrones.

"Alexander Hamilton Stephens, like the Savior of mankind, loved these and from them came his followers. You remember it was said on the hills of Judea that the 'common people heard Him gladly,' and so it could be written of the great Georgian who dwelt at 'Liberty Hall.' He saw what the world is more and more beginning to discern—the value, worth and dignity of the common people who do its work. He came from their ranks and fought their battles; and the Georgia wealth wasted, as well as the heroic lives crushed out from Manassas to Appomattox, bear witness to the truth

MONUMENT OF THE OLD GUARD OF THE GATE CITY GUARD.
Dedicated October 10, 1911, Piedmont Park, Atlanta, Ga.

of his prophetic counsel at the Secession Convention. His opponents felt the weight of his argument and bore tribute to it as well as to his personal worth in making him Vice-President of the Southern Confederacy.

"He lived a life of singular purity and over his dead form the State can mourn with no blush of shame and no need for the veil that she must sometimes use at the bier of her strong sons. It is good, therefore, that we of the Old Guard, under command of his personal friend, should add this tablet to the memory of the distinguished dead."

Extract from the speech of Hon. J. R. Smith:

"Daughters of the Confederacy, Comrades and Friends: The sentiment that brings us together is so delicate and so beautiful that it would be difficult to express it in words. It is better expressed in the labor and sacrifices made in the erection of the beautiful tablets which the Old Guard have erected as an expression of love and esteem of one whose life work was devoted to his State and his country.

"Each day and generation has produced its great men, great because they have contributed one way or another to civilization. And it is unnecessary to call the roll of the strong men who held the center of the stage during these most interesting chapters in our country's history. The period was one remarkably productive of statesmen and leaders of the first magnitude; men whose names will live in history when the monuments erected in their honor shall have crumbled under the touch of time. Not the least of these— not least in intellect, nor in love of his people nor in inflexible integrity and loyalty to his cause—stood Alexander H. Stephens, of Georgia.

"Although a believer in and consistent advocate of the principles of State's rights, he opposed secession to the last, not because it was not right, but because it was not wise. With many other of the best men of the day, he believed that the questions involved could be settled without disruption of the Union. Yet none could doubt the course he would take when civil conflict could no longer be averted. Called to the Vice-Presidency of the Confederate States, he did his part faithfully and well.

"We can not contemplate the life of this man without being impressed not only with his intellect, which amounted to genius, but also with the fact that he gave it unselfishly and unreservedly to his people. His life was one of public service from youth 'til the day of his death; as a school teacher, as a young lawyer, who never advocated any but a just cause; as a member of

Congress, and in his State Legislature; as a wise counsellor during the most trying period in the history of our State, and as Governor during his declining years, he may be said to have devoted his whole life to the public welfare. Yet he found time to write and publish his 'Constitutional View of the War between the States,' a voluminous work which, without question, is the ablest defense of the doctrines of State sovereignty and justification of secession from the pen of any author.

"Almost since the birth of the human race, men have sought to inspire the living by perpetuating the memory of the honored dead. We have met here today to dedicate a monument to this great man—this man of lofty patriotism, broad humanity, profound wisdom and ingrained honesty, who, though beyond the reach of mortal honors, still serves his people by the illustrious example he has left to them."

Extract from the address of Genl. Andrew J. West:

"Ladies, Gentlemen, My Friends, and Confederate Comrades: It is esteemed a distinguished honor, and great personal pleasure to be accorded the privilege of participating today in these interesting exercises.

"The splendid people of this beautiful city of Crawfordville, and of this historic county of Taliaferro, tell us in enthusiastic tones, by their presence here, that in honoring the memory of Alexander Hamilton Stephens, no token of esteem can be too profuse; no mark of respect can be too emphatic; and no rendition of honor can be too conspicuous.

"The hand upon the dial can not be seen as it moves, but it does move nevertheless, and so surely as it keeps pace with the circling sun, so surely is the fame of the Great Commoner safe in the hands of the patriotic Daughters of the Confederacy.

"We honor ourselves today in honoring the memory of the great Georgian, the friend and helper of young men, the lawyer, the statesman, and the Vice-President of the Confederate States. He was the friend of the man who walked in the new-ploughed furrows, and through the rustling corn. He gave the helping hand to the men whose faces were made radiant by the glare of the furnace, and to the delvers in the deep, dark mines.

"His powers as an orator in Congress never received a more genuine tribute than when Abraham Lincoln wrote to his law partner in Illinois, in 1848: 'I take up my pen to tell you that Mr. Stephens, of Georgia, a little, slim, pale-faced, consumptive man, has just concluded the very best speech

DR. WILLIAM LEAK GILBERT.

THOS. COWAN ERWIN.

LIEUT. WALPOLE BREWER, M. D.
Assistant Surgeon.

JAMES R. SMITH.

of an hour's length I ever heard. My old, withered, dry eyes are full of tears yet.'

"We honor ourselves in honoring the man who was greatest in his simplicity. Being once asked, late in life, what he considered the highest compliment he had ever received, Mr. Stephens gravely replied by telling how a white-haired old negro at Crawfordville, in answer to the inquiry of a stranger as to whether he knew the master of 'Liberty Hall', said: 'Yas, suh, I knows Marse Aleck—I knows him mighty well; he's kinder to dawgs than other men is to people.' Sentiment causes the heart-strings to play hide and seek around the sweet memories of the old oaken bucket that hangs in the well at 'Liberty Hall'. And sentiment, coupled with a pleasant duty, quickened the foot-steps of the Old Guard in hastening to accept the summons of our distinguished and beloved commander, Col. Joseph F. Burke, in being present today to unveil this monument to the memory of the Great Commoner —their friend, Alexander H. Stephens.

"Handicapped by physical weakness, and frequent attacks of severe illness, he wrote many histories; amongst them, his 'Constitutional View of the Late War between the State.'

"Mr. Stephens served the South with great ability before the war and during the war, and after the war he directed his efforts towards bringing an end to the era of passion and despotism. For his people he wrought mightily when they were most imperiled. He was a great factor in making the history of Georgia, and ranked high among the South's constructive statesmen. He did much in the dark days of reconstruction in lifting up the fainting people of the South, binding their wounds, and suggesting to them how they might do the best for themselves amid almost unparalleled misfortunes.

"He served in Congress from the period of the Mexican War to the secession of the Southern States, and died in the Governor's mansion, in Atlanta, Georgia, the idol of his people."

After the speaking the Old Guard marched to the grave of Stephens. Standing at "present arms," in a circle around the grave the Old Guard solemnly paid honor to Stephens as their commander, Colonel Burke, drew away the veil from the tablet. As the veil was drawn three volleys as a salute rang out under the somber skies. The ceremonies were fittingly closed when Frank Meader, Jr., a lad of a dozen years, bugler of Marist College, blew "taps."

The inscription on the granite tablet is surmounted by the coat of arms of the Old Guard battalion, and reads as follows:

This Tablet
is a tribute from the
OLD GUARD,
of the
Gate City Guard,
in the memory of their
departed friend,
Alexander Hamilton Stephens,
Statesman and Patriot,
Vice-President
of the
Confederate States of America.
Born, February 11, 1812.   Died, March 4, 1883.
Dedicated, October 19, 1913.

Mrs. Myrta Lockett Avary's Tribute to Alex. H. Stephens

"October 19, 1913.

"Colonel Burke: You were one of the last whom Mr. Stephens asked to see in his dying hours. In your family vault, his remains found rest before committal to their final repose at Liberty Hall. Years after, when his home —once a mecca for distinguished visitors—and its master seem like to be forgot by all the world—the ever-faithful Old Guard, under your command, goes thither to unveil the monument they raised to his memory.

"In his name, I present to the keeping of his Old Guard, this tribute to the Southern soldier written by him in his 'Prison Journal,' which may be called his 'Testament to the American People':

" ' More intelligent, patriotic, or braver body of men than those who filled the Southern armies never went to battle for their country's cause in any age or clime; and never were any men animated by loftier, purer principles and sentiments; it was with no view of aggression upon others, but simply to defend their own rights; not to make war on the Union, but to maintain the sovereignty of their own States, which had quit the Union but

PHILIP BETHEA GREEN.

GEORGE HARRINGTON.

WALTER C. TAYLOR.

THOS. H. MORGAN.

had rescued the Constitution. * * * It was to preserve this that they rushed to the ranks as soldiers never did before—not even in the days of Peter the Hermit and the Crusades.'

Yours faithfully,

MYRTA LOCKETT AVARY"

COL. J. F. BURKE RETIRES FROM ACTIVE COMMAND

For more than a year past it was known to the members that Col. Burke desired to be relieved of the active command of the Old Guard Battalion. For thirty-five years his connection with the organization was a period of activity that made the name of the Old Guard, of the Gate City Guard, a synonym of unselfish patriotism throughout the Union. The members determined to create a special office in the battalion for Col. Burke, to be known as "Honorary Colonel," and that he should have an honorary staff. By this new law, Col. Burke and his staff, in addition to their active membership in the corps, were to serve on the Executive Committee whenever called on, and in the councils of the battalion. All this was the unanimous action of the battalion at their fifty-sixth anniversary, on January 21, 1914. The members were in full dress uniform and following the meeting they adjourned to the ball-room which was profusely decorated, and where their ladies awaited them.

Miss Louise Williams entertained the assembly by her excellent recitations of old time negro lore in native dialect, recalling memories of antebellum days on the plantation. Dancing and refreshments followed, interrupted by a delightful incident which surprised Col. Burke, who was suddenly called to the stage to receive a large and handsome silver loving cup, elaborately embossed and bearing the names of the members of the battalion. It was their gift to their old commander, and was presented by Hon. Jos. A. McCord, on behalf of his comrades, in an appropriate speech in which he dwelt on Col. Burke's boyhood and his part in the Civil War at the very outset, his long connection with the Gate City Guard and its Old Guard, and the nation-wide praise for their patriotic work. Col. Burke made a feeling response on receiving the gift, and his thanks to the members of the battalion for this evidence of their regard for him found sincere expression in fitting terms. Several members also spoke; among them, Col. A. J. West, Dr. Jno. H. Powell, and others.

Silver Loving Cup presented to Col. J. F. Burke on his retirement from active command of the Old Guard after thirty-five years of active service. The inscription on the cup is as follows: Presented to Colonel Joseph F. Burke by members of the Old Guard Battalion, upon his retirement from its active command and his acceptance of the rank of Honorary Colonel of the Old Guard, and as a token of the affectionate regard of the donors, January 19, 1914.

The inscription on the loving cup is just below the engraved coat of arms of the battalion and is as follows:

"Presented to Col. Joseph F. Burke, by members of the Old Guard Battalion, upon his retirement from active command and his acceptance of the rank of Honorary Colonel of the Old Guard, and as a token of the affectionate regard of the donors.   January 19, 1914."

Col. George M. Napier was elected to succeed Col. Burke in the active command.

A. D. 1914

ANSLEY HOTEL, January 21, 1914.

GENERAL ORDER NO. 1

At the annual meeting of the Old Guard Battalion, the following officers were elected and appointed to serve the battalion for the ensuing year, or until their successors are elected.

This order is published for the information of the battalion that these officers may be obeyed and respected accordingly.

GEO. M. NAPIER,
J. W. MURRELL,   Major Commanding.
Capt. and Adjutant.

OLD GUARD

HONORARY STAFF

J. F. Burke, Colonel

Col. F. J. Paxon   Major F. J. Cooledge
Col. A. J. West   Major B. H. Jones
Col. W. M. Crumley   Major A. H. Davis
Col. E. L. Connelly   Major C. P. Byrd
Col. Louis Gholstin   Major B. B. Crew

COL. GEORGE M. NAPIER.

Active Staff

George M. Napier, Major Commanding
John W. Murrell, Capt. and Adjt.
Wharton Wilson, Capt. and Qt.
A. McD. Wilson, Capt. and Com.
E. J. Spratling, Capt. and Surgeon
Dr. J. H. Powell, Lst. Lt. and Asst. Sur.

"A" Company

Peter F. Clark, Captain
W. D. Ellis, 1st Lieut.
W. M. Camp, 2nd Lieut.

"B" Company

Ed. L. Wight, Captain
A. H. Bancker, 1st Lieut.
W. E. Hancock, 2nd Lieut.

"C" Company

Harrison Jones, Captain
J. A. Kemp, 1st Lieut.
Frank Ridge, 2nd Lieut.

Non-Commissioned Staff

Ben Lee Crew, Sergeant-Major

E. L. Bergstrom, Col. Srgt.   W. A. Haygood, Col. Srgt.
Battalion Colors   U. S. Colors

Non-Commissioned Line Officers

"A" Company

W. B. Cummings, 1st Srgt.
S. Paul Burkert 2nd Srgt.

"B" Company

A. P. Coles, 1st Srgt.
W. M. Stephenson, 2nd Srgt.

A Medal for Mrs. Jno. W. Murrell.

At a quarterly meeting of the Battalion on October 21, 1914, held at the University Club, to arrange for a midsummer outing, a pleasing episode centered the proceedings when Col. J. F. Burke detailed the work of the past year, and paid tribute to Mrs. John W. Murrell, the accomplished wife of Adjutant Murrell, for her many courtesies to the members and her valuable suggestion in forwarding the work of the Corps. It was unanimously voted that a Battalion Medal be made and presented to Mrs. Murrell, with the thanks of all the members. The committee appointed to carry out the resolution lost no time in having a medal made and it was sent to Mrs. Murrell about three weeks afterward. Mrs. Murrell's gracious response was written on the minute-book of the Guard.

The Annual Election.

The regular election for officers for the ensuing year was held on January 28, 1915. A large number of members were present to enjoy the usual elaborate luncheon that has become a feature at all meetings. The following officers were elected:

> Major Edwin Leigh Wight, Commander
> Capt. Jno. W. Murrell, Adjutant
> Capt. Wharton O. Wilson, Quartermaster
> Capt. A. McD. Wilson, Commissary

Company A	Company B
Capt. George Hope	Capt. Harrison Jones
1st Lieut. T. A. Kemp	1st Lieut. Frank F. Ridge
2d Lieut. F. M. Berry	2d Lieut. E. L. Bergstrom

Battalion Surgeon
Dr. J. H. Powell

Assistant Surgeon.
Dr. Walpole Brewer*

*Dr. Brewer is now serving in the Italian Army with the American Red Cross.

COL. EDWIN LEIGH WIGHT,

ANOTHER MONUMENT TO BE ERECTED—THE OLD GUARD'S
TRIBUTE TO THE ANTE-BELLUM NEGROES.

The indomitable spirit of the Old Guard was again in evidence in their meeting on May 28, 1915. After the business of the meeting was finished, and the members were enjoying the tempting repast that is a part of the proceedings at every meeting, Col. J. F. Burke, in a reminiscent mood, referring to "old times," spoke feelingly of the old time negro, of his fidelity to his "white folks," the many manifestations of love that bound master and servant in the old days—and the guardianship they displayed in cultivating the fields and the garden, from which came the support of the women and children in the family residence, when there was not a white man, old or young, on the plantations to protect them—the men and boys of the South, clad in gray, were in the ranks of the Confederate Army—but such was the relation from birth to death, between master and servant, under the old *regime* that they had no fear of harm to their loved ones at home. Col. Burke stated that there was one more work to be accomplished by the Old Guard, and that was to erect a fitting monument in Piedmont Park, to transmit to posterity the story of the close attachment of the old servants to their masters in those days.

Instantly, the whole meeting were on their feet clamoring their approval of the project. Col. Ed. L. Wight, Commander of the Old Guard, related an instance of his mother's maid servant, who took all the jewelry of her mistress and buried it before the "blue coats" reached the plantation, and travelling for miles, found the commanding officer and, with tears, begged him to save the "home place" from destruction. A guard was placed on the premises and the residence was saved. Capt. Ed. W. Martin recited a similar instance by which his old home was saved. Col. Walter P. Andrews added further interesting facts and Secretary J. Cleves Symmes spoke of the good effect a monument would have on the colored race of the present day. It was resolved to make Col. Burke chairman of such committee as he may appoint, to carry this work to a successful termination. A committee was selected without delay and designs from various sculptors requested, which will be received by the committee and passed upon without delay. It will require about six months to make the model and bronze casting and granite pedestal. When erected, the dedication ceremonies will be elaborate and there will be representatives from all the States invited to be present.

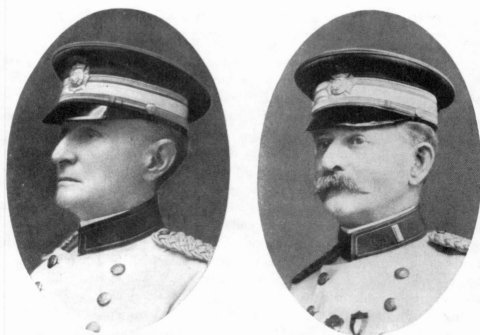

MAJOR BENJAMIN B. CREW.   LIEUT. WM. M. CAMP.

The following beautiful tribute to the old time Southern negro, in days before the war, is from the pen of Peter Francisco Smith, of Atlanta, Ga.

"He was a true and faithful friend, true to his master, true to the children and the children's children unto the third and fourth generation. God bless the forlorn and ragged remnants of a race now passing away. God bless the old black hand that rocked our infant cradle, smoothed the pillow of infant sleep and fanned the fever from our cheeks. God bless the old tongue that immortalized the nursery rhyme, the old eyes that guided our truant feet and the old heart that laughed at our childish freaks. God bless the dusky old brow, whose wrinkles told of toil and sweat and sorrow. May the green turf rest lightly on their ashes, and the wild flowers deck every lonely grave where 'He giveth His beloved sleep.' May their golden dreams of golden slippers, of golden streets, of golden harps and golden crowns, have become realities."

The following list shows the names of officers from the reorganization of the company, in July, 1876, as far as can be ascertained, owing to the incomplete records:

CAPTAINS

A. Leyden, July 25, 1876; resigned September 24, 1877.
T. J. Dabney, September 26, 1877; resigned December 6, 1877.
J. F. Burke, March 21, 1878; resigned August, 1882.
Henry Jackson, October 3, 1882; resigned May, 1886.
J. F. Burke, July 23, 1886; resigned July 8, 1887.
C. L. Anderson, August 5, 1887; resigned June 29, 1888.
Lyman Hall, July 5, 1888; resigned January 5, 1890.
A. C. Sneed, February 4, 1890; resigned August 28, 1891.
W. J. Kendrick, September 25, 1891; resigned January 23, 1893.

In the early part of 1893 the Gate City Guard withdrew from the service of the State, and joined the "Old Guard," of the Gate City Guard, composed of the old members, and formed the Old Guard Battalion.

J. F. Burke, commander; retired January 19, 1914.
Geo. M. Napier, comdr., January 19, 1914; retired January 19, 1915.
Ed. L. Wight, comdr., January 19, 1915.

LIEUTENANTS

J. W. Butler, July 25, 1876; resigned September 24, 1877.
J. G. Scrutchin, October, 1876; resigned February 25, 1879.
W. C. Sparks, March 4, 1879; resigned.
Joseph H. Lumpkin, March 4, 1879; resigned.
M. B. Spencer, February 3, 1885; resigned.
Hooper Alexander, November 29, 1887; resigned May 30, 1888.
F. H. Ellis, July 30, 1888; resigned January 8, 1891.
B. M. Goldsmith, November 17, 1891; resigned May 25, 1892.
C. M. Roberts, June 6, 1892; resigned January 24, 1893.
E. W. Hewitt, March 26, 1883; resigned December, 1884.
W. M. Camp, February 3, 1885; resigned.
Chas E. Sciple, February 3, 1885; resigned.
W. T. Kuhn, October 6, 1885; resigned July 12, 1886.
Geo. L. Lowman, August 16, 1892; resigned April 17, 1893.
G. C. Crawford, August 21, 1888; resigned May 16, 1889.

The active company of the "Old Guard," composed of the younger members, elected officers in 1893-94-95, as follows:

> Capt. J. B. Hollis, 1893.
> Capt. L. D. White, 1894 and 1895.
> Lieut. Gabriel Beck.
> Lieut. Herbert Storer.
> Lieut. Robert Schmidt.

In August, 1896, some of the members of the younger company withdrew from the Old Guard and formed a separate company and enlisted in the State troops under the name of the Gate City Guard. This company is a part of the 5th Regiment of the Georgia State Troops, and designated as Company "L."

Adjutant's Roll of Active Members, August 1, 1915

AKERS, F. M.

ANDREWS, WALTER PEMBERTON — Lawyer

ASHE, H. M. — Real Estate

AUSTELL, W. W.

BANCKER, A. H. — Lawyer

BEERMAN, HENRY C. — Retired

BENNETT, W. C. — Printer

BERRY, FRANK M. — Assistant Cashier

BEUSSE, JESSE HOYT — Broker

BERGSTROM, ERNEST LAMAR

    Int. Rev. U. S. Dep. Col.

BEUTELL, H. M. — Bank Fixtures

BIDWELL, CHARLTON B. — Auditor

BLACKSHEAR, PERRY GREENFIELD — Bank Clerk

BLECKLEY, HARALSON — Architect

BOWEN, CHAS. A. — Insurance

BREWER, WALPOLE — Physician and Surgeon

BRITTAIN, MARION LUTHER — State Supt. Schools

BROWN, S. B.

BURKE, JOS. FRANCIS — Retired

BURKE, WM. M. — Broker

BURKERT, PAUL — Undertaker

BYRD, CHAS. P. — Pres. Byrd Printing Co.

CALLAWAY, EUGENE C.

    Pres. Gate City Coffin Co.

CAMP, W. M. — Asst. Supt. Pullman Co.

CARY, DAN

CLARKE, PETER F. — Bank Cashier

CLARKE, THOS. M. — Retired

COKER, FRANK M. — Banker

COLEMAN, WALTER SCOTT — U. S. Official

COMER, RANSOM HOGUE — Grocer

CONNALLY, DR. E. L. — Realty

COOLEDGE, FRED J. — Merchant

CREW, BENJAMIN B. — Merchant

CREW, BEN LEE — Salesman

CRUMLEY, WM. M. — Hardware Merchant

CUMMINGS, W. B.

DANIEL, L. J. — Merchant

DAVIS, ARCHIBALD H. — Lawyer

DISOSWAY, J. J. — Pres. C. S. Belt'g & Sup. Co.

DONNELL, M. C. — Lawyer

DONOVAN, GEORGE R. — Bank Cashier

ELLIS, JR., A. D. — Lawyer

ERWIN, THOS. C. — V-Pres. 3d Natl. Bank

EUBANKS, GEO. F. — Merchant

FLOYD, JAMES S. — Banker

FULLER, JAMES MARSHALL — City Marshal

FLEMMING, THOS. — Railroad

GAVAN, J. CHARLES — Books

GHOLSTIN, LOUIS — Manufacturer

GILBERT, WM. L. — Physician

GOREE, C. P. — Lawyer

GRAHAM, WM. ALEXANDER — Physician

GREEN, PHILIP BETHEA — Linotype Operator

HANCOCK, WALTER EUGENE — Real Estate

HANCOCK, WILL L.

HARRINGTON, GEORGE — Insurance and Banking

HARRIS, JR., LUCIUS JACK — Asst. Cashier

HILLYER, JR., GEORGE — Engraver

HIRSCH, H. H. — Insurance

HOLLEMAN, J. T. — Banker

HOOPER, FRANK ARTHUR — Lawyer

HOPE, GEORGE MELVILLE — Gen. Mgr. Life Ins.

JACOBS, JOSEPH — Druggist

JONES, BOLLING H. — Postmaster

JONES, HARRISON — Lawyer

KEMP, THOS. ARDELL — Paint and Paper Dlr.

KREIGSHABER, V. H. — Merchant

KUHNS, WM. THEODORE — Photographer

LOKEY, M. D., HUGH M. — Oculist and Aurist

McMILLAN, WM. VERNON — Com. Merchant
McCORD, JOS. ALEXANDER
         Banker, Fed. Res. Bank
McELREATH, WALTER

MARTIN, EDMUND WELLBORN — Lawyer
MASSENGALE, ST. ELMO — Advertising Agent
MEYER, JR., SAMUEL
      Treas. Schlessinger-Meyer Baking Co.
MORGAN, THOS. H. — Architect
MORROW, GILHAM HOYLE
        Pres. Morrow Trans. Co.
MURRELL, JOHN W. — Diamond Merchant

NAPIER, GEORGE M. — Lawyer

OWENS, JOHN S. — Banking

PAXON, FREDERIC J.
        Davison-Paxon-Stokes Co.
PITT, THOS H. — Real Estate
POMEROY, EDGAR E. — Lawyer
PORTER, WM. LOWRY — Real Estate
POWELL, M. D., JOHN H.
        Eye, Ear, Nose and Throat

RIDGE, FRANK T. — Traveling Salesman
REID, W. W. — Insurance
RUSHTON, W. W. — Lumber
RANDOLPH, HOLLINS NICHOLAS — Lawyer

SCOTT, JAMES TOMPKINS
        Com. Agent Clyde Line
SCOTT, HENRY FORT — Physician
SCHLESSINGER, HARRY L. — Manufacturer
SHARP, MACON CRAWFORD — General Agent
SHIELDS, J. A.
SMILLIE, F. C. — Traveling Salesman
SMITH, J. R. — Real Estate
SMITH, CHAS. ALONZO — Druggist
SPRATLING, E. J. — Physician
STEPHENS, W. M. — Photographer
STOVALL, W. H. — Trust Company
SYMMES, JOHN CLEVE — Sou. Bell Tel. Co.

TIDWELL, CHAS. W. — Photographer
THROWER, M. L. — Real Estate
THOMAS, C. C.
TURMAN, SAMUEL — Rl. Est. and Mort. Loans

WEST, ANDREW J. — Real Estate
WHITE, W. WOODS — Insurance
WIGHT, GEORGE ALDEN — Real Estate
WIGHT, ED L. — Marine Insurance
WILSON, A. McD. — Wholesale Grocer
WILSON, WHARTON O. — Lawyer
WINSHIP, GEORGE — Retired Capitalist
WITHAM, W. S. — Banker
WOODSIDE, JOHN JAMES — Rent and Storage
WRIGHT, JAMES THOMAS — Lawyer
YANCEY, JR., GOODLOE HARPER — Salesman

Conclusion

This page closes the history of a remarkable organization, remarkable in war and in peace—historic in both, while from our point of view, we applaud the unselfish patriotism that moved them at the very beginning to take places in the serried columns of the battle-field. Yet, after all, we must give them greater applause for manfully accepting defeat, and, with a true patriotism, taking the flag of a reunited country and with confidence in their hearts invading the territory of their former adversaries, and eloquently demanding that sectionalism shall cease, and that there shall be but one flag and one country.

No military organization ever had such a history. Their movements often seem like inspirations—asking nothing for themselves—their influence and service were ever for the public good.

But a few of the members who served in the war between the States are in life, but their memories are ever green with the members of the Old Guard, and the evening shadows draw closer as the years wear on.